XML FOR REAL PROGRAMMERS

LIMITED WARRANTY AND DISCLAIMER OF LIABILITY

XML FOR REAL PROGRAMMERS

REAZ HOQUE

AN IMPRINT OF ACADEMIC PRESS
A Harcourt Science and Technology Company

San Diego San Francisco New York Boston
London Sydney Tokyo

This book is printed on acid-free paper. ♾

ACADEMIC PRESS
A Harcourt Science and Technology Company
525 B Street, Suite 1900, San Diego, CA 92101-4495 USA
http://www.academicpress.com

Academic Press
Harcourt Place, 32 Jamestown Road, London NW1 7BY, UK

Morgan Kaufmann
340 Pine Street, Sixth Floor, San Francisco, CA 94104-3205 USA
http://www.mkp.com

Library of Congress Catalog Card Number: 94-68563
International Standard Book Number: 0-12-355592-2

Printed in the United States of America
00 01 02 03 04 IP 6 5 4 3 2 1

Contents

Dedication

To Faez, the brother I never had the pleasure to get to know; Faez and to the five most important people in my life: my parents, Bhaia, Chris, and Tannie. I love you all with all my heart!

Preface

The web is changing every day. It is not only a place for nifty web pages, but also a communication medium where businesses can perform daily routines. Thus the buzz of e-business is everywhere. "e-business" is not about creating a shopping center on the web. Rather, it is about how a business can communicate with its partners, customers and suppliers.

This kind of scenario demands a new set of technologies. Many companies, including Netscape, Sun and Microsoft, have done a great job inventing some of the major technologies that are making e-business possible. Java, a good asset, has changed the web in many ways. With HTML you create content, but with Java you connect to your server side technology to display dynamic data. As HTML is limited to its set of semantics, it does not let you define data with your own arbitrary structure for more complex applications.

Although HTML is a widespread standard for the presentation of simple documents, it does not disclose anything about either the content or context of the data. By contrast, XML delivers information that separates content from presentation. By separating content from presentation, XML provides the recipient of the data with a business context that allows the recipient to act intelligently on the data.

Much like HTML, XML can be used as a format to deliver data from the application server to the client. However, XML goes far beyond HTML; XML clients can take advantage of both client and server side processing. Because XML can be used to do anything ranging from collaboration and dynamic data generation to seamless application integration, intelligent searches and agents are enabled . It is not limited as is the case with HTML but it also is not as complicated as SGML, making it the developer's choice for next generation applications on the internet.

What To Expect from This Book

We start first with the XML specification. In Chapter 1 we examine the XML specification in detail. If you are very new to XML and need more assistance with the specification, pick up a more introductory level book to familiarize yourself with it.

Chapters 2 and 3 cover the essential parts of the XML family: DOM, XSL, Xlink and Xpointer. These two chapters try to show what these technologies are all about and provide small examples of how to use them. It is important to understand these technologies as clearly as possible because these technologies are used in the core application of this book.

After you have become familiar with the XML family members we talk about the applications that can be created with XML. Chapter 4 describes the types of application that should be created with XML and where each fits well.

Chapters 5–7 are the core chapters of the book. We demonstrate how XML should be used to create a whole e-commerce site. We show how to use XML with Java and demonstrate XML's strengths and weaknesses. For complete understanding we walk you through each line of code.

In our last chapter, we talk about the next phase of the XML technology: what is to come and what is envisioned in the near future. In this chapter you will get to know more of the "X" technologies that are still in the works.

Who Should Read This Book?

This book requires prior knowledge of Java, databases, and the World Wide Web. Because this book is an advanced book, it does not present extensive details on the XML specification, but it covers how to use this technology in the real world. Our goal in this book is to show you how you can benefit from using XML in your e-business venture.

This book is for you if you are:

- eager to know how XML can be used to explore new ways of doing business on the internet;
- interested in learning how to use Java and XML together;
- an intranet/internet/extranet application developer who wants to create mission critical e-commerce applications; and/or
- students and researchers who want to keep up with cutting edge net technology.

Acknowledgments

First of all I would like to thank my publisher, who has done a great job to make this book a success. I thank especially, my editor, Thomas Park, for his constant help and feedback.

I would like to thank the team I have worked with. Without Vishal Anand, Mike Alexander, and Bruce Weber (you really saved me!), this book would not have been possible. Special thanks goes to John Baum who helped me get the team together. He is a true friend who came to my rescue when I needed him the most.

I would like to extend my thanks to IBM for giving me permission to use their software for the CD.

Thanks to my family and friends—you have been my constant support. As always, my parents, Faisal Hoque (my big bro who is always watching out for me) and his wife Christine, and my dearest girl friend Tannie will always have a special place in my heart. Finally, thanks to the Almighty for giving me the strength to do so much.

CHAPTER 1

The Core of XML

1.1 Introduction to XML

The abbreviation XML stands for Extended Markup Language. It was developed by an XML Working Group (originally known as SGML Editorial Review Board) under World Wide Web Consortium (W3C) in 1996. Standard Generalized Markup Language (SGML), now an ISO standard, enables you to define a grammar for marking up documents in terms of semantic tags and their attributes. This means that SGML is a "metalanguage," that is, a language used to define other languages. Thus XML is a dialect of SGML. The consortium defining the standard for XML has attempted to remove everything that was difficult about defining new markup languages in SGML, while retaining most of what was useful about it in the first place.

Before providing XML details, it is important to start with HTML. Hypertext Markup Language (HTML), developed during the world wide web's infancy, is the best-known language defined using SGML. It is the language of the web that provides us with a wonderful medium to share information. With its standard nametags it allows a web page to be accessible from any browser that can read and understand those nametags. A drawback to HTML is that the standard set of nametags limits the language. Some browsers use browser specific tags, which make the web page look different in that browser; this incompatibility serves to reduce the value of the web page.

XML solves this problem of language extension in a unique way. It is a markup language for documents containing structured information. Documents having structured information include both the content as well as what the content stands for. Content can be words, pictures etc. Based on where the content is located in the document, it carries a different meaning. For example, content as part of regular text is different from content in a table.

A markup language is a mechanism to identify structures in a document and XML specification defines a standard way to add markup to documents.

Regarding language extension, XML allows us to use any nametag we want. These independent nametags allow us to write documents meaningful to the context of the document. The problem, however, is that no predefined semantics exist. Therefore, if we choose <H1> in a document to designate the height of a wall instead of a standard HTML header, it would be perfectly legitimate to do so.

To comprehend these tags, XML provides various methods that include Document Type Definitions, Style Sheets, Parsers, and Extensible Linking Language, etc. These methods will be discussed later in this book. The importance of user defined tags and displaying methods is that the content and the description is divided. The XML documents store content—thus leaving the possibility of content being displayed in relevant medium based on the requirement. An example would be the value of a stock stored over a period of time. One parser could display it in a table and another in the form of a graph. This allows XML to be extended as a universal format for any number of applications. As the document is also storing tags, it is probably not the best medium for a large number of records. In those cases we can use traditional databases and convert the data into XML when required, thus again allowing data to be displayed in a user specific medium.

XML on its own specifies neither the semantics nor a tag set. It provides only a facility to define tags and the structural relationship between them. In this way it acts as a metalanguage for describing markup languages. As there is no predefined tag set, there cannot be any preconceived semantics. All the semantics of an XML document are either defined by the applications that process these documents or by style sheets, in Extended Style Language (XSL), to be defined later in next chapter.

XML describes a class of data objects called XML documents and partially describes the behavior of the computer programs that process these documents. By construction XML documents conform to the SGML standards.

1.1.1 Scope of the Standard

As already described, XML is a standard for defining markup languages. An instance of an XML-compliant language merely specifies a data representation syntax, which may or may not be accompanied by a set of specifications for visual layout in a client browser. Currently, the specification is purely vendor-neutral and any XML editing tool or parser should be mutually compatible.

Unlike some other standards for business-to-business communication, there is no proprietary transport protocol for exchanging XML documents. Network transfer occurs with standard HTTP over TCP/IP, leveraging security mechanisms like SSL for encryption of sensitive data.

The chapter tries to describe different aspects needed to understand and implement XML. The following topics will be presented in the coming sections:

- **XML Documents**—how they are made and different constituents of the document.
- **The Physical** as well as the **Logical structure** of the document. Physically the document is composed of *entities*. Logically the document is made up of components, character references, declarations, and elements and processing instructions, all of which are indicated in the document by explicit markup. All entities contain either unparsed or
- **Parsed Entities**.
- Finally some currently available **XML tools** are discussed. These tools include Parsers, Server software, Database software, and authoring tools.

We start with XML documents.

1.2 Documents

XML 1.0 specification defines an XML document as a data object that conforms to the rules of a well-formed document. Well-formed documents have to meet a minimum set of requirements defined in the specification for them to be considered well-formed. A well-formed document is not necessarily **valid** until it also meets the constraints defined by SGML specification. An XML document usually comprises two parts—the prolog and the body. As shown in the figure here, Prolog information has version declarations and DTD. The body contains the rest of the XML markup.

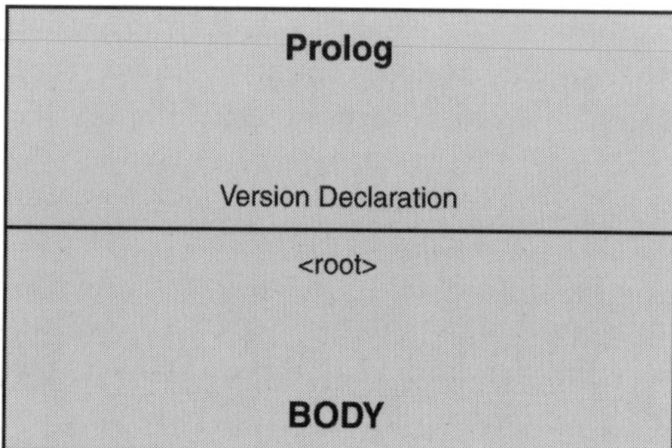

Figure 1.1 An XML document.

1.2.1 Prolog and Document Type Declaration

XML documents should begin with XML declaration, which specifies the version of XML being used in the document. The version number should be used to indicate conformance to this version of this specification. It is an error for a document to use a value for a version number that does not conform to this version in this specification. The processor may signal an error if it receives documents labeled with versions it does not support.

The markup in an XML document is used to describe its storage and logical structure and to associate attribute-value pairs with its logical structures. **Document Type Declaration** is used both to define constraints on the logical structure and support the use of predefined storage units. As mentioned previously, an XML document is said to be valid if it has an associated document type declaration and if the document complies with the constraints expressed in it. A document type declaration is defined by using DOCTYPE tag and is in the form: `<!DOCTYPE tagname [...]>`.

For example:

```
<!DOCTYPE tagname
[ <!ELEMENT tagname ...>
<!—Element declarations and associated attributes-->
] >

<tagname>
<!—-body for rest of the document-->
</tagname>
```

The document type declaration must appear before the first element in the document.

The XML document type declaration contains or points to markup declarations that provide a grammar for a class of documents. This grammar is known as **document type definition (DTD).** The DTD can point to an external subset (a special kind of external entity) containing markup declarations, contain the markup directly in an internal subset, or do both. The DTD for a document consists of both subsets taken together.

A markup declaration is an element type declaration, an attribute-list declaration, an entity declaration, or a notation declaration. The markup declarations may be made up in whole or in part using the replacement text of parameter entities. Parameter-entity replacement text must be properly nested with markup declarations. That is to say, if either the first character or the last character of a markup declaration is contained in the replacement text for a parameter-entity reference, both must be contained in the same replacement text. In the internal DTD subset, parameter-entity references can occur only where markup declarations can occur, not within markup declarations.

As with the internal subset, the external subset and any external parameter entities referred to in the DTD must consist of a series of complete markup declarations of the types allowed by the non-terminal symbol markup declarations, interspersed with white space or parameter-entity references.

However, portions of the contents of the external subset or of external parameter entities may conditionally be ignored by using the conditional section construct; this is not allowed in the internal subset.

The external subset and parameter entities also differ from the internal subset in that, in them parameter-entity references are permitted within markup declarations, not only between markup declarations.

Example of an XML document with a document type declaration:

```
<?xml version="1.0"?>
<!DOCTYPE greeting SYSTEM "hello.dtd">
<greeting>Hello, world!</greeting>
```

The system identifier "`hello.dtd`" gives the URL of a DTD for the document.

The declarations can also be given locally, as in this example:

```
<?xml version="1.0" encoding="UTF-8"?>
<!DOCTYPE greeting [
   <!ELEMENT greeting (#PCDATA)>
]>
<greeting>Hello, world!</greeting>
```

If both the external and internal subsets are used, the internal subset is considered to occur before the external subset. In effect the entity and attribute-list declarations in the internal subset take precedence over those in the external subset.

1.2.2 Standalone Document Declaration

When declaring an XML document, the **standalone** attribute of the document is used to indicate if the document has any markup declarations that are external to the document that would affect the contents of the document when passed from an XML processor to an application.

If the standalone declarations is assigned the value "yes", then the document has no markup declarations external to the document entity and the document is self-contained. There are no references to an external DTD or in an external parameter entity referenced from an internal subset.

The value "no" indicates that there might be markup declarations external to the document, either in external DTD or in an external type parameter entity.

If a document has external markup declarations and no standalone document declarations then the default value of "no" is assumed. On the other hand if there are no external markup declarations, the standalone document declaration has no meaning. Note that the standalone document declaration denotes only the presence of external declarations. The presence in a document of references to external entities when those entities are internally declared does not change its standalone status.

The standalone document declaration must have the value "no" if any external markup declarations contain declarations of:

- attributes with default values, if elements to which these attributes apply appear in the document without specifications of values for these attributes, or
- entities (other than amp, lt, gt, apos, quot), if references to those entities appear in the document, or
- attributes with values subject to normalization, where the attribute appears in the document with a value, which will change as a result of normalization, or
- element types with element content, if white space occurs directly within any instance of those types.

An example XML declaration with a standalone document declaration:

```
<?xml version="1.0" standalone='yes'?>
```

1.2.3 Well-Formed XML Documents

A textual object is said to be a well-formed XML document if the following conditions are met by the document:

1. The document is taken as a whole, and it matches the production labeled document.
    a. It contains one or more **elements**. Elements in XML usually identify the nature of the content they surround. They are tags that start with delimiting brackets, <*tag name*> and end with </*tag name*>. For example, <TEMPERATURE>65</TEMPERATURE>.
    b. It must contain a uniquely named element, known as the **root element**, no part of which appears in the content of any other element.
    c. Nonempty tags must be nested properly.

2. Each of the **parsed entities**, which are referenced directly or indirectly within the document, is well-formed. If a document has markup characters that cannot be parsed or are invalid, then the document is not considered well-formed.

As a result of this, for each non-root element C in the document, there is one other element P in the document such that C is in the content of P, but C is not in the content of any other element of P. P is referred to as the **parent** of C, and C as a **child** of P.

Logical structure of an XML document is made up of Elements and Attributes.

1.2.4 Elements

As mentioned before, each **XML document** is made up of one or more elements. An element in XML is defined by a start tag, an end tag, and data in between. Using the same example as used before:

```
<TEMPERATURE>65</TEMPERATURE>
```

constitutes an element.

It is important to note that both the start and the end tags must be the same. XML is case sensitive, therefore `<Temperature>` and `<TEMPERATURE>` are not the same.

The specification defined by W3C does not place any restrictions on the number of characters to be used for defining the tag, although that can be dependent on the individual parsing program.

An **element** usually has **character data** and the **markup**. For our example "65" is the character data and the `<TEMPERATURE>` tag on the either side is the markup tag.

1.2.4.1 Start Tags, End Tags, and Empty-Element Tags

As already mentioned, the start tag is defined by `<tag_name>`. An end tag is defined the same as start tag except for a prefix of '/'. For the start tag defined as *<tag_name>*, the end tag will be `</tag_name>`. The end of every element that begins with a start tag must be marked by an end tag containing a name that echoes the element's type as given in the start tag.

The text between the start and the end tag is defined as **content**.

If an element is empty, it must be represented either by a start tag immediately followed by an end tag or by an empty-element tag.

Empty-element tags may be used for any element that has no content, whether or not it is declared using the keyword EMPTY. **For interoperability**, the empty-element tag must be used, and can only be used, for elements that are **declared** EMPTY.

Example of empty elements:

```
<WEATHER temperature="65" />
or <TEMPERATURE></TEMPERATURE>
or </TEMPERATURE>
```

When declaring the attribute name, it should be kept in mind that no attribute name may appear more than once in the same start tag or empty-element tag. The attribute must also have been declared; the value must be of the type declared for it. Attribute values cannot contain direct or indirect entity references to external entities and, finally, the replacement text of any entity referred to directly or indirectly in an attribute value (other than "<") must not contain a <.

1.2.5 Element Type Declarations

The Element Type Declaration defines the 'type' of the **content** of the **element**, thus putting a type constraint on the **element**.

Element type declarations often constrain which element types can appear as **children** of the element. At user option, an XML processor may issue a warning when a declaration mentions an element type for which no declaration is provided, but this is not an error.

An element type declaration is defined as:

```
<!ELEMENT element_name Element_Type>
```

where the **element_name** gives the element type being declared. The specification imposes a constraint that no element type may be declared more than once. Possible `Element_Type` values are—`'EMPTY'`, `'ANY'`, **`Mixed`**, **`children`**.

Examples of element type declarations:

```
<!ELEMENT br EMPTY>
```

```
<!ELEMENT p (#PCDATA|emph)* >
<!ELEMENT %name.para; %content.para; >
<!ELEMENT container ANY>
```

1.2.5.1 Element Content

The element content is defined through element content model, which lists the child elements that an element can contain. The model defines the allowed types of the child elements and the order in which they are allowed to appear. Regular expressions shown below are used for defining the grammar used in the content models.

Parameter-entity **replacement text** must be properly nested with parenthesized groups. That is to say, if either the opening or closing parentheses in a **choice, seq**, or **Mixed** construct is contained in the replacement text for a **parameter entity**, both must be contained in the same replacement text. **For interoperability**, if a parameter-entity reference appears in a **choice, seq**, or **Mixed** construct, its replacement text should not be empty, and neither the first nor last non-blank character of the replacement text should be a connector (| or ,).

The table provided here shows content model operators and their uses.

Symbol	Usage
,	Strict ordering
|	Selection
+	Repetition with minimum of 1
*	Repetition
?	Optional
()	Grouping

For example:

```
<!ELEMENT cylinder (radius, length, color?, content+)>
```

In the document instance it would appear as:

```
<cylinder>
    <radius>...</radius>
```

```
    <length>...</length>
    <color>...</color>
    <content>...</content>
</cylinder>
```

The regular expression "+" used with **content** indicates that there can be more than one type of content present in the cylinder. The symbol "?" with color indicates that the color element is optional. Going by this rule, another instance the document could be:

```
<cylinder>
    <radius>...</radius>
    <length>...</length>
    <color>...</color>
    <content>...</content>
    . . .
</cylinder>
```

the symbol "," stands for strict ordering therefore the elements defined must follow one another in the order defined.

The content of an element matches a content model if and only if it is possible to trace out a path through the content model, obeying the sequence, choice, and repetition operators and matching each element in the content against an element type in the content model.[1]

1.2.5.2 Mixed Content

The element content model defines mixed content model where order of the child elements defined is not important and they must not contain the same name twice. The elements of this type may contain character data but they must be separated by "|" character.

Examples of mixed content declarations:

```
<!ELEMENT p (#PCDATA|a|ul|b|i|em)*>
<!ELEMENT p (#PCDATA | %font; | %phrase; | %special; | %form;)* >
<!ELEMENT b (#PCDATA)>
```

1. It is an error if an element in the document can match more than one occurrence of an element type in the content model.

1.2.6 Element's Attributes-List Declaration

Attributes are used in XML to define properties of an element. The element is associated with an attribute through a name-value pair defined within the start and end tags. Attribute-list declarations specify the name, data type, and default value (if any) of each attribute associated with a given element type. For example:

```
<!ATTLIST FORECAST date CDATA #REQUIRED>
```

In the example here the date is an attribute for FORECAST. FORECAST is an element. It is important that at the time of declaring the attribute list, the element should have been declared. If it has not been declared then the XML processor may issue a warning on encountering the element name (FORECAST in our case).

Element attribute lists are generally used to

1. define a set of attributes for a given element type;
2. define type constraints for the attributes; or
3. provide default values for the attributes.

When more than one attribute-list declaration is provided for a given element type, the contents of all those provided are merged. When more than one definition is provided for the same attribute of a given element type, the first declaration is binding and later declarations are ignored.

An XML processor may, at user option, issue a warning when more than one attribute-list declaration is provided for a given element type, or more than one attribute definition is provided for a given attribute, but this is not an error.

1.2.6.1 Attribute Types

An attribute type for an element defined in the Attribute-List declaration can be of three types—String, tokenized, and enumerated.

The values for a **string type attribute** can be any literal string.

A **tokenized type attribute** can be – `ID` or `IDREF(S)` or `ENTITY(IES)` or `NMTOKEN(S)`. The tokenized types have the following lexical and semantic constraints.

1. A name must not appear more than once in an XML document as a value of this type; that is, ID values must uniquely identify the elements which bear them.
2. No element type may have more than one ID attribute specified.
3. An ID attribute must have a declared default of #IMPLIED or #REQUIRED.
4. Each **Name** must match the value of an ID attribute on some element in the XML document; that is, values must match the value of some ID attribute.
5. Values of type ENTITY must match the **Name** production, values of type ENTITIES must match **Names**; each **Name** must match the name of an **unparsed entity** declared in the **DTD**.
6. Values of type NMTOKEN must match the **Nmtoken** production; values of type NMTOKENS must match **Nmtokens**.

Enumerated attributes can take one of a list of values provided in the declaration. There are two kinds of enumerated types—**Notation type and Enumeration**.

A NOTATION attribute identifies a **notation**, declared in the DTD with associated system and/or public identifiers, to be used in interpreting the element to which the attribute is attached. The specification enforces a constraint that values of this type must match one of the **notation** names included in the declaration; all notation names in the declaration must be declared.

For **enumeration**, values of this type must match one of the Nmtoken tokens in the declaration.

For **interoperability**, the same **Nmtoken** should not occur more than once in the enumerated attribute types of a single element type.

1.2.6.2 Attribute Defaults

As mentioned above, the attribute declaration list defined also includes information whether the attribute has any default value. This value is used if the attribute is missing from the document. The XML processor uses the three directives—#REQUIRED, #IMPLIED, or #FIXED, to decide the necessary action for the element's processing.

In an attribute declaration, #REQUIRED means that the attribute must always be provided, #IMPLIED that no default value is provided. If the declaration is neither #REQUIRED nor #IMPLIED, then the **AttValue** value contains the declared **default** value; the #FIXED keyword states that the attribute must always have the default value. If a default value is declared, when an XML processor encounters an omitted attribute, it is to behave as though the attribute were present with the declared default value. The declared default value must also meet the lexical constraints of the declared attribute type.

If the default declaration is the keyword #REQUIRED, then the attribute must be specified for all elements of the type in the attribute-list declaration. If an attribute has a default value declared with the #FIXED keyword, instances of that attribute must match the default value.

Examples of attribute-list declarations:

```
<!ATTLIST termdef
          id      ID      #REQUIRED
          name    CDATA   #IMPLIED>
<!ATTLIST list
          type    (bullets|ordered|glossary)   "ordered">
<!ATTLIST form
          method  CDATA   #FIXED "POST">
```

1.2.6.3 *Attribute-Value Normalization*

XML processor normalize the attribute values before it is passed to the application for validity checks. The normalization process includes certain tuning of the document so as to reduce the misinterpretation of data by the application. The following actions are taken while normalizing:

- all new lines and or returns are replaced by spaces. Multiple white spaces are also replaced by single spaces.
- the character reference is processed by appending the character to the attribute value.
- the entity reference is processed by recursively processing the replacement text for the entity.

A non-validating parser should treat any attribute for which no declaration has been read as a CDATA. The parsers that do not have case sensitivity implemented should change all NMTOKEN values to upper case letters.

1.2.7 Conditional Sections

Conditional sections help in providing clauses that can help define the flow of the document based on the requirements. You can use them to activate/de-activate certain sections based on the requirements. They can only be used in the external subsets of the DTD.

A conditional section may contain one or more complete declarations, comments, processing instructions, or nested conditional sections intermingled with white spaces.

There are two types of conditional sections—INCLUDE and IGNORE.

An INCLUDE defines a section as part of the DTD at the time of processing. IGNORE makes a section not a logical part of the DTD at the time of processing. No action is taken for the declarations defined inside the IGNORE section. If an INCLUDE section is nested inside the IGNORE section then the outermost conditional section is taken into consideration, and, in this case, the INCLUDE section is IGNORE(d) too.

Example of a Conditional section:

```
<!ENTITY % headlinenews 'IGNORE' >
<!ENTITY % nationalnews 'INCLUDE' >

<![%headlinenews;[
<!ELEMENT news (national, international, sports)>
]]>

<![%nationalnews;[
<!ELEMENT news (national)>
]]>
```

In this example we have specified that we want to `"INCLUDE"` `nationalnews` section and `"IGNORE"` `headlinenews`. If later we want to process news in the `headlinenews` section and not the `nationalnews` section then we simply switch the values of the two entity declarations.

At the time of parsing the document, the conditional sections are parsed completely to ensure proper behavior of nested sections. If the keyword of the conditional section is a parameter-entity reference, the parameter entity must be replaced by its content before the processor decides whether to include or ignore the conditional section.

1.3 *Physical Structures*

An XML document is made up of one or more entities. Each of these entities is identified by name and has associated content. Every XML document has one **document entity**, which serves as the starting point at the time of document processing. This may contain the whole document also.

Entities can be parsed or unparsed. The entities that have been parsed act as an integral part of the document. The content of parsed entity is referred to as **replacement text**. They are invoked by using entity references.

An **unparsed entity** may or may not be **text**. It is identified by a name and has an associated **notation**. XML places no constraints on the contents of the unparsed entities. They are referenced by using the name.

There are two types of entities—**general** and **parameter**. General entites are declared in the document type declaration but are used only for the document's content. Parameter entities are valid for the scope of the document type declaration.

An example of a general entity would be:

```
<!ENTITY name "some replacement name like John Doe">
```

in this case the replacement text for the entity "name" is :

```
some replacement name like John Doe
```

An example of a parameter entity would be:

```
<!ENTITY %params "length|width|height|volume|area">
```

The % marks the entity as the parameter entity. It can be used further as :

```
<!ELEMENT rectangle (Name|%params;)>
```

1.3.1 Character and Entity References

The content of the entity defined in the document is referred to as **Entity References**. When writing an XML document, it is important to keep in mind that the entity should be declared before any reference to that entity name is made; otherwise the parser will flag an error.

An entity reference is made by using the "&". The symbol "," acts as a delimiter. Following is an example of an entity:

&entityparam;

Parameter Entities are referenced using "&", for delimiters "," is used.

For standalone documents, or documents with no DTD, or with only internal DTD subset that contain no parameter entity references, the Entity Reference Name must match the entity declaration for the same. For entities declared in external subset or in external parameter entities, an XML parser only needs to check the well-formed-ness constraint if the standalone property is set to "yes".

Well-formed documents do not need to declare following entities. They are also a part of predefined entities.

Entity Name	**Name**	**Symbol**
<	Less than	<
>	Greater than	>
&	Ampersand	&
"	Quote	"
&apos	Apostrophe	'

Character references are also entity references. Character references are defined from the subset of ISO/IEC 10646-character-set. The character reference uses the symbol "&#x" or "&#" to define the Unicode that is equivalent to the character from the 10646-character-set. The symbol "&#x" is used for hexadecimal character code and the symbol "&#" is used for decimal codes.

Example of character and entity references:

```
<?xml version+"1.0">
<!DOCTYPE mycontact [
<!ENTITY hm        "Home">

<!ENTITY num  "Number">
```

```
<!ENTITY ph        "Phone ">
]>

<mycontact>My &hm; contact: &ph;&num;</mycontact>
```

1.3.2 Entity Declarations

The section on Physical Structure in this chapter discusses entities briefly. An entity is declared with the help of the ENTITY keyword. The syntax for the ENTITY, is the keyword followed by the name and a value. It is recommended that the same entity is not declared more than once in a document. The XML parser binds the first entity definition that it encounters. The parser can then be instructed to issue warnings if more than one declaration is made.

From the previous example:

```
<!ENTITY name "some replacement name like John Doe">
```

1.3.2.1 Internal Entities

An Internal Entity declaration indicates that the content of the parsed entity (**replacement text**) lies inside the document. The replacement text itself can be a location. Internal entities are **parsed entities**.

Example of an internal entity:

```
<!ENTITY     entityname        "corresponding value">
```

1.3.2.2 External Entities

In external entities, unlike their internal counterparts, the contents of the replacement text for the entity reside in a file separate from the XML document. The content can be accessed using either a **system identifier** or a **public identifier**. System Identifier is a URI (Uniform Resource Identifier) address, which may used to retrieve the content. The URI can be relative to the document or to some other external parameter entity like an HTTP address.

The other method of accessing the content is through the public identifier. An XML processor in this case tries to generate an alternative URI to retrieve the entity content. If the processor is unable to do so then it uses the URI defined by the system identifier.

Examples of external entities:

```
<!ENTITY entityname SYSTEM "http://www.myserver.com/XML/contnet.xml">
<!ENTITY entityname PUBLIC "-//home//johndoe//content"
        "http://www.mydrtbr.vom//XML//content.xml">
```

1.3.3 Parsed Entities

Parsed entities as defined by XML specifications can only contain character data or XML markup. The entity should be well-formed obeying the rules of a well-formed XML document. An internal parsed entity is said to be well formed if the replacement text matches the production labeled content. By definition, all internal entities are well formed.

External entity is well formed if it matches the production labeled **extParsedEnt**. A document entity is well formed if it matches the production labelled **document**.

1.3.4 Predefined Entities

Few entities are predefined in the system. As mentioned in Section 1.3.2, they include amp, lt, gt, apos, and quot. Corresponding numeric references in the form of hexadecimal or decimal can also be used for these symbols. All XML processors must recognize these entities whether they are declared or not, though valid documents should still declare them for interoperability with older processors.

1.3.5 Notation Declarations

Notations are used to associate certain actions with the certain entities. For example, file formats can be associated with a corresponding application for interpreting the file, or an extension can be used to perform certain actions. Notations identify by name the format of these actions.

Notation Declarations are used to provide an identifying name for the notation. They are used in entity or attribute list declarations and in attribute specifications.

Notations are defined using the NOTATION keyword. Following is an example of a notation declaration:

```
<!NOTATION  txt  SYSTEM  "notepad.exe">
```

which can be further used as:

```
<!ATTLIST    document
             file.name     ENTITY       #REQUIRED
             file.format   NOTATION     txt>

<!ENTITY     docfilename   SYSTEM       "c:\temp\chapter.txt"   NDATA txt>

<document    file.name="docfilename"    file.format+"txt"/>
```

It is mandatory for an XML processor to provide the name and the external identifiers of any notation declared or referred to in an entity declaration, attribute declaration or an attribute value to the application. It is not an error though, if the associated applications are not available on the system where the XML processor is running.

1.3.6 Document Entity

As briefly mentioned in Section 1.3, Physical Structures, each XML document has one **document entity** that acts as a starting point for the XML processor. It is considered to be the root of the entity tree. Unlike general entities, the document entity has no name and can be used without any identification.

1.3.7 Comments, Processing Instructions, and CDATA Sections

Comments, Processing Instructions (PIs), and CDATA sections act as data fillers in an XML document.

1.3.7.1 Comments

Comments make the documents more meaningful for the programmer. They help in explaining the complexities of the document without getting in the way of the processing logic. Comments are written in XML using the double hyphen (--) characters.

An example of a comment:

```
<!-- declarations for temperature data -->
```

The text should not include the character "_" or "--" to avoid the parser getting confused.

Comments can appear at places allowed by the grammar. Comments are not allowed inside element tags within declarations. For example.

```
<tag <!--comment at wrong place --> >
        incorrect value now
</tag>
```

1.3.7.2 Processing Instruction

Processing instructions provide instructions to the applications using the XML data. They are not part of the document's character data but are passed through to the application. They are defined in the following manner:

```
<?PICommand    Instructions for command ?>
```

PICommand is used to identify the application to which the instruction is directed. "XML" and "xml" cannot be used and are reserved tokens.

1.3.7.3 CDATA Sections

CDATA Sections are used for skipping character blocks in a document at the time of processing. The blocks in this case are sections that might be taken as markup unless otherwise skipped. For example, if we would like to skip:

```
<YEAR>1999</YEAR>
```

it can be done using the CDATA sections in the following manner:

```
<![CDATA[<YEAR>1999</YEAR>]]>
```

The sections are defined by beginning the section with string "<![CDATA[" and end with string "]]>".

1.4 Tools for XML

1.4.1 XML Parsers

Computer Science Dept. – University of Trier, Germany, fxp. fxp stands for functional XML parser and is a validating XML parser written completely in functional programming language Standard ML. It includes support for XML catalog syntax, support for retrieval of nonlocal URLs and an application called **fxviz,** which is a sample document tree visualizing application.

IBM, XML Parser for Java. It is a validating XML parser written in pure Java. It includes a package called com.ibm.xml.parser that contains classes and methods for parsing, manipulating and validating XML document.

Microstar, AELfred. It is a small, fast, DTD-aware Java-based parser. It is designed essentially for applets and applications that want to add XML support. It is small (26K) and consists of two core class files—XmlParser.class and XMLProcessor.class.

Oracle, XML parser for Java, C, C++, PL/SQL. Oracle has various products on XML that include parsers for Java, C, C++, and PL/SQL. These are all standalone components that allow parsing in the language they support.

Sun, XML Library. Sun's XML library includes a document parser with optional validation, in-memory object model tree for manipulating and writing XML structured data, and preliminary support for customizing in-memory XML object tree for application-specific data structures and behaviors using JavaBeans with XML—XML beans.

DataChannel Inc., XJParser. Includes 100% XML 1.0 and DOM level 1 compliance, SAX and W3C interfaces, validation against both DTDs and XML-Data schemas, built in XSL transformation engine, and some XSL pattern matching facilities.

Clark Cooper, XML Perl Module. Module for processing XML documents in perl scripts.

Lars Marius Garshol, xmlproc -Python XML parser. XML parser written in python.

1.4.2 Server Software

Many server software vendors have already built XML support, for many different purposes, including:

- business-to-business communication;
- XML-HTML/XML-Database Translation;

- publishing; and
- push Content.

webMethods, B2B Integration Server. An XML-based solution that automates the exchange of data between applications, websites, and legacy data sources. For companies that are seeking to implement automated business-to-business linkages, the B2B Integration Server makes it possible to encapsulate key business services for automated access by their customers, partners, and suppliers. The server leverages webMethods' own Web Interface Definition Language (WIDL) to create a service-based architecture over the document-based web.

CrossRoute, Alliance Server. CrossRoute's tools allow two or more organizations to map out the business processes they share, defining what information needs to be shared at each stage and where that information is to be found in a company's databases or ERP. The business objects sent from company to company are represented in XML.

DataChannel, RIO. By combining open Web standards, the advanced browser access, IP multicasting (making it "bandwidth-friendly" when compared to PointCast or Marimba), and XML technology, DataChannel RIO represents the new breed of corporate "push" intranet environments. RIO melds ongoing employee communications and an existing information structure into a single Active Content routing system. With RIO, XML content becomes Active Content and can be repurposed, reducing the custom software development necessary today in connecting the once isolated "information islands."

Enigma, Insight 4.0. A professional electronic-publishing software solution for publishers of large documents. Enigma's SGML/XML Style Sheet Editor, currently bundled with Insight, is also available as a standalone product.

Hynet Technologies, Digital Library System. The Digital Library System (DLS) manages documents and document components as standard software objects, allowing import of documents created in Adobe FrameMaker and Microsoft Word, or SGML/XML files.

Inso, DynaBase Professional Publishing System. This indexing, searching and scripting software is available for Microsoft Internet Information Server and Netscape Enterprise and FastTrack servers running Windows NT 3.51 or

4.0, or Sun Solaris 2.5. The DynaWeb companion server converts SGML or XML content into HTML "on-the-fly" for viewing by web browsers. DynaWeb is "client-aware" and customizes content for different browsers. In this manner, DynaWeb can also automatically deliver XML directly, with the appropriate style sheet, to XML-compliant browsers.

Open Market, Folio. Open Market's Folio 4 information management and distribution products already import XML documents into an indexed database for content delivery over IP networks or to CD-ROMs. Recently Open Market announced increased XML support to allow documents to be indexed and made secure in their native formats. Also, Folio products will interoperate with other standards-based solutions that author, parse, distribute, and render XML documents. Products include Folio SiteDirector (distribution), Folio SecurePublish (transaction management software), and Folio Publisher (electronic publishing).

Vignette, StoryServer. StoryServer 3.2 delivers XML-enabled applications and content on the Web. It combines tools for relational database, multimedia and XML content creation. StoryServer is a Web-content application platform for building, managing, and delivering service-based Web applications, such as online publishing, knowledge management, and e-commerce systems.

1.4.3 Database Software

POET. The architecture of object databases is ideally suited to handling XML data, so the widespread adoption of XML data could potentially be the "killer application" for the object database market. POET is currently the major player in the convergence of XML and object database technology. With POET's Object Server and XML Repository, the goal was to move beyond mere XML data storage, offering tightly integrated XML-specific tree navigation, versioning, management of arbitrary links, import/export, publishing of structured content on the web, and support for object-oriented programming languages and common scripting languages.

IBM. IBM has implemented a tool called **DataCraft**, which provides XML views of databases and makes it easier to publish XML forms on the Web. The current tool works with IBM's DB/2 and Microsoft Access.

1.4.4 Authoring Tools

Tools for creating, managing, and delivering XML are already on the market or in development by a number of companies.

Adobe. In mid-1998, Adobe introduced interim versions of FrameMaker and FrameMaker+SGML that can export to XML. The next full release of these products will be able to import XML. Adobe has a representative on the W3C's XML working group, and is also involved with XLink, Cascading Style Sheets and RDF, so it makes sense to expect these technologies to appear in future Adobe products. Eventually, customers will be able to use a single tool to create content that can be automatically published to all major standards for print and electronic formats, including HTML, SGML, PDF, Adobe PostScript(R), and XML.

ArborText. A longtime player in the SGML arena, ArborText released XML Styler, a free Java-based XSL editor. Its graphical user interface allows editing without the need to know XML syntax. In the future, ArborText will integrate XML Styler into Adept, the company's XML authoring tool for print publishing.

Balise. Balise can be described as a "middleware" component for building XML/SGML-based information systems. As a standalone product, Balise aids with structured document manipulation in a large number of applications:

- conversion of legacy documents into structured SGML form, DTD to DTD transformation;
- conversion of XML/SGML documents into HTML;
- content validation and document quality assurance;
- information extraction and dynamic document assembly;
- connection to databases, merge of various information sources, document formatting; and
- electronic publishing of XML/SGML documents.

DataChannel. A free, Java-based validating parser called DXP (DataChannel XML Parser; based on Norbert Mikula's well-known NXP) is available from the company's website. Just released is the free XML toolkit, XML Development Environment, which includes a set of components for people who want to get started with XML.

Inso. Inso offers what it calls "the first integrated, end-to-end publishing solution for creating, converting, storing, managing, indexing, searching, and publishing XML content to the Web, CD-ROM, and print." Products include DynaTag 4.0, DynaBase 3.0, DynaText 3.1, and companion tool DynaWeb.

IBM. The XML Editor maker from IBM automatically generates visual editors from DTDs. It also has **PatML**, a pattern match and replacement tool, and **TeXML**, which turns XML into the TeX formatting language.

Microsoft. Office 2000 has XML support.

Microstar. ActiveSG/XML is a set of tools and techniques for design and deployment of XML/SGML transaction-based systems on the Internet. Microstar also offers a free XML parser, SoftQuad. HTML editor HotMetal Pro will soon offer Live Data Base Pages, an add-on that lets developers drag and drop HTML data into a database and have it returned as XML.

1.5 *Conclusion*

In this chapter we described the basics of XML and the specification as described by the World Wide Web Consortium. XML as of now has a great future. It allows developers and users to manage data in ways that take advantage of the power of information exchange. It has the ability to solve the problems currently present in HTML and make data more useful. From an e-commerce perspective, XML will allow consumers to search effectively for products and services that meet their specific needs. This could lead to huge advantages to consumers in that it will increase awareness in the marketplace and provide momentum to drive price and quality competition on the web.

Not mentioned so far are risks—if there are any. The consensus among the XML gurus right now is that XML version 1.0 compliance by itself will not guarantee interoperability between data formats, which is supposed to be the beauty of XML in the first place. XML lets developers choose their own markup tags to determine how data should be categorized. However, in doing so there needs to be some coordination, or XML may usher in a whole new era of non-interoperable metadata.

CHAPTER 2

DOM and XSL

2.1 Introduction

This chapter presents the Document Object Model (DOM) and Extensible Style Language (XML). The DOM section also has a basic DOM example where I try to use a few common DOM functions to explain things as defined by W3C for the DOM specification. DOM is recommended by W3C for transformation and manipulation of XML documents. For formatting the documents, it is either XSL and/or CSS. The XSL section briefly explains some important concepts and has one example to elaborate further.

2.2 The Document Object Model

The Document Object Model (DOM) is a language and platform independent programming interface that permits scripts to access and modify the content, structure, and style for HTML and XML documents. It provides an object-oriented view of the documents by representing a document as a tree of nodes. Each node is considered as an object with its own set of properties and methods. This will be discussed in detail later in the chapter.

It is also a step towards resolving browser differences. Browsers currently have their own methods of representing web-page entities. These entities are maintained internally in the browser in a different manner, thus creating differences in web pages based on how they implement each object. W3C is trying to resolve these differences through its DOM Level 1 Recommendation. DOM defines a high-level set of objects that provide an interface between the developer and the browser's internal objects. Each DOM-compliant browser must support a core set of XML objects (DOM Core) and an additional set of HTML objects (DOM HTML).

W3C has defined three parts of DOM: DOM Core; DOM HTML; and DOM XML. DOM Core, which as already mentioned, has a core set of XML objects, a "must-have" part of every DOM implementation. DOM HTML has a set of classes to provide HTML support. DOM XML classes provide XML support. Our book covers only XML-related DOM.

XML is increasingly being used as a way of representing and storing information stored in diverse systems. XML presents this data as "documents." DOM is used to manage this data. It provides methods to define the logical structure of the documents and the way a document is accessed and manipulated. Using DOM, programmers can build documents, navigate their structure, and add, modify, or delete elements and content. Anything found in an HTML or XML document can be accessed, changed, deleted, or added using the Document Object Model. The API that DOM provides, as per W3C specification, can be used in a wide variety of environments and applications. DOM has been designed to be used with any programming language. The Document Object Model is not a binary specification. DOM programs written in the same language will be source code compatible across platforms, but the DOM does not define any form of binary interoperability.

2.2.1 Origins of Document Object Model

DOM was originally designed as a specification to allow JavaScript scripts and Java programs to be portable among web browsers. Dynamic HTML (DHTML) was the immediate ancestor of the Document Object Model and thought of largely in terms of browsers. When the DOM working group was formed at W3C, various vendors who had worked with SGML before XML was developed influenced it. Many were already working or had already developed their own object models for documents in order to provide an API for SGML/XML editors or document repositories, and these object models have also influenced the DOM.

2.3 Document Object Model (Core) Level 1

2.3.1 Overview of the DOM Core Interfaces

DOM provides a minimal set of interfaces and objects for accessing and manipulating XML documents. It provides interfaces to traverse the document and make changes to the content based on requirements. The specification, though, does not provide a mechanism to create or save a document. It is left to the product that implements the DOM API.

2.3.2 The DOM Structure Model

The DOM Core defines a tree-like structure of `Node` objects. The idea behind defining a tree is that it breaks up the document into a hierarchy. The Document object becomes the root of the tree and Node objects become the nodes for the tree. These `Nodes` may either be a subclass or a leaf `Node`.

Each node of the document tree may have a number of child nodes. The specification numbers these nodes sequentially. The nodes also can be named. Each of these nodes has its own set of properties and methods and each is an atomic unit by itself. Using reference to any node you can traverse to any other node in the tree.

DOM establishes two basic kinds of relationships between nodes. The first, using any node object, allows you to locate where in the document tree it is located. This helps in traversal of the list. DOM defines a `NodeList` interface, which is an ordered collection of nodes, to help in these kinds of traversals.

The second relationship is based on names. It allows the user to access a collection of objects by names. This is made possible through another interface called `NamedNodeMap`.

DOM is a container of all the objects defined in HTML and XML document. For XML documents, it provides methods to access the Document Type Definition (DTD). It provides methods and interfaces to access root element, the use of which allows you to traverse across the document tree. In case of HTML documents this root is the <HTML> tag. For XML documents it is the outside or top-level element. As already mentioned in Chapter 1, an element is defined as an object that contains the content between the start and the end tag of the element as object, as well as any set of attributes defined for the element.

Before going into the details of interfaces defined in Core DOM, a list of possible node objects in XML and HTML documents is provided.

The primary object types are **Nodes, Documents, Elements** and **Attributes.** In addition to these, the specification also defines the following objects.

- **Processing Instruction (PI):** instructions for the parser as defined between `<?` and `?>`.
- **Comment:** ignored by the parser, defined as the characters between `<!--`and `-->`.
- **Entity Reference:** used for named entities and parameter entities. When a '&' character prefixes a token, then a replacement string is placed in place of the token.
- **Text:** contains data for the element.
- **Cdata section:** text content that does not include markup characters.
- **Document fragment:** portion of a document.
- **Document type:** the grammar that defines the tags and attributes supported in an XML document that constitutes a DTD.

The interfaces defined in what follows use the specification as defined at http://www.w3.org/TR/REC-DOM-Level-1. The DOM-level-1 specification is now final a draft recommendation, and W3C is currently working on level-2 specification.

2.3.3 Primary Object Model Types

2.3.3.1 Interface `DOMImplementation`

The `DOMImplementation` interface provides methods for performing operations that are independent of any particular instance of the document object model (see Table 2.1).

The DOM level 1 does not specify a way of creating a document instance, and hence document creation is an operation specific to an implementation. Future levels of the DOM specification are expected to provide methods for creating documents directly.

Table 2.1 DOMImplementation Methods

Method Name	Parameters	Return Value	Comments
`hasFeature`	`Feature` The package name of the feature to test. In Level 1, the legal values are "HTML" and "XML" (case-insensitive).	`true` if the feature is implemented in the specified version.	Test if the DOM implementation implements a specific feature.
	`Version` This is the version number of the package name to test. In Level 1, this is the string "1.0." If the version is not specified, supporting any version of the feature will cause the method to return true.	`false` if not implemented.	

2.3.3.2 Interface Node

Interface Node is the primary datatype for the DOM specification. All node tyes in DOM inherit its basic properties from this interface. It represents a single node in the document tree. Each node that implements the Node Interface exposes methods for dealing with its children, though they may not necessarily have one. See Figure 2.1 for node hierarchy information and Table 2.2 for different interface node attributes.

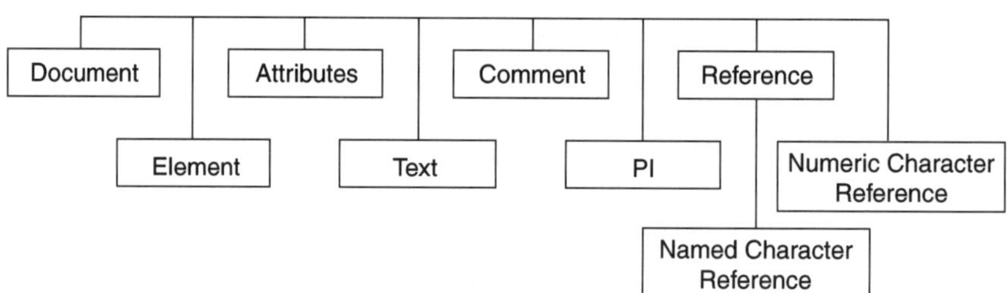

Figure 2.1 Node Hierarchy.

Table 2.2 Node Attributes

Attribute	Comments
`nodeName`	The name of the node; varies with its type. See Table 2.4 for different node types and corresponding node names.
`nodeValue`	The value of this node. For most cases this value is `'null'`.
`nodeType`	Returns a code representing the type of the underlying object.
`parentNode`	Returns the parent of this node. If there is no parent then returns a `null`.
`childNodes`	The returned `NodeList` is the indexed list of children nodes. The content is live, in the sense that changes to the children of the node object that it was created from are immediately reflected in the nodes returned by the `NodeList` assessors.
`firstChild`	The first child of this node. If there is no such node, this returns `null`.
`lastChild`	The last child of this node. If there is no such node, this returns `null`.
`previousSibling`	The node immediately preceding this node. If there is no such node, this returns `null`.
`nextSibling`	The node immediately following this node. If there is no such node, this returns `null`.
`attributes`	A `NamedNodeMap` containing the attributes of this node (if it is an `Element`) or null otherwise.
`ownerDocument`	The `Document` object associated with this node. This is also the `Document` object used to create new nodes. When this node is a `Document` this is null.

2.3.4 Definition Group NodeType

A node type is an integer constant that defines the type of node. Given below are different node types with their integer values and descriptions.

Table 2.3 NodeType Constants

Defined Constants	Integer Value	Description
ELEMENT_NODE	1	The node is an Element.
ATTRIBUTE_NODE	2	The node is an Attr.
TEXT_NODE	3	The node is a Text node.
CDATA_SECTION_NODE	4	The node is a CDATASection.
ENTITY_REFERENCE_NODE	5	The node is an EntityReference.
ENTITY_NODE	6	The node is an Entity.
PROCESSING_INSTRUCTION_NODE	7	The node is a ProcessingInstruction.
COMMENT_NODE	8	The node is a Comment.
DOCUMENT_NODE	9	The node is a Document.
DOCUMENT_TYPE_NODE	10	The node is a DocumentType.
DOCUMENT_FRAGMENT_NODE	11	The node is a DocumentFragment.
NOTATION_NODE	12	The node is a Notation.

The values of nodeName, nodeValue, and attributes vary according to the node type as illustrated in Table 2.4.

Table 2.4 nodeType, nodeName, nodeValue and Their Attributes

nodeType	nodeName	nodeValue	attributes
Element	tagName	null	NamedNodeMap
Attr	name of attribute	value of attribute	null
Text	#text	content of the text node	null
CDATASection	#cdata-section	content of the CDATASection	null

Table 2.4 nodeType, nodeName, nodeValue and Their Attributes (Continued)

nodeType	nodeName	nodeValue	attributes
`Entity-Reference`	name of entity referenced	`null`	`null`
`Entity`	entity name	`null`	`null`
`Processing-Instruction`	target	entire content excluding the target	
`Comment`	`#comment`	content of the comment	`null`
`Document`	`#document`	`null`	`null`
`DocumentType`	document type name	`null`	`null`
`Document-Fragment`	`#document-fragment`	`null`	`null`
`Notation`	notation name	`null`	`null`

Some types of nodes may have child nodes of various types, and others are leaf nodes that cannot have anything below them in the document structure. The node types, and which node types they may have as children, are as shown in Table 2.5.

Table 2.5 Node Methods

Method Name	Parameters	Returned Values	Comments
`insertBefore`	`newChild` The node to insert. `RefChild` The reference node, that is, the node before which the new node must be inserted.	The node being inserted.	Inserts the node `newChild` before the existing child node `refChild`. If `refChild` is null, insert `newChild` at the end of the list of children. If `newChild` is a `DocumentFragment` object, all of its children are inserted, in the same order, before `refChild`. If the `newChild` is already in the tree, it is first removed

Table 2.5 Node Methods (Continued)

Method Name	Parameters	Returned Values	Comments
replaceChild	NewChild The new node to put in the child list. OldChild The node being replaced in the list.	The node replaced.	Replaces the child node oldChild with newChild in the list of children, and returns the oldChild node. If the newChild is already in the tree, it is first removed.
removeChild	oldChild The node being removed	The node removed.	Removes the child node indicated by old-Child from the list of children, and returns it
appendChild	newChild The node to add.	The node added.	Adds the node new-Child to the end of the list of children of this node. If the newChild is already in the tree, it is first removed. If the node added is a DocumentFragment object, the entire contents of the document fragment are moved into the child list of this node.
hasChildNodes	No parameters.	Returns true if the node has any children, false if the node has no children.	This is a convenient method for easy determination of whether a node has any children.
cloneNode	deep If true, recursively clone the subtree under the specified node; if false, clone only the node itself (and its attributes, if it is an Element.	The duplicate node.	Returns a duplicate of this node, that is, serves as a generic copy constructor for nodes. The duplicate node has no parent (parentNode returns null).

Table 2.5 Node Methods (Continued)

Method Name	Parameters	Returned Values	Comments
			Cloning an `Element` copies all attributes and their values, including those generated by the XML processor to represent defaulted attributes, but this method does not copy any text it contains unless it is a deep clone, as the text is contained in a child `Text` node. Cloning any other type of node simply returns a copy of this node.

2.3.4.1 *Interface* `Document`

`Document -- Element, ProcessingInstruction, Comment, DocumentType`

The document can have only one element node, the root node. The `Document` interface represents the entire HTML or XML document. As there are no methods to create a document, it is left up to the user agent to create a document object. It is responsible for providing primary access to the document objects.

A document's name value is `#document` and it has a `null` value. Child nodes are allowed in a document object. See Figure 2.2 and Tables 2.6 and 2.7 for document hierarchy, attributes, and methods, respectively.

2.3.4.2 *Interface DocumentFragment*

`DocumentFragment -- Element, ProcessingInstruction, Comment, Text, CDATA-Section, EntityReference`

`DocumentFragment` allow you to build a subsection of various nodes, and then insert it into the document. The only thing to be kept in mind is that the document must remain well formed even after the fragment is placed

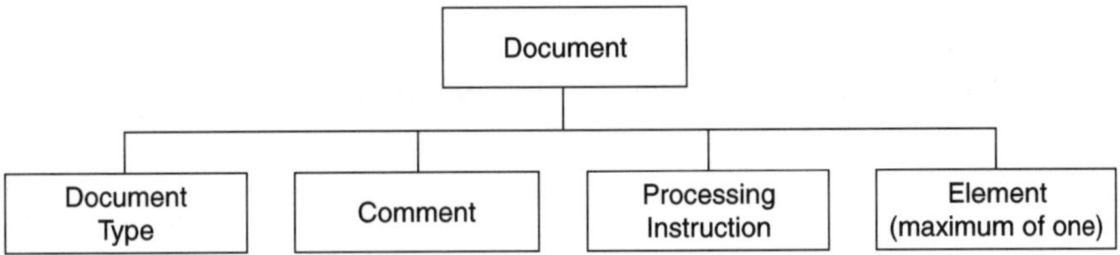

Figure 2.2 Document Hierarchy.

Table 2.6 Document Attributes

Attributes	Comments
`doctype`	Used to provide access to the DTD associated with a document. The specification does not provide any way of editing the document therefore, it can be altered in any way, including use of methods like insertNode or removeNode.
`implementation`	Of type DOMImplementation, it returns an object of this type that handles this document.
`documentElement`	Is used to return the root element. For HTML documents this is the element with the `tagName` "HTML."

Table 2.7 Document Methods

Method Name	Parameters	Return Value	Comments
`createElement`	`tagName` The name of the element type to instantiate. For XML, this is case-sensitive.	A new `Element` object.	Creates an element of the type specified.
`createDocument-Fragment`	None.	A new `DocumentFragment`.	Creates an empty `DocumentFragment` object.
`createTextNode`	`data` of data type string.	The new `Text` object.	Creates a `Text` node given the specified string.
`createComment`	`data` of data type string.	The new `Comment` object.	Creates a Comment node given the specified string.

Table 2.7 Document Methods (Continued)

Method Name	Parameters	Return Value	Comments
`createCDATASection`	`data` of data type string.	The new `CDATASection` object.	Creates a `CDATASection` node whose value is the specified string.
`createProcessingInstruction`	1. `target` The target part of the processing instruction 2. `data` The data for the node.	The new `Processing Instruction` object.	Creates a Processing-Instruction node given the specified name and data strings. <? And ?> are automatically added.
`createAttribute`	`name` of data type string.	A new `Attr` object.	Creates an Attr of the given name. Note that the Attr instance can then be set on an Element using the setAttribute method.
`createEntityReference`	`name` The name of the entity to reference. Of data type string.	The new `EntityReference` object.	Creates an EntityReference object.
`getElementsByTagName`	`tagname` of data type string.	A new `NodeList` object containing all the matched Elements.	Returns a NodeList of all the Elements. Can be accessed by index.

within its final position. When a `DocumentFragment` is inserted into a Document (or indeed any other Node that may take children) the children of the `DocumentFragment` and not the `DocumentFragment` itself are inserted into the `Node`. This makes the `DocumentFragment` very useful when the user wishes to create nodes that are siblings; the `DocumentFragment` acts as the parent of these nodes so that the user can use the standard methods from the `Node` interface, such as `insertBefore()` and `appendChild()`.

A document fragment's name is `"#document-fragment"` and it has a `null` value.

2.3.4.3 Interface DocumentType

`DocumentType - Notation, Entity`

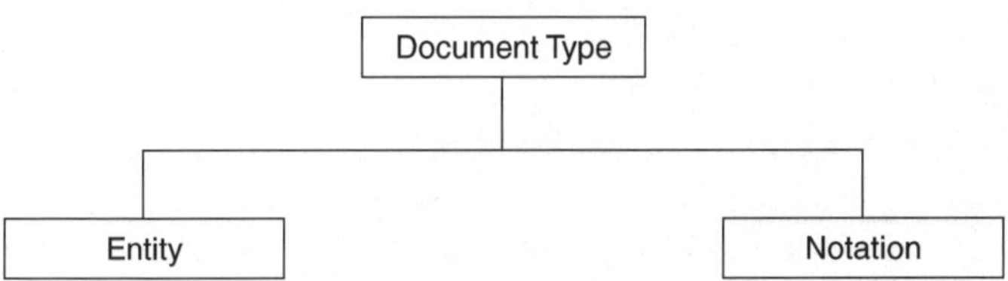

Figure 2.3 DocumentType Hierarchy.

`DocumentType` gives access to the methods and notations contained in the DTD, but in the DOM's Level 1 Core specifications there is no attempt to support element and attribute declarations.

The `DocumentType`'s name is the string that immediately follows the tag `<!DOCTYPE`. For example:

```
<!DOCTYPE mydoc ..some declaration>
```

The name of the `DocumentType` in this case is `mydoc`. `DocumentTypes` have a `null` value. Child nodes are allowed in a document object. The allowed child nodes are DocumentType. Figure 2.3 shows DocumentType hierarchy and Table 2.8 provides DocumentType attributes.

Table 2.8 DocumentType Attributes

Attribute Name	Comments
`name`	The name of DTD; that is, the name immediately following the DOCTYPE keyword. Can also be obtained using the `nodeName` attribute of `Node`.
`entities`	A `NamedNodeMap` containing the general entities, both external and internal, declared in the DTD. Duplicates are discarded. Can be accessed using index, although the order is not significant. The DOM Level 1 does not support editing entities, therefore entities cannot be altered in any way.
`notations`	A `NamedNodeMap` containing the notations declared in the DTD. Duplicates are discarded. Every node in this map also implements the `Notation` interface. The DOM Level 1 does not support editing notations, therefore notations cannot be altered in any way.

2.3.4.4 *Interface EntityReference*

```
EntityReference -- Element, ProcessingInstruction, Comment, Text, CDATA-
Section, EntityReference
```

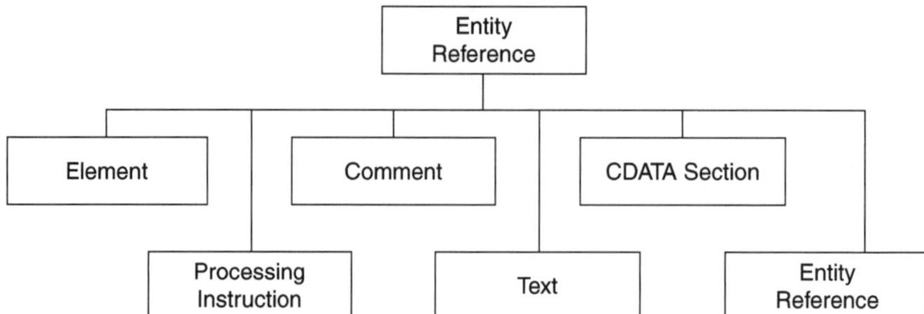

Figure 2.4 EntityReference Hierarchy.

An `EntityReference` can have its child node complete document fragment including other `EntityReference`. An `EntityReference` has a `null` value.

2.3.4.5 *Interface Element*

```
Element -- Element, Text, Comment, ProcessingInstruction, CDATASection,
EntityReference
```

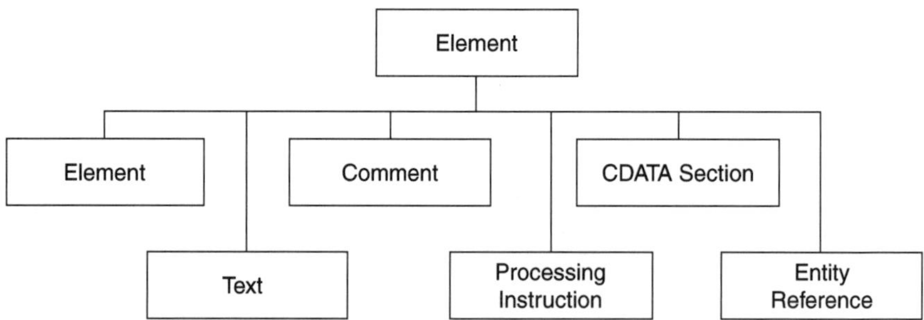

Figure 2.5 Element Hierarchy.

The majority of objects in a document are either text or element nodes. Element attributes are not considered children, but are considered properties of the given node. As node methods can be used for all elements, the only methods associated directly with the Element interface are concerned with attributes and their values. Figure 2.5 and Tables 2.9 and 2.10 show Element hierarchy, attributes, and methods, respectively.

An `Element's` name is its tag name and it has a `null` value. It also has an `attributes` property that is a `NamedNodeMap`.

Table 2.9 Element Attributes

Attribute Name	Comments
`tagName`	Will return the name of the element.

Table 2.10 Element Methods

Method Name	Parameters	Return Value	Comments
`getAttribute`	`name` The name of the attribute to retrieve.	Returns the `Attr` value as a string.	Retrieves an attribute value by name.
`setAttribute`	1. `name` The name of the attribute to create or alter. 2. `value` Value to set in string form.	No return value.	Checks to see if the attribute name is allowed by the DTD. If yes, then adds a new attribute or changes the existing value if the attribute is already present. Raises an error if the attribute name is not allowed.
`remove-Attribute`	`name` The name of the attribute to remove.	None.	Removes an attribute by name.
`get-AttributeNode`	`name` The name of the attribute to retrieve.	The `Attr` node with the specified attribute name or null if there is no such attribute.	

Table 2.10 Element Methods (Continued)

Method Name	Parameters	Return Value	Comments
set-AttributeNode	newAttr The Attr node to add to the attribute list.	If the newAttr attribute replaces an existing attribute with the same name, the previously existing Attr node is returned, otherwise null is returned.	Adds a new attribute. If an attribute with that name is already present in the element, it is replaced by the new one.
remove-AttributeNode	oldAttr The Attr node to remove from the attribute list.	The Attr node that was removed.	
getElements-ByTagName	name The name of the tag to match on. The special value "*" matches all tags.	A list of matching Element nodes.	Returned NodeList can be accessed by index.
normalize	No parameters.	No return value.	Combines all **Text** nodes that are children of this Element into a "normal" form (e.g., tags, comments, processing instructions, CDATA sections, and entity references) separates Text nodes, i.e., there are no adjacent Text nodes.

2.3.4.6 Interface Attr

`Attr -- Text, EntityReference`

Attr is a property of the element contained in Attr node. It has been shortened to remove confusion between the attributes keyword in the IDL interface. See Figure 2.6 for the Attr hierarcy.

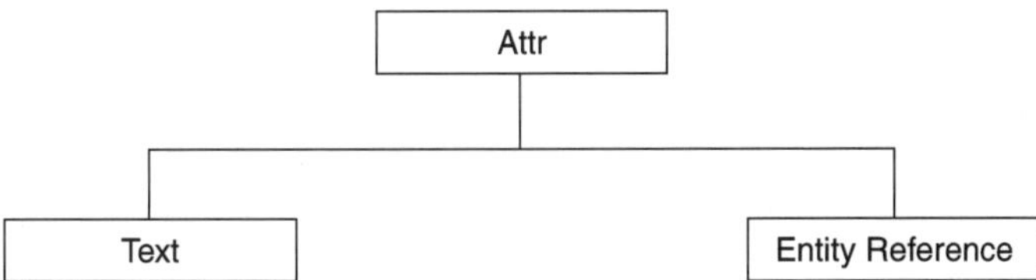

Figure 2.6 Attr Hierarchy.

The `Attr` interface represents an attribute in an `Element` object. Typically the allowable values for the attribute are defined in a document type definition.

Table 2.11 Attr Attributes

Attribute Name	Comments
`name`	Returns the name of this attribute.
`specified`	The returned value is `true` is the attribute was explicitly given a value in the original document. If the attribute has a default value then `false` is returned.
`value`	The value of the attribute.

2.3.4.7 Interface ProcessingInstruction

No children present. The `ProcessingInstruction`'s name is its target. Its value is its entire content, that is, everything between <? and >.

Table 2.12 ProcessingInstruction Attributes

Attribute Name	Comments
`target`	The target of this processing instruction. XML defines this as being the first token following the markup that begins the processing instruction.
`data`	The content of this processing instruction. This is from the first non-white space character after the target to the character immediately preceding the ?>.

2.3.4.8 *Interface Comment*

No child nodes allowed. A `comment`'s name is `#comment`. It is everything between `<!--` and `-->`. Note that this is the definition of a comment in XML, and, in practice, HTML, although some HTML tools may implement the full SGML comment structure.

2.3.4.9 *Interface Text*

No other nodes present. A `Text` node's name is `"#text"` and its content is its string value. The Text interface represents the textual content (termed `character data` in XML) of an `Element` or `Attr`. If there is no markup inside an element's content, the text is contained in a single object implementing the Text interface that is the only child of the element. If there is markup, it is parsed into a list of elements and Text nodes that form the list of children of the element.

Table 2.13 Text Methods

Method Name	Parameter	Return Value	Comments
`splitText`	`offset` The offset at which to split, starting from 0.	The new Text node.	The method breaks the exiting text node into two text nodes. It takes offset as the parameter and divides the original string from the offset location.

2.3.4.10 *Interface CDATASection*

It is named `"CDATASection"`. CDATA sections are used to escape blocks of text containing characters that would otherwise be regarded as markup. The only delimiter that is recognized in a CDATA section is the "]]>" string that ends the CDATA section. CDATA sections can not be nested. The primary purpose is for including material such as XML fragments, without needing to escape all the delimiters.

The `CDATASection` interface inherits the `CharacterData` interface through the `Text` interface. Adjacent `CDATASections` nodes are not merged by use of the `Element.normalize()` method.

2.3.4.11 *Interface Entity*

Interface Entity does not have any other nodes. `Entity`'s name is the entity name and it has no value.

The DOM Level 1 does not support editing Entity nodes. Entity declaration modeling has been left for a later Level of the DOM specification. If a user wants to make changes to the contents of an Entity, every related `EntityReference` node has to be replaced in the structure model by a clone of the Entity's contents, and then the desired changes must be made to each of those clones instead. All descendants of an Entity node are read-only. An Entity node does not have any parent. Table 2.14 gives Entity attributes.

Table 2.14 Entity Attributes

Attribute Name	Comments
`publicId`	The public identifier associated with the entity, if specified. Default value of null is assumed otherwise.
`systemId`	The system identifier associated with the entity, if specified. Default value of null is assumed otherwise.
`notationName`	For unparsed entities, the name of the notation for the entity. For parsed entities, this is null.

2.3.4.12 *Interface Notation*

Does not have any other nodes. A `Notation`'s name is the `NOTATION` name. It has no value. The DOM Level 1 does not support editing Notation nodes; they are therefore read-only. A Notation node does not have any parent. See Table 2.15 for Notation attributes.

Table 2.15 Notation Attributes

Attribute Name	Comments
`publicId`	The public identifier of this notation. Default value of null is assumed otherwise.
`systemId`	The system identifier of this notation. Default value of null is assumed otherwise.

2.3.4.13 *Interface CharacterData*

The `CharacterData` interface provides methods and attributes to access and modify character data present in nodes such as text nodes or a comment node. Tables 2.16 and 2.17 provide `CharacterData` attributes and methods, respectively. No DOM objects correspond directly to `CharacterData`, although the nodes that do have `CharacterData` do inherit from it.

Table 2.16 CharacterData Attributes

Attribute Name	Comments
`data`	String content of the node.
`length`	The number of characters that are available through `data`.

Table 2.17 CharacterData Methods

Method Name	Parameters	Return Value	Comments
`substringData`	1. `offset` Start offset of substring to extract. 2. `count` The number of characters to extract.	The specified substring. If the sum of `offset` and `count` exceeds the length, then all characters to the end of the data are returned.	Extracts a range of data from the node.
`appendData`	1. `arg` The `DOMString` to append.	None.	Append the string to the end of the character data of the node.
`insertData`	1. `offset` The character offset at which to insert. 2. `arg` The DOMString to insert.	None.	Insert a string at the specified character offset. Raises exception if offset is negative or greater than length of the node.

Table 2.17 CharacterData Methods (Continued)

Method Name	Parameters	Return Value	Comments
`deleteData`	1. `offset` The offset from which to remove characters. 2. `count` The number of characters to `delete`.	None.	Remove a range of characters from the node. Raises exception if offset is negative or greater than length of the node or if the count is negative.
`replaceData`	1. `offset` The offset from which to start replacing. 2. `count` The number of characters to replace. 3. `arg` The DOMString with which the range must be replaced.	This method returns nothing.	Replace the characters starting at the specified character offset with the specified string. If the count is more than the number of characters beyond the string, then all characters starting from the offset are replaced.

2.3.4.14 Exception DOMException

DOM interfaces usually provide a mechanism to handle errors as part of the return values for functions. This is also useful for cases when some object systems do not support the concept of exceptions. Return values then also provide error codes. Examples include out of bound errors in case of `NodeList`.

In DOM, exceptions are raised when the system has no way of processing the instruction, for example, in cases when data is lost, null value being passed or even if the implementation becomes unstable. Some of the exceptions may be implementation specific, but the intention is to help recover the system, or exit cleanly.

2.3.5 Definition Group `Exception Code`

This is an integer indicating the type of error generated.

2.3.5.1 *Defined Exception Code Constants*

Table 2.18 Exception_Code Constants

`INDEX_SIZE_ERR`	If index or size is negative, or greater than the allowed value.
`DOMESTIC_SIZE_ERR`	If the specified range of text does not fit into a DOM string.
`HIERARCHY_REQUEST_ERR`	If any node is inserted somewhere it does not belong.
`WRONG_DOCUMENT_ERR`	If a node is used in a different document than the one that created it (that does not support it).
`INVALID_CHARACTER_ERR`	If an invalid character is specified, such as in a name.
`NO_DATA_ALLOWED_ERR`	If data is specified for a node that does not support data.
`NO_MODIFICATION_ALLOWED_ERR`	If an attempt is made to modify an object where modifications are not allowed.
`NOT_FOUND_ERR`	If an attempt was made to reference a node in a context where it does not exist.
`NOT_SUPPORTED_ERR`	If the implementation does not support the type of object requested.
`INUSE_ATTRIBUTE_ERR`	If an attempt is made to add an attribute that is already in use elsewhere.

2.3.6 Auxiliary Types

DOM also specifies a few interfaces that act as helpers to other interfaces.

2.3.6.1 *Interface NodeList*

`NodeList` provides interface to handle unordered sets of `Nodes`. The items in the `NodeList` are accessible via an integral index, starting from 0. As mentioned before, NodeList interface essentially keeps track of a node's child nodes and their positions. It is responsible for maintaining the structure of the document in the memory. In other words, whenever the structure of the document changes, because of additions, deletions and updates on the nodes, the `NodeList` updates itself automatically. Tables 2.19 and 2.20 give NodeList methods and NodeList attributes, respectively.

Table 2.19 NodeList Methods

Method Name	Parameters	Return Value	Comments
`item`	`Index` Index into the collection.	The node at the indexth position in the `NodeList`, or null if that is not a valid index.	Returns the indexth item in the collection. If index is greater than or equal to the number of nodes in the list, this returns null.

Table 2.20 NodeList Attributes

Attribute Name	Comments
`length`	The number of nodes in the list. The range of valid child node indices is 0 to length-1 inclusive.

2.3.6.2 *Interface NamedNodeMap*

`NamedNodeMap` provides an interface to access unordered lists of `Nodes` and it is handled through their `name` attribute. Tables 2.21 and 2.22 illustrate methods and attributes, respectively. Objects contained in an object implementing `NamedNodeMap` may also be accessed by an ordinal index, but this is simply to allow convenient enumeration of the contents of a `NamedNodeMap`, and does not imply that the DOM specifies an order to these Nodes. Like `NodeLists`, `NamedNodeMaps` are live too. If any change is made to the structure of the document, it is updated automatically.

2.3.6.3 *Interface NodeEnumerator*

`NodeEnumerator`: The interface is used for iterating over a set of nodes.

Table 2.21 NamedNodeMap Methods

Method Name	Parameter	Return Value	Comments
`getNamedItem`	`name` Name of a node to retrieve.	A `Node` (of any type) with the specified name, or null if the specified name did not identify any node in the map.	Returns an Attr node object.
`setNamedItem`	`arg` A node to be added in a named node map.	If the new `Node` replaces an existing node with the same name the previously existing `Node` is returned, otherwise null is returned.	.
`removeNamedItem`	`name` The name of the attribute to remove.	The node removed from the map or null if no node with such a name exists.	Removes a node specified by name. If the removed node is an Attr with a default value it is immediately replaced.
`item`	`Index` Index into the map.	The node at the indexth position in the `NamedNodeMap`, or null if that is not a valid index.	Returns the `indexth` item in the map. If `index` is greater than or equal to the number of nodes in the map, this returns `null`.

Table 2.22 NamedNodeMap Attributes

Method Name	Comments
`length`	The number of nodes in the map. The range of valid child node indices is 0 to length-1 inclusive.

2.3.7 A Basic DOM Example

An example is provided here to facilitate more in-depth discussion of that which was presented in foregoing text. The basic skeletal structure is provided first and then built upon. The example has no purpose other than to demonstrate the mechanics of the syntax. Please refer back to relevant topics when necessary.[1]

2.3.7.1 Framework

```
<HTML>
<H1>DOM Concepts example</H1>

<XML id= "exIsland">
<?xml version="1.0"?>

<FORECAST date="01/01/2000">
    <OUTLOOK>Cloudy with chance of Rain</OUTLOOK>
    <TEMP>55</TEMP>
    <SUNRISE>5:27 AM</SUNRISE>
    <SUNSET>7:50 PM</SUNSET>
</FORECAST>
</XML>
<SCRIPT>
    var myDoc=exIsland;
    <!--default error check. the parseError method is IE 5.0 only and-->
    <!--is not part of DOM specs.-->
    if(myDoc.parseError.reason != "")
    {
       <!--this will display what error happened-->
       alert(myDoc.parseError.reason);
    }
</SCRIPT>
</HTML>
```

IE 5.0 gives you two different ways to create an XML document. The first method, as already shown, is though an XML island. The second method is via an ActiveX control.

1. This section uses IE 5.0 (http://www.microsoft.com/ie) as the basic browser for testing the code. Save this file as `main.htm`. We will be adding code to this as we move along.

XML Island is defined using the `ID` of the `<XML>` tag as already shown here. The code of the XML document is included with this HTML file in this case. It is also possible to use the SRC attribute to save the XML document object in another file. This is what the code will look like in that case:

```
<HTML>
<H1>DOM Concepts example</H1>

<XML id="exIsland" SRC="forecastXMLfile.xml"></XML>
<SCRIPT>
    var myDoc=exIsland;
    <!--default error check. the parseError method is IE 5.0 only and-->
    <!--is not part of DOM specs.-->
    if(myDoc.parseError.reason != "")
    {
       <!--this will display what error happened-->
       alert(myDoc.parseError.reason);
    }
</SCRIPT>
</HTML>
```

The second method of creating XML documents, mentioned in the preceding, is through XML ActiveX control. Here is how the code would look:

```
<HTML>
<H1>DOM Concepts example</H1>

<SCRIPT>
    var myDoc=new ActiveXObject("microsoft.XMLDOM");

    myDoc.load("forecastXMLfile.xml");

    <!--default error check. the parseError method is IE 5.0 only and-->
    <!--is not part of DOM specs.-->
    if(myDoc.parseError.reason != "")
    {
       <!--this will display what error happened-->
       alert(myDoc.parseError.reason)
    }
</SCRIPT>
</HTML>
```

2.3.7.2 XML Element

An XML element is represented by a start tag, an end tag and data in between. For example, in our document

```
<TEMP>55</TEMP>
```

is an element. It is important to note that XML tags are case sensitive. Try changing the </TEMP> to </temp> to see the error message that comes up.

2.3.7.3 Accessing XML Objects

IE 5.0 allows you to access the Data Island through the ID attribute. In our example "exIsland" becomes the name of the document object. We can then use the methods and properties of this object to access various elements and if required modify element's content. In our example we have <FORECAST> as the root node, and <TEMP>, <OUTLOOK>, <SUNRISE>, and <SUNSET> as child nodes. The root element can be accessed using the documentElement function. Table 2.23 shows what Application Programming Interfaces would be needed to see the values of different nodes.

Table 2.23 Value Access APIs

Node	DOM function needed to access it
<FORECAST>	myDoc.documentElement.nodeName
date	myDoc.documentElement.attributes.item(0).nodeName
"01/01/2000"	myDoc.documentElement.getAttribute("date") or
	myDoc.documentElement.attributes.item(0).nodeValue
<OUTLOOK>	myDoc.documentElement.childNodes.item(0).nodeName
Cloudy with...	myDoc.documentElement.childNodes.item(0).text
<TEMP>	myDoc.documentElement.childNodes.item(1).nodeName
55	myDoc.documentElement.childNodes.item(1).text
xml	myDoc.childNodes(0).nodeName
version	myDoc.childNodes(0).nodeValue

Try to determine the nodeType of a variety of nodes and compare each with the integer values defined previously in this chapter.

Given in what follows is the code for the preceding example. Please note that we have assigned the root node to a variable called rootelement to avoid retyping code.

```
<HTML>
<H1>DOM Concepts example</H1>
```

```
<XML id="exIsland">
<?xml version="1.0"?>

<FORECAST date="01/01/2000">
    <OUTLOOK>Cloudy with chance of Rain</OUTLOOK>
    <TEMP>55</TEMP>
    <SUNRISE>5:27 AM</SUNRISE>
    <SUNSET>7:50 PM</SUNSET>
</FORECAST>
</XML>
<SCRIPT>
    var myDoc=exIsland;
    var rootelement = myDoc.documentElement;

    <!--default error check. the parseError method is IE 5.0 only and-->
    <!--is not part of DOM specs.-->
    if(myDoc.parseError.reason != "")
    {
       <!--this will display what error happened-->
       alert(myDoc.parseError.reason);
    }

    document.write(rootelement.nodeName + "<BR>");
    document.write(rootelement.attributes.item(0).nodeName + "<BR>");
    document.write(rootelement.attributes.item(0).nodeValue + "<BR>");
    document.write(rootelement.getAttribute("date") + "<BR>");
    document.write(rootelement.childNodes.item(0).nodeName + "<BR>");
    document.write(rootelement.childNodes.item(0).text + "<BR>");
    document.write(rootelement.childNodes.item(1).nodeName + "<BR>");
    document.write(rootelement.childNodes.item(1).text + "<BR>");
    document.write(myDoc.childNodes(0).nodeName + "<BR>");
    document.write(myDoc.childNodes(0).nodeValue + "<BR>");

</SCRIPT>
</HTML>
```

Figure 2.7 shows what output for the preceding code will look like.

2.3.7.4 *Modifying Nodes*

Add the following line of code in the `<SCRIPT>` section and obtain the output to determine what the result is.

```
rootelement.appendChild(myDoc.createElement("Humidity"));
```

Add this function at the end to obtain a list of all child nodes of the document. Call this function after you have added the preceding line of code:

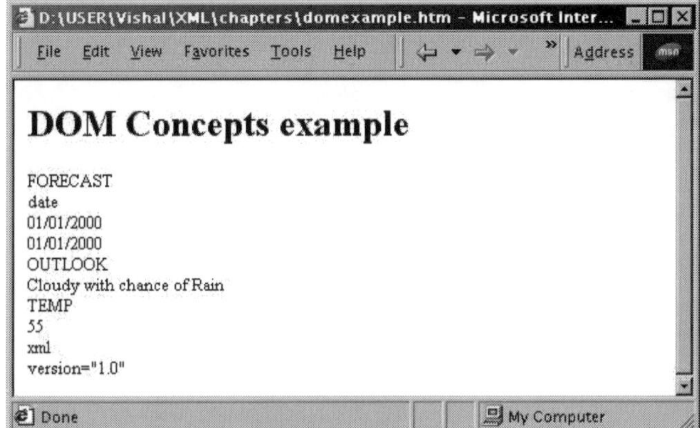

Figure 2.7 DOM Concepts Example output.

```
function getChildNodeNames()
{
    var nlist=myDoc.childNodes;
    var len=nlist.length;
    for(var x=0; x<len; x++)
    {
        document.write(nlist(i).nodeName + " | ");
    }
    document.write("<BR>");
}
```

Here is how the code would look:

```
<SCRIPT>
    var myDoc=exIsland;
    var rootelement = myDoc.documentElement;

    <!--default error check. the parseError method is IE 5.0 only and-->
    <!--is not part of DOM specs.-->
    if(myDoc.parseError.reason != "")
    {
       <!--this will display what error happened-->
       alert(myDoc.parseError.reason);
    }

    document.write(rootelement.nodeName + "<BR>");
    document.write(rootelement.attributes.item(0).nodeName + "<BR>");
    document.write(rootelement.getAttribute("date") + "<BR>");
    document.write(rootelement.childNodes.item(0).nodeName + "<BR>");
    document.write(rootelement.childNodes.item(0).text + "<BR>");
```

```
    document.write(rootelement.childNodes.item(1).nodeName + "<BR>");
    document.write(rootelement.childNodes.item(1).text + "<BR>");
    document.write(myDoc.childNodes(0).nodeName + "<BR>");
    document.write(myDoc.childNodes(0).nodeValue + "<BR>");

    getChildNodeNames();

    rootelement.appendChild(myDoc.createElement("Humidity"));

    getChildNodeNames();

    function getChildNodeNames()
    {
        var nlist=rootelement.childNodes;
        var len=nlist.length;
        document.write("<BR>");
        for(var x=0; x<len; x++)
        {
            document.write(nlist(x).nodeName + " | ");
        }
    }

</SCRIPT>
```

See Figure 2.8 for how the output will look.

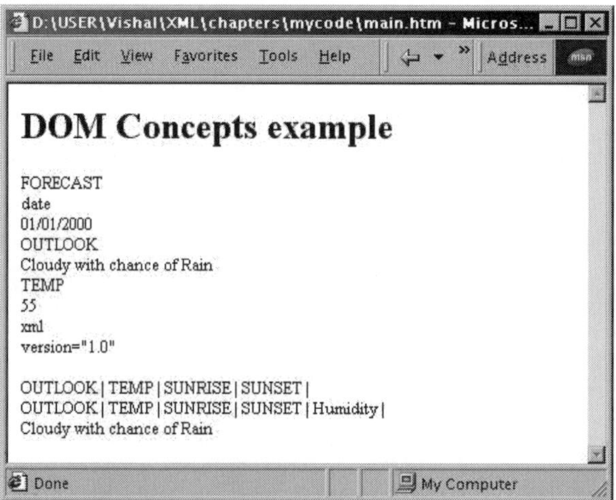

Figure 2.8 Output after changing values.

Try other node manipulation functions using this code.

2.4 *Extensible Style Language—XSL*

Extended Style Language (XSL) is the style language for XML. A style sheet contains the instructions to interpret the logical structure of the source document into a presentable structure for a medium-sized window in a web browser, or a set of pages in a book, memo etc. The XSL Style sheet is an XML document that also conforms to standards of a well-formed document. XSL is not a programming language but a declarative language. XSL declarations do not do anything, but describe the state of the transformed document in relation to the original document.

2.4.1 What It Does

As already mentioned, the style sheet instructs a processor as to how to translate the logical structure of a source document into a presentable structure. As there is no underlying mechanism for presenting the XML document, XSL must specify how each element should be presented and what the element is. This includes displaying definitions for every formatting object.

2.4.2 XSL Processing Model

The mechanism of XSL can be explained with a style sheet processor. An XSL *stylesheet processor* accepts a document or data in XML and an XSL stylesheet and produces the presentation of that XML source content as intended by the stylesheet. The result of the transformation engine is a structured result tree. The process of presenting the document is broken into two parts—constructing the tree out of the input data for interpretation and then displaying the data based on the formatting requirements.

The process of constructing a tree is called *tree transformation*. It is possible that the structure of the result tree is completely different from the source tree. Making this process modular allows you to add, filter, and reorder the generated content. The tree transformation also adds the information necessary to format the result tree.

The second process of displaying and formatting is called *formatting*. The formatting information is expressed through the use of *formatting objects*. All the nodes of the result tree are instances of formatting objects. The objects are of type page, paragraph etc. with their respective *formatting properties, including* font, margin, table, pagination etc. The output tree can be of any specified format like HTML or can be rendered to a hard copy, or to a screen device.

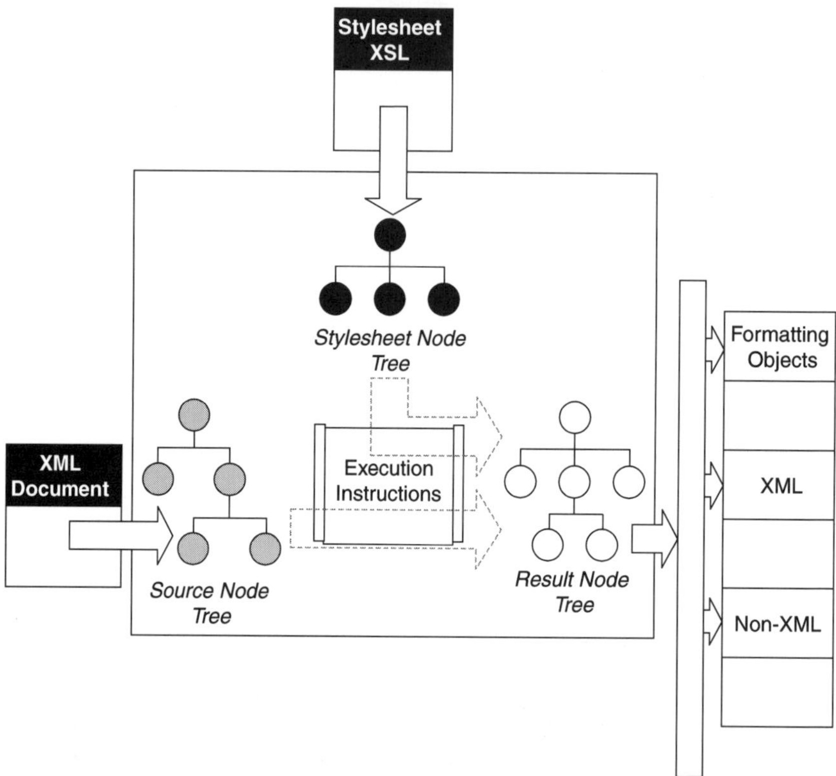

Figure 2.9 XSL Processing Model Tree.

To process the document the stylesheet processor starts at the root node in the source tree and processes it by finding the respective template in the style sheet that describes how the element should be displayed. Subsequent nodes are then processed one by one until there are no more nodes left to be processed. It is also possible that one node could be processed more than one time.

2.4.3 Cascading Stylesheet (CSS) and XSL

Cascading Stylesheet (CSS) provides features similar to those of XSL, in a way that allows rendering of information to a browser screen. CSS works with HTML 4.0 and with the use of divisions `<DIV>` and spans `<SPAN>` allows you to paint the browser screen with the source information. It can also be used with XML to extend functionality even further.

The main difference between CSS and XSL lies in the ability to rearrange components of the document. Although CSS allows you to render the text and the images from the source, it does not allow the rendered tree to be enhanced with custom information. In other words, the organization of the information for rendering is very tightly bound with the organization of the XML tree.

CSS provides the ability to select and display element with the use of a selector and its associated properties. Those properties allow you to use a range of display characteristics for display purposes. For example:

```
code {
    display: block;
    margin-left: 0.75in;
    margin-right: 0.75in;
    font-size: 90%
}
```
[2]

To accomplish the same thing XSL requires that you specify both the result object and its properties. It uses patterns and formatting objects to show how the elements are going to be displayed. For the same formatting requirement, XSL would look like this:

---

2. In the above example `"code"` is the *selector* and data between `{}` are its *properties*.

```
<xsl:template pattern="code">
    <fo:indent-start="0.75in"
        indent-end="0.75in"
        block font-size="90%">
     <xsl:process-children/>
    </fo:block>
</xsl:template>
```
[3]

When you specify/construct both the object and the properties are specified/constructed, it provides the ability to change the order of elements for display, display one element in one place and hide it in another, or change the order of elements and add generated text to the presentation. For example, for XML,

```
<employee>
    <first_name>John</first_name>
    <last_name>Doe<last_name>
    <emp_id>000321456</emp_id>
</employee>
```

If the requirement is to show the records in the format of employee id (`emp_id`), first name and last name, then the XSL would look like the following:

```
<xsl:template pattern="employee">
    <xsl:sequence>
        <xsl:process select="emp_id"/>
        <xsl:text>, </xsl:text>
        <xsl:process select="first_name"/>
        <xsl:process select="last_name"/>
    </xsl:sequence>
    </xsl:sequence>
</xsl:template>
```

CSS will only allow you to assign properties to different elements but will not permit reordering.

Currently the XSL draft uses many of the semantics defined in CSS and Document Style Semantics and Specification Language (DSSSL). The formatting objects defined have been defined in conjunction with the CSS

3. In this example everything between tag `<xsl:template>` is a *formatting object*, and the *pattern* is defined with the `<xsl:template> tag`.

working group. The final goal is to define a single formatting model for both systems that, when used, makes it possible to write style sheets on different devices with comparable results.

2.4.4 XSL Basics

With the information to date, I will explain a few basic rules one needs to get started. The complete working draft can be found at http://www.w3.org/TR/WD-xsl.

- XSL is a XML document too; therefore it must follow rules for well-formed documents. There must be unique opening and closing tags, and all the other tags must be nested.
- As mentioned before, an XSL element node is made up of two parts: a pattern part and an action part, which is made of formatting objects. Patterns select the element node from the source document using the following criteria:
  - name;
  - inheritance of the element;
  - ID assigned;
  - wildcards;
  - attributes of the source element;
  - an element's position relative to its siblings; and
  - an element's uniqueness relative to its siblings.

The action (formatting objects) part contains the following:

- An element meant to create a formatting object in the result tree will create a formatting object of the block type - `<fo:block><fo:block>`. `'fo:'` namespace is called a flow object and is a formatting object.
- Properties of the formatting object are applied in the form of attributes. For example: `<fo:block font-weight="bold">`. Here the `'font-weight'` property is applied to the block.
- Every element in the template is either an XSL processing instruction or is copied literally into the result tree. When a processing instruction like `"xsl:process-children"` is encountered, the processor processes each

of the children of current node. For each node it finds the matching template and instantiates it. The instantiated element is substituted for the processing instruction in the result tree.

- Extra literal text.
- Instructions to create fresh style objects if required.

2.4.5 Using XSL

An example will be provided here to clarify material already mentioned. For example, sake the output is an HTML file, but as mentioned before, the medium can be anything. I will use the example used in the DOM section to explain the styling part described by W3C. Please note that the example uses IE 5.0 (http://www.microsoft.com/ie) as the basic browser for testing code. The code that follows is from an example given on page 73.

```
<?xml version="1.0"?>

<FORECAST date="01/01/2000">
    <OUTLOOK>Cloudy with chance of Rain</OUTLOOK>
    <TEMP>55</TEMP>
    <SUNRISE>5:27 AM</SUNRISE>
    <SUNSET>7:50 PM</SUNSET>
</FORECAST>
```

The preceding input code when passed through the style sheet

```
<?xml version="1.0"?>
<xsl:stylesheet
  xmlns:xsl="http://www.w4.org/TR/WD-xsl">

    <xsl:template match="/">
    <HTML>
    <HEAD>
        <TITLE>Weather Forecast</TITLE>
    </HEAD>

    <BODY>
        <TABLE border="0">
        <TR>
          <TH>Forecast</TH>
          <TH>Outlook</TH>
          <TH>Temperature</TH>
          <TH>Sunrise Time</TH>
```

```
        <TH>Sunset Time</TH>
      </TR>
      <xsl:apply-templates/>
      </TABLE>
  </BODY>
  </HTML>

  </xsl:template>

  <xsl:template match="FORECAST">
  <TR>
      <TD><EM><xsl:value-of select="@date"/></EM></TD>
      <xsl:apply-templates select="OUTLOOK"/>
      <xsl:apply-templates select="TEMP"/>
      <xsl:apply-templates select="SUNRISE"/>
      <xsl:apply-templates select="SUNSET"/>
  </TR>

  </xsl:template>

  <xsl:template match="OUTLOOK | TEMP | SUNRISE | SUNSET">
      <TD><xsl:apply-templates/></TD>
  </xsl:template>
</xsl:stylesheet>
```

will produce the following HTML code :

```
<HTML>
    <HEAD>
        <TITLE>Weather Forecast</TITLE>
    </HEAD>
    <BODY>
        <TABLE border="1">
        <TR>
          <TH>Forecast for</TH>
          <TH>Outlook</TH>
          <TH>Temperature</TH>
          <TH>Sunrise Time</TH>
          <TH>Sunset Time</TH>
        </TR>
        <TR>
            <TD><EM>01/01/2000</EM></TD>
            <TD>Cloudy with chance of Rain</TD>
            <TD>55</TD>
            <TD>5:27 AM</TD>
            <TD>7:50 PM</TD>
```

```
        </TR>
        </TABLE>
    </BODY>
</HTML>
```

See Figure 2.10 for what the output will look like on the browser.

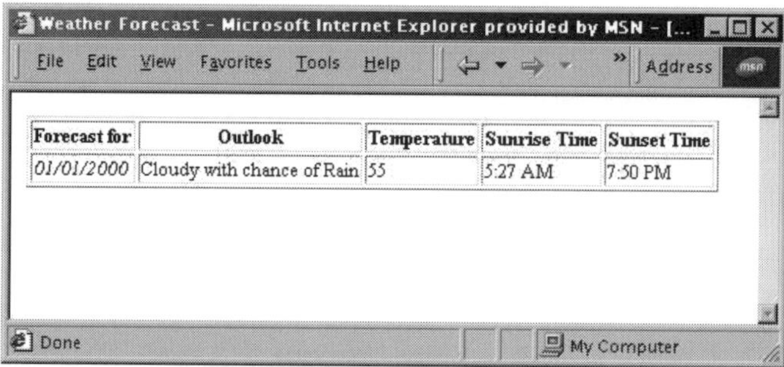

Figure 2.10 XSL Example Output.

In the example given here the processor uses the XSL to interpret the XML input. It parses the file until it finds `<xsl:apply-templates/>`. As already mentioned, each element is copied onto the result tree until it finds a processing instruction, `<xsl:apply-templates/>` in this case. When found, it processes each of the children of the current node. For each node, it finds the matching template and instantiates it. All the instantiated templates are placed in the result tree at the location of `<xsl:apply-templates/>` element in the template.

As an exercise try writing the XML for forecasts for other days and see how the HTML is formed later for comparison.

2.4.6 XSL and the Future

XSL in its second draft provides an extensive specification for both the styling and rendering of XML documents. XSL currently includes a standard vocabulary of formatting objects, with well-defined CSS properties to control them. Future versions promise to extend the vocabulary so as to use a single set of stylesheets that will work in multiple media with different applications. Future research directions include solutions for interactivity, support for a more powerful scripting language if required, and definitions for more formatting objects.

2.5 Conclusion

In this chapter I have tried to explain the two important features of XML, transformation and manipulation through DOM, as well as styling and formatting using XSL. Different sections cover some important features, but do not go into the details of each draft. The complete draft for DOM can be found at http://www.w3.org/TR/REC-DOM-Level-1. The XSL draft can be found at http://www.w3.org/TR/WD-xsl.

CHAPTER 3

XLink and XPointer

If there is one thing we have learned from the Web, it is the importance and value of interconnectivity. Whether it is people interconnected via email, web applications interoperating with one another, or simply information on websites interconnected via hyperlinks, it is interconnectivity that brings real value to the system. For example, the simple HTML `<A>` linking tag enables users to access and traverse resources located around the world simply with the click of a mouse. The Web is undergoing a transition from HTML to XML. XML provides powerful facilities for describing and structuring data; however, the core XML facilities only provide facilities for structuring standalone hierarchical data. In order for XML to provide real value to the Web, it must incorporate rich Web- and document-aware linking capabilities. XLink and XPointer are the XML-related technologies that provide this capability.

XLink is a third key component in the W3C's XML-based initiatives, which consist of:

- **Extensible Markup Language (XML)**—a W3C recommendation for expressing the structure and content of information in a text-based format.

- **Extensible Style Language (XSL)**—a W3C draft proposal for specifying how XML documents should be displayed.
- **XML Linking Language (XLink)**—a W3C draft proposal for specifying rich hypertext functionality in XML documents.

XLink is used to create links that are far richer than is possible with HTML, as you will soon discover. XPointer, the XML Pointer Language, is a key technology designed to work in conjunction with XLink. XPointer adds further richness to the basic XLink capabilities by making it easier to address individual elements within XML documents. When combined with XLink, XPointer gives you much finer granularity in terms of the types of resources that can participate in links.

In this chapter we will explore the rich hypertext functionality made possible by XLink and XPointer. Some of the more powerful—and more useful—XLink capabilities require an understanding of XPointers. We will begin our discussion with an overview of the type of functionality you can expect from both XLink and XPointer, without going into the syntax in detail. Next, we will cover the fundamental XLink capabilities and its syntax, primarily those core facilities that make XLink what it is. We will then cover XPointer in detail, and then come back to XLink to see how it can be combined with XPointers to provide very expressive linking capability.

3.1 XLink: The XML Linking Language

XLink is a syntax that enables you to express linking relationships between Web resources. These relationships may be between XML documents, between elements within a single XML document, or perhaps between XML elements located in multiple XML documents. XLink also enables you to express linking relationships between non-XML resources; for example, you could express the fact that two JPEG images are related to one another. Before we delve into the details of XLink syntax, we will first take a high-level survey of the type of functionality that XLink provides and discuss some of the ideas that have motivated its development.

3.1.1 XLink at a Glance: What Is New (and What Is Not)

XLink is guided by about a dozen design principles. As with other XML-related technologies, XLink must be usable over the Internet and must be both human-readable and human-writable. We will not cover all of the design principles here (they are nicely described in the W3C document NOTE-xlink-req-19990224) but will mention the following two and discuss their overall influence on XLink's design:

- XLink will support HTML linking constructs; and
- XLinks may reside within or outside the documents in which the participating resources reside.

The first of these design principles should be a comfort to those of you who are familiar with HTML's linking model; not surprisingly, the XLink linking model extends and generalizes that of HTML. The second design principle, however, begins to get at some of the differences between XLink and HTML's linking models. In HTML, linking information is embedded directly within documents that participate in links. The first design principle given in the preceding indicates that XLink will continue to support such "in-line" linking as you are used to in HTML, but the second one says that with XLink it should also be possible to keep linking information separate from the data that it serves to link.

With XLink, linking information need not be embedded directly in-line in one of the documents being linked (as HTML currently requires); rather, it can be maintained "out-of-line" in a separate document. This design principle is very much in keeping with the overall flavor of XML technologies thus far: XSL keeps presentation separate from XML content, and now XLink can keep information about relationships between XML content separate from the XML content itself.

As we will see, XLink also has implications for content presentation, in particular specifying what is to happen when a browser or other application program traverses a link. XLink provides a greater degree of control than does HTML over whether the data referenced by a link should be displayed in place of the current document, whether the referenced data should be embedded into the current document, and so on. The relationship between XML, XSL and XLink is depicted in Figure 3.1.

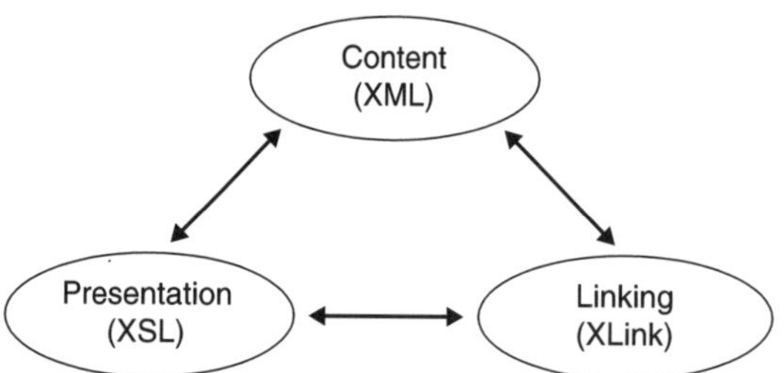

Figure 3.1 Relationship between XML, XSL, and XLink.

Although XLink still provides HTML-like linking behavior, there is more to XLink than that it is able to maintain HTML-like linking relationships separate from their associated content. Perhaps the largest change, conceptually, is in the very nature of what we mean by a "link." In effect, XML generalizes the concept of a link as we have come to know it from HTML. In HTML, a link is unidirectional relationship between two data objects; for example, in HTML we often add links from one document to another, as shown in Figure 3.2. Here we happen to be linking the contents of the <A> element in file xxx.html (i.e., the word "Link"), to a location, indicated by the `name="zzz"` attribute of an <A> element in file yyy.html. In XLink terms, this type of unidirectional link is now known as a "simple link."

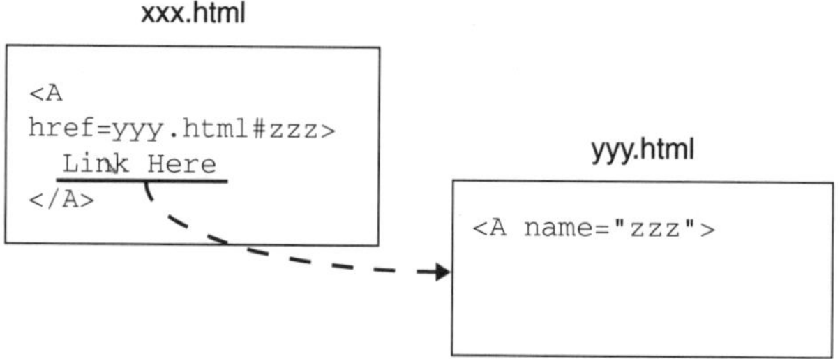

Figure 3.2 Unidirectional HTML-style link.

As you know from the first of the design principles, you will still be able to create this type of simple link with XLink; however, XLink will also allow you to create bidirectional links (we will cover the syntax for this later). Conceptually, you can think of a bidirectional link as behaving as shown in

Figure 3.3. Although they may seem similar on the surface, bidirectional links are quite different and more powerful than unidirectional (e.g., HTML-style) ones. As you know, when you browse an HTML document and follow a simple unidirectional link to another document, the browser lets you return to the previous document with the "Back" button, even though the link being traversed is unidirectional. It is important to keep in mind that the behavior of the browser's "Back" button is only a result of the browser caching pages as they are accessed and remembering "where it has been," thereby allowing users to backtrack along unidirectional links they have already traversed in the forward direction.

One way to confirm that the browser is simply caching unidirectional links and not actually implementing bidirectional links for HTML-style links is to consider what happens when you encounter a file that is the destination of a unidirectional link in your web browsing. For instance, if you loaded file yyy.html from Figure 3.2 in your browser, there would be no way to find the "other end" of the link shown in the figure, for example, to find the `<A>` element containing "Link Here" in file xxx.html, because the link to tag `"zzz"` is unidirectional.

On the other hand, a browser's behavior would be quite different if this were a bidirectional link as is now possible with XML and XLink. XLink allows you to create bidirectional links that are just as easily traversable in either direction regardless of which end you start from, as depicted in Figure 3.3. In this case, if we were to begin by browsing file xxx.xml and came across `<SomeLink>`, we would be able to follow the link to `<AnotherLink>`. As this is a bidirectional link, if we started with file yyy.xml and came across `<AnotherLink>`, we would just as easily be able to traverse the link to find `<SomeLink>` in file xxx.xml.

Bidirectional links are examples of what XLink calls "extended links"; an extended link associates together some fixed number of resources, which for a bi-directional link means two resources. One way to think of extended links is as sets, in the mathematical sense, whose members are the resources being linked. That is, an extended link in Figure 3.2 (which we had previously referred to as a bidirectional link) could be thought of as a set containing two resources, and could be denoted mathematically as { Resource1, Resource2 },

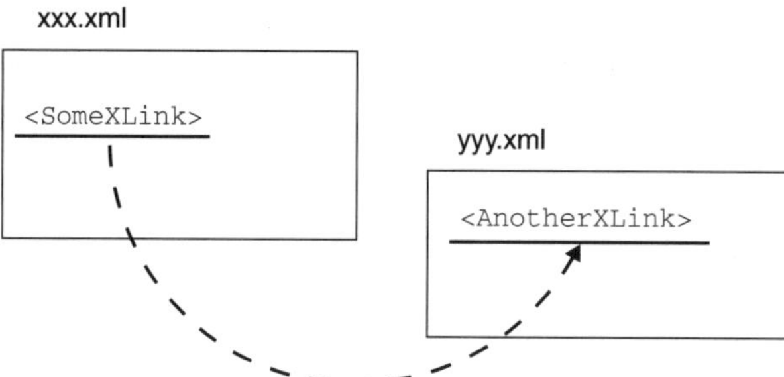

Figure 3.3 Example of bidirectional link implemented with XLink extended link.

where Resource1 refers to `<SomeXLink>` and Resource2 refers to `<AnotherX-Link>`. What happens if we want to use an extended link to "link together" three or more resources, say adding a link to a `<YetAnotherLink>` element in a third document? This would be denoted mathematically as { Resource1, Resource2, Resource3 }, where Resource3 refers to `<YetAnotherLink>` in file zzz.xml, and is shown pictorially in Figure 3.4. XLink's extended links enable you to create this type of multiresource link.

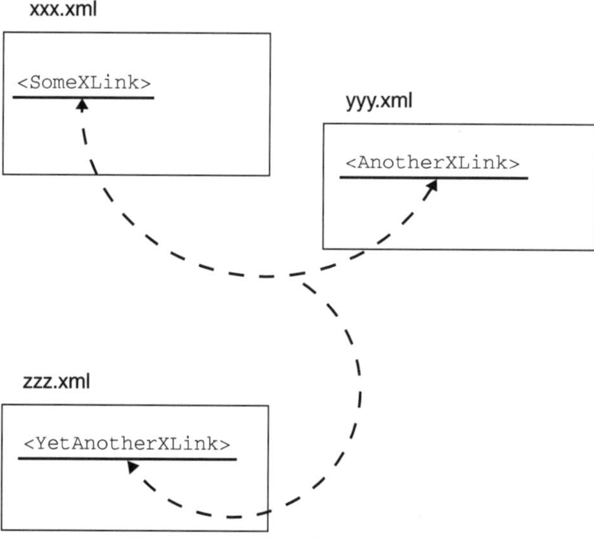

Figure 3.4 Multiresource XLink extended link.

You may be curious as to how a browser might behave if you were to navigate a set of XML documents such as the ones in Figure 3.4. If you began by browsing document xxx.xml and encountered the link at `<SomeLink>`, you are probably asking how the browser would know which of the two other resources (i.e., elements `<AnotherLink>` and `<YetAnotherLink>`) should be accessed when the link is traversed. One thing the browser could do in this situation would be to produce a pop-up menu that would allow you to select your destination from a list of the resources participating in the extended link.

The advantages of extended links over simple links become apparent when we consider documents with rich cross-related information content. A good example of the type of functionality that XLink's extended links provide, in a non-Web setting, would be the index for a technical book. Think for a moment how useful the index often is in helping you find interrelated information in a book and note how each index entry, in particular the ones that reference multiple pages, could be made into an extended link. For example, you might find a book on Java programming whose index entry for "DataOutputStream class" says that information on this topic can be found on pages 206, 398, and 404. If this book were made available on-line in XML format, it would be a simple matter to link the three references on these pages together with an extended link and also perhaps to an index page. This would allow the user to easily navigate between them without first having to consult a separate index page.

As you may have guessed from these introductory examples, XLink does not force you to use a specific "linking element" to create links, as HTML does with the `<A>` element. Rather, with XLink any element can serve as the starting point or end point of a link, simply by setting the appropriate attributes in that element. As you will see later, these attributes include our familiar friend `href`, plus a number of new attributes.

XPointer, the XML Pointing Language, is a new capability that works closely with XLink. Frequently we want to directly reference subresources within documents—for instance, to cross-reference elements buried in separate XML documents by linking them together in an extended link. XPointer enables you to precisely reference subresources such as elements within XML documents so that they may participate as resources in XLinks. XPointer gives you language constructs that let you "reach inside" an arbitrary XML document to specify a precise location within that document.

The final comment we will make in this overview of XLink functionality is that XLink lets you provide meta-information about links to both application software that will be processing the links, and to the end user as well. As you will see, link meta-information allows you to indicate the roles that the source and destination resources play in the link, as well as the role of the link itself. Link meta-information will be particularly useful for extended links, where a link can lead to multiple destinations, and it becomes a necessity to tell the user, in simple terms, the purpose or role of each of the possible destinations.

As an example, imagine an on-line automotive-parts catalog that uses an extended link to relate part names located in one document, with detailed part descriptions located in another document, with pricing information located in a third document as shown in Figure 3.5 here. Meta-information describing the role of each of the resources in the link could be used to help a browser populate a pop-up menu that lists the other resources that participate in the link. For example a pop-up menu might display "Part", "Description" and "Pricing", each of which would direct you to the appropriate resource when the user traverses this multiresource link.

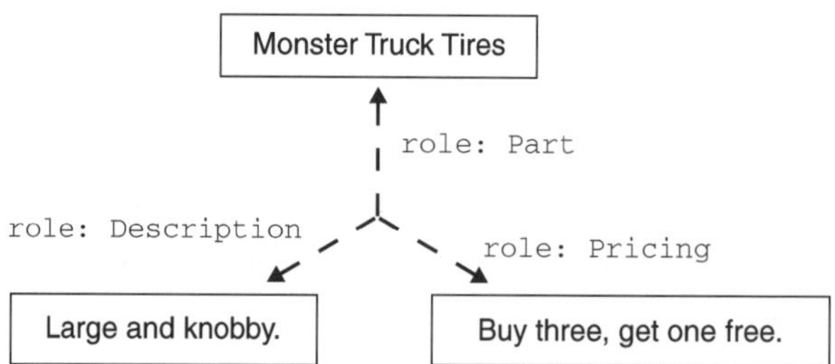

Figure 3.5 XLink metainformation may be added to links.

This first glance at XLink's capabilities is not meant to be comprehensive, but rather to give you a rough idea of what XLink is all about, and how it relates to HTML. As we have seen, XLink begins with a basic foundation that preserves HTML's linking capabilities, but generalizes and extends the underlying model in a number of significant ways, resulting in a far more powerful, and extensible linking language. In the following sections we will explore these concepts in more depth and cover the syntax in detail.

3.1.2 Basic XLink Terminology

Before we get into the details of XLink, it is best that we define some terminology.

- **Resource**—A data object such as a file, image, document, program or query result, or an identifiable portion of such a data object. Resources are the data objects that participate in links. XML documents and elements within XML documents will frequently be the resources that participate in links.
- **Locator**—Information, typically in the form of a URI plus an XPointer, that identifies a resource.
- **Linking Element**—An XML element that asserts the existence of a link and describes its characteristics. For HTML, the <A> element serves the function of a linking element; for XLink, any element with the appropriately set attributes (e.g., `href` and others to be discussed shortly) may serve as a linking element. XLink is essentially the syntax that is used to describe linking elements in XML.
- **Link**—An explicit relationship between two or more resources, which are then said to participate in the link (See boxed text for an explanation of "participating in a link"). A link may be "inline," in which case the linking element is a resource that participates in the link. If a link is not inline, it is "out-of-line," in which case the linking element is not a participating resource. With an out-of-line link, the linking element typically describes the set of resources that participate in the link.
- **Traversal**—The action of using a link to access a resource. A typical example of a link traversal occurs when a user clicks on a highlighted link in a browser, and is taken to that resource.

3.1.3 What Constitutes a Simple XLink?

With HTML it is easy for application software to identify links: the software merely has to identify <A> elements in documents. Let us look at how the <A> element operates in HTML and see how this type of functionality

> ***What does it mean for a resource to "participate in a link?"***
> For the moment, think of a link as an arrow that logically connects two (or perhaps more) resources. Very simply, the resources at the head(s) and the tail(s) of the arrow are said to participate in the link; they are what the link logically connects. But what about the arrow itself? As you will see, with XLink "out-of-line" links it is possible for the "arrow" to be defined separately from the resources at the "head(s)" and/or the "tail(s)" of the arrow; that is, the linking element (see above terminology) is not required to be one of the resources that participates in the link, but rather can be maintained as a separate resource, sort of "off to the side." In short, it is best to think of what falls at the head(s) and tails(s) of the linking "arrow" as the resources that participate in the link, noting that the definition of the arrow itself may be located in another (nonparticipating) resource.

could be expressed with XLink. In XLink terminology, we would say that the HTML `<A>` element serves as a linking element: it both asserts the existence of a link and describes the characteristics of that link. The content of the `<A>` element identifies the starting point or "source" of the link, and the value of the `href` attribute identifies the endpoint or destination of the link. In the example that follows, the content of the linking element is the text "Visit the W3C!", which would typically be underlined in a browser and denotes the starting point of the link. Similarly, the attribute `href="http://www.w3.org"` identifies the destination resource of the link, where a browser would take you if you traversed the link by clicking on it.

```
<A href="http://www.w3.org">
      Visit the W3C!
   </A>
```

In XML, any element can serve as a linking element, not just the `<A>` element as in HTML. So, how does an XML element identify itself as a "linking element?" The answer is very simple: in XLink, linking elements are identified by the presence of an `xml:link` attribute, which may take the values `"simple"` or `"extended"` (plus several others to be discussed later). For now we will discuss simple links, whose semantics follow those of the HTML-style links your are already familiar with; we will discuss the remaining types of links later.

We will start converting the simple line of HTML code above into XML that uses XLink. To do this we would first have to add the `xml:xlink` attribute to the <A> element so that an XLink processor would be able to identify the <A> element as a linking element.

```
<A xml:xlink="simple" href="http://www.w3.org">
   Visit the W3C!
</A>
```

As you may have guessed, the `href` attribute is also a required attribute for linking elements. Except for the addition of the `xml:link` attribute, this XML code looks just like the HTML <A> element with which you are already familiar. If we wanted to use an <A> element such as this for simple links in our XML code, we might want to make the `xml:link` attribute a fixed value that is always set to the value `"simple"`. We can do this when we define the characteristics of the <A> element in XML: as with all XML code, we need to define our element types with a Document Type Definition (DTD). The DTD is where we indicate which attributes are necessary (`xml:link` and `href` in this case), which ones are optional (more on this later), and so forth. We could do this for the <A> element as we have used it in the preceding with the following DTD:

```
<!ELEMENT A ANY>
      <!ATTLIST A
         xml:link    CDATA    #FIXED "simple"
         href        CDATA    #REQUIRED >
```

Note that we have specified that the value of the `xml:link` attribute must be `"simple"`, because we intend to use our XML <A> element only for simple links. This type of declaration will automatically set the `xml:link` attribute to the value `"simple"` in our <A> element instances without having to specify it explicitly. That is, every occurrence of an <A> element that does not otherwise set the `xml:link` attribute will behave as if it contained the attribute setting `xml:link="simple"`. (Note that setting this attribute value to anything except `"simple"` in an <A> element instance would cause a parse error to occur.) The DTD allows us to revert to a more concise syntax when creating our <A> elements in XML, as we are picking up the default `xml:link="simple"` setting. Using the DTD given here, the following HTML-like syntax is again possible:

```
<A href="http://www.w3.org">
        Visit the W3C!
     </A>
```

If you were wondering how XLink provides compatibility with HTML-style links, which we noted it did in the beginning when we reviewed XLink's guiding design principles, you have probably just figured out the answer. The use of default attributes in DTDs, and the choice by XLink to use the `href` attribute to designate target resources for links, make this possible.

As we are now in the process of converting this simple one-line example over to XML, we can begin to use some of XLink's additional capabilities. XLink does not restrict linking elements to the element `<A>`; any element with properly specified `xml:link` and `href` attributes will do. If you were creating a DTD for a document that provided information about organizations such as the W3C, it might make sense to define an element called `<AdditionalInfo>`, whose purpose would be to provide additional information about organizations that are being described. We could easily make an `<AdditionalInfo>` element function as a simple linking element with the following DTD definition:

```
<!ELEMENT AdditionalInfo ANY>
      <!ATTLIST AdditionalInfo
         xml:link    CDATA    #FIXED "simple"
         href        CDATA    #REQUIRED >
```

This DTD would allow us to code `<AdditionalInfo>` instances as follows, again automatically picking up the fixed value of `"simple"` for the `xml:link` attribute from the DTD:

```
<AdditionalInfo href="http://www.w3.org">
   Visit the W3C!
</AdditionalInfo>
```

We have said that an element must contain `xml:link` and `href` attributes in order to be recognized as an XLink linking element. This does not mean, however, that a linking element must have *only* these attributes, or that a linking element cannot contain additional subelements. For example, we could change the definition of the `<AdditionalInfo>` element in our DTD to allow it to contain optional subelements `<Member>` and `<Sponsor>` for each member and sponsor in the organization. We could also have added an optional (or just as easily, required) attribute such as "status" to indicate whether the organization is active or inactive. The resulting DTD might look as follows:

```
<!ELEMENT AdditionalInfo ( #PCDATA ( Member*, Sponsor*) )>
<!ATTLIST AdditionalInfo
   xml:link   CDATA   #FIXED "simple"
   href       CDATA   #REQUIRED
   status     CDATA   #IMPLIED  >
<!ELEMENT Member   (#PCDATA)>
<!ELEMENT Sponsor (#PCDATA)>
```

This type of DTD would support more complex <AdditionalInfo> elements that would function as simple links, such as the following:

```
<AdditionalInfo status="Active" href="http://visit.them.here">
      More info is available!
      <Member>Snoop E. Dog</Member>
      <Sponsor>Happy Go Lucky, GmbH</Sponsor>
   </AdditionalInfo>
```

The point here is that XLink's simple links, while similar in concept to the <A> element in HTML, allow complex unidirectional links to be constructed. In fact, with XML and XLink, any element can be made into a simple linking element merely by including the xml:link and href attributes in the element.

3.1.4 More on Link Attributes

The previous section should have given you a good sense as to how linking functionality similar to the familiar HTML <A> linking element can be implemented with XLink. Now we are going to turn our attention more closely to the additional attributes that are understood by an XLink processor for simple links, and look at the range of values they may take. You will see later that the same attributes that apply to XLink simple links also apply to multiresource XLink extended links.

The following DTD shows XLink attributes that apply to simple-link linking elements. Although here we are defining a new element called <SimpleLink>, remember that you can create elements with any name, and make them into simple linking elements by giving them the attributes we are using here:

```
<!ELEMENT SimpleLink ANY>
<!ATTLIST SimpleLink
   xml:link         CDATA                #FIXED "simple"
   href             CDATA                #REQUIRED
   inline           (true|false)         "true"
   role             CDATA                #IMPLIED
   title            CDATA                #IMPLIED
   show             (embed|relace|new)   #IMPLIED
   actuate          (auto|user)          #IMPLIED
   behavior         CDATA                #IMPLIED
   content-role     CDATA                #IMPLIED
   content-title    CDATA                #IMPLIED >
```

We will cover one-by-one the attributes we have not seen thus far. We have already discussed the `xml:link` and `href` attributes in the preceding, so we will begin with the `inline` attribute and cover the remainder in turn.

3.1.4.1 Inline versus Out-of-Line Links

Before we define what it means for a link to be inline (or not inline), we first note that all of the examples of simple links that we have seen thus far have been inline links, including the HTML-like `<A>` elements. A link is inline if the link element is a resource that participates in the link, and out-of-line if the link element is not a resource that participates in the link. (If a link is inline, it is not out-of-line, and vice versa. Thus, if we say a link is not inline, we are saying it is out-of-line.) The simple links we have seen, for example both of the forementioned `<AdditionalInfo>` examples, are inline links because the `<AdditionalInfo>` element participates in the link (the contents of this element serve as the starting point of the link), and also defines the characteristics of the link through its attributes (the `href` attribute of the `<AdditionalInfo>` element defines the destination resource for the link). As the following specification from the DTD already given here indicates, the default for a simple link is inline:

```
inline          (true|false)        "true"
```

The simple links we have seen thus far have all been inline links, but that does not have to be the case. As you will see, there are advantages to maintaining linking information separately from the content it serves to link, and out-of-line links serve this purpose. Just as you may decide to provide multiple style sheets for viewing the same content (e.g., on different output devices, for different users, etc.), out-of-line links make it simple to apply different linking characteristics to the same content (perhaps targeting different output devices or different users).

3.1.4.2 XLink Roles and Titles

The `role` and `title` attributes are a way to specify the intended purpose of the link to the application software and to the end user, respectively. For example, a browser could use the information in the `title` attribute to build a "tool tip" window that pops up whenever the mouse passes over the link, in order to let the user know, perhaps, that a link leads to "Pricing Information," or that it leads to a "Detailed Description," and so forth. Similarly, the `role` attribute could be used to pass information to an application program that processes XML data to let it know that these same links contain "Price" and "Description," where these two words ("Price" and "Description") have specific meaning to the application program. (The values of the `role` attributes could just as easily have been "foo" and "bar," if these less descriptive strings had meaning to the application.) Both the `role` and `title` attributes are optional and consist of `CDATA`, as seen from their specification in the definition given:

```
role            CDATA           #IMPLIED
title           CDATA           #IMPLIED
```

As we saw in our first glance at XLink, the `role` and `title` attributes will be particularly useful for extended links, where a link leads to multiple resources; these attributes will allow the application and end user to know the intended purpose of each resource participating in the link.

3.1.4.3 Link Traversal Semantics: Embed, Replace and New

The `show` attribute defines the semantics of what happens when the link is traversed; this behavior is specified by the three possible values the `show` attribute can take: `embed`, `replace` and `new`.

```
show            (embed|relace|new) #IMPLIED
```

The semantic meanings of these three values are as follows:

- **`embed`**—When the link is traversed, the destination resource is embedded into the current document at the point where the link started.
- **`replace`**—When the link is traversed, the destination resource replaces the current document.

- **new**—If this attribute is specified, the destination resource should be processed with a new instance of the processing application.

The various values for the `show` attribute will be useful at different times and for different applications. For example, the `show="embed"` attribute could be used to embed a picture in the document when the user clicks on the link. On the other hand, the `show="replace"` attribute setting could be used to provide the type of behavior you normally associate with a browser, where clicking on a link displays that resource in the browser's window in place of the current one. Finally, if `show="new"` were specified in an XLink, for a browser this would typically mean launching a new browser to explore the destination resource, leaving the current document unchanged in the present browser.

3.1.4.4 When Is a Link Traversed: Auto versus User

The `actuate` attribute specifies whether the link should be traversed automatically when it is encountered in an application program, or whether the link should only be traversed when it is specifically activated by the end user. These behaviors are controlled by the following possible values for the `actuate` attribute:

```
actuate           (auto|user)          #IMPLIED
```

We will look at when `actuate="auto"` and `actuate="user"` might each be appropriate. Automatic traversal of a link would be useful to provide functionality like the HTML `<IMG>` tag, where another file such as an image would be automatically embedded in a document when the link is encountered (and automatically traversed) by an application program. For instance, "boilerplate" text could automatically be pulled into a document using an appropriately defined `<BoilerPlate>` element, which might then be used as follows:

```
<BoilerPlate actuate="auto" show="embed"
             href="TermsAndConditions.xml">
```

On the other hand, `actuate="user"` is useful if a link should only be traversed when the user requests it; this is the way HTML `<A>` links operate in browsers, where the user requests that a link be traversed by clicking on it. Traversal that is only initiated upon user request is provided by specifying `actuate="user"` in the simple linking element.

3.1.4.5 *Detailed Processing Instructions: the Behavior Attribute*

The behavior attribute is an optional attribute that can be used to pass to an application program detailed information about how a link should be processed.

```
behavior          CDATA              #IMPLIED
```

One use of this attribute could be to inform an application as to what type of format the data at the other end of the link contains, or even name the program that should be used to process the data. For example, the behavior attribute could be used to specify the MIME type of the resource data, or the specific application program that should be used to process the data, as shown here:

```
<Video actuate="user" show="new" behavior="Mpegplay.exe"
                                        href="SomeMovie.mpg">
     Sneak Preview!
  </Video>
```

Here we are indicating that the application should show an MPEG-encoded file SomeMovie.mpg using a new instance of the Mpegplay.exe application when the user clicks this link.

3.1.4.6 *What Role Does the Destination Resource Play?*

The `content-role` and `content-title` attributes are much like the `role` and `title` attributes, except that these attributes pertain to the destination resource as opposed to the link itself. Both of these attributes are optional, as indicated by the `#IMPLIED` keyword:

```
content-role      CDATA              #IMPLIED
content-title     CDATA              #IMPLIED
```

These attributes allow the creator of the XML data to indicate the role played by the destination resource, as well as a title that could be displayed for this resource.

3.1.5 Accessing HTML Resources From XML: Fragment Identifiers

Up to this point, the primary means we have been using to address resources is the Universal Resource Identifier (URI); URIs have served as locators for identifying resources that participate in links. We saw that one of the design goals of XLink was that of support of HTML-style linking constructs, primarily the `<A>` element. One reason to have XLink support HTML-style constructs is that XML files can then make references to HTML files: HTML will be around for a long time and XML must be able to interact with it. Toward this end, XLink supports the concept of fragment identifiers from HTML, which means that `href="ThatFile.html#RightThere"` would be a valid way of addressing the location `"RightThere"` in file ThatFile.html. This is depicted here:

```
file: ThisFile.xml

   <SimpleLink href="ThatFile.html#RightThere">
      Link to HTML file
   </SimpleLink>



   file: ThatFile.html

      ...
   <A name="RightThere">
   <P>This line of HTML code can be referenced from XML
   using a fragment identifier.</P>
      ...
```

We will see in the following section that XPointers allow you to use a syntax that significantly extends HTML fragment identifiers in order to reference elements within XML documents.

3.2 *XPointer: The XML Pointing Language*

The primary means we have used to address XML resources is the Universal Resource Identifier (URI). As you know, a URI can be used to indicate the location of a complete resource, for instance an XML document, an image file, an entire website, and so forth. We have noted many times how XML adds structure to data. If we think of an XML document as an entire "resource," we can view it as being composed of subresources (e.g., elements) that are logically held together by the hierarchical structure of the document. Using a URI, we can easily reference an entire document as a resource; for example, `href="SomeFile.xml"`. Frequently we want to directly reference subresources within documents—for instance, to cross-reference elements buried in separate XML documents by linking them together in an extended link. XPointer, the XML Pointing Language, enables us to precisely reference subresources within XML documents, so that they may participate as resources in XLinks.

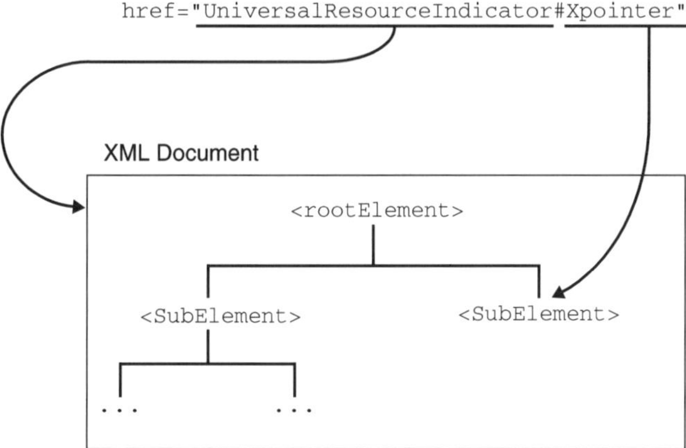

Figure 3.6 Relationship between URI and XPointer.

XPointer is a language for addressing the internal structures of XML documents. XPointer allows you to specify locations inside XML documents, allowing you to create subresource locators that can then participate in links. As you will see, XPointer gives you the ability to reference specific elements, character strings, and other parts of XML documents regardless of whether or not they have been explicitly marked with an identifying attribute. In effect, XPointer gives you language constructs that let you "reach inside" an arbitrary XML document to specify a precise location within that document.

3.2.1 What Does an XPointer Look Like?

A locator that references elements within an XML document generally consists of two parts, a Universal Resource Identifier and an XPointer, as

> ***The XML Path Language (XPath): A Foundation for XPointer***
> Although this chapter focuses on XLink and XPointer, the ability to precisely identify locations within documents is required by other XML facilities including the Extensible Style Language (XSL), and in particular XSL Transformations (XSLT). The W3C is currently working on the XML Path Language, referred to as XPath (see the Working Draft WD-xpath-19990709 at the W3C website), which seeks to provide a common syntax and semantics for functionality shared between XSLT and XPointer. XPointer is intended to be a superset of XPath; XPointer will provide additional addressing capabilities that are specific to link identification, in addition to the core capability set provided by XPath.

shown in Figure 3.6. An XPointer is a list of terms, called *location steps*, that are separated by the "/" character. The following pattern illustrates the general format for a locator containing an XPointer:

```
href="URI#LocStep1/LocStep2/LocStep3"
```

We will cover the format of XPointers and location steps in a moment, but first we need a conceptual understanding of how XPointers and location steps operate. You can think of the XML document as a tree made up of the various elements in the document, and of the XPointer as an abstract "pointer" that the location steps serve to move about and position in this tree. The pointer starts at an initial position, which is the root element of the document; then, the location steps in the list are processed one-by-one from left to right. Each location step advances the abstract pointer (i.e., causes it to take a "step") toward its final position, where it will point at one or more of the document subresources (or perhaps back at the root itself). The final pointer position, which is arrived at when there are no more XPointer location steps to process, identifies a subresource, which can then be made to participate in a link using the normal XLink syntax. You can think of the series of XPointer location steps as a list of tree-traversal commands that are applied to the pointer to position the pointer on the document tree. When the XPointer location steps have all been processed, the subresource that is indicated by the pointer is returned as the reference.

Knowing that location steps are processed one-by-one in turn, we will take a look at the format of an individual location step and see how it is processed.

Each location step has the following form consisting of three terms, indicated here by the placeholders `AxisName`, `NodeTest` and `[Predicate]`, where the `[Predicate]` term is optional. A location step takes the form:

```
AxisName::NodeTest[Predicate]
```

The first term, `AxisName`, defines what is known as a "relative axis" and is used to generate a sequence of what are called *candidate locations*, which are relative to a current location that is termed the *context node*. The general idea for processing a location step is that we start with a *context node list* as input, and use the `AxisName`, `NodeTest` and `[Predicate]` terms (as described in what follows) to generate a new context node list as output, which may be passed on to a following location step for further processing, and so on. The document content returned by the final location step is what is referenced by the XPointer.

It is important to understand how each of the terms within a location step affects the context node list so we will look at this in detail. The processing within a single location step is as follows. Using the current context node list as its input (which will contain only the single root node of the document if this is the first location step being processed), a temporary list of nodes that have a specific relationship to nodes of the context list is first generated by the `AxisName` term; for example, a specific relationship might be that of being a child of a given node, or being an ancestor of that node, and so forth. We will cover the valid `AxisName` terms shortly, but for the moment it is sufficient to say that a list of all nodes that are children of the nodes on the context node list will be generated if we use `child` as our `AxisName`.

When an `AxisName` term such as `child` is processed, it causes a new list of nodes to be generated, nodes that can be thought of as being "under consideration" for inclusion in the output context node list. Which of these "candidate" locations are retained and which are discarded? Very simply, that is the job of the `NodeTest` and `[Predicate]` terms; these terms act as filters to retain only nodes that meet criteria you have specified and discarding those that do not. The `NodeTest` term is used to test whether nodes on the candidate list are of the designated type; if a candidate node is not of the specified type it is automatically eliminated from the list. If a node passes that first screening, the `[Predicate]` term can be used to apply further screening. The optional `[Predicate]` term may be used to test the element type, attributes, positions or other properties of nodes, and multiple predicates can be specified and serve as successive filters. If we wished, for example, to filter the candidate list for the last node of type `<Chapter>`, we might code the `NodeTest` *and* `[Predicate]` terms as `Chapter` and `[position()=last()]`, respectively. Thus, given a context node list as input (e.g., output from the preceding location step), we could select the last node whose type is `<Chapter>` that is a child node of the (input) location list using the following location step. In the example here we are then sending the resulting context node list on to a following location step for further processing:

```
precedingLocStep/child::Chapter[position()=last()]/followingLocStep
```

Let us see how this might work with a simple example. Here we have built a tiny color palette in the document palette.xml, and given it three color elements corresponding to Red, Green, and Blue. Under each color element we have included elements for various shades of that color; note that the number of shades under each color is not the same. We have purposely given two of the color elements, Red and Green, identifier attributes in the form of `ID="R"` and `ID="G"`, respectively. However, the third color, Blue, has not been given an `ID` identifier attribute, nor have several of the shades of color. (Question: Will we be able to reference the Blue `<Color>` element if it does not have an `ID` identifier attribute? The Sky `<Shade>` of Blue? Answer: Yes, with XPointers!)

```
file: palette.xml

   <Palette>
      <Color ID="R">Red
         <Shade ID="001">Scarlet</Shade>
         <Shade>FireTruck</Shade>
      </Color>
      <Color ID="G">Green
         <Shade ID="002">Forest</Shade>
      </Color>
      <Color>Blue
         <Shade>Sky</Shade>
         <Shade ID="003">Indigo</Shade>
      </Color>
   </Palette>
```

The structure of the palette.xml document is depicted in Figure 3.7, where the contents and attributes of each <Color> and <Shade> element are shown beside the elements.

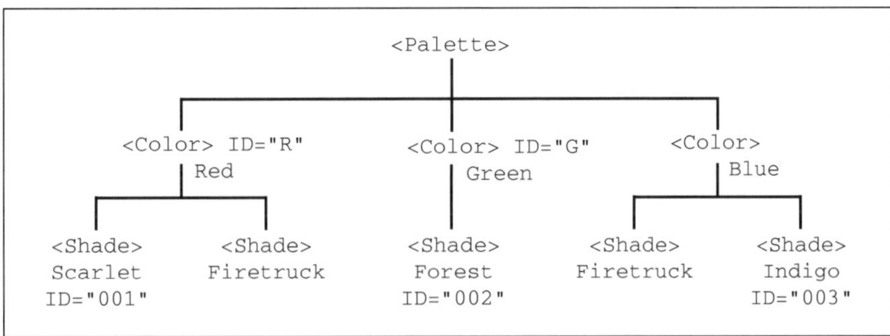

Figure 3.7 Structure of palette.xml document.

Given that the palette.xml document exists, our goal in this example will be to construct a separate document called ChooseAColor.xml that contains links to each of the <Color> elements in palette.xml, as well as links to each <Shade> of color. One of our constraints is to create these links without modifying the document palette.xml; this might be required if palette.xml was owned by someone else (e.g., if it was read-only), was located remotely, etc. In order to link to each of the <Color> and <Shade> elements in the palette.xml document, we will need locators that specify their precise location in file palette.xml. First we will take a look at how we might do this for the Red <Color> element. One way to code a locator for the Red <Color> would be the following:

```
href="palette.xml#child::Color[position()=1]
```

The locator in this case is made up of a leading URI portion consisting of the filename `"palette.xml"`, followed by the separator character `"#"`, followed by an XPointer that contains a single location step, `child::Color[position()=1]`. We will go over each of these items in turn. First, the URI is used to set the initial context for the pointer; that is, the URI indicates to which XML document the XPointer terms that follow will be applied. Here the URI indicates that the document being referenced is palette.xml, meaning that the XPointer terms will be applied to traverse the element tree for this document. The separator character "#" simply delimits the URI from the XPointer.

The XPointer follows next and consists of a single location step. Recall that the initial context node, which serves as input to this location step, is the document element node, namely the <Palette> element at this point. The AxisName::NodeTest terms, which are child::Color in this case, instruct the XPointer processor to generate a list of all child nodes of the <Palette> element whose node type is <Color>. Clearly, this list will contain all three <Color> nodes at this point; when the [Predicate] is applied, [position()=1] in this case, the node that is the first child of the <Palette> element is retained, and the remaining <Color> nodes are discarded. As desired, the Red <Color> element has been selected; as this is the last (and only) location step, this result is returned as the final XPointer. Thus, we could code a simple XLink that would take users directly to the Red <Color> element in palette.xml as follows:

```
<SimpleLink href="palette.xml#child::Color[position()=1]">
   Click Here for Red!
</SimpleLink>
```

As you may have noticed, we did not make use of the ID attribute, which was present for the Red <Color> element. XPointer has an abbreviated syntax that allows you to directly reference elements that contain an ID attribute. This is known as the "bare name" form of addressing, and would be coded as follows to reference the Red <Color> element, whose ID equals "R"______:

```
href="palette.xml#id(R)"
```

Thus the previous simple XLink that takes users directly to the Red <Color> element in palette.xml could also be coded as follows:

```
<SimpleLink href="palette.xml#id(R)">
   Click Here for Red!
</SimpleLink>
```

At this point you should be able to construct simple links to all of the <Color> elements, regardless of whether or not they have an ID attribute. The Green <Color> element could be addressed much like the Red <Color> element, but using a [position()=2] predicate, or a bare name form of address, such as id(G).

Creating links to the various shades of colors is not much more difficult; here we have our choice of using the bare name form of addressing for those <Shade> elements that have an ID attribute (namely Scarlet, Forest, and Indigo) or using an XPointer consisting of two location steps, the first of which locates the appropriate <Color> element, the second of which then locates the proper shade under that color. We will look at how each of these could be coded.

First, the bare name form of addressing is quite straightforward. Much like for the Red or Green <Color> elements we saw before, we simply need to indicate to the XPointer processor which ID we are looking for. To reference the Sky <Shade> of the Blue <Color>, which has an ID attribute of "001," we can do the following:

```
href="palette.xml#id(001)"
```

Referencing the Forest and Indigo shades is analogous. Now we will look at how we could address the FireTruck <Shade> of Red using a series of location steps. Recall how we created a reference to the Red <Color> element on page 115; this is actually half our solution to referencing the FireTruck <Shade> element. In fact, all we need to do is append the following location term to that previous XPointer:

```
child::Shade[position()=2]
```

The resulting reference would then be coded as follows:

```
href="palette.xml#child::Color[position()=1]/child::Shade[position()=2]
```

Note that we could just as easily combined the bare name form for addressing the Red <Color> element with the location step that locates the Scarlet <Shade> element, as follows:

```
href="palette.xml#id(R)/child::Shade[position()=2]"
```

At this point we have enough knowledge to code the ChooseAColor.xml file that we set out to create. It might look like the following:

```
file: ChooseAColor.xml

   <ChooseAColor>
      <SimpleLink href="palette.xml#id(R)">
         Click Here for Red!
      </SimpleLink>
```

```
    <SimpleLink href="palette.xml#id(001)">
       Click Here for Scarlet!
    </SimpleLink>
    <SimpleLink href="palette.xml#id(R)/
                      child::Shade[position()=last()]">
       Click Here for FireTruck!
    </SimpleLink>

    <SimpleLink href="palette.xml#id(G)">
       Click Here for Green!
    </SimpleLink>
    <SimpleLink href="palette.xml#id(G)/
                      child::Shade[position()=1]">
       Click Here for Forest!
    </SimpleLink>

    <SimpleLink href="palette.xml#child::Color[position()=last()]">
       Click Here for Blue!
    </SimpleLink>
    <SimpleLink href="palette.xml#child::Color[position()=last()]/
                      child::Shade[position()=1]">
       Click Here for Sky!
    </SimpleLink>
    <SimpleLink href="palette.xml#id(003)">
       Click Here for Indigo!
    </SimpleLink
</ChooseAColor>
```

Although this was a short example, it demonstrated some key XPointer concepts. It is important for you to note, for example, that we were able to reference elements that had not explicitly been set up beforehand as the intended destination of links, for example by giving them a unique `ID` attribute. This ability to reach into an XML file to reference an arbitrary element is very powerful, and effectively allows you to create links that reference documents for which you cannot change the source code.

There are many scenarios in which the ability to precisely reference elements in a document whose content you cannot change will prove essential. Consider a document that for legal reasons cannot be edited or modified, but to which you would like to add a link. For example, consider what would happen if United States Government regulations were posted as XML documents on the Web; you may wish to reference not just a particular section, but a very specific element in such a document. Think of the impracticality that would result if these documents were posted in HTML format rather than XML, and you wished to reference a specific line or item in the regulation. You could hardly expect the maintainer of these documents to add an `<A name="YourHook">` element every time someone wanted to link to a new location in the HTML document. If this data were maintained as XML, using an XPointer each "client" document (e.g., the documents that wish to link to the "server" US regulations document) would have the ability to directly address and reference locations in the server document without requiring the server document to be modified.

3.2.2 XPointer Relative Axes

Now that you have a general understanding of how XPointers work, we can take a closer look at the syntax. We will start by looking at what values may be used for the relative axis term (`AxisName`) in a location step; in the following sections we will review the values that may be used for the node test (`NodeTest`)and predicate (`[Predicate]`) terms. Earlier we noted that XPointer is closely related to another W3C standard, the XML Path Language XPath (see the Working Draft WD-xpath-19990709 at the W3C website). Relative axes are a concept that is common to both XPath and XPointer, and thus XPointer relative axes are in effect XPath relative axes as well.

The following terms are valid XPointer relative axes terms; given a context node list (e.g., the document root node if this is the first location step, otherwise the context node list output by the previous location step), each of the relative axes terms that is given here locates a list of nodes that are candidates for inclusion in the resulting context node list. The candidate nodes for a given axis are placed on the candidate node list ordered by distance from the context node.

- **`child`**—Selects direct child nodes of the context node.
- **`descendant`**—Selects nodes appearing anywhere within the content of the current node.
- **`descendant-or-self`**—Same as the `descendant` axis except that the context node itself is included as a candidate, preceding all descendants.
- **`parent`**—Selects the element nodes directly containing the context node.

- **ancestor**—Selects element nodes containing the current node.
- **ancestor-or-self**—Same as the `ancestor` axis except that the context node itself is included as a candidate, preceding all ancestors.
- **preceding-sibling**—Selects nodes that share the same parent as the context node that appears before (preceding) the context node.
- **following-sibling**—Selects nodes that share the same parent as the context node that appears after (following) the context node.
- **preceding**—Selects nodes that begin before (preceding) the entire context node.
- **following**—Selects nodes that begin after (following) the entire context node.
- **self**—Selects for each context node in the context node list a singleton node list containing that same context node.
- **attribute**—Selects the attributes of the context node.

The output that results from applying a relative axes term to the (input) context node list is a candidate node list, which is then passed on to the node test and (optional) predicate terms in that same location step.

3.2.3 XPointer Node Tests and Predicates

Once a list of candidate nodes has been generated by an XPointer relative axis term, nodes on that list are fed through a node test, and then finally (if they have survived that far) through a predicate screening test. As with relative axes, the syntax for node test terms (`NodeTest`) and predicate terms (`[Predicate]`) is common to both XPath and XPointer. The XPointer node test and (optional) predicate term in a location step are used to filter the nodes on the candidate list. The filtering performed by the node test is quite straightforward, as is the syntax for expressing a node test: exactly those nodes on the candidate node list whose node type matches the specified NodeTest type are retained. That is, if the node test returns "true," then the candidate node is retained. For example, the following example will select exactly those child elements (produced by the relative axis `child`) whose type is `<Keeper>`.

```
child::<Keeper>
```

In addition, XPointer provides the functions `comment()`, `text()` and `processing-instructions()`, which may be used as node tests, and which return true if the context node is of the corresponding type. Finally, a node test may be the wild-card character "*," which returns true for any node that is of the principal type of the axis. The principal type of all axes is element, with the exception of the attribute:: axis, whose principal type is attribute. Thus the following example selects all elements that are direct children of the node whose `ID` attribute is "PartDescription" (e.g., `ID="PartDescription"`):

```
id(PartDescription)/child::*
```

The predicate term is optional; if no predicate term has been specified, then those nodes that remain on the candidate node list become the nodes on the output context node list for that decision step. However, if a predicate has been specified, it is used to further filter the list of remaining candidate nodes before the output context node list is produced. As with the node test, only those candidate nodes whose test results in a "true" are retained on the list. There is a rich set of functions that may be invoked for predicates; these include node-set functions, Boolean functions, string functions, numeric-conversion functions; these functions are described in detail in the W3C XPath specification (see the Working Draft WD-xpath-19990709 at the W3C website). We will focus on the node-set functions and describe several commonly used ones here:

- **`last()`**–Returns the number of nodes in the context node list;
- **`position()`**–Returns the position of the context node in the context node list; and
- **`count()`**–Returns the number of nodes in the argument node-set.

The following examples illustrate how these predicates may be used with one another. The position() and last() predicates are often used together; for example, to select the last `<Paragraph>` child of the context node:

```
child::Paragraph[position()=last()]
```

Similarly, the first `<Paragraph>` node that is a sibling occurring before the context node may be selected as follows:

```
preceding-sibling::Paragraph[position()=1]
```

The `count()` function accepts a location path as an argument and returns the number of nodes in the resulting node list. For example, the following example selects <Customer> nodes that are descendants of the context node that have three or more <LatePayment> child nodes and do *not* have an <ElectronicsFundsTransfer> child node:

```
descendant::customer[count(child:LatePayment) >= 3 and
                        not(child:ElectronicFundsTransfer) ]
```

This example also illustrates the use of logical Boolean operators such as `and` and `not()`.

3.2.4 Another Example of XPointers in Action

To try some of the more esoteric XPointer relative location terms, we have created here a document whose elements and structure reflect a legal document, such as Articles of Incorporation. The structure of this document is shown in Figure 3.8 and the XML code appears in what follows. We have purposely given each element a `TAG` attribute, but note that the `TAG` attribute does not necessarily uniquely identify each element (as a necessarily unique `ID` attribute would be required to do).

```
<Document TAG="DOC">
      <Title TAG="TT">
      <Definitions TAG="D1">
         <Term TAG="T1"/>
         <Term TAG="T2"/>
      </Definitions>
      <Article TAG="A1">
         <Section TAG="S1"/>
         <Section TAG="S2">
            <SubSection TAG="SS1"/>
            <SubSection TAG="SS2"/>
         </Section>
         <Section TAG="S3"/>
      </Article>
      <Article TAG="A2">
         <Section TAG="S1"/>
         <Section TAG="S2"/>
      </Article>
      <Article TAG="A3">
         <Section TAG="S1"/>
```

```
      <Section TAG="S2"/>
      <Section TAG="S3"/>
      <Section TAG="S4"/>
    </Article>
  </Document>
```

TAG attributes are primarily added for exposition, to allow us to informally refer to, for example, Section 1 of Article 2 as `"A2,S1"`, or the second term under the definitions as `"D1,T2"`. Using this terminology, see if you can understand how each of the following XPointer references was arrived at. (Note that some of them hop around the tree quite unnecessarily and are meant to test your knowledge, rather than serve as examples of ideal practices.)

- **Article A1:** `child::/Article[position()=2]/ preceding-sibling::Article`
- **Section A2,S2:** `descendant::Section[position()=5]`
- **Section A3,S4:** `child::Article[position()=last()]/ child::Section[position()=last()]`
- **Subsection A1,S2,SS2:** `descendant::Article[postion()=1]/ descendant::Subsection[postion()=2]`
- **Article A3:** `following::*[position()=last()]/parent::*`

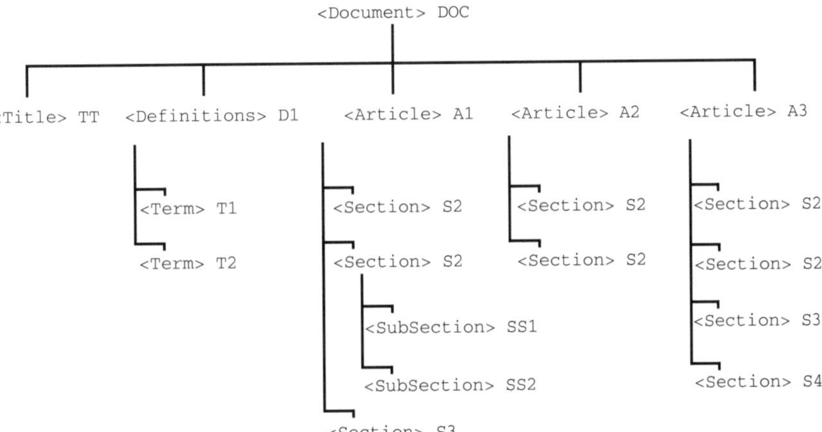

Figure 3.8 Sample XML document.

3.3 XLink Extended Links

Extended links are where XLink's linking model truly begins to differentiate itself from its HTML heritage. Extended links generalize the linking model from being simple unidirectional relationships between two resources (as we saw with the simple links) to encompass multi-resource links between an arbitrary number of resources.

We will start off with an example of an inline extended link that could be used to present information about a book. When viewed with a browser, the following XML code would display the text "My Book!" as a link, underlining this text to indicate that it represents a traversable link.

```
<MyExtendedLink xml:link="extended" inline="true"> My Book!
      <MyLocatorElement xml:link="locator" title="Chapter One"
                        href="ch1.xml">
      <MyLocatorElement xml:link="locator" title="Chapter Two"
                        href="ch2.xml">
      <MyLocatorElement xml:link="locator" title="Chapter Three"
                        href="ch3.xml">
      <MyLocatorElement xml:link="locator" title="References"
                        href="refs.xml">
</MyExtendedLink>
```

Clicking on the "My Book!" link in a browser might produce a pop-up menu listing the four possible destinations of this link; selecting one of these choices would take you to that location. The syntax for an extended link is somewhat different than for a simple link, and is driven by the fact that extended links can link together multiple resources. With an extended link, the linking element acts as a wrapper element that encloses locator elements that identify the actual resources participating in the link. In the preceding example, the `<MyExtendedLink>` element serves as the linking element. As the name suggests, each locator element contains a locator for one of the resources participating in the link. In the example already given, there are actually five resources that participate in the link: the four resources referenced by `<MyLocatorElement>` locator elements, as well as the contents of the `<MyExtendedLink>` element, namely, the text "My Book!" Since the extended link is declared to be inline, the contents of the extended linking element also participate in the link.

Sample definitions for extended link elements and locator elements are shown in what follows. Once again, you can name your linking elements anything you like; they need not be named `<ExtendedLink>` and `<Locator>` as was done here. Extended links are indicated by setting the `xml:link` attribute to `"extended"`; locator elements are identified by the presence of an `xml:link` attribute with the value `"locator"` and the presence of an `href` attribute.

```
<!ELEMENT ExtendedLink ANY>
   <!ATTLIST ExtendedLink
      xml:link          CDATA                 #FIXED "extended"
      inline            (true|false)          "true"
      role              CDATA                 #IMPLIED
      content-role      CDATA                 #IMPLIED
      content-title     CDATA                 #IMPLIED >

   <!ELEMENT Locator ANY>
   <!ATTLIST Locator
      xml:link          CDATA                 #FIXED "locator".
      href              CDATA                 #REQUIRED
      role              CDATA                 #IMPLIED
      title             CDATA                 #IMPLIED
      show              (embed|relace|new)    #IMPLIED
      actuate           (auto|user)           #IMPLIED
      behavior          CDATA                 #IMPLIED
```

The meanings of the attributes (e.g., `role`, `content-role`, `href`, `show`, etc.) are the same as they were for simple links. As you can see, the attributes that apply to the link as a whole are coded in the extended link element, and those attributes that pertain to the individual resources are coded in the locator elements. However, XLink provides intelligent default behavior for extended links and locators as follows: If a locator attribute is included in the extended link element, its value becomes the default value for that attribute in each of the locator elements it encloses. Individual locator elements are still free to specify a value for this attribute, which will then override the default value supplied by the enclosing extended link element.

For example, if we wanted the default `show` behavior for every link in an extended link to be `"replace"` (as opposed to the other possible values of `"embed"` or `"new"`), we could specify the locator attribute `show="replace"` in the enclosing extended link element. Then, if we decided that one of the links would function better if it had the "new" show behavior, we would need only to override the default value from the enclosing extended link. Consider the following XML code:

```
<ExtendedLink xml:link="extended" inline="false">
      <Locator xml:link="locator" href="ch1.xml"  show="replace">
      <Locator xml:link="locator" href="ch2.xml"  show="replace">
      <Locator xml:link="locator" href="ch3.xml"  show="replace">
      <Locator xml:link="locator" href="refs.xml" show="new">
   <ExtendedLink>
```

This could be coded to take advantage of default locator attributes stored in the extended linking elements as follows:

```
<ExtendedLink xml:link="extended" inline="false" show="replace">
      <Locator xml:link="locator" href="ch1.xml">
      <Locator xml:link="locator" href="ch2.xml">
      <Locator xml:link="locator" href="ch3.xml">
      <Locator xml:link="locator" href="refs.xml" show="new">
   <ExtendedLink>
```

3.3.1 Combining Extended Links and XPointers

Extended links, in particular those that are maintained out-of-line, work very well in combination with XPointers. In the following example we are using an out-of-line extended link to create a multiresource link between three <Section> portions of a chapter of a book:

```
file ch1.xml:

   <ExtendedLink xml:link="extended" inline="false">
      <Locator xml:link="locator" title="Section 1"
               href="child::Section[position()=1]">
      <Locator xml:link="locator" title="Section 2"
               href="child::Section[position()=2]">
      <Locator xml:link="locator" title="Section 3"
               href="child::Section[position()=3]">
   <ExtendedLink>

   <Section>
      <P>Here's some text for the first section.</P>
      <SubSection>And some text in a subsection.</SubSection>
      <SubSection>And more text in another subsection.</SubSection>
   </Section>
```

```
<Section>
   <P>Here's text for the second section.</P>
   <SubSection>This section has only one subsection.</SubSection>
</Section>
<Section>
   <P>Finally, text for the last section.</P>
   <SubSection>This section has two sub-sections.</SubSection>
   <SubSection>This is the last subsection.</SubSection>
</Section>
```

Note how the attributes of the `<ExtendedLink>` element declare it to be an extended linking element, and declare that it is not inline (meaning that it is out-of-line). Because it is out-of-line, the link itself does not participate in the link; it merely describes those resources that do participate in the link. In this case the resources that are participating in the link are the three `<Section>` elements in the document.

What type of behavior could we expect from a link such as this? If this document were viewed in a browser, clicking on any of the Sections might bring up a menu that would let you choose between "Section 1," "Section 2," and "Section 3." Of course, these are the `title` attributes associated with each of the three resources that participate in the link; selecting "Section 2," for example, would take you directly to that section.

The beauty of XLink extended links, in particular, when combined with XPointers, is that they allow you to separate information about links from the content that they serve to link. Each of the `<ExtendedLink>` elements is used to define a set of resources that participate in a particular extended link. There may be many extended link elements associated with an XML document, as there will be one for each multiresource link. For example, we could enrich the linking functionality of the previous example by making it so that each set of subsections under a particular section participated in its own extended link; this could be done as follows:

```
file ch1.xml:

<Chapter>
   <ExtendedLink xml:link="extended" inline="false">
      <Locator xml:link="locator" title="Section 1"
               href="child::Section[position()=1]">
      <Locator xml:link="locator" title="Section 2"
               href="child::Section[position()=2]">
```

```
    <Locator xml:link="locator" title="Section 3"
             href="child::Section[position()=3]">
  <ExtendedLink>

  <ExtendedLink xml:link="extended" inline="false">
    <Locator xml:link="locator" title="Subsection 1.1"
             href="child::Section[position()=1]/
                   child::Subsection[position()=1]">
    <Locator xml:link="locator" title="Subsection 1.2"
             href="child::Section[position()=1]/
                   child::Subsection[position()=2]">
  <ExtendedLink>

  <ExtendedLink xml:link="extended" inline="false">
    <Locator xml:link="locator" title="Subsection 3.1"
             href="child::Section[position()=3]/
                   child::Subsection[position()=1]">
    <Locator xml:link="locator" title="Subsection 3.2"
             href="child::Section[position()=3]/
                   child::Subsection[position()=2]">
  <ExtendedLink>

  <Section>
    <P>Here's some text for the first section.</P>
    <SubSection>And some text in a subsection.</SubSection>
    <SubSection>And more text in another subsection.</SubSection>
  </Section>
  <Section>
    <P>Here's text for the third section.</P>
    <SubSection>This section has one subsection.</SubSection>
  </Section>
  <Section>
    <P>Finally, text for the last section.</P>
    <SubSection>This section has two sub-sections.</SubSection>
    <SubSection>This is the last subsection.</SubSection>
  </Section>
</Chapter>
```

Note that we did not create an extended link for the single subsection under Section 2; in this context, doing so would not make sense, as there is no other subsection in this section with which to associate it.

3.3.2 Maintaining Links and Content Separately

In the preceding example of an out-of-line extended link, we succeeded in separating linking information from content, but only *within* the confines of the document. What we would really like to be able to do is to completely separate the linking information from content by keeping linking information and the content it serves to link in separate documents. In essence, we would like to have a "content" document, and a "link" document that work in conjunction with the content document.

There are a number of reasons for separating content and link information. For example, when different people use information content, different sets of links may be appropriate. For example, a single business document could have multiple uses, each of which would dictate the type of links it included. It could have a set of "internal use only" links that reference proprietary information, as well as a set of "general use" links that reference only publicly available information. In both cases the document content would be identical, yet the linking information could be vastly different.

Recall from Figure 3.1 at the beginning of the chapter that we noted how XLink enables linking information to be maintained separately from the content it serves to link, much like XSL separates presentation from content. Just as you can have multiple XSL sheets to provide different "views" of the same data, XLink allows you to have multiple sets of links (maintained as separate documents) that provide different linking behavior for the same information content. This is illustrated in Figure 3.9.

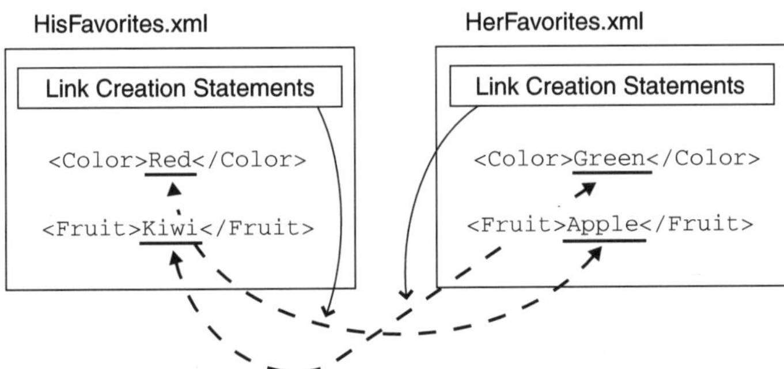

Figure 3.9 XLink enables content, linking information and presentation to be maintained separately.

When linking information spans multiple documents, or when linking information is maintained as a separate document, it is useful to be able to indicate to a link processor those documents that should be processed together as a group. In particular, if extended links are present in two documents that reference one another, it is not until both documents have been processed that all links become available to the end user. For example, consider the documents HisFavorites.xml and HerFavorites.xml in what follows. You will notice that both documents contain extended links that link elements from both documents together. This relationship is depicted in Figure 3.10.

```
file: HisFavorites.xml:

  <Favorites>
    <ExtendedLink inline="false">
      <Locator href="HisFavorites.xml#id(Red)">
      <Locator href="HerFavorites.xml#id(Apple)">
    <ExtendedLink>
    <P>His favorite color is <Color ID="Red">Red</Color>
      and his favorite fruit is the
      <Fruit ID="Kiwi">Kiwi</Fruit>.</P>
  <Favorites>


file: HerFavorites.xml:

  <Favorites>
    <ExtendedLink inline="false">
      <Locator href="HerFavorites.xml#id(Green)">
      <Locator href="HisFavorites.xml#id(Kiwi)">
    <ExtendedLink>
    <P>Her favorite color is <Color ID="Green">Green</Color>
      and her favorite fruit is the
      <Fruit ID="Apple">Apple</Fruit>.</P>
  <Favorites>
```

What links would become available if we loaded HisFavorites.xml into a browser? The extended link in this document would create a link in which the Red `<Color>` element in this document and the Apple `<Fruit>` element in the HerFavorites.xml document participate. Question: At this point would, the Kiwi `<Fruit>` element in HisFavorites.xml be an active link? The answer is no—if HisFavorites.xml were the only file processed by the browser, the browser would have no way of knowing that the Kiwi `<Fruit>` element in this document participates in a link. This is true

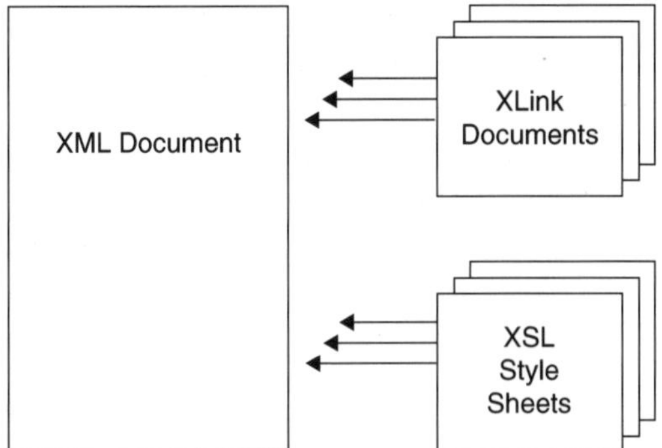

Figure 3.10 Link creation when links are stored in multiple documents.

because the linking information that creates this link resides in HerFavorites.xml, and will only be discovered by the XLink processor when HerFavorites.xml is processed. In a situation like this, we would like to be able to indicate to the XLink processor that it should process both HisFavorites.xml and HerFavorites.xml together as a group of documents.

Fortunately, XLink provides a mechanism for specifying that a group of documents should be processed together using XLink `group` linking elements and `document` linking elements. The syntax for declaring that the documents in the preceding example should be processed as a group would look like this:

```
<Group xml:link="group" steps="1">
      <Document xml:link="document" href="HisFavorites.xml">
      <Document xml:link="document" href="HerFavorites.xml">
   </Group>
```

This declaration could be added to the file HisFavorites.xml, and similarly to HerFavorites.xml, as follows:

```
file: HisFavorites.xml:

   <Favorites>
      <Group xml:link="group" steps="1">
         <Document xml:link="document" href="HisFavorites.xml">
         <Document xml:link="document" href="HerFavorites.xml">
      </Group>
      <ExtendedLink inline="false">
```

```
            <Locator href="HisFavorites.xml#id(Red)">
            <Locator href="HerFavorites.xml#id(Apple)">
         <ExtendedLink>
         <P>His favorite color is <Color ID="Red">red</Color>
            and his favorite fruit is the
            <Fruit ID="Kiwi">Kiwi</Fruit>.</P>
      <Favorites>


   file: HerFavorites.xml:

      <Favorites>
         <Group xml:link="group" steps="1">
            <Document xml:link="document" href="HisFavorites.xml">
            <Document xml:link="document" href="HerFavorites.xml">
         </Group>
         <ExtendedLink inline="false">
            <Locator href="HerFavorites.xml#id(Green)">
            <Locator href="HisFavorites.xml#id(Kiwi)">
         <ExtendedLink>
         <P>Her favorite color is <Color ID="Green">green</Color>
            and her favorite fruit is the
            <Fruit ID="Apple">Apple</Fruit>.</P>
      <Favorites>
```

This would cause the link processor to process the links in both HisFavorites.xml and HerFavorites.xml when HisFavorites.xml was loaded in a browser. (And similarly if HerFavorites.xml was loaded in a browser.) The result of this would be that the Kiwi `<Fruit>` element would now appear as a link because both of the extended links (one in each of the documents) would have been processed.

Sample declarations for an XLink group element and an XLink document element are provided here. (You could name your group and document elements anything, it is the values of the `xml:link` attribute that makes these `"group"` and `"document"` XLink linking elements.)

```
<!ELEMENT Group (Document*)>
   <!ATTLIST Group
      xml:link          CDATA                 #FIXED "group"
      steps             CDATA                 #IMPLIED >


<!ELEMENT Document EMPTY>
   <!ATTLIST Document
```

```
    xml:link            CDATA              #FIXED "document"
    href                CDATA              #REQUIRED >
```

The steps attribute of the group element is a required attribute that indicates how many layers of links the link processor should process before it stops looking for additional links. A steps value of 1 says to process only those documents that are immediately referenced, a steps value of 2 would indicate that any documents referenced by the first level of linked documents should also be processed for linking information, and so forth. The steps attribute is intended to prevent the link processor from pulling in an unbounded number of only marginally related documents for link processing; in general, the steps value will be a small integer value.

In the previous example, part of the difficulty we encountered was that linking information was spread across multiple documents; until we had processed all of the documents in the group we did not know all of the existing links. The approach we used to circumvent this shortcoming was to make sure that all related documents were processed, which we accomplished by using the group and document XLink elements. Is there a better way to organize this information? or is there some way for you to keep all of the linking information in a single document?

Ideally, we would like to keep all of the linking information in one place. As you can imagine, the simple 2-document example above, where links information was buried in just two documents, could become considerably more complex as the number of documents increased. One approach to taming this complexity would be to keep all of the linking information in a single "link" document. We could do this for the previous example as follows:

```
file: AllTheLinks.xml:

   <AllTheLinks>
      <ExtendedLink inline="false">
         <Locator href="HisFavorites.xml#id(Red)">
         <Locator href="HerFavorites.xml#id(Apple)">
      <ExtendedLink>
      <ExtendedLink inline="false">
         <Locator href="HerFavorites.xml#id(Green)">
         <Locator href="HisFavorites.xml#id(Kiwi)">
      <ExtendedLink>
   </AllTheLinks>
```

```
file: HisFavorites.xml:

   <Favorites>
      <Group xml:link="group" steps="2">
         <Document xml:link="document" href="AllTheLinks.xml">
      </Group>
      <P>His favorite color is <Color ID="Red">red</Color>
         and his favorite fruit is the
      <Fruit ID="Kiwi">Kiwi</Fruit>.</P>
   <Favorites>


file: HerFavorites.xml:

   <Favorites>
      <Group xml:link="group" steps="2">
         <Document xml:link="document" href="AllTheLinks.xml">
      </Group>
      <P>Her favorite color is <Color ID="Green">green</Color>
         and her favorite fruit is the
         <Fruit ID="Apple">Apple</Fruit>.</P>
   <Favorites>
```

Here we have pulled all of the linking information out of our content documents, HisFavorites.xml and HerFavorites.xml, and now maintain this information in a single document called AllTheLinks.xml. This approach will likely be very useful for creators and maintainers of XML content. What we have done is to take a very complex set of links that were being maintained across a large number of documents, and replace this set of links with a much less complex setup. A more general case of this approach is shown in Figure 3.11.

The final example we will cover for XLinks is how we can maintain different sets of links for a single content document, and allow users to access these alternative sets of links while viewing the same document content. The file BusinessPlan.xml is our brief content-only document, to which we will be applying multiple sets of links.

```
file: BusinessPlan.xml

   <BusinessPlan>
      <Description> Develop Next Gen E-commerce System.</Description>
      <Personnel> Good folks are hard to find.  </Personnel>
      <Financials> Charge a little, sell a lot. </Financials>
   </BusinessPlan>
```

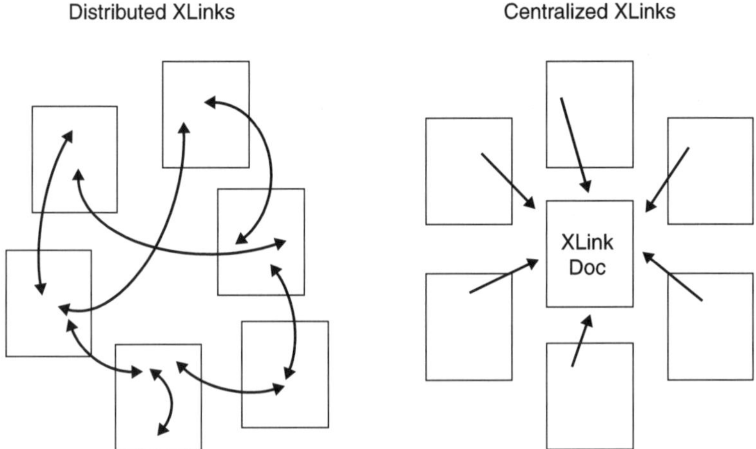

Figure 3.11 Complex sets of cross-document links may be maintained centrally.

The first set of links we are creating is for public consumption and will be maintained in a document called Public.xml. Here we are using extended links to link each of the three elements in BusinessPlan.xml to an appropriate XML file. For example, the `<Description>` element is linked to PressRelease.xml, and so forth. Of particular interest is the final element, `<SimpleLink>`, which links the document Public.xml to the original BusinessPlan.xml document. Note how the actuate attribute is set to `"auto"` and the show attribute is set to `"embed"`. The result of these attribute values will be that when the Public.xml document is processed, the extended links will be processed (creating links between the appropriate resources), and then the BusinessPlan.xml document will automatically be displayed. This second item happens because the Public.xml document contains no content for presentation (e.g., the extended links simply create links), so "embedding" the content of BusinessPlan.xml into Public.xml in fact replaces the view. Of course, since the extended links have been processed, the browser will enable the users to visit the PressRelease.xml document by clicking on the text in the `<Description>` element, and similarly for the other elements.

```
file: Public.xml

   <Public>
      <ExendedLink inline="false">
```

```
      <Locator href="BusinessPlan.xml#
                        descendant::Description[position()=1]">
      <Locator href="PressRelease.xml">
   </ExendedLink>
   <ExendedLink inline="false">
      <Locator href="BusinessPlan.xml#
                        descendant::Personnel[position()=1]">
      <Locator href="Employment.xml">
   </ExendedLink>
   <ExendedLink inline="false">
      <Locator href="BusinessPlan.xml#
                        descendant::Financials[position()=1]">
      <Locator href="Prospectus.xml">
   </ExendedLink>

   <SimpleLink href="BusinessPlan.xml" actuate="auto" show="embed">
</Public>
```

We have created next the Private.xml document in a manner similar to that used to create Public.xml already provided here. However, our extended links create links from the elements of the BusinessPlan.xml document to a completely different set of resources. Once again, loading this file in a browser would set-up the appropriate links (e.g., the <Description> element would be linked to the HowToGetRich.xml document in this case), but would still display the same content as for Private.xml, namely what is in BusinessPlan.xml.

```
file: Private.xml

   <Public>
      <ExendedLink inline="false">
         <Locator href="BusinessPlan.xml#
                           descendant::Description[position()=1]">
         <Locator href="HowToGetRich.xml">
      </ExendedLink>
      <ExendedLink inline="false">
         <Locator href="BusinessPlan.xml#
                           descendant::Personnel[position()=1]">
         <Locator href="GoodSalaryPlusOptions.xml">
      </ExendedLink>
      <ExendedLink inline="false">
         <Locator href="BusinessPlan.xml#
                           descendant::Financials[position()=1]">
         <Locator href="HowToRobABank.xml">
      </ExendedLink>
```

```
    <SimpleLink href="BusinessPlan.xml" actuate="auto" show="embed">
</Private>
```

3.4 Conclusion

As we have seen, XLink starts with a basic foundation that builds upon HTML's linking capabilities, but generalizes and extends the underlying linking model in a number of significant ways, resulting in a far more powerful and extensible linking language. The combination of XLink and XPointer permits an even greater degree of addressibility in terms of the XML document-content structures that can participate in links. These rich XML links provide an unprecedented degree of connectivity and interconnectivity for Web resources, and hold the promise of even richer user experiences for Web users.

CHAPTER 4

Web Applications with XML

XML holds tremendous promise as a core technology for building the next generation of Web applications. What will characterize these applications? If we listen to the hype and latch onto a few buzzwords, we might hear the following: global e-commerce; on-line shopping, intelligent search capability; and global interoperability. You would be wise to ask yourself, "Can XML provide all of this?" By the time you finish this chapter, we hope that your answer to this question will be a resounding "yes," that you have a solid understanding of why it can, and that your mind will be brimming with ideas for new Web applications that take full advantage of XML's capabilities. As you will see, the use of XML will be pervasive in Web applications of the future; also XML will play an important role not only on the client side but on the server side as well.

In order to orient you in terms of XML's possibilities, we begin in Section 4.1, *XML in Action*, with a scenario showing how XML-enabled technologies will make users more productive; this scenario is intended to give you a flavor of the types of Web-based applications that XML makes possible. In Section 4.2, *Anatomy of a Web Application with XML*, we will see how application developers can take advantage of XML by examining the architecture of a typical three-tier Web application and exploring the role that XML can play in each tier. In Section 4.3, *Interoperable Web Applications,* we discuss in more detail how the ability to share XML content makes Web applications interoperable and able to collaborate on behalf of the user. As we already laid the groundwork in the previous sections, in Section 4.4, *E-commerce Applications,* we explore in depth the exciting new area of electronic commerce, and discuss how XML provides support for it.

4.1 XML in Action

We will start out with a scenario of XML in action. Although some of this might seem fanciful, it is all possible within the realm of XML.

Sometime next year...

Mike arrives at work early because he wants to get a jump on the competition. He works in the business-development group of ANY Corporation ("A New You"), a booming architectural firm that specializes in designing creative work environments for expanding companies, and where workspace design requires creativity; the old "we'll put a few cubicles over there" approach is a thing of the past. Today's customers demand personalized solutions, and ANY's business is thriving because they deliver.

When Mike arrives at his workspace on the top floor of the New Millennium office building, his first stop is his electronic in-box. The first message he reads is from his colleague, Sally, who flew to Dallas the previous day to present design concepts drawn up by the firm's architects a week ago. Her presentation was generated automatically by the system from the actual architectural plans. (Whoever set up this system must be a genius. Remember when it used to take days to prepare a presentation like this one only to have one of the architects make a change at the last minute that did not quite make it into the final presentation?) The system is amazing: the architects work collaboratively on the CAD (Computer-Aided Design) drawings, which are linked into the system; these drawings contain references to the actual parts and materials to be used for the remodeling. When Mike or Sally wants to visit with the customer to go over the latest plans, they simply go to the "Generate A View" screen on the architecture application, and voila, they get an up-to-date document that gives them not only the drawings, but also a cost report that provides a detailed item-by-item cost breakdown. The system also tells them what kind of delivery date they are looking at as it is tied into their suppliers' systems, and about the availability of parts and materials. Fortunately for business-development folks such as Mike and Sally, the output of the system is not just some lifeless report they would have to spend days turning into a decent presentation. Instead, the system behaves as a multifaceted document, providing architects and business-development folks different customized views, allowing them to get any level of detail they want and in any format. Data can be seamlessly imported and exported to other applications. For large-screen presentations Sally likes to have the system create a view (i.e., a presentation) with plenty of graphics and really large fonts. For the handout documents she usually prepares to go along with a presentation, she has the system include additional detailed information, including, of course, information about the firm from the business-development database.

For the design concepts Sally presented to the customers, a 3D walkthrough of the floorplan on a large wall-size computer screen was included. (It is amazing how the system can generate walkthroughs from the floorplan data. One of the system designers mentioned something about Java making it possible. Do they drink a lot of coffee?)

Well, back to Sally's on-site presentation. Good news! The customer loved it! In particular, the jungle-flora boardroom and the saltwater aquarium in the reception area were nice touches. A question arose about the kind of delivery and schedule for beanbag chairs for the lunchroom. What if a decision was made to update to the more expensive ones? This was an easy question for Sally, even being off-site. Using one of the customers Web browsers during the presentation, Sally accessed ANY's automated supplier system to check on availability. A quick search turned up a trading partner located right there in Dallas who had the items on hand and ready for delivery. (Amazing how the system was smart enough to find a supplier whose location was near the customer, not only reducing the shipping cost but shortening the delivery time as well.)

With this final bit of good news the customer agreed to go ahead with the plans. Because the customer was interested in moving forward with this as quickly as possible, Sally proceeded to order the necessary materials for the work, and although she was off-site, it was not a problem. In fact, all that was involved in ordering the materials was dragging the icon for the floorplan onto the icon for the "Order" application on her desktop, and providing the Order application her authorization code. The Order application automatically read the floorplan document, performed a real-time search to find the best overall prices, and then ordered the materials directly from the selected trading partners. As the customer information, including shipping address, was included in the floorplan, the trading partners' systems knew to ship the materials to the customer's location in Dallas, rather than ANY's office. Of course, the applications knew to bill the ANY firm for the parts and materials, as ANY will bill the customer for them at a later date. Fortunately, the entire process is automated, traceable and auditable.

Very conveniently, after the parts and materials have been ordered, it is easy to check on the exact delivery status of particular items, because all of the shipping services that ANY's trading partners use are required to make tracking information available via the Web. In fact, ANY's customers can even check on the status of items that will be delivered to them. Because Mike and Sally do not have time to continually check on the status of orders, they both use an agent that automatically tracks the orders and notifies them if an item's delivery date is slipping. Mike is on the road a lot, and likes to know about these occurrences immediately. Therefore, he uses another agent to notify him via pager of the arrival of any messages that are tagged "urgent." (When he reads messages on the pager, they are displayed in an abbreviated format; he hates reading long messages on his tiny pager screen.)

Sometimes, Mike and Sally marvel that things that used to take days now take only minutes, and often even less. Oh well, there are more items in the in-box; time to get back to work!

... and so our story ends.

This scenario gives a glimpse of some of the exciting possibilities for Web applications through XML, including:

- collaborative, Web-aware documents;
- on-the-fly generation of customized documents;

- seamless application interoperability, both at the desktop and server levels;
- automated business-to-business electronic commerce;
- intelligent searching; and
- intelligent agent technology.

Before continuing, we need to understand of how current Web applications work and discuss why it would be difficult to develop the next generation of Web-based applications without a technology such as XML. In particular, we want to consider the problems faced by non-XML-based Web applications, and show how XML overcomes these limitations. As a result, you will be well equipped for our exploration later in the chapter of the new breed of Web-based applications and understand how XML makes them possible.

4.2 *Anatomy of a Web Application with XML*

In order to reap the full benefits of XML technology, it is important that Web application developers understand where XML fits in a three-tier application architecture. As we will see, XML has an important role to play on both the client and the server sides, and will play a key role on each of the following: client tier; middle tier; and back-end tier. As a Web developer you need to know when and how XML can best be used on each of these tiers. Keep in mind that much of the benefit of XML derives not only from its use within each of these tiers, but also from its central role as a data format that simplifies communicating between tiers.

4.2.1 XML's Role on the Client Tier

Because XML was originally envisioned as a replacement for HTML, it should come as no surprise that XML plays a significant role on the client tier. Much like HTML, XML can be used as a format to deliver data from the application server to the client. However, XML goes far beyond HTML in this respect; XML clients can take advantage of client-side processing.

Review: What Is A Three-Tier Architecture?
The de facto standard architecture for Web-based applications consists of three logical tiers that communicate with one another: (1) a client tier consisting of a Web browser, which communicates with (2) a middle tier that hosts application logic, which in turn communicates with (3) a back-end tier that hosts databases and data services.

Three-tier architectures are popular for a number of reasons. First, the widespread availability of Web browsers means that you as an application developer generally do not have to worry about developing and installing client software; the "browser wars" have taken care of this for you by ensuring that high-quality browsers are available on the user's desktop.

Second, the three-tier architecture serves to partition an application by functionality into pieces with well-defined interfaces and distinct roles: the client tier is responsible for presenting data on the user's desktop and gathering input data from the user; the middle tier hosts application-specific business logic; and the back-end tier handles databases and data services. Partitioning functionality across tiers makes it easier to reuse functionality, for example, sharing database resources among multiple applications running on the middle tier.

A Web server, which is a piece of software that runs on the middle tier, facilitates communication between client browsers and applications running on the middle tier. Because applications running on the middle tier can handle multiple clients, they are often referred to as application servers. The Hyper Text Transfer Protocol (HTTP) is used to transfer data over the Internet between browsers and application servers. Data transferred via HTTP from the middle tier to the clients contain Hyper Text Markup Language (HTML) in the form of web pages. HTML is the data that the browser displays for the user. Data can also be transferred in the other direction, from the browser back to the application, using HTTP-format GET and POST requests, which are then handled by the application servers.

An important aspect of client-side processing is the presentation of the data to the end user. There are a number of ways in which the client presentation of XML can be controlled and we will discuss them here. In addition, application interoperability is something that end users are coming to expect, and XML can certainly help application developers deliver this capability. End users routinely run multiple applications on their desktops—browsers tied to different websites, various business applications, etc.—and want to be able to exchange data between these applications directly on the desktop. As we will see, XML can be used to increase application interoperability on the client tier.

4.2.1.1 Getting Data to the Client and Back

In three-tier Web applications the client tier serves as the interface between the enduser and an application running on a server. The client tier is the means by which end users interact with the application; it allows end users to view information generated by the application server and to input new information and submit requests to the application server. In general, the client tier serves two purposes, namely: (1) displaying information that it has received from an application running on the middle tier; and (2) gathering information from the user, which is then relayed back to the application server for further processing.

Although we may not normally think of it this way, the client tier is one of the places where individual Web applications can interoperate with one another. At present, with HTML-clients as the front-end for applications, interoperability on the client tier really comes down to cutting and pasting simple text from one application screen to another, which is highly inefficient. As you will see, XML offers great improvements in this area by permitting much more intelligent interchange of data between Web-based applications, allowing documents or portions thereof to be passed between applications.

For Web-based applications, the HTTP protocol is used as the transport mechanism to move data back and forth between the front-end client and the application server running on the middle tier. For current Web applications in which the client is a Web browser, the data is sent to the client in HTML. For XML-based applications the format of the data sent to the client will be XML rather than HTML. The following sections discuss the benefits of using XML as the format to exchange data from the server out to the client. Figure 4.1 shows Web-based applications that use HTML and XML to communicate with clients.

4.2.1.2 Giving the Client Something to Work With

There are a number of advantages to shipping XML rather than HTML to the client. At this point it is important to understand the difference between HTML and XML. HTML is a widespread standard for the presentation of

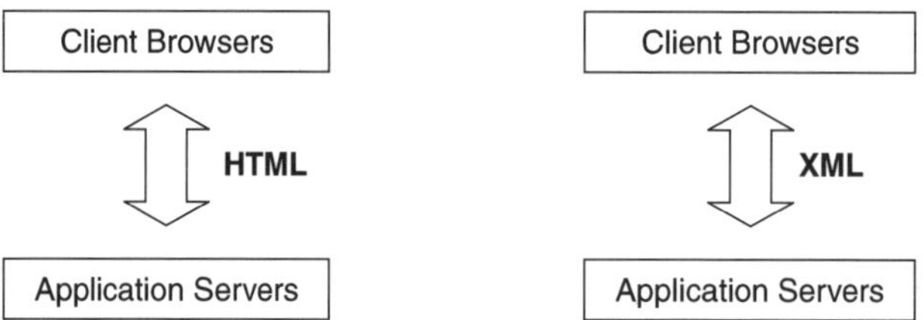

Figure 4.1 Web-based applications communicating with clients using HTML and XML.

> ***Note: XML or HTML on the Client?***
> Although this is getting a bit ahead of ourselves, we will see later that an XML application may choose not to use XML on the client, but could choose to use HTML instead. Why is this? Unlike HTML, at present not all core XML facilities are supported in browsers, although this situation is changing rapidly and should not be a concern in the near future. Even without full XML support on the client, there are many compelling reasons to use XML "server side," for example, within an application server. Thus a "server-side XML" application could choose to work with data in XML format on the middle tier and simply transform the XML data into HTML before shipping the data to the client.

simple documents, but it does not reveal anything about the content or context of the data. HTML simply provides formatting information for the data contained within the file; for example, it indicates whether a piece of text should be rendered by the client with a boldface font, italics, etc.

In the HTML approach to Web applications, an application running on the middle tier could extract data from a back-end database, build HTML from the data, and then ship the HTML to a client browser. An unfortunate consequence of this approach is that the process of creating HTML removes the distinction between data and presentation. Consider what happens when we want to display the results of a database query; if the result happens to be the price of an item, that price is simply embedded in the HTML file as a piece of textual data to be displayed. For example, if our query tells us that a pair of size 10 shoes costs 10 dollars, to a client browser these two "tens" are the same, simply text to be rendered for display even though semantically they represent vastly different kinds of values (e.g., shoe size vs price).

XML is very different from HTML in this respect; XML delivers information that separates content from presentation. With XML, data sent to the client are tagged, so that, for example, values representing prices can be indicated as such. By separating content from presentation, XML provides the recipient of the data with a business context that allows the recipient to act intelligently on the data. In the database query example in the foregoing, the first 10 could be tagged as the size (e.g., `<size>10</size>`), and the second 10 could be tagged as the price (e.g., `<price>10</price>`). The recipient, which could be an XML-enabled browser, would now have the opportunity to act upon the data intelligently, knowing precisely what each data value is meant to represent (e.g., size, price, etc.). Unlike HTML, XML delivers semantic meaning with each exchange of data, making data that are delivered to the client much easier to work with. XML allows the distribution of a chunk of information to the client for local processing, allowing the client to do more on behalf of the user without help from the server.

It has been said that unlike HTML, XML delivers the client "something to work with." In today's HTML-centric world, client applications that receive HTML-based Web pages with the intention of operating on the embedded data have a very difficult task ahead. As HTML embeds data within presentation markup, such programs must perform a "screen scrape" of the HTML file in order to recover the data, hoping that the positioning of data items within the page has not changed (which is a losing battle). Even after the HTML presentation markup has been removed, the program still can only guess as to the semantic meaning of the actual data values. As we have seen, XML solves both of these problems by separating content from presentation.

4.2.1.3 Controlling Presentation on the Client

We have been stressing the fact that XML does not specify how data should be presented on the client. This raises an interesting question: How does a browser know how to display the XML data? There are several mechanisms for this, including Extensible Style Language (XSL) documents, and client-side scripting languages such as JavaScript. An XSL document is an accompaniment to an XML document that specifies how the XML data should be formatted when displayed to the user. A single XML document can have multiple associated XSL documents, each providing the user with a different "view" of the data. Applications can allow users to dynamically switch between the multiple views by downloading multiple XSL files to the client along with the XML data, and making the various XSL formats dynamically selectable. Some types of XML, such as the Scalable Vector Graphics (SVG), may become directly renderable in browsers, because they are specifically designed as rendering languages; other types of XML will generally continue to be handled via XSL or via a task-specific application code. The reason for this is that much of the XML encountered in a browser will have been specified using a DTD that the browser authors have never seen; browser support for XML in such situations will be limited to displaying the structure of the XML data (which might not be very pretty), because XML describes the structure of data rather than the presentation of data.

Example 4.1

Figure 4.2 shows how client-side processing of XML data can be used to dynamically display data as either a bar graph or pie chart. In this case the client might be a Java, which receives XML data from the server; as the client receives semantically meaningful data in the form of XML data, the client can easily render the data in a variety of ways (using, for example, the Java Swing packages), without requiring further interaction with the server.

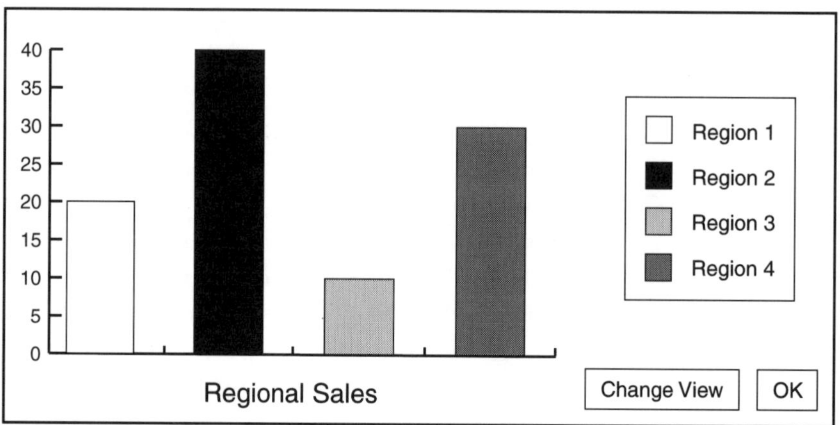

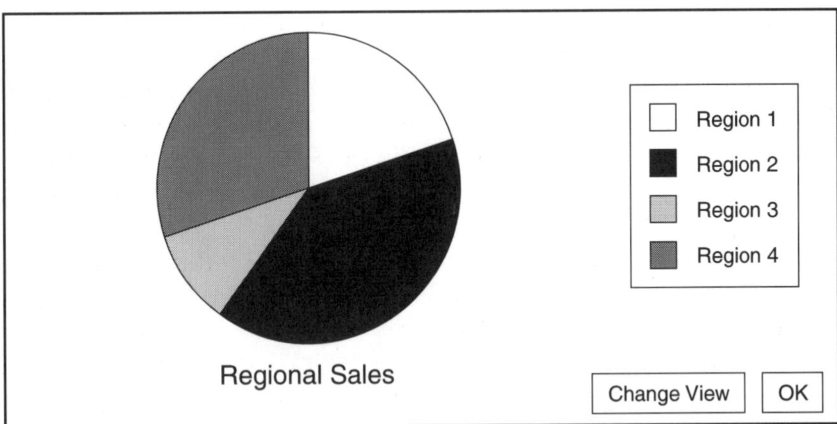

Figure 4.2 Client-side processing of XML data allows multiple views of the same data. (Continued)

There are a number of advantages to separating data and presentation on the client as done with XML. Clients have the opportunity to process the data, enabling, for example, intelligent client-side searching and sorting of the received data. In addition to the increased client-side interactivity that is possible, client-side processing of XML allows multiple views of the same data. Consider an application that is designed to support a variety of different users, or perhaps users with different types of computers (e.g., desktop computers vs palmtops). With XML it is possible to ship the same type of data to widely different clients, and allow the client to decide how the data should best be presented. For example, a desktop computer with high-resolution graphics could decide to display tabular data as a multidimensional graph, while a lower-resolution palmtop computer could choose to present these same data simply as rows and columns of numbers. Another application that wanted to display these same values could present them in a spreadsheet-like format, where columns are sortable, hideable and swappable. As yet another example, for a Web application that had many graphical images to display, one XSL sheet could choose to display the graphics as still pictures while another could employ animation.

Example 4.2

As with our opening scenario concerning the ANY Corporation's dynamic business presentation, an XML document such as a CAD drawing that is normally presented as 2D drawing (e.g., an architectural plan) could be rendered in three dimensions by an appropriately XML-enabled client. This is depicted in Figure 4.3, where a client in the form of a Java Applet has been served XML data that describe an architectural floorplan. As the client has received the floorplan data – rather than, for example, a particular rendering of that data—the client can easily render the data in a variety of formats. Here the Applet might be using Java 2D APIs and graphics routines for the flat view on the left, and a Java 3D APIs on the right to render the data accordingly.

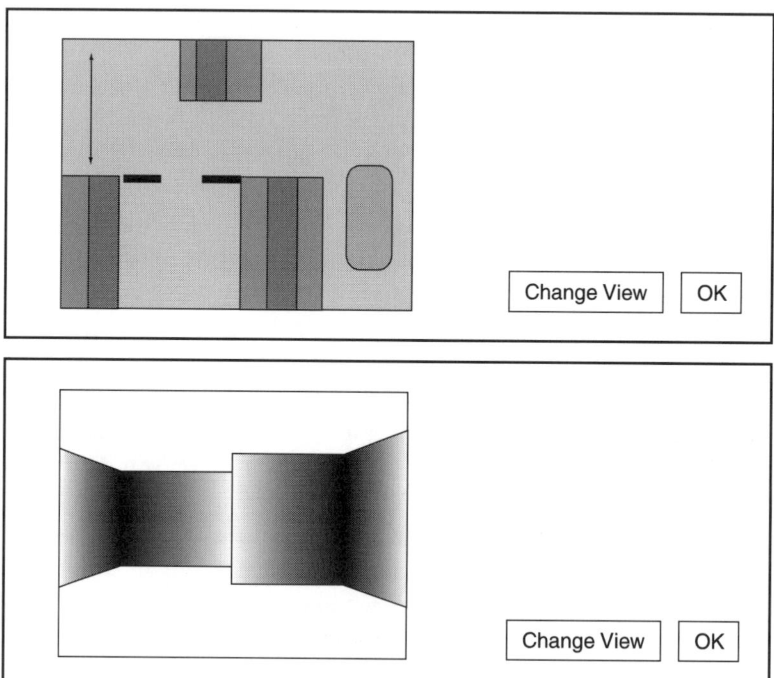

Figure 4.3 XML data presented to client as 2D and 3D graphics.

4.2.1.4 Client-Side Application Interoperability

Client-side processing of XML also allows semantically meaningful interchange of data between client applications. At present, data interchange is meaningful primarily on users native desktops; for example, dragging a file over to a word processing icon opens the file. XML has the ability to extend this paradigm to all kinds of applications by allowing data pulled from an unknown source (e.g., acquired via searches on the Internet) to be meaningfully plugged into another application. As a trivial example, just think how much time could you save in filling out HTML forms with your name, address, phone number, etc., if such forms were XML-interchange enabled. Imagine automatically populating an online order form with the result of a query from a completely different application, all with a single gesture of the mouse. For example, if the result of a database query for an item was delivered to a client-browser application as XML, the user might only need to drag the item over to the Order application to transfer the "data package" received from the query to the second application. This type of processing is depicted in Figure 4.4 below.

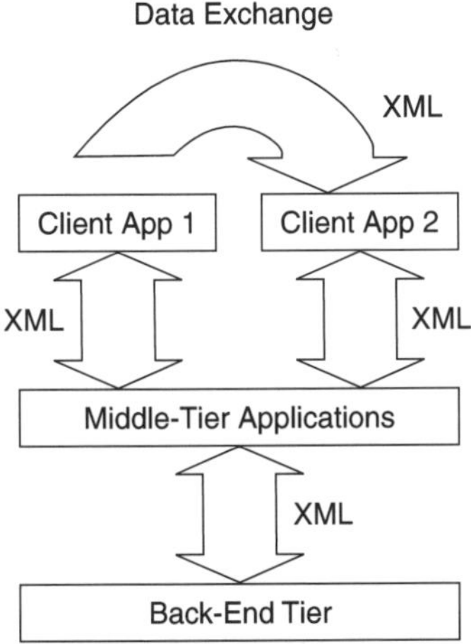

Figure 4.4 Improving application interoperability for the client by exchanging XML data.

4.2.2 XML's Role on the Middle Tier

When end users think about applications, they often do so in terms of the various screens, menu, etc.; in effect, the graphical user interface. As a Web application developer, you know that there is much happening "behind the scenes"—the application logic, interactions with multiple data sources, etc.—all of which must function seamlessly before any data can be presented to the user via the graphical user interface. As you know, these functions are often carried out on the middle and back-end tiers. With XML, the task of off-loading some or all of this processing to the client—using scripts, Applets and browser plug-ins—is greatly simplified. In addition to its role on the client, XML will play a very important role on the middle tier as well. Although the benefits of client-side XML are perhaps the most immediately visible to end users (e.g., more interactive Web pages, intelligent data interchange, etc.), the use of XML on the server side will have broad impact as well. Full support for XML from the server side is also necessary to fully realize the benefits of XML on the client tier. One of the thorniest problems that application developers face is integrating data from multiple sources. We will discuss how XML addresses this and other problems and give examples of what companies can do with XML on the middle tier.

4.2.2.1 Architecture of a Middle Tier

In the previous section we noted that browsers running on the client-tier typically serve as the user interface for Web-based applications. In three-tier architectures, application services generally run on the same logical tier, namely, the middle tier, which serves to separate the business logic from both the client tier and the back-end tier that houses databases and data services. A middle-tier application server exchanges data with the user-interface tier and interfaces to back-end data, aggregating information from the necessary sources, processing it with internal business logic, and creating a set of information to be sent to the client. This type of architecture is one of the most common for implementing Web-based applications. Although it is by no means the only approach, its major advantage is ease of implementation, which frequently becomes the determining factor when delivery schedules run into the realities of "Web time." The canonical three-tier architecture is depicted in Figure 4.5.

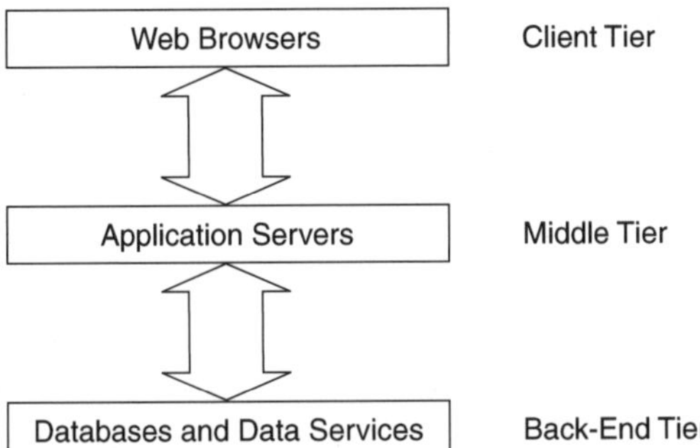

Figure 4.5 Three-tier Web-application architecture.

The middle tier simultaneously hosts many different application servers, each providing different application functionality to clients. In order to simplify the development of application servers, it makes sense to factor out common functionality that can be reused across multiple application servers. An example of such functionality is the need to communicate with clients using the HTTP protocol. For this reason the middle tier contains a piece of software called a Web server that facilitates communication between clients and applications servers. The Web server receives HTTP requests from clients and forwards them to the appropriate application server. The Web server then sends back to the client a HTTP response containing data generated by the application server. Applications are thus shielded from the low-level details of the HTTP protocol and syntax. The need for this sharable "front-end" processing on the middle tier seems clear, and is the motivation for Web servers; it would be inefficient to make each application server implement this low-level functionality independently.

What is becoming more and more apparent on the middle tier is the need for an analogous type of "back-end" processing, which would allow application servers to more easily access information that resides on the back-end tier. As we noted earlier, in broad terms an application server hosts the application's business logic and aggregates information from multiple sources. For large enterprises, these information sources can be many and often have widely different formats as they come from a variety of different databases and data sources.

Integrating the many different information sources with the application servers is one of the most costly problems faced by enterprise application developers. In the next section we discuss how creating an XML-based integration server addresses this problem. The integration server serves as a staging area where data from disparate sources are given a common format before being processed by the application servers. This is depicted in Figure 4.6.

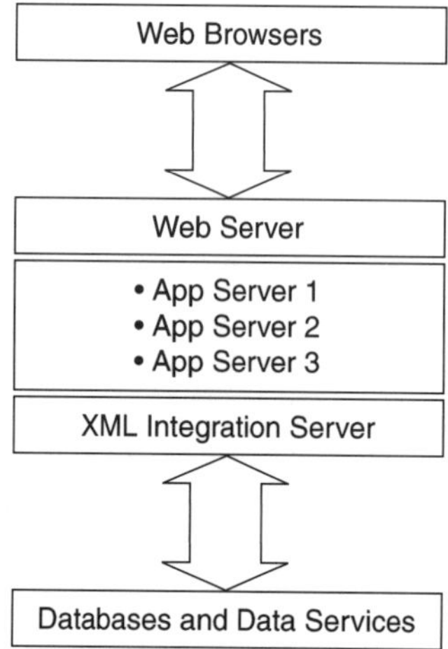

Figure 4.6 Architecture of middle tier.

4.2.2.2 The Data Integration Problem

Server-side XML holds the promise of being able to solve one of the most expensive and recurring problems experienced during enterprise application development; i.e., middle-tier data integration. One of the tasks that are typically performed by an enterprise application server is aggregating data from multiple sources, data that are more than likely arriving in different proprietary formats. This problem is difficult for several reasons. Data coming from different sources can have different formats, and if the application code is exposed directly to these different formats it becomes brittle to changes in the underlying data formats. It is bad enough that a single application has to have code to handle the multiple formats, but what compounds this problem is the many-to-many mapping required to map the many application servers to the many data sources. Modifications to a single data source have the potential to require changes in all application servers that directly access the data source. Although this is an unacceptable situation, it is all too common in many organizations.

Taking a cue from the role the Web server plays on the "front end" of the middle tier, the process of aggregating data ought to be separated from the application servers and viewed as an underlying infrastructure capability that is provided by an integration server. It is the duty of the integration server to provide to the application servers a consistent view of the various databases and data services. In order to be effective, an integration server must provide data in a common format, yet one that is rich enough to represent data of any type. This is where XML will play a critical role for application development on the middle tier; XML can easily represent data from relational, hierarchical and object databases, documents, images, various messaging formats, regular text, and Unicode data (in short, most structured data used by a business to share information), hence it makes a good hub language for conversion. Very importantly, XML's ability to represent such a wide variety of data formats means that application developers can readily integrate legacy databases.

The integration server provides a uniform format for all data, regardless of its sources, by converting all data to XML format and passing this XML-format data to the application servers. This has the benefit of insulating the application servers from proprietary and potentially changing formats of the underlying databases and data services. Applications can be written generically to handle this universal XML data format, allowing them to process the data uniformly regardless of its origin or original structure. An XML integration server lets applications access data as if it all came from a single, unified database. Of course, if an application requires that the data it receives from the integration server must be a specific (non-XML) format, the XML data from the integration server must be converted to that format. Nevertheless, as is illustrated in the example in what follows, the maximum number of data conversions that may be required if an integration server is *not* used grows proportionally to the square of the number of clients and databases. However, the number required if an integration server is used grows much less quickly, because it is proportional only to the number of clients and databases (and not their square).

Example 4.3

Information systems in the healthcare sector use a wide variety of data formats, and need to support interactions with national, state and local information systems. There are tremendous benefits to be realized by providing applications with a unified view of the information stored in the many separate internal systems. Doctors need to reference patient histories and be able to crosscheck medicine interactions. The pharmacy and accounting department have different information system requirements, but both clearly can benefit from integrated information sources. Integration servers can greatly simplify application development by providing application developers a unified, coherent view of available data resources as shown in Figure 4.7.

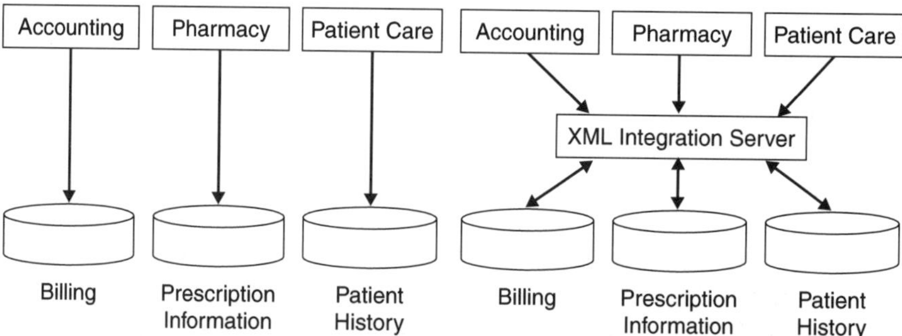

Figure 4.7 Data integration using XML integration server.

4.2.2.3 *Server-Side Application Interoperability*

Although XML was initially conceived as simply a better format for Web documents, its potential as a means to transfer information between application systems at the server level soon became apparent. The extensible nature of XML and the inclusion of self-describing metadata within documents enable XML to support an extremely flexible and dynamic environment for application interoperability and integration. XML documents may include embedded metadata that enable applications to readily examine and manipulate the data contained in the document. Thus, in addition to being an excellent medium for storing traditional documents, XML documents can be used as self-describing messages that can convey information between applications with access to the Internet. Use of XML data exchange for server-side application interoperability is illustrated in Figure 4.8.

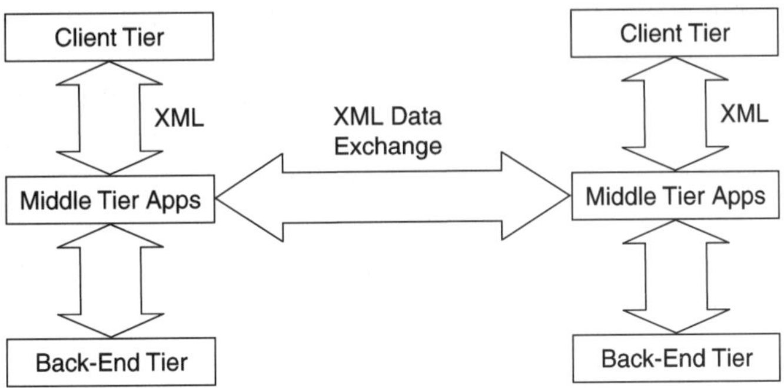

Figure 4.8 Server-side application interoperability using XML data exchange.

By relying on HTTP as the underlying protocol to transport data, XML-based middle-tier servers comply with the demands of existing firewalls and can take advantage of currently available Web security measures. XML provides a means for transferring data, as well as the corresponding data schemas, for databases and object repositories over existing HTTP-based infrastructures such as the Internet and Intranets. XML allows applications to easily transfer information across the web using pervasive open protocols.

In addition to being an easily transportable data structure, XML is also extremely robust. XML structures can absorb new fields without disrupting the existing data structures or programs that use these structures, meaning that database schemas do not need to be redesigned and applications do not need to be rewritten. These unique properties of XML make it an ideal format for the universal interchange of data. An application that publishes an XML document that is used by multiple other applications could choose to add a new attribute to the document. The original applications that used the document would be unaffected by the addition of the new attribute. Because each data element is self-described, each application need only extract the appropriate elements from the message as required. This approach enables different organizations to construct loosely coupled application integration schemes.

Using XML as the universal interchange format allows applications servers to look at all the data through a single logical view. Each integrated component need only provide a single XML adapter in order to interoperate with all other components, which means the amount of code that needs to be written and supported is limited to linear growth.

4.2.3 XML's Role on the Back-End Tier

We have seen how XML plays an important role on the client and middle tiers processing data. Next, we consider XML's role on the source of this data, namely, the back-end tier. There are a number of motivations for using XML on the back-end tier. XML on the back-end tier can simplify Web application development by offering an efficient means of storing data that lends itself to powerful query capability. Using XML on the back-end tier allows developers to easily integrate legacy data and provides a foundation for tuning the performance of data-driven applications.

4.2.3.1 Efficient XML Storage

A primary motivation for using XML on the back-end tier is to support the use of XML on the middle tier. As we discussed in the previous section, the adoption of XML on the middle tier will go a long way towards solving the data-integration problem. If an application handles data in XML format on the middle tier, it is only natural to consider storing this information in XML format on the back-end tier as well. Middle-tier XML data that are not stored in XML format on the back-end tier require repeated translation to and from an XML format on each access. For relational databases this involves decomposing XML into its constituent elements and mapping these elements to rows and columns in tables, and vice versa, to build and store the XML data. While these composition and decompositions are possible, they can be very costly in terms of performance. Fortunately, XML is also a convenient and efficient storage format for any richly structured data and a number of databases already support XML data formats.

4.2.3.2 *Querying XML Data*

There is growing industry support for a standard XML query language, similar in concept to the capability that SQL provides for relational databases. XML Query language (XQL) is a query language for XML document data that allows applications search and retrieve information from a document in much the same way as querying a database. Unlike HTML, in which a retrieval consists of pulling the entire HTML page, queries of XML structures can be structured so that they only return the relevant attributes.

Example 4.4

When the Web server receives a request for an XML-type document, it can easily react according to the requested file's type. For example, if the type of document requested is simply XML, the web server might merely return the contents of the document. If the type of document requested is XQL, the Web server might execute the XQL query and return the resulting XML.

It is interesting to note that XML Querying (of any flavor) does not assume XML-formatted data on the back end; only that the query can be understood in terms of an XML data model and retrieved data can be returned to the caller in XML format. That is, it is a query against the XML Information Set.

4.2.3.3 *Integrating Legacy Data*

In the previous section we discussed the role of an integration server. Clearly, if data are stored in XML format on the back-end tier the job of the integration server is greatly simplified. Even without a middle-tier integration server, however, legacy systems can continue to store data in their present format (e.g., relational database, etc.) if they provide an adapter that converts the data to XML format before being returned and vice versa. Because newer applications that use the XML adapter see only the logical XML data structure, they are insulated from changes occurring within existing databases and legacy applications. This approach is similar to the integration server discussed in the previous section, but here the responsibility for converting data to XML format remains with the data source on the back-end tier.

The use of XML on the back end is being driven by the adoption of XML as a universal data format on the middle tier. However, traditional non-XML technologies, such as relational databases, are very mature and represent large investments by many enterprises. As we noted, XML on the middle tier stands to resolve many of the data-integration problems. While the benefits of easier data integration will be considerable, it remains to be seen if the overall benefit will be compelling enough to cause enterprises to replace their many existing relational databases in favor of XML databases. For databases that interact heavily with XML-based applications on the middle tier, XML is clearly the way to go on the back-end tier. However, for many legacy systems it is likely that relational databases will remain common, with middle-tier integration servers and back-end XML data adapters playing key roles by transparently mapping between formats when these data are accessed by Web-based applications.

4.2.3.4 Performance Enhancements

Initial efforts to address XML on the back-end tier focused on using a simple XML adapter in front of a relational database. Although this direct approach works on smaller systems, there are significant opportunities to improve the performance and efficiency of demanding Web applications by caching data from the back-end tier in the integration server on the middle-tier. The approach of caching frequently used data is well known in database and other data-intensive applications, and lends itself well to XML data servers. Application servers require high-speed access to data, for example, when executing queries across large sets of aggregated data. In order to improve the performance of the back-end tier for such operations, a number of products provide data-caching mechanisms that temporarily store a copy of the data in XML format on the middle tier. An example of this type of architecture is depicted in Figure 4.9.

There are a number of advantages to caching a copy of XML objects on the middle tier. Aggregating and caching data on the middle tier enables applications to query data much faster, because navigating an XML structure in the middle tier requires only traversing pointers in memory. The middle-tier cache eliminates the need to construct and deconstruct the XML object at every access, potentially eliminating many time-consuming roundtrips to the back-end database. Of course, this type of middle-tier data caching must ensure the integrity and consistency of data, which is not trivial. Application developers who want to take advantage of middle-tier caching should consider purchasing middle-ware solutions that provide this capability rather than attempting to build this functionality themselves.

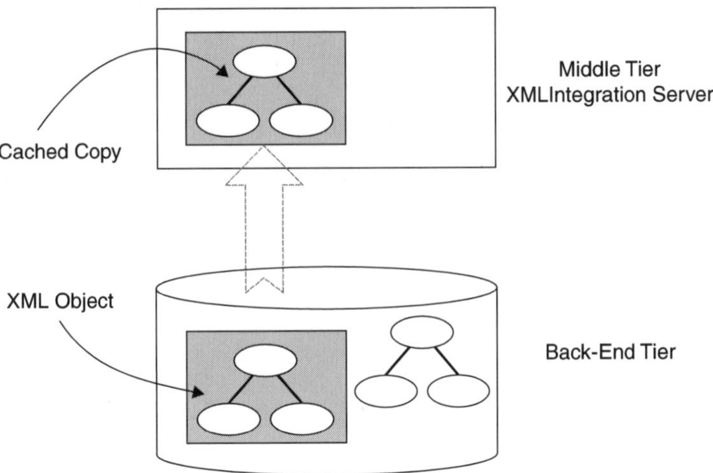

Figure 4.9 XML integration server caching XML objects on the middle tier.

4.3 Interoperable Web Applications

Now that we have an understanding of the role that XML can play in each of the three application tiers, we can take a look at how Web-based applications can become more interoperable and more powerful as a result. XML gives meaningful structure to data, and very importantly, allows this structured data to be shared not only among local users but across widely distributed sites as well. XML's ability to structure data meaningfully, and the ability to distribute this structured data across the Internet can add new capability and functionality to many Web-based applications. The application areas that can benefit from the use of XML are seemingly unlimited; we will explore three general application areas that each can benefit directly from XML: content syndication; on-line documentation and support; and personalized content. These examples should give you ideas about how interoperability can be improved with XML in those applications you are undertaking.

4.3.1 Content Syndication

The power of the Web comes from its ability to give users access to information and by providing users the means to share that information with each other. Following the lead of the previous media industries, we have come to refer to information that is available on the Web as content. In this section we discuss how XML simplifies the process of content syndication on the Internet. We begin by discussing content syndication in general and the issues it raises. Then we explore how XML can be used to address these problems.

4.3.1.1 What is Syndication and What Makes It Difficult

Syndication occurs when an owner of information sells that information or some portion of it to a second party so that the second party may use it. A classic example of this is the syndicated news services, such as the Associated Press (AP) and Reuters, whose stories newspapers have traditionally carried and which now appear on the Web.

Syndication benefits the Web in several ways. First, it benefits end users by increasing the amount of high-quality content that is available on the Web. Second, it benefits the providers of content by giving them another outlet for their information, which can become an additional revenue source. News services, as we mentioned, provide their services on the Web giving them an additional source of revenue. Although syndication currently takes place on the Internet, the techniques for supporting it are far from optimal and hinder its growth. This comes largely from trying to distribute content in the form of raw data or HTML files. Both of these distribution formats have their share of problems. Raw data are data that can only be interpreted by knowing the exact file format. One non-XML approach calls for content suppliers to ship raw data to content receivers; this has the advantage of allowing content receivers to decide on the presentation format. Unfortunately, transmitting raw data leads to brittle solutions; the content-receiver code becomes highly dependent on the content-supplier's data format, and seemingly insignificant changes to the data format can lead to significant work and rework on the part of the content receivers.

Distributing HTML, on the other hand, suffers from other problems. Although HTML is a well-known standard format, using HTML as the distribution format essentially dictates the presentation format to the content receivers unless they are willing to invest significant resources to reformat the information. However, this is error-prone because the data are tagged only with presentation information. Both distribution techniques, that is, raw data and HTML, suffer from another shortcoming. If only a portion of the content has changed, how easy is it for the content provider to send only the content that has changed? In order to do this, the content receiver must have a reliable way of merging the updated content with the existing content. In the absence of content-oriented tags this can be very difficult. Due to the very dynamic nature of syndicated content, content receivers continually need to update their web pages. Manual or nonautomated solutions are clearly not cost-effective solutions to this problem.

4.3.1.2 *How XML Addresses The Problems*

As you know, XML lets data be represented in a structured format and lets users tag these structures in terms of their content. Meaningful content-oriented tags can be applied at any level in the structure, all the way from individual elements, to portions of the structure, or even the entire structure. Content-oriented tags enable the recipient of an XML document to act intelligently upon the data, which has a number of implications for content syndication.

Tagging data in terms of its content means that the recipient of the data is not dependent on the specific format of the data, leading to more flexible robust solutions. Content receivers no longer simply receive "files" of data but rather decipherable content. Thus, when content changes and web pages must be updated, the content supplier has the option of shipping only those portions of the content that actually changed. Because they are tagged in terms of content, when these portions are received they can easily be integrated into the local content, thus replacing the previous data with the updated data. This approach is supported by XML "content repositories," which are database-like programs typically resident on the back-end tier. Such programs give content providers the ability to automatically provide content updates to downstream content receivers. Using XML as the distribution format, content syndication does not have to use a batch-oriented, all-or-nothing approach. Instead, only those portions of the content that have changed need to be transmitted, and the receiver can easily and reliably merge the new content with the previously received content. Of course, there is nothing to preclude using XML in a batch-oriented approach where all content, whether it has changed or not, is shipped to the receiver. Although this wastes bandwidth, it could simplify the receivers job if they only want to refresh their content periodically.

Whether the content receiver is getting all of the content or just a portion as an update, the receiver always has the option of filtering the received content, selecting perhaps only the content that has been tagged as modified after a specific time to be used to update the local information. XML allows the interface between content provider and content receiver to be much less tightly coupled than with other content-distribution approaches; such flexibility is essential in real-world applications. XML solves the problem of updating out-of-date content by enabling meaningful information to be transferred between sites. This allows sites to correctly and automatically update the necessary local data.

For publishers whose primary source of income comes from syndication, XML will broaden the ability to include or link to related content, thereby increasing revenues. Towards this end, the Information Content and Exchange (ICE) protocol is an emerging standard based on XML that is designed to allow content providers to share their information by syndicating parts of it to other parties on the Web. ICE is designed to enforce traditional business rules for content including access rights to the data, expiration dates, and the means for updating the data automatically at specified intervals or when content changes.

4.3.1.3 Syndication Application Example

Figure 4.10 illustrates how content syndication can be performed using XML. All of these systems are middle-tier applications, running on different servers via the Web. At the highest level we see two content providers: the first of these provides content related to home mortgage interest rates, which are updated daily; the second content provider is a national real estate company with home listings nationwide. At the second level in the content-syndication chain we see a content consumer that also serves as a content provider. This entity takes content in the form of interest rate information from the first content provider and information on homes for sale within a specific geographic region from the second content provider. This content provider/consumer aggregates this information, which it then offers as content to its own subscribers. On the third level of this chain we see a human resources system for a major corporation, which strives to provide its new employees with the latest information on homes for sale during employee relocation. Because the corporation provides the employees with discounts not available to the general public, it takes the content from the second-level provider and adds additional information to the local content.

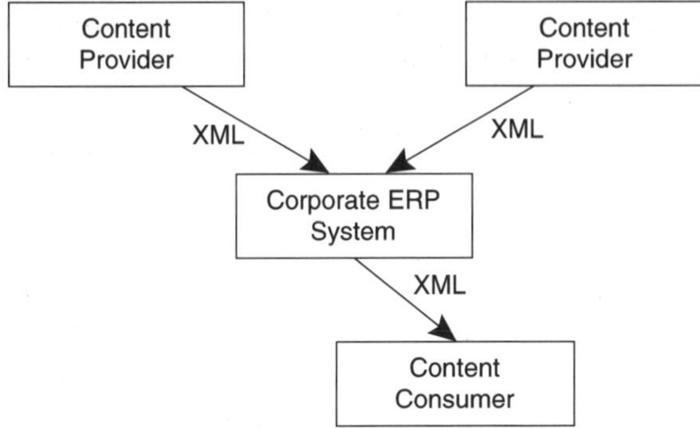

Figure 4.10 Content syndication using XML.

4.3.2 On-Line Documentation and Support

Another application area that can be made more interoperable through the use of XML is online documentation and support. XML provides a particularly effective infrastructure for this application area, which calls for managing documentation (back-end tier), distributing information (middle tier) and presenting information to the end user (client tier).

Because XML lets entire pieces of information within a document to be identified with content-oriented tags, XML gives users the ability to request a semantically meaningful portion of a document rather than simply "pages" of information. The use of XML in online documentation is a good example with which to explore this idea further. At present, many technology companies provide information about their products via the web. In fact, some software companies have taken this a step further by choosing to provide technical documentation strictly online. There are a number of advantages to this approach, both from the company's perspective as well as that of the users of the products. For the company it is far less expensive to distribute documentation electronically over the Web than it is to physically ship manuals or even CDROMs with the same information. End users, on the other hand, want access to the most current information, and they want this information in a format that is easy to use. The same content may drive many distinct renderings: websites; application built-in documentation; CDROM; hardcopy, voice-response systems; and so forth. In each of these cases the rendering may be performed by the supplier, by the server (based on knowledge about the needs of this particular user), by the client, or by some combination of these. XML is ideally suited as a means for managing, distributing and presenting online documentation. We will cover each of these in turn.

4.3.2.1 Managing Documentation

XML provides the means to structure and manage highly complex information. The hierarchical structure of XML, combined with the ability to nest structures arbitrarily deeply, allows information that is hierarchical in nature to be represented readily. However, XML does not require that the information it represents be strictly hierarchical; the use of XLink and XPointer enable XML to represent highly complex, nonhierarchical structures as well.

The tagging ability of XML allows these structures to be given meaningful labels; that is, semantically meaningful portions of a document can be referenced in their entirety and manipulated as such. In particular, a specific section of a document can be referenced as the Installation section (e.g., <section>Installation</section>), rather than as simply a collection of paragraphs.

4.3.2.2 Distributing Information

Documentation comes in many sizes and levels of detail. While one product's documentation may correspond to a small pamphlet, that of another may represent thousands of pages. XML permits meaningful portions of documentation to be requested and distributed to the end user. XML will allow client applications to request portions of the documentation, such as a Table of Contents or a section on installation, and know that they will receive a meaningful piece of information in return rather than simply a collection of pages that (hopefully) correspond to what was requested. What is sometimes called the "zip file" approach to online documentation distribution requires that the user download the documentation in its entirety even if only a small portion is desired. This is especially frustrating if the user merely wants to update his or her local documentation by downloading only the modified sections. Neither the zip-file approach nor the HTML-based approaches addresses this common problem. XML, on the other hand, enables portions of a document to be meaningfully tagged with information such as "last revised" dates, making it simple for only the most recently changed information to be identified. And, due to XML's ability to represent data structure, only the updated sections need to be downloaded; these updated sections can be downloaded and merged far more easily than with a technology such as HTML.

4.3.2.3 Presenting Information to the User

Downloading meaningful portions of a document enables the client to act intelligently upon the data. Unlike static HTML pages, whose presentation is fixed, XML allows the document's presentation to be modified dynamically on the client. For example, a document could initially present itself in outline format, simply showing the highest-level headings such as sections. The user would have the ability to expand these items as fully as necessary, in the same way as with ordinary desktop data (that is the key). The XML data behave exactly like desktop data on the client. Not every navigation requires a roundtrip to the server, providing a much greater level of interactivity.

4.3.3 Personalized Content

End users are increasingly demanding customized solutions. A solution that meets one user's needs may not meet the needs of the next user. This situation is particularly true for applications that primarily deliver content. Fortunately, XML can be used to create content that is tailored specifically for an individual user. We will discuss personalized content and its creation using intelligent search agents, and then by an example of personalized content in the form of a tailor-made newspaper.

4.3.3.1 What is Personalized Content

The Web is all about information, or more precisely access to information. Information exists on the Web concerning almost every conceivable subject and then some. The only problem is: can you find it when you need it? It is no wonder that the Internet search-engine sites remain some of the most popular sites on the web. What other recourse do you have when you want to find information on a particular topic on the web?

Although interactive search engines are the de facto means of locating information on the web, they suffer from a number of problems. Enter a search term such as "rock" and you are just about as likely to be steered to a website on "Geologic Rock Formations" as you are to find yourself at a website dedicated to the "Legends of Rock Music." What do these sites have in common? They both use the word "rock," though in a different context. As you probably know, the reason both of these pages turned can be said to reside more with the way the web pages containing these terms were constructed out of HTML than with the search engine, which is primarily informing you where it found the word "rock" in a web page. With XML's ability to tag information semantically, pages can be tagged in terms of content, such as `<geology>Rock</geology>` or `<music>Rock</music>`. Clearly, this situation will make web searching more productive.

This brings us to personalized content which is content that has been tailored to an individual user. In order to be practical, this personalization should be performed automatically. That is, it is conceivable that you could hire someone to continuously search the Web, find information they think will interest you and then forward it to you. However, this approach is not practical. (I guess you could team up with a colleague and search for each other on alternate days, but your boss is not likely to approve.) In the next section we will discuss how software agents can be created that will perform this type of searching for you automatically.

As an example of personalized content, consider the following. We will say that you have indicated to your system (how is not important at the moment) that you are interested in, among other things, buying and selling stocks. Would not it be convenient if, when you read an article that mentioned a company's name, the first occurrence of the company's name in the article always be followed by that company's stock symbol (e.g., MSFT, IBM), and a click on that symbol would show the current stock trading price? Now, you have probably seen this type of functionality on web pages belonging to stock information sites. However, it would be interesting if this type of "personalization" could automatically be applied to any article you accessed regardless of the source. (Of course, you would probably want to give the user the option to turn off this type of processing in the event they tired of seeing the stock symbols or were having a bad day on the market.) The key idea of this example is that a piece of content, in this case a news article, could be processed by adding information (or perhaps removing information) that personalized the content to an individual user.

4.3.3.2 Intelligent Searching Via Agents

Personalized information sounds very appealing and there are ample opportunities for it, but how can it be performed automatically? The example we cover later considers a newspaper whose articles are selected based on an individual's specified preferences. How do we go about generating the personalized content? One way is to employ intelligent agents, which are simply programs that run on behalf of the user in order to perform a task. Using the improved searching capability of XML, which permits searching based on content tags, it is possible to set up an agent program to periodically search any number of information sources for information that matches the selection criteria that have been indicated by the user. Because XML allows much more precise queries and searching of content than is possible with HTML, for example, the information gleaned by the intelligent agent is likely to be of much higher quality and of more value to the end user. Intelligent agents are not unique to XML; instead, XML simply provides a structured representation of data for the agents to manipulate, making agents easier to implement. Although they still have to understand the structure of the documents they are accessing, they have some hope of negotiating a small set of standard representations as provided possibly by a single XML DTD.

4.3.3.3 Data Reuse

As we previously noted, intelligent agents can easily be used to locate information on the Web. Once this information has been located, however, it may not be in a format that is suitable for presentation to the user, or perhaps long-term storage by the user. For example, consider an agent whose purpose is to locate financial statements for public corporations that have been posted on the Web. However, the user does not wish to read the entire financial statement, but rather is only interested in the net income portion of the statement for these corporations. This situation provides an opportunity for data reuse. The XML financial-statement document can be converted to a much smaller XML net-income document by having a program extract the net-income elements and create a separate document discarding the original. This concept of on-the-fly filtering of data should be quite familiar to Perl and Unix shell programmers, where commands (grep, awk, etc.) are routinely used to extract and reformat data. XML permits this type of processing to be performed on the data, allowing data to be filtered, merged and ultimately reused.

4.3.3.4 Personalized Newspapers

Figure 4.11 shows how a personalized newspaper can be constructed with the use of an intelligent search agent. The intelligent search agent employs the user's preferences to sift through the information provided by numerous content providers, thus identifying relevant information. This information is aggregated by the search agent and formatted for display on the user's desktop. The agent can be programmed to periodically remove news items from the personalized newspaper after they have been included in the newspaper for a specified length of time. In this way the size of the personalized newspaper does not grow too large, and the content that is displayed to the user is always up to date.

4.4 E-commerce Applications

Ask someone what the next "killer app" is going to be and chances are their answer will involve e-commerce. Aspects of e-commerce have been around for quite some time, but only recently with the advent of the Web and even morey recently XML has the true promise of e-commerce seemed within grasp. The focus of this section is on how XML can be used for e-commerce, in particular, how XML can make the Web a conduit for business

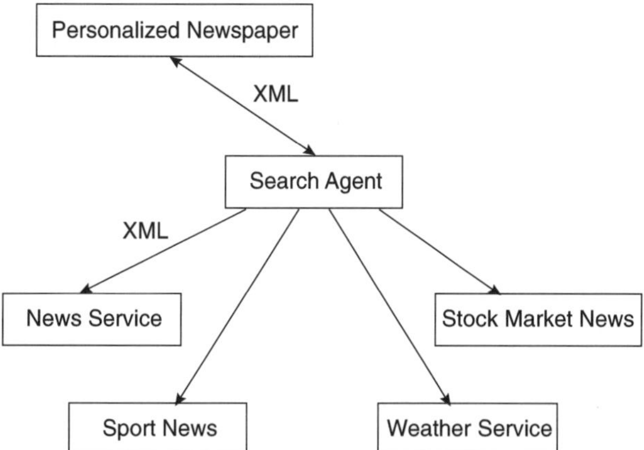

Figure 4.11 Personalized newspaper created by intelligent search agent.

transactions. There are many aspects to business and commerce that involve using the Web, including topics you are no doubt familiar with, such as advertising, service, support and of course sales. As you will learn in this section, there are many opportunities for performing business transactions using the Web, perhaps some you had not thought of. We will focus on how XML enables both businesses and end consumers to perform e-commerce transactions using the Web.

E-commerce is a large subject, so it is important that we come to a common understanding of what we mean by the term. A number of standardization efforts are underway relating to both business-to-consumer and business-to-business e-commerce.

4.4.1 E-commerce: the Broader Picture

If you ask five people to describe what an e-commerce application should do chances are you will get five very different answers. E-commerce means one thing to an Internet shopper and probably something quite different to an executive with a major automotive manufacturing firm. Thus, where do we find e-commerce? What is business process automation? These are only some of the questions relating to e-commerce that we explore here.

4.4.1.1 Where Do We Find Electronic Commerce?

Electronic commerce, better known as e-commerce, refers to the transaction of business using electronic networks. If you stop to think about it, it is hard to imagine a business sector that does not transact business in some way using electronic networks. Is there a business sector where companies do not try to gain a competitive advantage through the use of electronic networks, or where companies are not directly involved in transacting business using electronic networks? Perhaps ten or twenty years ago you could find such a sector but probably not today, and in the future you almost certainly will not be able to. This section of the book focuses on e-commerce, how companies can perform internal and external business functions and, in general, conduct business using the web. Interestingly, if you ask people to tell you what e-commerce means to them, the answer you will probably hear is Internet shopping. Most of you have probably done this yourself: browsed one of the many shopping websites in order to locate a particular book or music CD, added it to your "shopping cart" by clicking a button, and perhaps authorized payment for the item online with your credit card. To many people, this is what e-commerce means.

While this is certainly one example of e-commerce, by the time you finish this section, we think you will see that e-commerce goes much, much deeper than simply Internet shopping, and in fact, that e-commerce has already become an integral part of traditional commerce today. Wait a minute, you are probably saying. We all know that at present, the amount of goods bought by consumers over the Internet is only a tiny percentage of total consumer spending. Although this percentage seems to be growing rapidly, how can you claim that "e-commerce" is already an integral part of commerce today?

Well, as you may have guessed, the justification for our claim is not the Internet-shopping example. In fact, the reason for our claim is often not immediately visible to the consumer. The basis is the increasingly large role that e-commerce plays in automating business-to-business transactions, and the increasing reliance of businesses on these interbusiness electronic transactions. What is an example of a business-to-business transaction? We will cover these in detail shortly, but for starters think of how a retailer might order products from a wholesaler or manufacturer. The two businesses must come together to perform a transaction, say order some goods, and this transaction is increasingly being done via electronic networks. This is where XML will play a key role. As we will see, this type of e-commerce is somewhat different and currently much more pervasive than the Internet-shopping example. Internet shopping is an example of business-to-consumer e-commerce; here a business is using an electronic network (the Web in this case) to perform a business transaction directly with a consumer, the end user who will pay for and hopefully enjoy the product. From the consumer's perspective, on the other hand, business-to-business e-commerce happens "behind the scenes," and the consumer may not even be aware that it is happening. The fact that the consumer is not aware of these e-commerce transactions does not mean they are unimportant; in reality, they will ultimately serve the consumer by reducing the final cost of the product.

Why should you as a Web developer be interested in business-to-business e-commerce? Is knowing about the business-to-consumer variety not enough? Well, the answer to the first of these questions is easy: money. While the online shopping scenarios, where an individual purchases several items, are certainly exciting and will be covered here as well, the real money to be made in e-commerce will come from automating the many business processes that lead up to the final purchase by the consumer. The final purchase by the consumer, which could likely take place online, is only one of the many e-commerce transactions that occurs leading up to the final sale of the item to the consumer.

To give you a flavor of the types of transactions that increasingly are being performed electronically as commerce, we will explore a business that you might consider the last place on earth you would find e-commerce: your local supermarket. With this example you will understand how pervasive e-commerce is, even in "traditional" marketplaces. This should be a good way to get you thinking of how e-commerce can be introduced into the industry sector in which you work, regardless of what it may be.

Keep in mind that at present, although most of these business transactions are performed with the assistance of electronic networks, many of them are not fully automated. In later sections we will explore the benefits of using XML for business-to-consumer e-commerce, as well as how business-to-business e-commerce can be automated using XML. First, however, we take a bird's-eye view of a traditional business process, keeping an eye out for examples where business transactions are not fully automated, and viewing them as opportunities that may be addressed with XML.

4.4.1.2 Business Process Automation

What happens when you buy a common item such as a tube of toothpaste from a supermarket? Think for a minute of all the business transactions that had to take place for your simple purchase of this item to take place. By business transaction we mean not only the final transaction that occurs when you pay for the item, but also all of the transactions that must have occurred between the various businesses involved (the supermarket, wholesalers, manufacturers, etc.) before your final business transaction was even possible.

As the cashier runs the tube of toothpaste over the scanner at the checkout, the Universal Product Code (UPC) identifies the product and allows the cash register to look up the item in the supermarket's database to retrieve its price. Paying for the items with a credit or debit card, you have just performed a significant electronic transaction, that is, a money transfer involving perhaps your credit card company, your bank and the supermarket. While at present these credit-card transactions are performed primarily using private dial-up networks rather than a medium such as the Internet, the important point is that the card authorization and payment transfer represents a complex e-commerce transaction of they type for which XML is ideally suited.

Next, we ask you to think of all the things that had to happen to put those tubes of toothpaste on the shelf so you could lift one and place it in your basket. Toothpaste does not just magically appear on the shelf, at least not where we happen to live; instead, something must have caused it to be there. Clearly, the store must have ordered the toothpaste and surely it had to have paid for it as well. There is a very good chance that both the ordering of this product, and the payment of it were handled by electronic networks rather than using the US postal system for example. How did the supermarket know to order the toothpaste? Using the supermarket's inventory system, which keeps track of the amount of each product the supermarket has on-hand, the supermarket can monitor the level of items and reorder them when they run low. The store may order from a wholesaler, a business that keeps large quantities on hand and sells them in bulk at a discount to local retailers such as the supermarket. How is this supermarket-to-wholesaler order transacted? Again, there is a good chance it is performed using an electronic network. When the supermarket orders from the wholesaler, information about the order is probably also sent electronically to the supermarket corporate headquarters. This type of information is valuable to the corporation for it allows them to monitor at regional and national scales the level at which specific products, or types of products (e.g., toothbrushes, toothpastes), are selling. This type of information can be used to negotiate more favorable prices from suppliers, monitor whether suppliers are meeting schedules, and so forth.

Returning to the electronic order that the supermarket retailer placed with the wholesaler, a number of things will happen as a result of the receipt of this order. If the requested product is in stock, the wholesaler must arrange for its delivery and for payment from the supermarket. Again, this transaction will likely occur using an electronic network. The wholesaler will arrange for the product to be picked up and delivered, hopefully along with other items that need to go to the same final destination to reduce shipping costs. The wholesaler already will have a billing arrangement worked out with the supermarket, and billing for the shipment will be handled by this process, perhaps automatically at month's end.

Now consider the wholesaler's business for a moment. The wholesaler must also manage his level of inventory, a process that is similar in concept to what the retail store does, only concerning much higher volumes. The wholesaler will have an information system that allows the levels of products on hand to be monitored, and that enables items to be ordered from the manufacturer's distribution center when quantities of items run low. Once again, the two parties will have to perform a business transaction that specifies price, quantity, payment and delivery. In order to make this transaction as timely and efficient as possible, it too will likely be handled by an electronic network that connects the two parties. Here again we have an example of (or clearly an opportunity for) e-commerce.

Thus, we have followed our tube of toothpaste from the store shelf all the way back to the manufacturer. Does the use of electronic networks to transact business end here? Almost certainly not, because the manufacturer of the product will have to deal with its suppliers, which provide raw materials, for example. As you can see, the more you dig, the more opportunity you find for e-commerce, even in industries you may never have thought of as being candidates for e-commerce.

4.4.1.3 Automated Supply Chains

When we look closer at the scenario we have just covered, we see that a large part of commerce, in general, involves business-to-business transactions, and not just business-to-consumer transactions. In the example cited we saw how raw materials had to be supplied to the manufacturer, that the manufacturer supplies goods to the wholesaler, who in turn supplies goods to the retailer, who in turn supplies goods to the consumer. This chain of business parties, each supplied by its predecessor, is often referred to as a supply chain and is depicted in Figure 4.12.

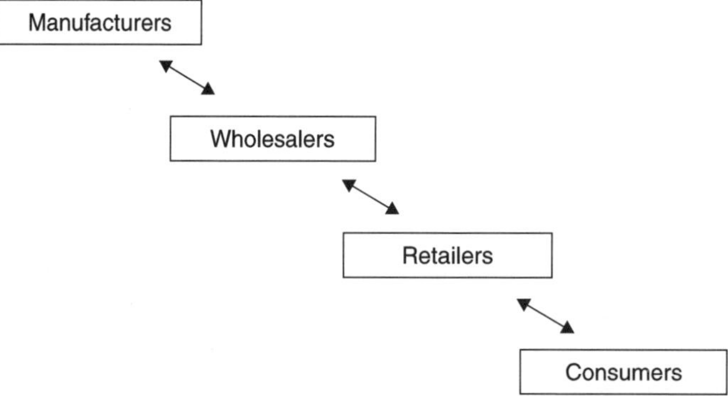

Figure 4.12 Supply Chain.

Figure 4.12 shows the basic relationship among business partners; however, considerable detail has been omitted. It is important to keep in mind that the relationship between these business parties is generally not one-to-one but rather many-to-many. For example, a single retailer will have relationships with many wholesalers; conversely, each wholesaler will have relationships with many retailers. This same relationship exists at the final supplier level, where the customer meets the retailer. We all shop at many stores and each of those stores serves many customers.

What are the implications of these many-to-many relationships for e-commerce, and what does this have to do with XML? First, we all know that the many-to-many relationship has existed for a long time in most businesses. However, due to the difficulty of obtaining information about suppliers and the subsequent difficulty of working out detailed automated-supplier arrangements, businesses tend to continue working with the same suppliers, even if these suppliers are not the most ideally suited ones. Why is this? Part of the problem is the many-to-many relationship, which makes it difficult for businesses to find the best supplier. Then how exactly do we define "best supplier?" The best supplier is not always the one that offers the best price and selection; rather there are many value-added opportunities with which suppliers can compete. Suppliers may add intangible value through guarantees for parts availability or preference during shortages; suppliers may have favorable relationships with other suppliers, who can collaborate on behalf of the purchaser, perhaps enabling the purchaser to buy partially assembled units rather than individual components. In terms of sheer information overload, if there are relatively few suppliers, then the task may not be too difficult. However, for commodity items, there may be hundreds or thousands of potential suppliers. At present, without an automated way to do so, it is very time consuming for a business to evaluate all possible suppliers in order to find the single supplier that provides the best price on a given item and to do this for every item. The difficulty of performing this type of search is also evident at the consumer level; do you know right now who has the best price on denim jeans in your town? E-commerce holds the promise of making it easy for consumers to locate the best possible price for an item; this is what some of the Internet-shopping sites promise you as the end user. However, e-commerce holds the same promise at all levels of the supply chain. For example, e-commerce should allow a manufacturer to locate a raw materials supplier that best meets the manufacturer's needs. Similarly, a retailer can find the wholesaler that provides the best possible price and delivery schedules. E-commerce promises to bring a new level of efficiency to many levels of the market.

4.4.1.4 Cross-Level Supply Chain Interactions

Another implication of the many-to-many relationships among suppliers and consumers in e-commerce is perhaps more subtle, but could have an even more profound effect. Figure 4.12 shows the relationship between, for example, manufacturers and wholesalers. This figure does not say anything about the relationship between retailers and manufacturers; it implies that the retailer must go through the wholesaler in order to receive items. Now, we stop to consider this for a moment in the context of the Web. An amazing thing about the Web is that everyone is connected to everyone else. If a manufacturer is set up to handle automated order processing, why should the retailer bother to go through the wholesaler instead of going directly to the manufacturer? This is an extremely interesting question, and it can be generalized to other levels of the supply chain. If the retailer can skip one level over the wholesaler and order directly from the manufacturer, is there anything preventing the end user from skipping two levels over the retailer and wholesaler and interacting directly with the manufacturer? Given an appropriate e-commerce infrastructure, in which the end user can work directly with the manufacturer, there appears to be nothing standing in the way. Figure 4.13 shows the result of these cross-level supply chain interactions. In this type of scenario, what becomes the role of the traditional wholesaler? The traditional retailer? These are extremely profound questions, and exploring them is beyond the scope of this book. However, you should be aware that the network economy is likely to have significant impacts on commerce, not only from the end users perspective but at all levels of the supply chain.

4.4.1.5 Just-In-Time Business Practices

It is interesting to consider the effects that e-commerce will have on just-in-time business practices. Traditional business practice calls for maintaining a level of inventory that is adequate to ride out any short-term demands that exceed resupply times. Because it normally takes a while for items to be ordered, processed and delivered, it makes sense to keep extra items on hand. Just-in-time manufacturing, on the other hand, calls for maintaining little or no inventory. Instead, parts are ordered or produced only as needed, "just in time" for them to be used by the next process. A clear advantage of this approach is that the business can maintain less inventory, thereby reducing costs. Of course, the business must truly be able to

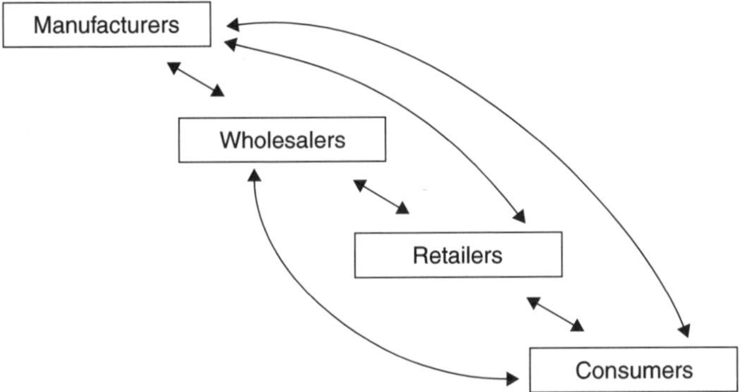

Figure 4.13 Cross-level supply chain interactions.

produce all the necessary items "just in time" to reap the benefits; if items are not produced "in time," the whole operation stands to suffer. Businesses that adopt this approach are relying more heavily upon the efficiency and reliability of their business processes and information systems (including external order and delivery systems) than are businesses with more traditional inventory approaches. It is noteworthy that many businesses have been able to achieve significant savings by moving to a just-in-time approach. The new level of efficiency and faster turnaround times that are possible through XML-based business-to-business e-commerce promises to make just-in-time business practices even more appealing.

4.4.2 E-commerce Standards

Although XML is a relatively new technology, work is already underway to standardize its use in e-commerce. XML holds the promise of application interoperability, and it is likely that the standards that are based on XML will in fact deliver upon this promise. In this section we examine a number of existing and emerging e-commerce standards including Electronic Data Interchange (EDI) and the Open Financial Exchange (OFX).

4.4.2.1 Electronic Data Interchange (EDI)

Electronic Data Interchange, or EDI, is the basis for much of the current automated business-to-business processing. Although it seems clear that XML-based specifications will be the natural successor to EDI, we should not dismiss EDI lightly. In particular, EDI has accomplished a great deal, and any reader wishing to seriously pursue automated business-to-business processing using XML would do well to study EDI as a reference point for their own implementation. As always, a great deal can be learned from the successes and shortcomings of related technologies.

EDI is a process that allows companies to exchange data representing business transactions between heterogeneous computer systems, allowing these computer systems to process business transactions without human intervention. EDI is also a set of rules dating back to the 1970s that businesses can follow to automate their business-to-business transaction processing. Created by the Transportation Data Coordinating Committee, EDI was originally designed to enable vendors within industry sectors to electronically process purchase orders and billing with one another. EDI is based on the concept of transaction sets, which specify data fields and their format, as well as business rules for the processing of these data.

The concepts promoted by EDI seem to be in principle what forward-looking businesses are seeking, namely automated business transaction processing, and the businesses that have implemented EDI solutions report significant savings, as might be expected. However, experience has shown that creating and maintaining EDI-based solutions is, in practice, quite difficult and quite costly. There are a number of reasons for these shortcomings. EDI-based solutions generally require that the companies entering into the business-to-business processing agreement write significant amounts of custom software for the solution, mapping their internal data formats to that of the EDI specification. In addition, transaction sets specify business rules, which may or may not be appropriate for the particular partners. Finally, EDI runs on top of Value Added Networks (VANs) rather than the Internet, which adds significantly to the overall day-to-day cost of operation. Despite the promise of EDI, these shortcomings have conspired to keep EDI beyond the realm of many small and medium-sized businesses.

XML addresses the shortcomings of EDI with self-describing data whose structure is flexible, and which can be transported over the Internet using standard protocols such as HTTP. With XML as the universal data exchange format that runs on top of the Internet, business-to-business transaction-processing systems based on XML seem destined to replace those based on EDI, significantly lowering the barrier to entry and opening up interbusiness automation opportunities to many small and medium-sized businesses.

4.4.2.2 Open Financial Exchange (OFX)

Open Financial Exchange (OFX) is a specification for the exchange of financial data between financial institutions, businesses and consumers using the Internet. OFX is designed to facilitate a number of business-to-business and business-to-consumer exchanges relating to money including consumer and small-business banking and bill payment. It is also designed to facilitate the exchanges and presentation of information related to investments such as stocks, bonds and mutual funds. OFX is a publicly available specification that has support from a number of major players in the software industry.

4.4.2.3 Emerging Standards

There are a number of emerging standards for XML that will assist its adoption for e-commerce. A common vision of the organizations supporting these standardization efforts is to see XML become the basis for a set of common business languages for the Internet economy.

The goal of the eCo Framework project is to develop a common framework for interoperability among XML-based applications and e-commerce environments. Working groups within the project are currently developing a specification for content names and definitions in e-commerce documents, as well as an interoperable transaction framework specification. Along the same lines, the Graphical Communications Association Research Institute (www.gca.org) and the Data Interchange Standards Association (DISA) (www.disa.org) are considering constructing libraries of XML Document Type Definitions that will enable businesses to automatically process e-commerce messages that conform to the these formats.

4.4.3 Business-to-Consumer E-commerce

As we noted earlier, business-to-consumer e-commerce is what comes to the minds of most people when they hear the word e-commerce. There are a number of forces driving the movement toward business-to-consumer e-commerce. One of the reasons for the diversity of forces is that economic benefits can be realized by both businesses and consumers, not just one or the other. We will explore some of these forces and cover two examples of business-to-consumer e-commerce that may become the norm rather than the exception in the near future—on-line shopping and at-home financial services.

4.4.3.1 Goals of Business-to-Consumer E-commerce

There are many things a business must have in order to be successful, with perhaps two of the most important being a product and customers. In many respects, the goals of a business that is trying its hand at business-to-consumer e-commerce are the same as those for any business—to sell products or services to customers, and to make a profit doing so. The types of products that can be bought and sold over the Internet include many of those found in traditional markets. This would include consumer products (with books and music CDs coming to mind immediately), as well as consumer services (with personal banking and financial services such as on-line stock trading falling in this category). In order for e-commerce to compete successfully with markets that offer these products and services through traditional channels, the e-commerce approach must offer the consumer greater value for their money than is available via traditional channels. Here we take a moment to look at some of the ways that e-commerce markets for products and services can distinguish themselves from traditional markets.

An obvious way to distinguish a product or service to the consumer is through price, and e-commerce has some clear advantages in this area. For starters, e-commerce malls have much lower overhead than their traditional physical counterparts. Indeed, a "shopping area" consisting of several server machines that serve the entire world is much less expensive than having storefronts in major malls across the United States. Clearly, the reduced overhead costs can be translated into reduced prices for the consumer. It is interesting to note that several retail operations whose focus are technical books and software have already moved completely online. Furthermore, as we noted earlier, e-commerce permits consumers to deal directly with manufacturers in many cases, thus reducing the number of middlemen, and further, reducing overall cost.

In addition to lower cost, e-commerce can also be more convenient than traditional commerce. Shopping can certainly be a social experience, and there is no doubt that traditional markets and shopping malls will continue to exist well into the future, even if only to serve this important purpose. Online shopping can be extremely convenient for people who do not have the time or the desire to fight the crowds at the shopping mall on a Saturday afternoon. There are segments of society that rely heavily on catalog-order shopping to make their purchases and business-to-consumer e-commerce that targets such market segments will likely be successful.

Online shopping also gives consumers something that is hard to take away once it has been experienced: increased variety and selection. The notebook computer on which parts of this manuscript were written happens to have been purchased online. In our experience, the selection of notebook computers that can be found online far exceeds that which is found in retail stores. And as you are dealing directly with the manufacturer, in many cases the final price is actually less, and with better selection and lower price what more do you want? Thus we see that the goal of business-to-consumer e-commerce is to provide products or services to consumers that offer more value than is possible for the same products or services offered through traditional channels.

4.4.3.2 Online Shopping

This section presents online shopping as an example of business-to-consumer e-commerce that can benefit from XML. The objective of an online shopping site should be to provide the consumer with a richer shopping experience than can be found through a traditional channel. Enriching the shopping experience would include ensuring that the consumer can easily find the items they are seeking, at a better price and with wider selection than through traditional channels. And, due to the ease with which an online shopping site can be reached (right from the user's desktop) and the 24-hour-a-day store hours (this type of mall does not close at 9:30 pm), the user's shopping experience is made more convenient. We have already addressed how e-commerce can lower prices by reducing business overhead and eliminating middlemen. We will not delve further into aspects of convenience other than to reiterate that online shopping can save the end user time, allowing him or her to find and purchase the items they desire more quickly, from the comfort of home.

We will examine how an online shopping site that is powered by XML can help consumers find what they are looking for more quickly, and how such a site will give them a much larger selection than is possible in a traditional market.

As you know, XML allows data to be tagged according to content, thus greatly simplifying the problem of searching for and retrieving information. Recall also that XQL, the Extensible Query Language, allows XML structures to be queried, much like a relational database. Recall that XML Querying will enable XML data stores (and other data stores that support an XML data model) to be queried, returning results in the form of XML data. A typical setup might involve using an XML content repository as the back-end data source for storing information about items that are for sale, and a middle tier that formulates queries based on user input gathered from the client. This type of setup is shown in Figure 4.14.

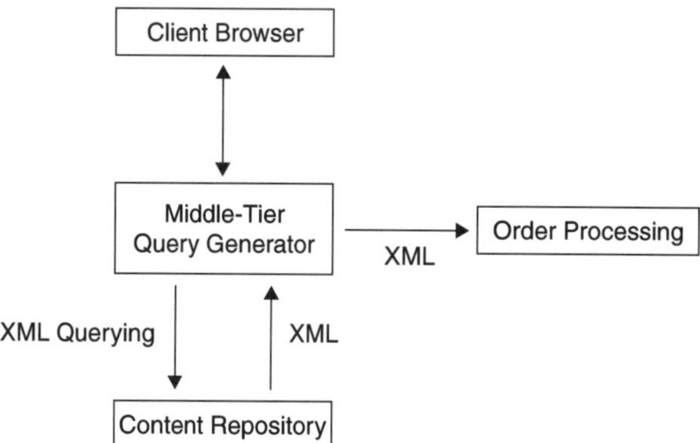

Figure 4.14 Online shopping architecture using XML.

Using this type of approach, a manufacturer can set up an online shopping site that allows products to be sold directly to the consumer. Of course, this approach only works well if people are already familiar with the company or brand and know to go to the company's website to find the product. In reality, however, consumers cannot be expected to be aware of individual companies' websites, and certainly for smaller or less well-known products or services this problem is compounded. Finally, even if the consumers were aware of the many individual manufacturer and retailer websites that offer the product they are interested in purchasing, it simply would take too much time for them to visit every site. Fortunately, with XML there is a better way.

Because XML is a universal format for data exchange, and because business sectors are coming to agreement as to the meaning of specific content tags (such as `<price>`), the problem of searching multiple sites for the same information is greatly simplified. The results of numerous searches of individual sites can meaningfully be compared, and the best price across all of the sites readily determined. Thus XML supports the creation of meta-shopping sites, that is sites that serve as directories for individual sites such as those provided by manufacturers and retailers. Of course, there is also potential for meta-meta-shopping sites, which would perform even more comprehensive searches. Figure 4.15 illustrates these concepts.

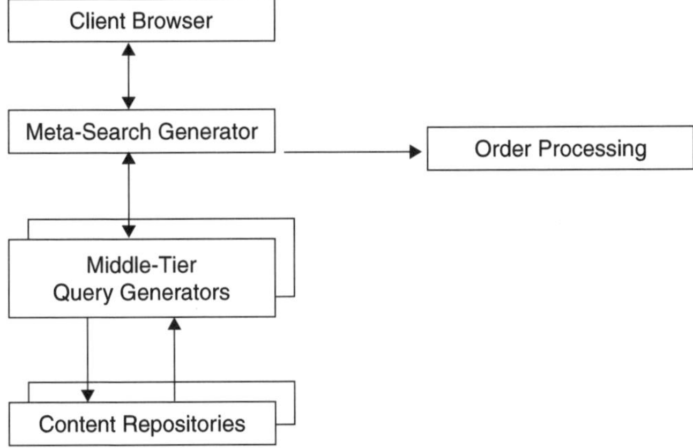

Figure 4.15 Online shopping architecture that queries multiple sites using XML.

One of the largest "consumers" of goods is the United States government. Thus it should not be surprising that branches of the US government such as the Government Services Administration (GSA), the nation's largest procurement organization, are actively implementing online search and acquisition capabilities using XML. The GSA's XML-based pilot system currently enables authorized government buyers to search across multiple electronic catalogs, not only to locate specific items but also to find the best prices. This system demonstrates how an interoperable electronic catalog system can help reduce the enormous costs and inefficiencies associated with proprietary electronic catalogs for both buyers and sellers.

4.4.3.3 *At-Home Financial Services*

As with other online businesses that compete with traditional businesses, at-home banking must differentiate itself from the competition in order to succeed. As with our previous example, at-home banking offers benefits to both the business and the consumer. At-home banking is attractive to banks because it can reduce their operational costs. For example, day-to-day operations that would normally be handled by tellers, such as balance inquiries and funds transfers, can be handled directly by the end user without assistance from the bank. The resulting reductions in operational costs can be passed along to the customer.

At-home banking also provides the added convenience for the customer of paying bills online without the need to write and physically mail personal checks. And all of these convenient services are available outside normal business hours, which provides an additional level of service to the customer. Figure 4.16 shows an example architecture for an at-home banking application.

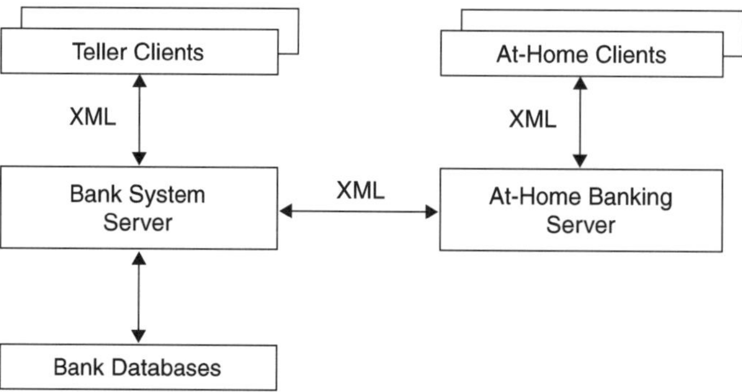

Figure 4.16 Example architecture for Web-based at-home banking application.

We have discussed the intelligent data interchange capabilities that XML will provide on the users desktop. Although present non-XML-based systems permit customers to perform his or her personal banking online, XML will allow such at-home banking operations to interact intelligently with other personal-finance applications. For example, a user could pay their credit card bill using an application that connects the user to the credit-card company and interacts with the at-home banking application directly on the user's desktop. Here again the end user will be able to have applications that know nothing about each other and interoperate and collaborate on behalf of the end user through the end user's interactions on the desktop.

4.4.4 Business-to-Business E-commerce

It is widely believed that the true promise of XML will be realized in powering and simplifying business-to-business e-commerce. It is important to understand the forces that are driving the move towards business-to-business e-commerce and to understand how XML provides the basis for a suitable infrastructure. An area that is receiving increasing attention in terms of business-to-business e-commerce is automated Enterprise Resource Planning (ERP), and XML is already playing a significant role in such business-critical applications.

4.4.4.1 Goals of Business-to-Business E-commerce

The goal of business-to-business e-commerce is to automate intercompany activities and transactions in order to reduce costs for both business parties, increase the responsiveness to business needs, and to reduce errors. In the section Business Process Automation and the section Automated Supply Chain we hit upon many of the concepts that motivate businesses to electronically incorporate their business partners in their day-to-day business operations. In order to remain competitive, companies increasingly are finding the need to open their internal business process applications to suppliers, partners and resellers in order to streamline the business process and increase profit margins.

4.4.4.2 Automated Enterprise Resource Planning (ERP)

Automated enterprise resource planning and supply-chain automation can be readily addressed with XML. As is known, XML allows companies not only to communicate with one another, but also to interoperate and work together towards common business goals. In the past decade, many large corporations have implemented enterprise resource planning (ERP) systems, whose purpose is to help the corporation reduce inventory and manufacturing costs, improve product quality, and improve relationships with both customers and partners. By investing in these ERP systems, corporations have realized increased operating efficiency, greater return on assets, and have gained global competitive advantage.

Despite the promise of such returns, many corporations have been slow to implement ERP systems. This is due in large part to the sizable investments both in time and in money required to make such systems work and continue to work in a dynamically changing business environment where suppliers and trading partners come and go.

Although there is a growing need for companies to share data, both internally and across the extended supply chain, the job of doing so has been extremely difficult, as most business process applications have been developed independently of standards or guidelines. Without the common ground of standards or interoperable data formats, sharing data becomes very difficult. At the application development level the lack of a common data format has the unfortunate and costly consequence of requiring that translation routines be maintained individually at both the source and receiving systems. Of course, these translation routines must be maintained and may require tedious but painstaking modification even for relatively simple changes or upgrades. These types of cross-business application development issues have conspired to make cross-business application interoperability more of an elusive goal than a reality.

As we discussed in the section Server-Side Application Interoperability, XML has the ability to eliminate much of this difficulty by becoming the universal data exchange format. A number of the largest ERP system providers are opening up their systems by providing XML interfaces, which should greatly simplify the process of integrating these systems across both application and company boundaries.

Figure 4.17 shows how the ERP systems for a number of businesses can be linked using XML to provide automated enterprise resource planning across the boundaries of individual companies, thereby providing integrated supply-chain automation. The benefits of such cross-enterprise integration, made much simpler by XML, will be reflected on the bottom line of these corporations.

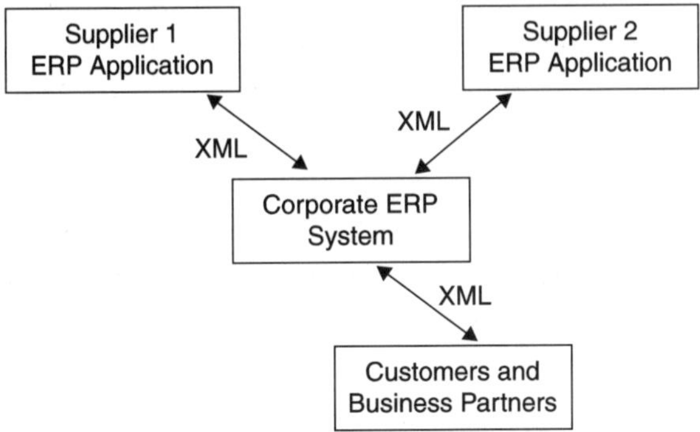

Figure 4.17 Automated enterprise resource planning (ERP) using XML.

4.5 Conclusion

In this chapter we have explored how XML will enable developers to build the next generation of interoperable web applications. Although XML was initially envisioned as simply a replacement for HTML, its impact is turning out to be far greater, affecting the client-, the middle- and the back-end tiers. As we have seen, XML enables intelligent client-side processing, including the ability to dynamically change data presentation without cumbersome and time-consuming interaction with the server as was required with HTML. On the middle tier, XML is ideally suited to address many of the chronic data-integration problems that plague enterprise application development. And finally XML is also well suited as a data storage and retrieval medium for the back-end tier. XML enables applications to readily exchange data with one another on both the client and the server side, which will allow developers to construct a new generation of highly interoperable web-based applications. The decision to use XML in your application is but the first of many decisions you will need to make subsequently. Chief among these decisions is how to structure your data once you have decided to go with XML. We have noted a number of application areas where XML is already beginning to take hold, for example, e-commerce, content syndication, documentation, etc. In order to save time—and to ensure interoperability with similar applications—it is important to look for and work with emerging standards in these and other business areas.

E-commerce is one of the promising application areas in which XML is already playing a key role. We have seen that e-commerce can take many forms, ranging all the way from large-scale business-to-business process automation down to individual business-to-consumer transaction processing. It is difficult to guess which industries will be most affected by e-commerce. However, regardless of the industries involved, it seems certain that XML will play a critical role in the underlying application infrastructure.

CHAPTER 5

Using the Document Object Model

5.1 *Your mission, if you choose to accept...*

"Wake up!" says your boss as you quickly snap your head back and realize that you have dozed off in another boring meeting in which your company's financial situation is being discussed. After sitting up straight, you notice you are the center of attention among your peers (and the next topic of the weekly joke email). Realizing that an explanation for your siesta is in order, you begin to explain to your boss how you have been staying up really late reading this book on XML and Java. After a short pause, the silence in the room pressures you into a more in-depth explanation, so you begin to suggest how the company can create an Electronic Commerce website using Java and XML.

You continued by explaining how you could create a Java Servlet that could use JDBC to communicate with the company's existing database of products, and output XML to the browser, or any XML-processing client application for that matter. Hoping that this was all that was needed for redemption, primarily because you have read only the first few chapters of the book, you sit back and glance around the room. Although everyone in the room is still starring at you, your friends have stopped snickering and everyone's facial expressions have turned to amazement. After a pause, your boss finally breaks the silence by enthusiastically saying "WOW! Now that's a good idea! Let's meet after this meeting to discuss the business requirements!"

5.1.1 Key Concepts

This chapter will cover the following essential concepts and technologies:

- creating an implementation-independent document factory to create XML documents;
- creating a generic framework for writing XML Documents; and
- using the Document Object Model (DOM) Level 1 Recommendation with Java.

5.1.2 Business Requirements

Initially, the business requirements will be very simple to get a feel for the new technologies we are introducing to the company. After discussing the requirements with your supervisor, these are the high-level list of requirements agreed upon:

1. Utilize the existing Personal Data Assistant (PDA) database structure.
2. Display all of the products in company's PDA catalog.
3. Provide the ability to create a customer account.
4. Provide the ability to log into an existing customer account.
5. Provide the ability to add, change, and remove a product to a shopping cart.
6. Adhere to the W3C DOM (level 1) recommendation.
7. Design the site such that our Marketing team can independently develop the User interface while we develop the logic and data gathering.

At the time of this writing, the Extensible Stylesheet Language (XSL) is only in draft form. Although Microsoft Internet Explorer 5™ provides XML support, the functionality it provides for stylesheet transformations (XSLT) does not conform to the current XSLT working draft at the time of this writing. As a stopgap solution, we will be providing a mechanism to transform the XML documents on the web server before it is delivered to the web browser. This will allow all HTML browsers to view the website. Ultimately, when XSL becomes a recommendation and more browsers implement the specification, we would send the XML document to the browser. This is still very important; however, because the release of browsers will never be coordinated, websites will need to support HTML and XML browsers for some time.

> **NOTE:** If you are developing an intranet site that needs to support only Internet Explorer 5 browsers, these coding examples are still applicable. Although we will be implementing server-side processing, we will also provide a mechanism to disable server-side processing so that browsers, such as IE5, can perform the stylesheet transformations. These areas will be pointed out as we proceed through the examples. To find out more about the W3C working draft, or IE5's implementation, you can visit to following websites:
>
> W3C XSL working draft: http://www.w3c.org
>
> Microsoft XSL implementation: http://msdn.microsoft.com/xml

Realizing that we squirmed out of the siesta only to dig ourselves a deeper hole with a number of business requirements, we decide to negotiate with our boss. Remembering some of the complexities and issues involved from the previous chapters, we explain how we will need to do some initial work to build a foundation before we can actually proceed to website development. Acknowledging our plea for more time, the boss agrees to limit our initial focus on building this foundation and implementing the business logic—at least for the purposes of this chapter!

5.2 *Technology Requirements*

Before we get started, we will review the necessary technologies to complete the examples in this chapter. First, we will be using the Java 2 JDK to implement all of the coding examples throughout the book. If you do not already have this installed, you can download it from http://

java.sun.com. We have not gotten to the database overview yet, but we will need Microsoft™ Access© 97 to communicate with the PDA database. Last, but most important, we will be using IBM's XML for Java toolkit for parsing XML documents and creating them. Although we will be adhering to the DOM recommendation, some examples are coded using IBM's API. If you really want to use a different XML implementation, we recommend using the XML4J with the examples and testing our approach with the implementation of your choice. You can get the latest release of XML4J at http://developer.ibm.com/xml. In conclusion, here is a summarized list of tools that you will need before getting started:

1. Java 2 JDK version 1.2.1
2. Microsoft Access 97
3. IBM's XML for Java toolkit (XML4J) version 2.06
4. Configure ODBC Data Source Name (DSN)

The versions listed here are the actual ones we used when developing the code for the examples. If you already have JDK 1.2.0 installed on your system, you should be fine. Likewise, IBM frequently releases minor fixes to XML4J so there should not be a problem using any of the version 2.x installations.

To set up the database access, first make sure Microsoft Access is installed. Although having Microsoft Access is not an absolute requirement, it does provide a user interface for viewing and manipulating the database. We will still be able to communicate with the database using JDBC; however, you will not be able to view the schema of the database. Next, create a directory where we will store the source code we will be creating in the subsequent chapters (*i.e.c:\dev\xmlbook*). This is our project directory. Now, create a new subdirectory, called database, below the project directory. This directory will be used to store the Microsoft Access database. Once the directory is created, copy the xml.mdb database from the CD-ROM to this new database directory.

Before we can programmatically communicate with the database, we need to configure an Open Database Connectivity (ODBC) Data Source Name (DSN). As we will be using the JDBC-ODBC Bridge to communication with the database, this is required so that ODBC knows where to locate the database when we request a connection. To do so, follow these steps for creating a new ODBC DSN:

1. Goto Start | Control Panel | ODBC Data Sources
2. Select the System DSN tab
3. Click the Add button
4. Select Microsoft Access Driver (if you do not have Microsoft Access installed on your computer, you may need to download the driver from www.microsoft.com.)
5. Click the Finished button
6. Type in XMLBook for the Data Source name
7. In the database group, choose the Select button
8. Browse to find the XML.mdb file where you placed it on your hard drive
9. Click the OK button

Make sure all of the software is installed and configured before you proceed.

5.3 *Application Overview*

There is a good amount of logic to what we have claimed to our boss is possible, so we had better review the system in a little more detail before we dive into the coding. First, we are ultimately creating a dynamic website centered on a Java servlet. Although it is not necessary to focus on the servlet during this chapter, the servlet will need to interact with the PDA database and send data back to the browser. At some point, it will be necessary to implement business logic to provide authentication, account creation, and the various shopping basket activities.

If we can impress our boss with this project, this code will most likely be reused many times over to implement similar projects (and we should get a big fat raise). Drooling over the thought of more money, we will apply some object-oriented design to make our code more reusable in future projects. In addition, this is an opportunity for us to shine by providing an elegant solution that addresses a weakness in the Level 1 DOM recommendation.

As you have seen in Chapter 2, the Level 1 Recommendation does not address dynamically creating and printing XML documents. As part of laying the foundation, we will take some philosophies from a well-known design pattern to provide an elegant way to separate the proprietary implementation from the application code. This could serve to be a big factor in the raise if our company standardizes on a different DOM/XML implementation!

> **NOTE:** Near the end of this writing, the W3C created a working draft for Level 2 of the Document Object Model. This draft contains specifications for standardizing document creation. We will still provide a document creation mechanism because this is still a working draft that could change before it becomes a recommendation. Furthermore, the philosophies we use can be applied to many different programming tasks. For more information on the DOM Level 2 drafts visit http://www.w3c.org.

We will begin the chapter by looking at that elegant solution we are expecting to bring in some extra cash. In doing so, we will create a reusable API that provides the ability to create XML documents and print them. In addition, we add a couple of convenience-oriented methods to provide a more convenient API for common operations to the DOM tree. Once this is in place, we will put our new API to the test by creating the business objects that will implement the business rules and interact with the PDA database. Of course, before we do that we will review the PDA database to get a better understanding of how to implement the business logic.

Well, from 50,000 feet, this does not look too difficult. This chapter will lay the foundation for the entire system that will then grow in subsequent chapters. Although we will not look at the actual servlet code in this chapter, do not underestimate the importance of the DOM work we will be performing. Working through these examples will provide you with practical, hands-on knowledge of the DOM recommendation that will complement what was already covered in Chapter 2. Finally, while we are working through the examples concepts to implementing mission-critical systems will be provided in the hope that these concepts will assist your day-to-day programming tasks as well. Refill your coffee cup because there is a lot to cover!

5.4 W3C Level 1 Document Object Model (DOM) Recommendation

When the XML recommendation was finally released (well, actually well before the official recommendation) the technical community was ecstatic. The possibilities were considered endless with a standard markup language we could use to describe our data independent of its presentation. Now that all programs will be able to interact across the Internet, it is a revolution! Right? Well, equipped with the proper tools yes—but not so fast. The strength and promise of XML can be undone if it is not supported properly. XML is a relatively complex protocol that would not be cost-effective to implement for most systems. If not for its widespread acceptance, open standards of XML parsers and multiple implementations from different software vendors, this revolution would have been viewed as another one of Stephen King's esoteric plots for a terror film!

The XML Recommendation described the proper format of an XML document and indicated how parsers were to react under various conditions when processing an XML document. Among many other topics, the recommendation provided for two different levels for parsers: nonvalidating and validating. Nonvalidating parsers were only required to check the well formedness of the document whereas validating parsers were required to validate the document based on a document-type definition (DTD) in addition to the well formedness checks. By providing the two distinct levels, many eager software vendors were able to implement the nonvalidating parser well before the official recommendation was released, which ultimately provided a little more fuel for the XML revolution! Similarly, these two separate levels provide multiple entry points for software companies to get involved in creating XML toolkits. As you will soon see, with a good XML parser, we can develop applications or even entire systems very quickly and the cost of ownership and maintenance is considerably reduced because it is extensible and open standard-based. If the implementations failed to adhere to the open standard then many of these advantages would not exist.

This was a good start, but there was no recommendation for how our applications were supposed to interact programmatically with an XML document. Without a standard, programmers would have to learn all the idiosyncrasies of a vendor-specific API whenever they used a different implementation. In essence, this nullified many of the benefits of using XML because, from a programmatic standpoint, we would still be using a proprietary API.

Concurrently, the HTML programmers were in a little debate of their own. They needed a common way of client-side scripting between the two dominant browsers, Internet Explorer and Netscape Navigator. Shortly after the XML recommendation was released, the DOM recommendation was released as well. This recommendation provides an open standard for programmatically manipulating and accessing the various elements within a document and the document itself. It was limited to HTML documents; however, XML documents were included as well. For Java, this recommendation becomes reality with the `org.w3c.dom` package that is usually included with most of the software vendor's implementations of XML parsers and toolkits.

As we have already seen from Chapter 2, the `org.w3c.dom` package contains interfaces for all of the different types objects found in the DOM, such as `Documents`, `Elements`, `CDATASections`, `Comments`, `Attributes`, etc. These are only interfaces. They still require software vendors to provide the actual implementation of the API. For the most part, these implementation details can now be hidden from our code because of the open standard.

The Level 1 Recommendation left document creation and persistent storage to the specific implementation. This is understandable because interfaces alone can not be instantiated. The class that implements the interface must be instantiated. For many of the interfaces described in the DOM recommendation, this is not a problem because the Document interface provides methods to instantiate all the different types of nodes within the DOM tree. Unfortunately, it is still necessary to use the proprietary APIs to create the class that implements the `Document` interface.

> **NOTE:** Think of an interface as a contract. For example, consider a marriage license/contract. It describes all of your responsibilities of being a good spouse but it does not meet them for you. When a class says that it "implements" a given interface, it is agreeing to perform all of the responsibilities of that contract. For Java classes, this means that we must provide identical methods that the interface provides. As the contract does not actually do anything by itself, the class must provide its own implementation for the methods described in the interface. Just ask my wife about this, she would probably agree that I have stopped "implementing" my marriage interface ever since I began to write this book!

Typically, the object-orientated solution to instantiating interfaces to an application is to use what is known as the Factory Design Pattern. Design patterns are a common way of accomplishing a task. Essentially, this design pattern describes an independent object that is used to produce other objects. Thus, it was named the Factory pattern. This pattern is not new to programming. It has been used extensively as the solution to many different programming problems, including for complex tasks such as remote object creation in distributed computing environments.

Providing a single class to create a document object will accomplish isolating the proprietary API; but while we are at it, we might as well design this to support any number of DOM implementations. To accomplish this, we need to add another layer of abstraction to our design. Instead of a single class, we will create a single interface. In doing so, we will be able to write classes that implement the interface, and provide implementation specific code to create documents. As such, we will call these adapters because we will essentially be able to "plug" them into the program. It is important to note however that in doing so we will need to place a lot of emphasis on the interface. If the adapter class is referenced within the program logic code, then the proprietary code will not be isolated.

5.4.1 DOMFactory interface

Attempting to create a generic way of constructing an XML document independent of implementation can be a daunting task. Although there are many different ways of implementing the code to accomplish the same result, the ultimate success will be how close we design our API to support current and future versions of XML and the DOM recommendation.

The first things to consider are all the possible combinations of parameters that may be used during the creation of an XML document. Ultimately, it would be best to sample some other implementations in the industry to get a better understanding of the different parameters required to perform this task across many implementations. In reality, though, this is usually not a possibility due to time constraints and project deadlines. Another way of approaching this is to go directly to the source. As we are really only concerned with how XML documents are created we can learn a great deal from the XML specification.

The XML recommendation is very important because it is the basis for all XML documents. Examining the requirements of an XML document will give us the information necessary to design our factory interface. Referring to the symbols we have seen in Chapter 2, an XML document consists of the following expression:

```
document = prolog element Misc*
```

The expression states that an XML document consists of a prolog, element, and zero or more Misc symbols. Without going into excruciating detail (If you are thirsting for the details, refer back to Chapter 2), if you explode out each of these separate symbols you find that they are primarily composed of processing instructions, comments, element tags, etc. It is not necessary to worry about these because the `Document` interface provides specific methods to create the different objects that these symbols represent. Once we create the Document, the program will be able to manipulate the `Document` interface to create these objects. Thus, we should not have to pass any parameters in order to create a new instance of an object that implements the `Document` interface.

Although the DOM API can perform all of the necessary actions, this does not mean they are the most convenient. For the most part, the XML declaration (`XMLDecl` symbol nested inside the prolog) is similar to a processing instruction that provides information such as the version of the document, the encoding type, and a standalone indicator. Although the DOM API provides a method for creating a processing instruction, it requires some ugly string manipulation to blend in attributes. This is necessary for a generic interface for handling all types of processing instruction nodes. Even though the `XMLDecl` symbol is not a processing instruction, we could use the method because it provides the correct output format. A more intuitive approach, however, would be to parameterize these attributes when creating the document. To provide this, we will create a few different overloaded methods to handle the different ways that an XML document can be declared.

Sticking with our plan to make a Factory that is completely abstract from the physical implementation of the DOM, we will first create a public interface that describes the methods that are required for objects to be considered a `DOMFactory`. Doing so will allow us to create implementation-specific factory objects that implement this common interface for creating new instances of `Document` objects. Finally, we will wrap all of this up in a container that will provide dynamic loading (at run time) of the implementation-specific factories for use within our application.

Example 5.1 DOMFactory.java

```
package com.ctp.dom;
import org.w3c.dom.Document;

public interface DOMFactory
{
  public Document createDocument( String strVersion, String strEncoding,
boolean bStandalone )
    throws DOMFactoryException;
  public Document createDocument( String strVersion, boolean bStandalone )
    throws DOMFactoryException;
  public Document createDocument( String strVersion, String strEncoding)
    throws DOMFactoryException;
  public Document createDocument( String strVersion )
    throws DOMFactoryException;
  public Document createDocument()
    throws DOMFactoryException;
}
```

As you can see from Example 5.1, we have created a few different overrides to create a document. The first method is the most elaborate, accepting the version, encoding, and a flag indicating if the document is standalone. Notice the version is present in all overrides except the method that has no parameters. If you remember back to Chapter 2, the `XMLDecl` symbol was optional, but if included in the document it must include the `VersionInfo` symbol. Likewise, this means when we use the `createDocument` method with no parameters we will be creating a document without the declaration. In contrast to the version info, the encoding and the standalone indicators are always optional so we provide a few different methods for handling all of the possible combinations of these parameters.

> **NOTE:** The standalone parameter we added to some of the overridden methods in the `DOMFactory` interface is defined as Boolean. The actual data type of the standalone attribute in the XML specification is either a string value of "yes" or "no." If you remember back to Chapter 2, the encoding and the standalone attributes are both optional. We created different overloaded methods to handle the cases if they were both passed or if only one of them was passed. In doing so, we could not define the standalone attribute as a string because two of our overridden methods would have the same signature. To alleviate the clash of signatures, we simply make the standalone attribute a Boolean value where true indicated "yes" and false indicated "no." Finally, we simply do not set the attribute in the declaration if we are performing the creating logic in a method that does not have the standalone parameter.

There are a couple points of interest in Example 5.1 that we should discuss. First, the interface is actually being defined as part of the `com.ctp.dom` package. This is our way of saying it is official. We are packaging this interface because we are creating our own little standard in which all applications that we write can be used simply by importing the package. This is how the JDK is distributed, in a series of packages. The difference is that our package is only meaningful to our development efforts. It has not been approved by the industry so it is official only to us. Furthermore, this will make creating factories and writing applications much easier. When we are all finished with the package we will Java Archive (JAR) the class files and include the JAR file in our classpath just as we did for the IBM toolkit. This will make it readily accessible when we start to build our XML application (and all others).

> **NOTE:** Packages are typically given the company name. The code we will be developing in the examples will use Cambridge Technology Partners (CTP) as the company name; however, you are free to use your own company acronym or abbreviation when you are typing in the examples yourself!

The last thing to note is that each method has been defined to throw a `DOMFactoryException`. This special exception class can be used to generate errors that pertain specifically to the operations involved with constructing new document objects. As we will see shortly, the design is similar to that of the `DOMException` class. We will cover this in more detail when we wrap this whole mechanism with a containing class to allow for dynamic loading of a specific DOM implementation.

With our common interface intact, we are ready to create the first class that will implement the `DOMFactory` Interface. We will call these classes adapters because we can create different classes for different DOM implementations. As previously discussed, this class will be responsible for encapsulating the proprietary API used to instantiate new objects that implement the `Document` Interface. As we will be working exclusively with IBM's XML4J toolkit, this class will provide the details for creating specific IBM Documents. We first review how to do this using IBM's API.

Nestled in the `com.ibm.xml.parser` package is a class called `TXDocument`. The `TXDocument` is one of IBM's classes that implement the `org.w3c.dom.Document` interface. The XML4J provides a few different implementations of parsers and DOM objects that vary in functionality and performance. For the book, we are going to stick with the "TX compatibility" objects because they provide the most functionality. If you have not yet guessed, all we have to do is code

```
TXDocument doc = new TXDocument()
```

to create a new instance of a document. As the `TXDocument` class implements the `Document` interface, simply typecasting the object reference to a `Document` hides the implementation details! The client or consumer code will never know the difference, or even that this is IBM's implementation of the DOM. (Actually, there is a way of revealing the objects identity, can you think of it?) Creating the XML declaration is just as simple. The `TXDocument` class provides the convenience methods `setVersion`, `setEncoding`, and `setStandalone` for setting the version, encoding, and the standalone attributes, respectfully. For example, the following code

```
TXDocument doc = new TXDocument();
doc.setVersion( "1.0" );
doc.setEncoding( "UTF-8" );
doc.setStandalone( "yes" );
```

would create a new instance of a document with the following declaration:

```
<?xml version="1.0" encoding="UTF-8" standalone="yes"?>
```

As it is shown, the document would still not be considered well formed because it does not contain a root element. We would still need to add the root element for the document to be considered well formed, but this is not the correct place to add this functionality. Instead, we will use the DOM API. These are the only details we really need before we start implementing a new `DOMFactory` provider that will create document objects using IBM's XML4J toolkit. Before you start thinking we are crazy for spending so much time on such an easy topic, remember that we are putting in the extra effort to keep the implementation details of document creating separate from our applications.

To implement the provider, we start by creating a new class that implements the `DOMFactory` interface we previously created. This is shown in Example 5.2.

Example 5.2 IBMDOMFactory.java

```
import com.ctp.dom.*;
import org.w3c.dom.Document;
import com.ibm.xml.parser.TXDocument;

public class IBMDOMFactory implements DOMFactory
{
  public Document createDocument( String strVersion, String strEncoding,
                                  boolean bStandalone )
    throws DOMFactoryException
  {
    TXDocument doc = new TXDocument();
    doc.setVersion(strVersion);
```

```
    doc.setEncoding(strEncoding);
    doc.setStandalone((bStandalone == true) ? "yes" : "no" );
    return doc;
  }

  public Document createDocument( String strVersion, boolean bStandalone )
    throws DOMFactoryException
  {
    TXDocument doc = new TXDocument();
    doc.setVersion(strVersion);
    doc.setStandalone((bStandalone == true) ? "yes" : "no" );
    return doc;
  }

  public Document createDocument( String strVersion, String strEncoding )
    throws DOMFactoryException
  {
    TXDocument doc = new TXDocument();
    doc.setVersion(strVersion);
    doc.setEncoding(strEncoding);
    return doc;
  }

  public Document createDocument( String strVersion )
    throws DOMFactoryException
  {
    TXDocument doc = new TXDocument();
    doc.setVersion(strVersion);
    return doc;
  }

  public Document createDocument()
    throws DOMFactoryException
  {
    return new TXDocument();
  }
}
```

As you can see, implementing the document creation functionality using the IBM's XML4J is relatively straightforward. Although we must provide for throwing the `DOMFactoryException` to fully implement the `DOMFactory` interface, we did not actually throw this exception within our provider class. Do not be alarmed, the `DOMFactoryException` we provided on the interface actually provides a safety net available in case we have to inform the client code of a problem.

As the `TXDocument` does not actually throw any exceptions, we did not need to perform any special exception processing. This may differ if we are using an implementation that throws exceptions during document creation. Ultimately, a client will either get a reference to a document or a nasty exception that can be used to determine why they did not get the document reference! As exceptions are simply classes that inherit from `java.lang.Exception`, the specific factory providers can extend the generic `DOMFactoryException` to provide implementation specific errors that are not already handled in the `DOMFactoryException` object. Thanks to polymorphism, the client code will not have to know the exact details of the exception, only that it *is a* type of our implementation-independent `DOMFactoryException`.

> **NOTE:** We did not need to include the `DOMFactoryException` in the `DOMFactory` interface because it (indirectly) inherits from `java.io.RuntimeException`. Runtime exceptions do not need to be explicitly defined in the throws clause of method declarations because they are used for unforeseen errors that may happen at runtime, such as null pointers. As these types of exceptions could happen in almost any method, the Java compiler does not require us to define them. The real reason it is included in the interface is to explicitly inform the programmer that our Factory implementation *may* throw this exception.

In contrast to the `DOMFactory` interface, we did not package the `IBMDOMFactory` class in the `com.ctp.dom` package because it provides a specific implementation to the problem we are solving. As we are creating an adapter-type architecture for creating documents, it would not make sense to include each provider implementation we create with the generic interfaces. If included, we would have to rebuild the package every time we create a new "plug-in" thereby leading to numerous versions of the package. This was not the intention of packages. Instead, the providers can be left in the unnamed package or packaged separately from the generic implementation. For the purposes of this book, we will leave the `IBMDOMFactory` class in the unnamed package to keep the coding as simple as possible. If you plan to implement many different providers, it may be advantageous to package these classes according to their specific implementations.

For example, the `IBMDOMFactory` class might be packaged in a package named `com.ctp.dom.impl.ibm` to indicate that it is a DOM implementation specific to IBM's Toolkit. Keep in mind that this will affect how we dynamically load and plug-in the provider class in the subsequent examples.

5.4.2 DOMManager class

We are not quite finished. Now that we can create documents independent from the actual DOM implementation, we also need to provide a mechanism so the client application can choose the DOM factory adapter to use. In doing so, this will allow us to hide or encapsulate the physical implementation of the provider class. This means that we will no longer need to provide import directives specifically for our provider class. Instead, we will create a mechanism in which we can dynamically load the provider, or plug-in, by passing a string parameter containing the name of the class.

This is similar to how the `java.sql.DriverManager` class connects application code to a specific database. If you have ever worked with JDBC, the `DriverManager` class connects application code to an implementation-specific JDBC driver that knows how to communicate with its associated database implementation. We simply pass a string containing the database URL to the `getConnection` method of the `DriverManager` class to connect to a database. Internally, the driver manager class interrogates each registered driver to determine the appropriate driver to use for providing a database connection. If it is not apparent, this is exactly what we are trying to do, in this case for XML documents.

> **NOTE:** Ever wonder why we always code the `Class.forName` ("driver class") before each call to `DriverManager.getConnection()`? The `DriverManager` only knows about drivers that have registered. If you dig into the JDBC specification, you will see that one of the requirements for JDBC drivers is to register itself with the `DriverManager` when the class is loaded. Because we are not sure if the driver has been loaded (and thereby registered), it is safe coding practice to attempt to load the driver prior to calling the `getConnection` method unless you know that it has been registered previously.

It is not necessary to worry about our drivers registering themselves with a manager. Instead, all we really need to do is provide the name of the class that will implement the document creation responsibilities we defined in the `DOMFactory` interface. This will enable our `DOMManager` class to dynamically load the class and instantiate it. Thus, the application will have the ability to choose the appropriate adapter. Although the applications will be able to change implementations at run-time, for the purposes of this book we will limit the application to a single factory provider at any given time.

Java has made dynamically loading classes simple. As we have seen, all we have to do is use the static `forName` method of the `Class` object and pass a string parameter indicating the name of the class to load. For example, the following code:

```
Class impl = Class.forName( "IBMDOMFactory" )
```

will load and return a reference to the `Class` object of the factory provider we just created so long as the name represents a valid class. If the JVM could not find the class, it will throw a `ClassNotFoundException`. It is important to note that this did not actually create a new instance of the `IBMDOMFactory`. It only loaded the class or definition of the object. To create a new instance of the `IBMDOMFactory` we call the `newInstance` method of the `Class` object as follows:

```
DOMFactory myFactory = (DOMFactory) impl.newInstance()
```

Notice that we had to typecast the result of `newInstance` to our generic `DOMFactory` interface. This is because the `newInstance` method is a generic way of creating any object and thus it must return a generic value. In order for this function to instantiate a Java class, it must return a reference to the base class of all Java classes- `Object`. Furthermore, we did not type cast the object to `IBMDOMFactory` because we want to keep this mechanism generic so we can reuse it for any implementation. The `DOMFactory` is the least common denominator to keep the `DOMManager` implementation-independent while providing document creation functionality

It is a risky endeavor to typecast a reference down the inheritance hierarchy. We can not be sure that the object implements the type we are expecting it to implement. Java does provide facilities for dynamically discovering the interfaces the object implements and the ability to retrieve the super class but this is not necessary in our case. We will not be so defensive, but will, instead simply perform the typecast and prepare ourselves for the consequences by catching the `ClassCastException`. (Of course, if you are playing the dating game, you would definitely want to take the defensive approach to ensure that your counterpart is someone you want to date.) The potential problems do not stop here. Simply providing the name of the class does not necessarily ensure that we can actually instantiate the class. This name could represent an interface or even a class defined as abstract. If we try to instantiate an abstract class or an interface, Java will throw an `InstantiationException`. Finally, do not underestimate the security features built into Java. Java will throw an `IllegalAccessException` if we do not have the appropriate permissions to access or instantiate the class.

The last thing to discuss before we actually look at the implementation is multithread support. As this class will be used in a servlet, we want to make sure that we can support multiple threads calling into the object at any given time. For the most part, the focus is on protecting the instance variable reference we maintain internally to the Factory implementation.

Although most of the activity within the `DOMManager` class will simply involve returning references to various adapters, we do allow the implementation to be switched at any time. This means we need to synchronize thread access to this object to ensure that one thread is not reading the reference while a different thread is changing it. To accomplish this, we use the `synchronized` keyword to provide mutually exclusive (one thread at a time) access to our internal factory object.

For thread synchronization, Java provides a special type of object called a monitor for each object instance. These monitors provide a mutually exclusive locking mechanism that can be used to synchronize access to shared resources. The synchronized statement can be included on a block of code or a function declaration. In the first case, a valid object reference must be provided so that the synchronized statement has a monitor to lock. In the second case, Java provides the convenience to modify any given method of an object by including the keyword in the method declaration. In this case, the entire method is synchronized and the monitor is acquired from the object instance. In the case of static methods, the monitor from the class object is used. Once the block of code has terminated, either normally or abnormally, the synchronized keyword will release the lock so other threads can acquire the lock.

> **NOTE:** A common misconception about the synchronized keyword is that it only synchronizes access to the method in which it is defined. This is not the case. The key to remember is that a thread must acquire a lock from the monitor of the object being synchronized. When the synchronized keyword is used to modify a method declaration, the monitor of the object instance is used (static methods use the `Class` object instance). This means the same monitor can synchronize two or more separate blocks of code. In the case of a class, this means only one thread will be permitted inside ALL of the synchronized methods of the class.

Example 5.3 DOMManager Factory methods

```
public class DOMManager
{
  protected static DOMFactory m_factory = null;
  private static final String ERR_IMPL_NOT_SET =
                                "No Implementation specified.";

  public static synchronized void setFactory( DOMFactory factory )
    throws DOMFactoryException
  {
    if (factory == null)
     throw new DOMFactoryException(DOMFactoryException.NO_IMPLEMENTATION,
                                   ERR_IMPL_NOT_SET);
    m_factory = factory;
  }

  public static synchronized void setFactory( String strClassName )
    throws DOMFactoryException
  {
    try
    {
      Class impl = Class.forName( strClassName );
      setFactory( (DOMFactory) impl.newInstance() );
    }
```

```
    catch( ClassCastException NoDOMFactory )
    {
      throw new DOMFactoryException(
                DOMFactoryException.INVALID_FACTORY_IMPL,
               "Specified class does not implement DOMFactory interface.");
    }
    catch( ClassNotFoundException BadDriver )
    {
      throw new DOMFactoryException(
                   DOMFactoryException.IMPLEMENTATION_NOT_FOUND,
                  "The class (" + strClassName + ") could not be found." );
    }
    catch( InstantiationException CantLoadit )
    {
      throw new DOMFactoryException(
                   DOMFactoryException.CANT_LOAD_IMPLEMENTATION,
                   CantLoadit.getMessage() );
    }
    catch( IllegalAccessException Access )
    {
      throw new DOMFactoryException(DOMFactoryException.ILLEGAL_ACCESS,
                                    Access.getMessage());
    }
  }

  public static synchronized DOMFactory getFactory()
    throws DOMFactoryException
  {
    if (m_factory != null)
      return m_factory;
    else
      throw new DOMFactoryException(
          DOMFactoryException.NO_IMPLEMENTATION, ERR_IMPL_NOT_SET);
  }
}
```

At first it may seem like a large amount of code, but the exceptions are what make these methods lengthy. We could have simply declared the exceptions in the throws clause of the method declaration to reduce some of the code but for a couple of reasons we chose not to do so. First, we wanted to provide a simple interface that could be used and that does not require 10 times more coding of exception handling (which will inevitability cause carpal tunnel syndrome) every time we call the `setFactory` method. Instead, we caught the exceptions and converted them into `DOMFactoryExceptions`. This allows the client to catch just the `DOMFactoryException` to operate safely.

The second reason is to improve debugging. Simply letting common exceptions, such as a `NullPointerException` through can sometimes be hard to track down, especially when we are developing the application code. By catching these exceptions, we can provide slightly better information to solve problems or at least associate them with the `DOMFactory` call.

As the operations that are performed in the factory are related to the Document Object Model, we have decided to design our new exception object similar to the `DOMException`. Of course, our exception object will provide different error types and messages. As you can see from Example 5.4, the `DOMFactoryException` is simply a new class that extends the `RuntimeException` class. This will allow the users to be a little more relaxed because the compiler will not require that these exceptions be caught. This is how the `DOMException` is implemented:

Example 5.4 DOMFactoryException.java

```
package com.ctp.dom;

public class DOMFactoryException extends RuntimeException
{
  public final static short NO_IMPLEMENTATION         = 1;
  public final static short IMPLEMENTATION_NOT_FOUND  = 2;
  public final static short CANT_LOAD_IMPLEMENTATION  = 3;
  public final static short ILLEGAL_ACCESS            = 4;
  public final static short INVALID_FACTORY_IMPL      = 5;

  private short  m_nCode = 0;

  public DOMFactoryException(short code, String message)
  {
    super(message);
    m_nCode = code;
  }

  public short getCode()
  {
    return m_nCode;
  }
}
```

In the constructor, all we need to do is pass the exception message to the `RuntimeException` instance and store the code in the instance variable `m_nCode`. When the exception is caught, the client code can call the `getCode` method to determine the error code. Likewise, the client can call the `getMessage` method (from the `java.lang.Throwable` parent class) to retrieve the exception description.

Notice, in Example 5.4, how we broke out the `setFactory` method into two separate overrides and provided public access to both of them. At first, this may seem strange because these two methods work together when the class name is passed as a parameter. This layered approach provides more versatility with the same amount of code. Furthermore, the inner layer that takes a reference to a `DOMFactory` interface may be used when an adapter requires more than a default constructor does. Although we could have gotten more elaborate in the process of constructing the class factory, ultimately this would have increased the complexity of the client interface. As most of the factory provider implementations should work fine with the default constructor, we decided to keep the interface simple and leave the object creation code intact. Because the inner `setFactory` method takes a `DOMFactory` reference, this provides for the most flexibility because all of the creation details are abstracted from the `DOMManager` class.

All of the methods have been defined as static so our application code will never have to create an instance of our `DOMManager`. It may not seem like much, but this is all that is required for encapsulating the creation of specific `DOMFactory` providers. Now all the client has to do is call up one of the `setFactory` methods to initialize the appropriate DOM implementation. This is typically done during the initialization of the application. After initialization, all the application code simply calls for the `getFactory` method to retrieve a reference to a `DOMFactory` interface. For example:

```
DOMManager.setFactory("IBMDOMFactory");          // Initialize the Factory
  Document doc = DOMManager.getFactory().createDocument();
```

The first line will load and instantiate the `IBMDOMFactory` provider and store a reference to it internally in the `DOMManager` class. The second line will first retrieve a reference to the `DOMFactory` implementation, and create a new `Document` instance by calling the `createDocument`. Notice that there are no objects other than our `DOMManager` and the `Document` required. Everything is DOM implementation-independent with the exception of the string passed to the `setFactory` method. This is acceptable because it is now manageable by storing its value in a properties file, or in the case of a Java Servlet in the Servlet configuration file. We will see more of this in the next chapter.

5.4.3 Writing Documents

We can use many of the same philosophies we applied creating the classes for producing documents to create custom objects that know intimate details of specific implementations and still keep our application code abstracted from these details. In particular, many of the different implementations provide methods for printing documents to standard Java `OutputStreams` or `Writers`. Printing, saving or writing documents from the DOM was not included in the DOM recommendation. Although this is not required for the DOM to function, there can be significant coding involved in creating a well-formed document using only the interfaces defined in the `org.w3c.dom` package.

Although this could be accomplished by writing a generic routine that would generate a well-formed document while walking the nodes in the document, the IBM's TX implementation provides this capability for us. Thus, it would be unreasonable not to use the printing functionality IBM has provided. Likewise, many other XML implementations are bound to provide similar functionality as a convenience to developers.

The `TXDocument` exposes a couple of `printWithFormat` methods that will stream a document to any of the numerous `java.io.Writer` super classes! Of course, this logic is proprietary to IBM's implementation. For the same reasons we created the document factory, we will add a layer of abstraction to isolate this implementation-specific code from our application code. As we covered many of these concepts earlier, we will move quickly and focus primarily on the interface and implementation details for writing a document. If a particular topic is still confusing, you may want to review the `DOMFactory` examples.

The first thing we need to do is define the standard interface that will provide the various implementations with the information they will need to accomplish this task. For simplicity, we will provide a bare-bones implementation that takes a reference to a `Document` and a `java.io.Writer` class shown in Example 5.5.

Example 5.5 DOMWriter.java

```
package com.ctp.dom;
import org.w3c.dom.Document;

public interface DOMWriter
{
  public void writeDocument( Document doc, java.io.Writer writer )
    throws DOMWriterException, java.io.IOException;
}
```

This interface will provide a single method, `writeDocument`. This method will take references to an `org.w3c.dom.Document` interface and a `java.io.Writer` interface. To handle unforeseen circumstances we explicitly defined the `DOMWriterException` and `IOException`. As we will see shortly, the `DOMWriterException` is similar to the `DOMFactoryException` we implemented recently. This provides a general mechanism that `DOMWriter` adapters can use to report errors to the client code related to the `Document`. Finally, the `IOException` is also thrown so the client can resolve issues related to the `Writer` parameter.

With the interface defined, we can now create an adapter class that implements the `DOMWriter` interface. As we are focusing on using IBM's XML toolkit, we will create a class that is focused solely on writing IBM `TXDocument` objects. In the process, we take advantage of the convenience methods `TXDocument` provides for printing.

We start by creating a new class that implements the `DOMWriter` interface as shown in Example 5.6. The implementation of the `writeDocument` method is relatively straightforward. In contrast to the document factory, we need to be defensive and ensure that the `Document` parameter truly is a `TXDocument` before we start to print. Thanks to the design of the Java API, this task is again very easy. Although our parameter is of `Document` type, we can access object instance's `Class` object to determine its true type. We can safely typecast the reference to the TXDocument if we recognize the class name as such. Otherwise, we need to throw an exception to notify the application code that this plug-in does not know how to print this type of Document.

Example 5.6 IBMDOMWriter.java

```
import com.ctp.dom.*;
import java.io.Writer;
import java.io.IOException;
import org.w3c.dom.Document;
import com.ibm.xml.parser.TXDocument;

public class IBMDOMWriter implements DOMWriter
{
  private static final String IBM_DOC_CLASS_NAME =
"com.ibm.xml.parser.TXDocument";

  public void writeDocument( Document doc, Writer writer )
    throws DOMWriterException, IOException
  {
    if (doc.getClass().getName().equals(IBM_DOC_CLASS_NAME) )
    //if (doc.getClass().isInstance(new TXDocument() ))
    {
      TXDocument IbmDoc = (TXDocument) doc;
      String strEncoding = IbmDoc.getEncoding();
      if (strEncoding != null)
        IbmDoc.printWithFormat( writer, strEncoding );
      else
        IbmDoc.printWithFormat( writer );
    }
    else
      throw new DOMWriterException( DOMWriterException
.UKNOWN_IMPLEMENTATION, "Do not know how to print document of type (" +
doc.getClass().getName() + ").");
  }
}
```

Once we have successfully typecast the Document reference to a TXDocument, the rest is straightforward. We simply call the printWithFormat method passing the writer parameter. If the encoding attribute was set on the document then we can pass that as well to have the writer print in the same encoding we used for the document. You will agree that the DOMWriter layer of abstraction saved us from having to write a hefty amount of code that is not even remotely related to the business problem.

Now we need to provide the ability to dynamically instantiate the `DOMWriter` adapter. Just like the `setFactory` methods we added to the `DOMManager` previously, we will add new `setWriter` methods to isolate the `DOMWriter` adapters from the application code. We will use the same concepts as before by giving two different methods, thereby providing the capability of either plugging in a `DOMWriter` implementation by class name or by object reference. Just as we did with the `setFactory` methods, the first or outer method will be responsible for loading the class and creating a new instance. The inner method will be responsible for merely setting a member variable to hold a reference to the implementation. If anything happens to go wrong inside one of these methods, we will throw a `DOMWriterException`. As with the `DOMFactoryException`, the `DOMWriter-Exception` extends `DOMException` to provide additional error types and messages. As you will notice from Example 5.7, the code is very similar to the `setFactory` and `getFactory` methods.

Example 5.7 setWriter/getWriter Methods

```
public static void setWriter( String strClassName )
{
  try
  {
    Class impl = Class.forName( strClassName );
    setWriter( (DOMWriter) impl.newInstance() );
  }
  catch( ClassCastException NoDOMWriter )
  {
    throw new DOMWriterException(
        DOMWriterException.INVALID_FACTORY_IMPL,
      "Implementation Invalid. Provider must implement DOMWriterImpl.");
  }
  catch( ClassNotFoundException BadDriver )
  {
    throw new DOMWriterException(
        DOMWriterException.IMPLEMENTATION_NOT_FOUND,
        "The DOMWriter class (" + strClassName + ") could not be found." );
  }
  catch( InstantiationException CantLoadit )
  {
    throw new DOMWriterException(DOMWriterException
.CANT_LOAD_IMPLEMENTATION,
                                 CantLoadit.getMessage() );
```

```
    }
    catch( IllegalAccessException Access )
    {
      throw new DOMWriterException(DOMWriterException.ILLEGAL_ACCESS,
                                   Access.getMessage());
    }
  }

  public static synchronized void setWriter( DOMWriter writer )
  {
      m_writer = writer;
  }

  public static synchronized DOMWriter getWriter()
    throws DOMWriterException
  {
    if (m_writer != null)
      return m_writer;
     else
      throw new DOMWriterException( DOMWriterException.NO_IMPLEMENTATION,
                                   "Writer Implementation not specified.");
  }
```

Like many managers in the corporate world (Please skip this paragraph if you are in management!), the `DOMManager` class does not do a whole lot. Although we have written a lot of code the manager delegates all of the nitty-gritty details to the `DOMWriter` and `DOMFactory` class implementations. Although this may resemble the way typical managers in the corporate world delegate by, simply hiring employees, it does not have to be this way for our Java classes!

If it is not apparent from the amount of code written so far, the `DOMManager` is going to see a lot of action within an application. This is primarily because the `DOMManager` is now the central point, where an application can go to both create and write documents. We can now shift our focus to the tasks we will needed to perform through the DOM tree.

5.4.4 Convenience Methods

This class is a good place to add some useful convenience methods to reduce the amount of application code required for manipulating the DOM itself. As you will soon see, writing XML applications will frequently require us to dynamically create new XML nodes on the fly. Although the `Document` interface provides methods for accomplishing these tasks, it is not always the most convenient mechanism. Sometimes we will need to create an element with an associated value. For example, to create an `Element` node of type "Title" with an associated "XML for Real Programmers" value would require the following code using the document interface alone:

```
Document doc = DOMManager.getFactory().createDocument();
Element e = doc.createElement("Title");
e.appendChild( doc.createTextNode("XML for Real Programmers") );
```

Although three lines of code may not seem like much, can you imagine coding the same three lines for each column from a database query? This type of task will occur so frequently while we are coding an XML-based application that it deserves a convenience method.

> **NOTE:** After working with the different types of Nodes in the DOM you may begin to think that you could simply call the `setNodeValue` method from the Node Interface to insert some text within an Element. Do not get caught in this trap! The `setNodeValue` will only work for specific types of nodes and `ELEMENT_NODE` is not one of them. Likewise, only nodes of type `ELEMENT_NODE` are allowed to have attributes.
>
> The rational W3C used for this design decision was to provide for both a "flat" and an Object-Orientated API. Consequently, the `Node` interface turned into a "Super" interface that provided access to all the functionality throughout the DOM. This design actually allows a significant number of operations to be performed on a node without requiring typecasting. This has some performance benefits because internally Java performs runtime-type checking to ensure safe typecasting. In other words, the JVM would allow you to cast an apple object to a fruit object, but the JVM would not allow you to cast the apple object to a nut object (although the JVM would think you are nuts for trying it!).

Although the Document Object Model is extremely powerful, the longer you work with it the more you will realize the amount of code that is involved, even with the trivial tasks described. We will provide a few convenience methods that will reduce the amount of code that we have to write for the website. Obviously, although there are many convenience methods we could implement, for the purposes of this book we will focus our efforts on creating an `Element` node with an associated `Text` node child. You are welcome to extend the class and add your own convenience methods as well.

First, we will add a few different ways to provide a more convenient mechanism to create `Element` nodes. To assist creating `Element` nodes with an associated `Text` node value, we will create a `createElement` method that takes a `Document` reference and two string parameters. The first `String` parameter will be for the `Element` type and the other for the content of the child `Text` node. This is shown in Example 5.8.

Example 5.8 DOMManager.createElement Method

```
public static Element createElement( Document doc, String strType, String
strValue )
{
  if ( strValue != null)
  {
    Element e = doc.createElement(strType);
    Node text = doc.createTextNode(strValue);
    e.appendChild( text );
    return e;
  }
  else
    return doc.createElement(strType);
}
```

The `createElement` method simply checks to see if a value for the text node was passed. If so, the method creates the outer element by calling the `createElement` method of the `Document` interface. Next, we use the `Document` interface again by calling `createTextNode`. Finally, we call `appendChild` to append the text node to the outer element and return a reference to it. If the value for the text node was not passed, we simply return a newly created element without any children. This will save numerous lines of code in the client application checking for null values.

A common misunderstanding of the DOM model is the concept of an owner. All nodes are created in the context of an owning document. In doing so, these nodes can only be appended to the owner's documents hierarchy. This means the node can only be appended to the document that created it or another node that was created by its owner document.

This can present a problem if you are coding a method and you do not have a reference to the owning document. The DOM provides a `getOwnerDocument` method on the `Node` interface that will retrieve a reference to the document owner. As the `Document` Interface is a descendant of the Node interface, you can call this method on the document also. Doing so will actually return a null reference to indicate that it is the document! Instead of dealing with the null references, we will add a new convenience method to the `DOMManager` class that encapsulates this task.

Example 5.9 DOMManager.getOwner method

```
public static Document getOwner( Node node )
{
  if ( node.getNodeType() == Node.DOCUMENT_NODE )
    return (Document) node;
  else
    return node.getOwnerDocument();
}
```

We create a new `getOwner` method that takes a `Node` interface as a parameter. With the `Node` interface, we first check the type of node by calling `getNodeType`. If the node is a document, we can simply return the node typecasted as a `Document`. Otherwise, we simply return the `Document` from the `getOwnerDocument` method.

That is all there is to the `DOMManager` class. Although simple, it provides some extremely important abstractions that will be very beneficial in terms of maintaining the XML-applications we build. The complete listing of the source is included on the companion CD-ROM in the chptr5\src directory.

Before continuing, make sure that all of the code covered so far has been successfully compiled and either JAR'd or nested in a subdirectory structure equivalent to the name of the package. For example, if you used the same package name as found in the book, all of the packaged code can be placed in the com\ctp\dom directory below your project directory. If you decided to JAR the package, make sure it is added to your classpath environment variable before continuing. The adapters (`IBMDOMFactory` and `IBMDOMWriter`) should be left in your project directory.

5.5 *PDA Database Overview*

The company's Personal Data Assistant (PDA) database is a Microsoft® Access 97© database consisting of four different tables as shown in Figure 5.1. As you probably expect, the `Customer` table contains one record for each customer account and the product catalog is stored in normalized form in the remaining three tables: `Catalog`, `Manufacturer`, and `Category`.

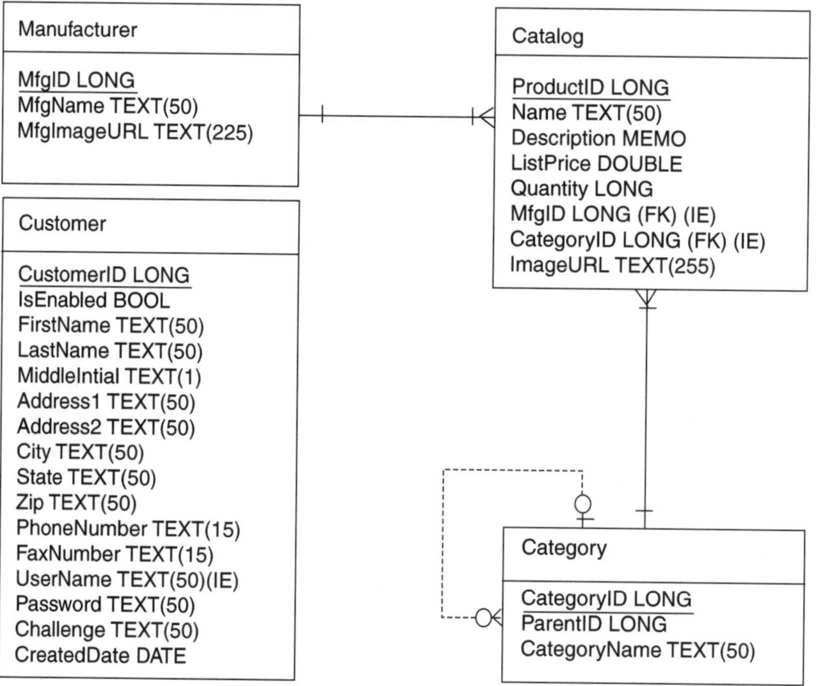

Figure 5.1 Entity Relationship Diagram (ERD)

The Customer table is uniquely keyed based on a system-generated value, CustomerID. We will not need to worry about creating these keys because the database engine takes care of this for us. All columns in the Customer table, except for the MiddleInitial, Address2, and FaxNumber columns, are required fields that must be populated in order to successfully insert a row in the table. In other words, the data values of the columns can not contain null values. The IsEnabled column signifies if the account is active or inactive. For our purposes, we will always be setting this value to true when registering new users. Furthermore, we will use the Username and Password columns to authenticate a user.

The Hint column contains a phrase to assist the user in remembering his/her password. We will need to display this to users when they attempt to authenticate with the wrong password for their Username. Finally, a unique index (primary key) has been built over the Username column to speed the authentication process and ensure these values remain unique.

The Manufacturer table is normalized to contain information pertaining to a given manufacturer of a product. The primary key of the table is the MfgID, which is also a system-generated number like the CustomerID column in the customer table. Of the remaining columns, the MfgName contains the name of the manufacturer and the MfgImageURL is used to store a relative URL to an image of the manufacturer's logo. Finally, any given record in the manufacturer table can be related to one or more records in the product table; however, any specific product record can (and must) be related to one manufacturer record.

The Category table is used to group related products. The unique identifier or primary key for the table is the CategoryID. The interesting thing about this table is the ParentID column. The ParentID column is a foreign key to the same (Category) table! Essentially this is a recursive reference to itself which models a hierarchical tree or node data structure. This allows us to nest categories below other categories. For example, we could implement a root level category called "Computers" with a child category of "Notebooks." To do so, we would first insert the record for Computers with a ParentID set to null, and then insert the category Notebooks with a ParentID set to the CategoryID of the Computers row. Do not worry about this too much right now; it will become simpler when we start implementing the code. Finally, any given `Category` row can be associated to one or more products, and a product must be related to one `Category` row.

The `Catalog` table contains all of the products that we will be displaying. The `ProductID`, a system generated number, is the primary key of the table. Each record in the table describes one product. The `MfgID` and `CategoryID` are foreign keys that associate the row with rows in the `Manufacturer` and `Category` tables, respectfully. The `ListPrice` is the price of the product and will be used to determine the price of the product. The `Quantity` field indicates the number of products our company has for sale. We can only sell products that have a quantity of greater than zero.

If you have not copied the database to your local hard drive or set up the ODBC DSN, you will need to do so now. Refer back to the Technical requirements section at the beginning of this chapter. If these steps are not accomplished, you will not be able to complete the remaining examples.

5.6 *Business Objects*

We start developing the site by implementing the business objects. This is our opportunity to get some hands-on experience with the Document Object Model and test our new `DOMManager`, related interfaces, and plug-in classes. As we work through the examples, you will notice that many of the classes operate independently of each other. Although the amount of code in the book is trivial to a full XML system, many of the objects have been developed to operate independently of each other. This was done to reduce dependencies between the objects and improve team development possibilities. This may not mean much for the book, but consider it the next time your boss asks you to have something done yesterday!

We will separate the business functionality into three separate classes. Based on the business requirements, it makes sense to separate the business objects into separate classes. We start with an account class that implements the business rules for creating a new customer account and handling the authentication requirements for logging into the site. Next, we create a

Catalog class to manage the products to be displayed to all of our users. Finally, we create a ShoppingBasket class that will interact with the Catalog class and maintain a list of the products that the user has selected to purchase.

5.6.1 Account class

From a high level, the Account class needs to interact with the PDA database to provide customer registration and authentication. When someone logs into the site, the authentication routine should retrieve the information about the account so that it can be displayed to the user. In the process of creating the authentication logic, we will add a nifty feature to assist users who forget their passwords by providing a hint. If the user does not already have an account set up, the Account object will need to provide the logic to register the user by creating a new record in our database.

We will use standard Java objects, such as String to store the account data internally within the class. To support the XML requirements, we need to provide a mechanism to convert the account data into XML markup. Example 5.10 shows how we will need to structure the various attributes that represent the account.

Example 5.10 Logical structure of the Account markup

```
<Account Status="..." CustomerID="1">
  <Address1>123 Main Street</Address1>
  <Address2/>
  <FirstName>Bruce</FirstName>
  <MiddleInitial/>
  <LastName>Weber</LastName>
  <City>Phoenix</City>
  <State>AZ</State>
  <Zip>85050</Zip>
  <PhoneNumber/>
  <FaxNumber/>
</Account>
```

Notice that we have encapsulated all of the various elements that describe the account as children to the parent account element. Furthermore, we will be creating two attributes, Status and CustomerID for the parent account element.

5.6.1.1 Creating an Account Class

Enough of the philosophical babble—it is time to write code. We will start by creating an `Account.java` file that will hold the source for our object. We will need to import class definitions for JDBC, DOM and the `DOMManager` we have recently completed. This is shown in Example 5.11.

Example 5.11 Account class imports

```
import java.sql.Connection;
import java.sql.ResultSet;
import java.sql.SQLException;
import java.sql.PreparedStatement;
import java.sql.Types;

import org.w3c.dom.Document;
import org.w3c.dom.Element;
import org.w3c.dom.NodeList;
import org.w3c.dom.Node;
import com.ctp.dom.DOMManager;
```

> **TIP:** We could have simply used the wildcard (*) instead of explicitly importing each class we will be using. Although both mechanisms work, taking the extra time now to define explicitly the classes we will be using will save a good deal of time in the future.

Next, we will create the `Account` class. In doing so, we will create some constant (final) members that will be used to create the various element types we saw in Example 5.11. This is a very important technique, especially when creating an XML application. This is shown in Example 5.12.

Example 5.12 Account class

```
public class Account
{
  public static final String ACCOUNT_TYPE     = "Account";
  public static final String CUSTOMER_ID      = "CustomerID";
  public static final String ATTRIB_STATUS    = "Status";
  public static final String ANONYMOUS        = "Anonymous";
  public static final String HINT             = "Hint";
  public static final String AUTHENTICATED    = "Authenticated";
```

```
    public static final String FIRST_NAME       = "FirstName";
    public static final String LAST_NAME        = "LastName";
    public static final String MIDDLE_INITIAL   = "MiddleInitial";
    public static final String ADDRESS_LINE1    = "Address1";
    public static final String ADDRESS_LINE2    = "Address2";
    public static final String ADDRESS_CITY     = "City";
    public static final String ADDRESS_STATE    = "State";
    public static final String ADDRESS_ZIP      = "Zip";
    public static final String PHONE_NUMBER     = "PhoneNumber";
    public static final String FAX_NUMBER       = "FaxNumber";

    public static final String CONFIRM_PASSWORD = "ConfirmPassword";
    public static final String USER_NAME        = "UserName";
    public static final String CHALLENGE        = "Challenge";
    public static final String PASSWORD         = "Password";
}
```

For the most part, the constants should be self explanatory. The first three lines describe the `Account` element and its two attributes. The next three lines describe the possible values of the `Status` attribute. These are covered in more detail later. The rest of the constants describe the child elements of the account object. Do not be alarmed to see more definitions than elements in the example logical structure. The last four elements will be used depending on the status of the account.

> **TIP:** All of the string parameters used to identify the element type/name, attribute names, and attribute values are all constant string values (defined with the `final` keyword). This is considered a good programming practice in general. It is even more important when working with XML documents because we have to use these values for creating and searching the DOM tree (Do not forget XML *is* case-sensitive). Save some time and trouble by using constants when naming nodes!

There is little logic needed to create the `Account` object. The only thing we need to do is set up some instance variables to hold the various properties of the account. To store the account properties, we will use a `Hashtable` object. Although this is slightly slower that simply using `String` objects, this provides an elegant solution for generating the XML markup. The last thing we want to do is set a default status when the object is instantiated. This is shown in Example 5.13.

Example 5.13 Account instance variables

```
private Hashtable m_hashElements  = new Hashtable();
private String    m_strStatus     = ANONYMOUS;
```

Notice that we did not code a constructor. As we only needed to initialize some objects, we simply did so when they were declared within the body of the `Account` object, just like the constant definitions where defined.

That is all that is necessary to initialize the `Account` object. Before we start implementing the business logic we need to create a way to retrieve the value of the `Status` attribute. Ultimately, the status of the account will have an impact on how the business rules are processed. For example, we should not allow a user of the website to reauthenticate himself or herself (or someone else) if he or she has already logged in. Although this is a business rule in itself, we will implement this rule in the Servlet because someday this account object may be used for administrative purposes that may need to provide impersonation capabilities.

To accomplish this, we will provide a convenience method to access the `m_strStatus` instance variable. This is shown in Example 5.14. This code is relatively trivial. To make this method thread-safe, we defined the method as `synchronized`. We discuss threading in detail when we create the `Catalog` class.

Example 5.14 getStatus Method

```
public synchronized String getStatus()
{
 return m_strStatus;
}
```

Now that we can retrieve the status of the account, it is time to implement the business rules.

5.6.1.2 Authenticate Method

Ultimately, the goal of authentication is to apply security filters that ensure users are who they say they are by making them identify themselves. Internally, the account object will verify the user is in the database and take the necessary actions. As this is going to be one of potentially several different business objects within an application, we need to ensure that the class does not tie up precious resources. In particular, we need to make sure the class uses database connections. For the most part, database connections are scarce (limited) resources. If we allowed each account object to reserve their own connection, we would exhaust them very quickly.

To get this rolling we will create a new public method that accepts a reference to live database connection, and two String parameters to represent the username and password parameters. This is shown in Example 5.15.

Example 5.15 Account.authenticate method

```
private static final String SQL_GET_CUSTOMER = "SELECT * FROM Customer
WHERE UserName = ?";

public synchronized String authenticate(Connection conn, String strUser-
Name, String strPassword )
  throws AccountException, SQLException
{
  if ( strUserName == null)
    throw new AccountException( AccountException.TYPE_MISSING_PARAM,
"Missing " + USER_NAME );
  if ( strPassword == null)
    throw new AccountException( AccountException.TYPE_MISSING_PARAM,
"Missing " + PASSWORD );

  PreparedStatement stmt  = conn.prepareStatement( SQL_GET_CUSTOMER );
  stmt.setString(1,strUserName);
  ResultSet rs = stmt.executeQuery();

  if (!rs.next())
  {
    throw new AccountException( AccountException.TYPE_INVALIDUSERNAME,
"The username '" + strUserName + "' does not exist.");
  }
  else
  {
    if ( !rs.getString( PASSWORD ).equalsIgnoreCase( strPassword ) )
    {
      storeColumn( rs, USER_NAME );
      storeColumn( rs, CHALLENGE );
      m_strStatus = CHALLENGE;
    }
    else  // Authentication was successful, set up the account fields.
```

```
        {
          storeColumn( rs, ADDRESS_LINE1);
          storeColumn( rs, ADDRESS_LINE2);
          storeColumn( rs, FIRST_NAME);
          storeColumn( rs, MIDDLE_INITIAL);
          storeColumn( rs, LAST_NAME);
          storeColumn( rs, ADDRESS_CITY);
          storeColumn( rs, ADDRESS_STATE);
          storeColumn( rs, ADDRESS_ZIP);
          storeColumn( rs, PHONE_NUMBER);
          storeColumn( rs, FAX_NUMBER);
          storeColumn( rs, CUSTOMER_ID);
          m_strStatus = AUTHENTICATED;
        }
      }
    return getStatus();
}
```

First we need to ensure that the username and password parameters are valid. Unfortunately, the only way we can do this is to query the database. Before we do that, however, we can do a preliminary check to make sure that the `String` objects are at least valid references. If either of the two `String` parameters is invalid (`null`), we will throw an `AccountException` to indicate what parameter was missing. This will provide information that is more useful than a `NullPointerException` which is bound to happen if we do not check. The `AccountException` will be covered in more detail later.

As long as the two `String` parameters passed our initial verification, we can query the database for a row matching the username. Instead of dynamically building the syntax for the query, we used a `java.sql.PreparedStatement.` The `PreparedStatement` object provides a solution that is more elegant than dynamically generating the SQL that is typically performed in many systems. Using the `PreparedStatement` in conjunction with the `SQL_GET_CUSTOMER` string separates the SQL statement from the Java logic nicely.

Using the `PreparedStatement` object is a matter of passing a generic SQL statement when created. If parameters need to be inserted into the SQL statement, question marks are used as placeholders for the parameters. Once the object has been instantiated, we simply bind the parameters to replace the placeholders. In our case, we called the `setString` method because our parameter was a string of characters. Once all the parameters have been appended, we simply call the `executeQuery` to return a `ResultSet` object that contains the results of the query.

More importantly, the `PrepareStatement` makes sure that the SQL statement if formatted appropriately. Remember from Chapter 2 how XML provides predefined entities, such as the < to represent a less than "<" character, to escape markup code from the content. SQL statements require similar formatting to separate properly the parameters from the command syntax.

Typically, database engines use an apostrophe or quotation marks (single or double quotes in programmer slang) to delimit character parameters from the SQL Keywords. Blindly concatenating SQL statements together with parameters could result in invalid SQL statements, such as the ones shown in Example 5.16. The database engine can not execute the query as the SQL keywords are intermingled with the parameters because the parameters also contain the delimiter character. Sometimes programmers will write a function to ensure that the parameter value will not invalidate the query but this would be like writing an XML document without using the Document Object Model! The `PreparedStatement` does this well and we do not have to write any additional code!

> **TIP:** You would be amazed at the number of applications that do not contain logic to handle delimiters in the parameter values. You have relatively high odds of making some extra cash (or at least winning some free lunches) on this topic by betting your peers that you can break their code—try it!

Example 5.16 Invalid SQL (Parameter values containing a delimiter)

```
SELECT * FROM CoolNames WHERE name = 'O'Connor'
SELECT * FROM FamousPhrases WHERE Phrases = "I said, "XML is Really Cool!""
```

The real substance of the authentication logic is buried in how we query and process the `ResultSet`. First, we did not include the password as a parameter in the where clause of the query. Although we need to make sure the password matches in order to successfully authenticate a user, we still want to retrieve the record when the user forgets his/her password.

This will allow us to provide a hint. Thus, we need to verify that the passwords match when we get a row back. Whether the password parameter matches the password from the database determines whether the user is successfully authenticated or the status is set to hint.

The outcome of the password comparison determines what information we actually store in our m_hashElements instance variable and the Status of the Account. This means there are three possibilities we must handle:

1. no records returned from the query;
2. record returned with a different password; or
3. record returned with a matching password.

First, if the query returns no records, either the user does not have an account or the username was incorrectly typed. In either case, we will throw an AccountException to interrupt the normal logic flow. In situations such as these, exceptions can improve the readability of the Java code because they interrupt the logical flow. In other words, the exceptions can be used to separate "the way it normally works" from all the "other situations." Usually, these "other situations" clutter code and hide the intentions of the code. We will look at the AccountException object once we are finished with the authenticate method.

In the second case, we will receive a row back from the database but the password provided is different from what's stored with the record. In this case, we store two columns from the ResultSet, UserName and Challenge, in our instance variable m_hashElements to update the status to CHALLENGE. You will soon see that the storeColumn method simply abstracts this process by ensuring that only nonnull columns are inserted into the Hashtable object.

In the third case, the user matched the username with the password in the database, so we will store all of the properties as elements in our m_hashElements instance variable and update the status to AUTHENTICATED. Inside the storeColumn method, shown in Example 5.17, we retrieve the value of a column by passing the name of the column to the getString method of the ResultSet object. There are other methods for accessing different data types; however, in our case we merely need to use the getString because the XML document will not be able to interpret the difference. As long as the value of the column is not null, we insert the value into the m_hashElements using the name of the column as the key.

Example 5.17 Account.storeColumn method

```
private void storeColumn( ResultSet rs, String strColName)
  throws SQLException
{
  String strValue = rs.getString( strColName );
  if (strValue != null)
    m_hashElements.put( strColName, strValue );
}
```

Before we get too involved in the rest of the Account class we will look at the AccountException. This exception class extends java.lang.Exception so the client code must catch this exception explicitly, whenever the authenticate method is called. For the most part, this object simply groups all of the different kinds of error messages that can occur in the Account object. As with the other exception classes we have implemented, the coding is rather trivial. This is shown in Example 5.18.

Example 5.18 AccountException.java

```
public class AccountException extends Exception
{
  public static final int TYPE_GENERAL          = 0;
  public static final int TYPE_DUPLICATEACCOUNT = 1;
  public static final int TYPE_INVALIDUSERNAME  = 2;
  public static final int TYPE_INVALIDPASSWORD  = 3;
  public static final int TYPE_MISSING_PARAM    = 4;

  public int m_nType = 0;

  public AccountException( int nType, String message )
  {
    super(message);
    m_nType = nType;
  }
  public int getType()
  {
    return m_nType;
  }
}
```

Finally, whenever we work with the JDBC classes we must handle the `java.sql.SQLException`. As we have used the `PreparedStatement` to set the parameter values, it is highly unlikely that our query would generate this exception. This exception is more likely to be generated because of a connection or change in the database. It would not make sense to attempt to resolve these types of exceptions because we did not allocate the connection. Instead, we will pass the exception up the call stack so that the client can catch and handle the exception.

5.6.1.3 *Create Method*

Now that we have written the authentication method, we have no records in the database to make sure that it works! Before you start thinking we are on a snipe hunt, think about what the `create` method should accomplish. Of course, a new record should be added to the customer table—but what about the status of the account? Usually, when you register yourself at a website, your automatically logged in. Because we have already implemented the authenticate method, we can now call it after successfully creating a new customer account.

There are a number of little things that will be required for the `create` method to function properly. Although they are straightforward, they will be tedious. For starters, a few more things can go wrong when inserting or updating a database. First, we need to make certain that a record with the same username does not already exist in the database. If there is an existing record, we will have to throw an exception because we can not create a duplicate record. In addition, we will also throw an exception if any of the parameters required to populate the customer table were not passed to the method (see Section 5.5, *PDA Database Overview* for more information). If we manage to get past all of these exceptions, we can insert the row in the database and call the `authenticate` method to update the `status` and `m_hashElements` accordingly.

We used a `Hashtable` object to store the properties of an account because we wanted to make it easy to add new properties to this class in the future. It does little good to go against the grain now so we will use another `Hashtable` to pass the parameters required for creating the account. This will make adding future properties much easier. There will be a lot of tedious work involved so we will make use of some helper methods to reduce the amount of code we must write.

For starters, we will make a new `create` method that makes a reference to a `Connection` and a reference to a `Hashtable` containing the properties of the account to be created. As we will be working with the database again, this method will need to throw the `SQLException`. Furthermore, we can also throw an `AccountException` if there is a business rule violation. This is shown in Example 5.19.

Example 5.19 Account.create Method

```
private static final String SQL_CREATE_CUSTOMER   = "INSERT INTO Customer
(IsEnabled, FirstName, LastName, MiddleInitial, Address1, Address2, City,
State, Zip, PhoneNumber, FaxNumber, UserName, Password, Challenge ) VALUES
(1, ?, ?, ?, ?, ?, ?, ?, ?, ?, ?, ?, ?, ?)";

public synchronized void create( Connection conn, Hashtable tblProperties
)
  throws SQLException, AccountException
{
  String strUsername = getRequired( tblProperties, USER_NAME);
  String strPassword = getRequired( tblProperties, PASSWORD );
  String strConfirm  = getRequired( tblProperties, CONFIRM_PASSWORD );

  if (!strPassword.equalsIgnoreCase(strConfirm ) || strPass-
word.length()==0)
    throw new AccountException( AccountException.TYPE_INVALIDPASSWORD,
"Passwords don't match.");

  if( isDuplicateAccount(conn, strUsername) )
    throw new AccountException( AccountException.TYPE_DUPLICATEACCOUNT,
"Account already exists." );

  int nParam = 0;
  PreparedStatement stmt = conn.prepareStatement( SQL_CREATE_CUSTOMER );
  BindHashString( stmt, ++nParam, true,  tblProperties, FIRST_NAME );
  BindHashString( stmt, ++nParam, true,  tblProperties, LAST_NAME );
  BindHashString( stmt, ++nParam, false, tblProperties, MIDDLE_INITIAL);
  BindHashString( stmt, ++nParam, true,  tblProperties, ADDRESS_LINE1);
  BindHashString( stmt, ++nParam, false, tblProperties, ADDRESS_LINE2);
  BindHashString( stmt, ++nParam, true,  tblProperties, ADDRESS_CITY);
  BindHashString( stmt, ++nParam, true,  tblProperties, ADDRESS_STATE);
  BindHashString( stmt, ++nParam, true,  tblProperties, ADDRESS_ZIP);
  BindHashString( stmt, ++nParam, true,  tblProperties, PHONE_NUMBER);
```

```
  BindHashString( stmt, ++nParam, false, tblProperties, FAX_NUMBER);
  BindHashString( stmt, ++nParam, true,  tblProperties, USER_NAME);
  BindHashString( stmt, ++nParam, true,  tblProperties, PASSWORD);
  BindHashString( stmt, ++nParam, true,  tblProperties, CHALLENGE);

  if (stmt != null && stmt.executeUpdate() == 1)
  {
    m_hashElements = tblProperties;
    m_strStatus = AUTHENTICATED;
  }
  stmt.close();
}
```

The first thing we must do is to extract the username, password, and confirmation password from the hashtable (`tblProperties`). If any of these parameters were not passed, we need to generate an `AccountException` of type `TYPE_MISSING_PARAM`. To accomplish this we will create a new method, `getRequired`, to encapsulate this processing. As you can see from Example 5.20, the `getRequired` method simply returns a `String` containing the value of the key parameter or it throws an `AccountException`.

Example 5.20 Account.getRequired method

```
private static String getRequired(Hashtable hash, String key)
  throws AccountException
{
  String strValue = (String) hash.get(key);
  if (strValue == null)
    throw new AccountException(AccountException.TYPE_MISSING_PARAM, "Miss-
ing " + key );
  return strValue;
}
```

After we have successfully retrieved the three required parameters, we need to perform two business rules to validate their contents. First, we need to check to see if the user entered a password and that they retyped it correctly for the confirmation. If the password does not match the confirmation password or the password is an empty string (zero length), we throw an `AccountException` with a type of `TYPE_INVALIDPASSWORD`.

The second business rule checks to see if there is already an account with the same username in the database. To do this we will construct a query that counts the number of records that have the same username parameter, as shown in Example 5.21. As this rule is a little more involved that the first rule, a separate method, `isDuplicateAccount`, was created to handle this rule. If the count that is returned from the query is greater than zero, we know if we try to create another account it will be a duplicate so we throw an `AccountException` with a type of `TYPE_DUPLICATEACCOUNT`.

We have implemented the `isDuplicateAccount` in a pessimistic fashion. The first line in the method sets the return value of the method to `true` to indicate that there is an existing account for the given username. Next, we construct a new `PreparedStatement` similar to the `authenticate` method except that we used the `SQL_DUPLICATE_CHECK` query. After executing the query, we set the return value to `false` only if the resulting column is set to zero, which indicates that there are no other accounts with the username. In contrast to the authenticate method's query, we used the `getInt` to retrieve the column value because it is a number.

Example 5.21 Account.IsDuplicateAccount Method

```
private static final String SQL_DUPLICATE_CHECK = "SELECT COUNT(*) FROM
Customer WHERE UserName = ?";

protected boolean isDuplicateAccount(Connection conn, String strUsername)
  throws SQLException
{
  boolean bReturnValue = true;

  PreparedStatement stmt = conn.prepareStatement( SQL_DUPLICATE_CHECK );
  stmt.setString( 1, strUsername );
  ResultSet rsCount = stmt.executeQuery();

  if (rsCount.next() == true && rsCount.getInt(1) == 0)
    bReturnValue = false;

  rsCount.close();
  stmt.close();

  return bReturnValue;
}
```

Once the initial checks have been done, we are ready to start building the SQL statement that will actually insert a new row in the Customer table.

Here we use another PreparedStatement object, as we did in the authenticate method. As we have a number of parameters to bind to the PreparedStatement, we will encapsulate most of this code in a private method BindHashString, found in Example 5.22. This function will primarily extract the parameter values from the Hashtable and insert them into the PreparedStatement object. Likewise, we set the parameter to null when the Hashtable does not contain a valid parameter value for the given hash key. In addition, we implement the business rules for checking for the necessary parameters by passing a boolean value indicating if the parameter is required or not.

Example 5.22 BindHashString Method

```
private void BindHashString(PreparedStatement stmt, int nParam,
                         boolean bRequired, Hashtable tbl, String strKey )
  throws MissingParameterException, SQLException
{
  String strValue = (String) tbl.get(strKey);
  if (strValue != null)
    stmt.setString( nParam, strValue );
  else if (bRequired != true)
    stmt.setNull( nParam, Types.VARCHAR );
  else
    throw new MissingParameterException( strKey );
}
```

This is the real workhorse of the create method. The purpose of this method is to take a parameter out of the Hashtable, using strKey as the hash key, and bind it to the statement by calling the setString method of the PreparedStatement object. The nParam parameter is used to indicate to which parameter (in the SQL query) we bind the value. Finally, the bRequired parameter is used to indicate what to do when the Hashtable does not contain a value associated with the hash key. Passing a value of false for bRequired indicates we should set the parameter to null, whereas true indicates we should throw an AccountException (TYPE_MISSING_PARAM) if the parameter was not in the Hashtable.

After all of the parameters are bound to the PreparedStatement, we insert the record into the database by calling the executeUpdate method. This method is different from the typical execute method because it does not return a ResultSet object. Instead, the executeUpdate method returns the number of records affected by the query. As long as the database reports that one record was inserted, which should always be the case, we simply reassign the m_hashProperties instance variable with the tblProperties Hashtable passed to the method.

This is for the business rules that pertain to the Account object. Now all we need to do is implement an intuitive way to retrieve our internal element and we are finished. This means we need to provide a mechanism to create the XML markup logical structure with the appropriate data values. Since DOM Nodes are always created in the context of an owning document, it is necessary to access this document in order to create the Account elements and append the document to another node.

To accomplish this we will create a new appendTo method that requires an Element parameter. This parameter will be used to determine the owning document and append the element. Although we could derive the owning document with merely a reference to a node, not all nodes can contain children elements. Because we are appending children to this Node, we have required a reference to an element to insure that we can successfully append our children elements. As you can see from Example 5.23, we used the getOwner convenience method from the DOMManager to retrieve the Document interface. Once the owning document has been retrieved, we can start creating the elements that represent the account and all of its properties.

Example 5.23 Account.appendTo

```
public synchronized void appendTo(Element parent )
{
  Document doc = DOMManager.getOwner(parent);
  Element eAccount = doc.createElement( ACCOUNT_TYPE );
  eAccount.setAttribute(ATTRIB_STATUS, getStatus() );
  eAccount.setAt-
tribute(CUSTOMER_ID,(String)m_hashElements.get(CUSTOMER_ID));

  eAccount.appendChild( DOMManager.createElement( doc, ADDRESS_LINE1,
(String) m_hashElements.get(ADDRESS_LINE1)));
  eAccount.appendChild( DOMManager.createElement( doc, ADDRESS_LINE2,
(String) m_hashElements.get(ADDRESS_LINE2)));
  eAccount.appendChild( DOMManager.createElement( doc, FIRST_NAME,
(String) m_hashElements.get(FIRST_NAME)));
```

```
  eAccount.appendChild( DOMManager.createElement( doc, MIDDLE_INITIAL,
(String) m_hashElements.get(MIDDLE_INITIAL)));
  eAccount.appendChild( DOMManager.createElement( doc, LAST_NAME,
(String) m_hashElements.get(LAST_NAME)));
  eAccount.appendChild( DOMManager.createElement( doc, ADDRESS_CITY,
(String) m_hashElements.get(ADDRESS_CITY)));
  eAccount.appendChild( DOMManager.createElement( doc, ADDRESS_STATE,
(String) m_hashElements.get(ADDRESS_STATE)));
  eAccount.appendChild( DOMManager.createElement( doc, ADDRESS_ZIP,
(String) m_hashElements.get(ADDRESS_ZIP)));
  eAccount.appendChild( DOMManager.createElement( doc, PHONE_NUMBER,
(String) m_hashElements.get(PHONE_NUMBER)));
  eAccount.appendChild( DOMManager.createElement( doc, FAX_NUMBER,
(String) m_hashElements.get(FAX_NUMBER)));
  parent.appendChild(eAccount);
}
```

To create the `Account` element, we call the `createElement` method of the `Document` Interface. In doing so, we pass the `ACCOUNT_TYPE` as the element type name. Once the `Account` element has been created, we can set the attributes for the element by calling the `setAttribute` method of the element interface. This method takes two parameters. As you might have guessed, the first parameter represents the name of the attribute and the second represents the value for the attribute.

The only thing left is to create the child elements of the `Account`. To do so, we first use the other convenience method of the `DOMManager` class, `createElement`. If you remember, this method enables us to create an element node with a child text node with one (rather lengthy) line of code. As the `DOMManager.createElement` method handles the possibility of nulls in the values, we do not need to worry about them in this method. Once each element is created, we simply call the `appendChild` method to append the `Element` created from the `DOMManager`.

Finally, once all of the account properties have been appended to the `Account` element, we simply append the whole `Account` element to the parent node that was originally passed to the method.

The `Account` class is now complete. If you did not type in all of the source code, you can find it in the `Account.java` file on the companion CD-ROM in the *chptr5\src* subdirectory. Make sure you have this file or the one you have been creating along with the examples saved in your project directory because we are going to take the code we have written so far for a test drive!

5.6.1.4 Testing the Account class

We first should make sure our Java compiler likes the code we have written, so if you have not done so already, fire up the Java compiler and work out the compilation issues now. If the compiler can not find some of the new classes we have been working with it is probably because we have forgotten to add the packages to our classpath. Once the code successfully compiles, we can unit test the code.

As the code we have written so far does not address any of the application functionality, testing may seem a little odd at this point. In actuality, the best time to start unit testing business objects, such as the `Account` object, is before it is integrated with the application functionality. This is the perfect time to catch bugs in the logic because we are in full control of the testing environment and the component is in its simplest state. In other words, there is not a lot of other code that may also have bugs that will increase your debugging and testing time. The downside, however, is we can not use all of that other, potentially buggy, code that was suppose to create our object and invoke its methods. Instead, we will have to create another small class we can use for testing.

It is not necessary to complicate things. We simply need to shift our mind set from providing functionality and business rules to trying anything you can thing of to break the implemented code! To do this, we need to provide an environment that the `Account` object expects. In particular, we need to set the `DOMFactory` and `DOMWriter` implementations and write the JDBC code necessary to connect to our PDA database. Once this is completed, we can create an instance of the `Account` object and call the public methods using various combinations and parameters. A sample testing class is shown in Example 5.24.

Example 5.24 TestAccount.java

```
import com.ctp.dom.*;
import Account;
import org.w3c.dom.*;
import java.sql.*;
import java.io.*;
```

```
public class TestAccount
{
public static void main( String strArg[] )
  throws Exception
{
  DOMManager.setFactory("IBMDOMFactory");
  DOMManager.setWriter("IBMDOMWriter");

  scenario( "Invalid Login", new Account(), "Invalid", "Account" );
  scenario( "NULL UserName", new Account(), null, "Account" );
  scenario( "NULL Password", new Account(), "bweber", null );

  Account acct = new Account();
  scenario( "Valid Login", new Account(), "bweber", "bammbamm" );
  scenario( "Already Logged in", new Account(), "bweber", "bammbamm" );
  scenario( "Already Logged in", new Account(), "bweber", "false" );

}

public static void scenario( String strHeader, Account acct, String
strUser, String strPwd )
{
  System.out.println( strHeader );
  try
  {
    Class.forName("sun.jdbc.odbc.JdbcOdbcDriver");
    Connection conn = DriverManager.getConnection( "jdbc:odbc:XMLBook" );
    long lStart = System.currentTimeMillis();
    System.out.println( acct.authenticate( conn, strUser, strPwd ));
    long lTime = System.currentTimeMillis() - lStart;
    Document doc = DOMManager.getFactory().createDocument("1.0");
    Element root = doc.createElement("root");
    doc.appendChild(root);
    acct.appendTo( root );
    doc.appendChild( doc.createComment("Total processing time: " + lTime +
"ms."));
    DOMManager.getWriter().writeDocument( doc, new PrintWriter( System.out
));
  }
  catch ( Exception e )
  {
    System.out.println( e.toString() );
  }
}
}
```

As you can see from the example, we did not get elaborate with the implementation. We simply created a new class and implemented all of the testing code in the main method. Furthermore, we used hard-coded values for all of the resources, such as the `DOMFactory`, `DOMWriter`, and parameters for JDBC that the `Account` object will require. We created a scenario method that allowed us to parameterize the relevant values to facilitate testing. This allows us to invoke the `authenticate` method in many different ways to test all possible combinations. We simply catch all types of exceptions and write them to `System.out`. Finally, if everything is successful, we add the `Element` from the account to a document and attempt to write it to `System.out`.

To perform a given test, we can simply add new calls to the scenario for the different parameter values you want to test. Then we simply recompile the code and run it. Spending a little time at this stage can reduce drastically the amount of time it takes to perform full system testing. This is because you will have encountered and resolved many of the bugs in an environment that is suited for your needs. Finally, keep this testing stub because if you ever make changes to the `Account` class you can reuse this as a starting point for regression testing.

This technique puts us in the shoes of the client developer who will have to use our objects. Of course, the key to this is keeping our objects simple and testing them thoroughly before application/system integration. We would spend too much time writing classes if our business objects are too complex. Furthermore, the complexity of locating problems through multiple layers of code is drastically increased. As you can see from the example, it is not necessary to be overly elaborate with the testing class. More complex or detailed testing could warrant a more elegant testing class but the only goal here is to show the concepts.

5.6.2 Catalog class

The `Catalog` class will be very similar to the `Account` class. Instead of creating and authenticating customers, though, we will focus on retrieving the products from the database and having them ready when the customers want to shop for our electronic toys! Unlike the `Account` object, a new instance of the `Catalog` object will not be created for each user. Think of the `Catalog` object as a shopping center. Shoppers are free to choose the product they want. If two shoppers pick up the same gadget, well, they have to fight over it! But we will avoid the virtual reality boxing match and take a less violent approach. The `Catalog` class will need to be implemented in a thread-safe manner so that the instance variables are not corrupted when multiple threads are manipulating them.

As the `Catalog` class will be servicing all of the clients browsing our site, its lifetime will also differ from the `Account` object. Although this is an implementation detail of the servlet code, it does drive certain design decisions regarding how we interact with the `Catalog` class. For the most part, the `Catalog` class needs to have the products ready for the customers when the store opens (i.e. the servlet starts accepting requests). Furthermore, we will reduce the number of database queries to retrieve the products by caching them within the internal structure of the `Catalog` class. In doing so, we need to provide a mechanism that the application layer code can use to refresh the cached products.

To simplify, we will delegate a fair amount of logic to a `Product` class that will manage each product in the catalog. Internally, the `Product` class will store the properties that describe the product.

For efficiency, we will cache the catalog to reduce the number of queries to the database. Keep in mind that this may not be realistic for large catalogs. Furthermore, caching in general can be problematic because the data is stored in memory; it is lost when a server crashes. A server crash will take the entire site offline. In our case, this approach is the most efficient because the products will rarely be changing in the database. Once the catalog is instantiated, we will need to provide mechanisms to retrieve all of the products or, in the case of a shopping basket, a specific product that can be used to validate and add products to a shopping basket.

To start, we need to create a new `Catalog.java` file to store the source code. Furthermore, we can add imports for the JDBC and DOM objects, as well as some utility classes as shown in Example 5.25. We have used the wildcard (*) on the imports for brevity.

In addition, we have defined a constant for the element type we will need when we convert the catalog to markup and a SQL statement that will be used to retrieve the products in the catalog. Unlike the previous prepared SQL queries, this one does not require any parameters because it will return all of the products from the database. Finally, the heart of the `Catalog` class is a `Hashtable` that we will use to manage all of the products in the catalog. A hash table works very well in this case because it provides a very fast keyed mechanism to look up a specific product. This will provide a very efficient mechanism for looking up products when they added to the shopping basket.

Example 5.25 Catalog.java

```
import java.sql.*;
import org.w3c.dom.*;
import com.ctp.dom.DOMManager;
import java.util.*;

public class Catalog
{
  public static final String  CATALOG_TYPE = "catalog";
  private final String CATALOG_QUERY = "SELECT * FROM catalog p, Manufac-
turer m, Category c WHERE p.MfgID = m.MfgID AND p.CategoryID = c.CategoryID
ORDER BY ProductID";

  private Hashtable           m_tblProducts = new Hashtable();

public Catalog(Connection Conn)
  throws SQLException
{
  refreshCatalog(Conn);
}
}
```

5.6.2.1 Creating the Catalog

Because the products must be available once the `Catalog` object is created, we need to retrieve the products before the constructor finishes. Sticking with the approach we took with the `Account` business object, a database connection must be passed to the constructor of the `Catalog` class. This will maintain control of the limited resources at the application level. Once inside the constructor code, we will create a `refreshCatalog` method and call it from within the constructor of the Catalog class. In doing so, we will also make this method public so that the catalog can be refreshed after it has been created. This is shown in Example 5.26.

Example 5.26 Catalog constructor

```
public Catalog(Connection Conn)
  throws SQLException
{
  refreshCatalog(Conn);
}
```

The refreshCatalog method is primarily responsible for querying the database for the products and storing them within the m_tblProducts Hashtable. In doing so, it will need to allocate a new Product object for each row in the ResultSet of the query. We will get to the Product class shortly, but for now the refreshCatalog method is shown in Example 5.27.

Example 5.27 refreshCatalog Method

```
public synchronized void refreshCatalog( Connection conn )
  throws SQLException
{
  m_tblProducts.clear();
  Statement stmt    = conn.createStatement();
  ResultSet rs      = stmt.executeQuery( CATALOG_QUERY );

  while ( rs.next() )
  {
    Product product = new Product( rs );
    m_tblProducts.put( product.getID(), product );
  }

  rs.close();
  stmt.close();
}
```

As we have done with the Account class, we define the refreshCatalog method as synchronized to provide mutually exclusive access. To implement the method, we simply call the clear method of our instance Hashtable variable to remove any products currently in the catalog. Although there will not be any products in the object initially, this is being done in case the refreshCatalog method is called after the object has been instantiated.

Now that the m_tblProducts variable has been reinitialized, we query the database using a Statement object. Calling the createStatement method of the Connection object does this. We did not need to use a PreparedStatement because there are no parameters to this query. Once the Statement object is created, the executeQuery method is used to query the database and return a ResultSet object containing the results of the query. In our case, this query returns a list of products contained within the catalog.

The real work of this function is nestled into the while loop. For each row in the ResultSet, we must create a new Product object and insert it into the m_tblProducts hashtable. We use the next method to iterate through the ResultSet. This method returns true if a record was successfully fetched, otherwise it returns false. Upon successfully fetching a row from the database, we will pass the ResultSet reference to the constructor of the Product class. This will allow the Product class to extract the properties that describe the product. Once the product constructor returns, we simply store the product in the Hashtable. Furthermore, we insert each product into the hashtable using its unique identifier (ID) as the key. This will allow for fast and efficient lookups when we start implementing the shopping basket. We will convert the Product class when we are finished with the catalog.

5.6.2.2 Searching the catalog

Now that we have populated the m_tblProducts instance variable, we need to provide a mechanism to look up a given product. The ShoppingBasket will need this to determine if a given product is valid. As we have keyed the products in the hashtable by ID, this becomes very simple. Example 5.28 show how to provide a new method to find the product.

Example 5.28 Catalog.findProduct method

```
private Product findProduct( String strProductID )
{
  return (Product) m_tblProducts.get(strProductID);
}
```

As you can see from the example, this code is relatively trivial. Searching for something is not only easy, but also very efficient within a Hashtable (As long as you are searching by the Key value). By passing in the key of the table, we simply pass the product ID to the get method of the Hashtable. If the Hashtable contains a matching object for the key a reference to the object is returned; otherwise, null is returned.

We could use this as a mechanism for determining if a product is valid; however, we are creating a potential security risk by handing out a direct reference to one of the products in the catalog. Instead, we have made this method private and we will use a separate method to access it. To keep the product reference internal to the Catalog class, we provide another method that merely returns a Boolean true or false to indicate if a given product exists in the catalog. This is shown in Example 5.29.

Example 5.29 Catalog.isValidProduct method

```
public boolean isValidProduct( String strProductID )
{
  return (findProduct(strProductID) != null) ? true : false;
}
```

The isValidProduct method is also relatively trivial. We simply encapsulate the call to findProduct. If the value returned from find product is nonnull, we return true to indicate there is a product in the catalog with the same product ID. As this is the only public access method for looking up products, we have successfully encapsulated the Product within the Catalog. While this may seem like a minor issue now, however, in multithreaded environments with multiple programmers hacking away this can be a lifesaver!

5.6.2.3 Generating the XML Catalog Element

The last thing to do is create the logic required to output XML markup for the catalog. Ultimately, the catalog will have limited responsibility for this because most of the content is encapsulated in the Product objects. The catalog is essentially a specialized wrapper, or collection of these products.

Because the catalog is merely a business object participating in a given application, it can potentially only be part of a larger XML document. Thus, we need access to the node to which we are expected to append the Catalog element. With the parent node, we have access to the owner document, so are be able to create the various nodes that constitute the catalog.

A new appendTo method will be created that is identical to the one we created for the Account class, which requires a reference to the parent Element. We will use this to element determine the owning document and insert our children. Once the owning document has been determined, we can create a shell catalog element. The details of describing the Product are delegated to the Product class, which we will cover very shortly. For now, we simply iterate through each of the products in the m_tblProducts Hashtable and instruct the Product class to generate the XML markup and append it to the Catalog element. This is shown in Example 5.30.

Example 5.30 Catalog.appendTo method

```
public void appendTo(Element parent )
{
  Document doc = DOMManager.getOwner( parent );

  Element catalog = doc.createElement( CATALOG_TYPE );
  for(Enumeration enum = m_tblProducts.elements(); enum.hasMoreEle-
ments();)
  {
    Product product = (Product) enum.nextElement();
    product.appendTo( catalog );
  }

  parent.appendChild( catalog );
}
```

From the example, we used the getOwner method from the DOMManager class to determine the document owner. With the Document reference, we simply call the createElement method. So far, this is very similar to the Account classes appendTo method.

Next, we retrieve an Enumeration of the objects within our m_tblProducts hashtable. With the Enumeration, we can iterate through each of the objects contained in the hashtable. The iteration continues until the Enumeration.hasMoreElements method returns false. If the method returns true, we call the Enumeration.nextElement to return a reference to the object. Since the Enumeration only returns references to an object, we have to typecast the reference to a Product class. Finally, we pass the newly created catalog Element to the appendTo method of the Product class. Just as if the application delegated the responsibility of appending the whole catalog element to the document, we will have delegated the details to the `Product` class.

Finally, when all of the products have been appended to the `Catalog` element, we append the `Catalog` element, with all of its product children elements, to the parent element that was originally passed to the method.

5.6.3 Product Class

Before we can say the catalog is complete, we have a fair amount of coding to complete the `Product` class. For the most part, the `Product` class is primarily a complex data structure that we can use to store all of the properties that describe a product. In doing so, it allows us to group all of the attributes into a single reference that can be added to a hashtable or other form of grouping object.

We can start by creating a new file, named `Product.java`, and add imports for JDBC, DOM, and our `DOMManager`. Before we get into coding the logic behind the `Product` class, we will cover the data properties that will be stored within the class as well as the element types that will be used when the class is output as XML elements. This is shown in Example 5.31.

Example 5.31 Product class

```
import com.ctp.dom.DOMManager;
import java.sql.ResultSet;
import java.sql.SQLException;
import org.w3c.dom.Document;
import org.w3c.dom.Element;
import org.w3c.dom.Node;

public class Product
{
  public static final String  PRODUCT           = "Product";
  public static final String  PRODUCT_ID        = "ProductID";

  public static final String  LIST_PRICE        = "ListPrice";
  public static final String  QUANTITY          = "Quantity";
  public static final String  NAME              = "Name";
  public static final String  DESCRIPTION       = "Description";
```

```
    public static final String  MFG_NAME          = "MfgName";
    public static final String  CATEGORY_NAME     = "CategoryName";
    public static final String  MFG_IMAGE_URL     = "MfgImageURL";
    public static final String  PRODUCT_IMAGE_URL = "ImageURL";

    private String  m_strID           = null;
    private String  m_strName         = null;
    private String  m_strDescription  = null;
    private String  m_strCategory     = null;
    private String  m_strManufacturer = null;
    private String  m_strImageURL     = null;
    private String  m_strMfgImageURL  = null;
    private int     m_nQuantity       = 0;
    private float   m_nListPrice      = 0;
}
```

First, we define the Element Type names and attribute names we use in describing a "Product" element in XML. Remember, this is very important in order to avoid case-sensitivity issues. We use static constant (`final`) variables because these values will not be changing. In an effort to making the overall system easier to understand, we decided to use the same database column names for the names of the elements in the XML elements. This means we will use the static variables when we extract column values from the database. The last group of declarations indicates all of the instance variables or properties of the product to be stored within the `Product` class instance.

5.6.3.1 *Instantiating a Product object*

We have already seen how the client code, in this case the `Catalog` object, will need to instantiate the `Product` class. It will be looping through a `ResultSet` from the database. For each record in the `ResultSet`, the `Catalog` class will create a new `Product` class and pass the `ResultSet` reference to the constructor. In doing so, the `Catalog` class is expecting the `Product` class to extract the relevant columns from the query and populate the properties of each product.

To accommodate this expectation, we must provide a constructor that requires a `ResultSet` as a parameter. Moreover, we also will declare that the constructor can throw an `SQLException` if the `ResultSet` does not contain the columns we are expecting. There is not much the `Product` class can do about this except inform the `Catalog` that it messed up the query!

As the Catalog will be responsible for looping through each row in the ResultSet, the only thing the Product constructor must do is extract the column values from the ResultSet. This is accomplished by passing the column name to one of the various getXXX methods of the ResultSet object. As you can see from Example 5.32, we have used the getString, getFloat, and getInt methods to extract the appropriately typed data values.

Example 5.32 Product constructor

```
Product( ResultSet rs ) throws SQLException
{
  m_strID             = rs.getString(PRODUCT_ID);
  m_strName           = rs.getString(NAME);
  m_strDescription    = rs.getString(DESCRIPTION);
  m_nListPrice        = rs.getFloat(LIST_PRICE);
  m_nQuantity         = rs.getInt(QUANTITY);
  m_strManufacturer = rs.getString(MFG_NAME);
  m_strCategory       = rs.getString(CATEGORY_NAME);
  m_strMfgImageURL    = rs.getString(MFG_IMAGE_URL);
  m_strImageURL       = rs.getString(PRODUCT_IMAGE_URL);
}
```

After extracting all of the properties from the database ResultSet, the Product class can accurately represent a single product within the catalog. Referring back to Example 5.27, the last thing the Catalog class needs is a way to access the Product ID so that it can be used as a key for inserting the Product in the Hashtable. More specifically, we implemented the Catalog class to call the getID method of a Product class to retrieve this value.

As shown in Example 5.33, this is merely a matter of providing an accessor method that simply returns a reference to the m_strID instance variable.

Example 5.33 Product.getID method

```
public String getID()
{
  return m_strID;
}
```

5.6.3.2 Generating the Product Element XML Markup

At this point, generating the various DOM Nodes to describe a data structure should start to become relatively easy. Staying consistent with the previous objects, we simply provide another appendTo method that requires a reference to an element. As before, we will use this element to append the Product data Element and its children. More importantly, however, we use the element to determine the owning document so that we can create the nodes that describe the products in the context of that owning document. This is shown in Example 5.34.

Example 5.34 Product.appendTo method

```
public void appendTo(Element parent )
{
  Document doc = DOMManager.getOwner(parent);

  Element product = doc.createElement(PRODUCT);
  product.setAttribute(PRODUCT_ID, m_strID );

  product.appendChild( DOMManager.createElement( doc, NAME, m_strName ));
  product.appendChild( DOMManager.createElement( doc, DESCRIPTION,
m_strDescription));
  product.appendChild( DOMManager.createElement( doc, LIST_PRICE,
Float.toString(m_nListPrice)));
  product.appendChild( DOMManager.createElement( doc, QUANTITY, Inte-
ger.toString(m_nQuantity)));
  product.appendChild( DOMManager.createElement( doc, MFG_NAME,
m_strManufacturer));
  product.appendChild( DOMManager.createElement( doc, CATEGORY_NAME,
m_strCategory));
  product.appendChild( DOMManager.createElement( doc, MFG_IMAGE_URL,
m_strMfgImageURL));
  product.appendChild( DOMManager.createElement( doc, PRODUCT_IMAGE_URL,
m_strImageURL));

  parent.appendChild( product );
}
```

To start the method, we pass the parent Element reference to the DOMManager.getOwner method to retrieve a reference to the owning Document. Next, we simply create our Product Element, using the previously defined PRODUCT constant, and add the PRODUCT_ID attribute by calling the setAttribute method.

For the remaining properties of the product, we will create Elements as children to the Product Element. We use the DOMManager.createElement method passing a reference to the (owning) `Document` and two Strings indicating the type of element and its associated text value. The `DOMManager` takes over and does a little bit of grunge work, and voila, the element is created. This returns a reference to the element, which is immediately passed to the `appendChild` method of the `Product` element. Although it is tedious and wordy, it is relatively trivial. Finally, the `Product` element is appended to the parent element that was originally passed to the method.

> **NOTE:** The XML recommendation does not contain concepts of data types. As such, all attributes are defined as strings so that they can contain alphanumeric character sequences. To support this, the DOM API uses String variables as the parameter data types. This means that we have to convert our numeric (integer) value to a string before assigning it to a node value.

This is all we need to do for the `Catalog` class! Again, if you did not type in the code while following along through the examples, you can find the complete source code for `Catalog.java` on the companion CD-ROM in the chptr5\src sub directory. Fire up your Java compiler and apply the techniques we discussed when we covered the `Account` class for testing the `Catalog` class.

5.6.4 ShoppingBasket class

The last thing we need to create is an object that can manage the products a customer wishes to buy. We saved this class for last because it must interact with the `Catalog` class in order to validate products, check pricing, etc. This class is very similar to the shopping basket you push around when you are grocery shopping. As you walk down the isle, you grab a couple of six packs of Mountain Dew and put them in your basket. When you finish shopping, you push your basket to the cashier and wait (and wait…) to be checked out. After the cashier calculates how much everything will cost, you suddenly realize that you do not have enough money for all of the items you placed in your basket. Embarrassed, you ask the cashier to remove one of the six packs so you can pay for the products and quickly escape the snickers and laughs from the rest of the people standing in line behind you. (So, maybe that only happens to me!)

I hope that your experiences are not as bad as that but the concept should be clear. Because the Internet does not provide shopping cars, we need to create a mechanism to add a product, remove a product, and change the quantity of products in the basket. Also we need to integrate with the `Catalog` class to ensure the products we add to the baskets are actually products in the Catalog. Similar to the account class, each user of the website will need their own instance of the shopping basket.

The `ShoppingBasket` class will provide a mechanism of associating products with a specific user who selected them. Furthermore, it needs to provide a count of the number of products the user has selected. As this class only needs to interact with the `Catalog` class, there is no need for accessing the database. We start by creating a new file, named `ShoppingBasket.java`, and identifying the final declarations that will describe the basket in XML markup as well as identifying the various instance variables we will use to manage the object's functionality. This is shown in Example 5.35.

Example 5.35 ShoppingBasket class

```
import java.util.Hashtable;
import java.util.Enumeration;

import javax.servlet.GenericServlet;
import org.w3c.dom.Document;
import org.w3c.dom.Element;
import org.w3c.dom.Node;
import org.w3c.dom.NodeList;

public class ShoppingBasket
{
  public static final String BASKET_TYPE  = "basket";

  public static final String PRODUCT_REF  = "Product-ref";
  public static final String PRODUCT_ID   = "ProductID";
  public static final String QUANTITY     = "Quantity";

  private Catalog        m_Catalog   = null;
  private Hashtable      m_Basket    = new Hashtable();
}
```

We have defined the BASKET_TYPE final String to identify the element type when the basket is output as XML. Furthermore, we have also defined a final PRODUCT_REF to indicate how products will be identified when they're output as children to the basket. We will not use the same mechanism as the Product in this case, because we are really only describing a relationship between a user and a product. For this reason, we have created a new element type altogether, named Product-ref. Furthermore, it will only contain the ProductID and Quantity attributes, but nothing else. This means that we will need to cross reference the products in the catalog if we want to display the name or price of the product. It is not necessary to be concerned about this right now, because it is the topic of the next chapter.

For instance variables, we have included a reference to a Catalog object, and allocated a new instance of a Hashtable to store the products that are in the shopping basket. A Hashtable works well in this situation because it is relatively fast for looking up products currently in the basket. This will be needed to change the quantities or potentially even remove products from the basket. Although Hashtables require an algorithm to index the objects when they are added, this is generally also a relatively quick and efficient also.

5.6.4.1 *Instantiating the ShoppingBasket*

In the real world, you typically yank a shopping basket out when you walk into a store. This is no different. The shopping basket will only be good while you are shopping our virtual store. For this reason, we need to pass a reference to the Catalog object when the ShoppingBasket is constructed. In doing so, the basket can cache this reference to validate when products are added to the basket. Thus, only the products in the Catalog object can be added to the basket. Example 5.36 shows the constructor for the shopping basket.

Example 5.36 ShoppingBasket constructor

```
public ShoppingBasket( Catalog catalog )
{
  m_Catalog = catalog;
}
```

Because we have already initialized our m_Basket when we declared it, the only thing left for the constructor is to assign a reference to the Catalog object we have recently created. Now that we have a Catalog reference assigned and the m_Basket ready to store products, we can move on to adding, removing, and changing the quantity of the products within the ShoppingBasket object.

5.6.4.2 Adding a product to the Basket

Once the basket is created, we can start adding products to the basket. Adding a product to the basket will be rather simple. As we have already created a Hashtable to store the products that are in the basket, all we will have to do is insert the Product identifier (ID) and the quantity into the Hashtable. Thus, we can use the product ID as the key to the table, and an Integer to represent the quantity that the user would like to purchase.

Before we can add a product to the basket, however, we must first make sure that it is in the Catalog. This is no problem because we have created the isValidProduct method on the Catalog class. By passing the unique identifier for the product (product id), the isValidProduct method will either return true or false to indicate whether or not the product is in the Catalog. If the product is valid, we simply need to insert the product and quantity into our m_Basket Hashtable, as shown here:

```
if (m_Catalog.isValidProduct(strProductID))
    m_Basket.put( strProductID, new Integer(nQuantity) );
```

When adding the product to the basket, we used the Product ID as the key to looking up its associated data. In this case, the associated data is the quantity that the user has selected. Because the Hashtable stores only objects, we have to allocate an Integer object to represent the quantity of the product.

On the other hand, we do not want to add a product to the basket that is not valid. If the catalog did not contain the product (indicated by the isValidProduct returning false), we can throw an exception to indicate that the product was not valid. To signify this, we will create a new InvalidProductException class that can be thrown when the application logic attempts to add a product that is not in the Catalog object.

As with most exceptions, the InvalidProductException class will primarily be used to provide a detailed description of the error that occurred. As this is a business-rule related exception, we will force the client code to catch the exception by extending the Exception class. The code necessary to implement this class is relatively straightforward. The entire source for the InvalidProductException is shown in Example 5.37. The constructor will require a String parameter to indicate the invalid product ID. In addition, we have overridden the getMessage method of the Throwable class to provide a customized message.

Example 5.37 InvalidProductException.java

```
public class InvalidProductException extends Exception
{
  private String m_strProductID = null;

  public InvalidProductException( String ProductID )
  {
    m_strProductID = ProductID;
  }
  public String getMessage()
  {
    return "Product " + m_strProductID + " is invalid.";
  }
}
```

With just a few lines of code, we have provided the ability to add a product to the shopping basket. What happens when the product we are trying to add is already in the basket? Right now, we could replace the existing Integer value with a new Value. A more intuitive approach, at least for the users, would be to add the new quantity to the quantity that already exists for the product in the basket.

This means that we first need to search for the product within our internal m_Basket hashtable. If we find the product within the basket element, we will simply add the additional quantity to the quantity that is associated to the product ID key. Furthermore, there is no need to verify that the product is valid; we can assume it is because it is already in the basket.

Example 5.38 addProduct Method

```
public void addProduct( String strProductID, int nQuantity )
  throws InvalidProductException
{
  Integer Quantity = (Integer) m_Basket.get(strProductID);
  if (Quantity != null)
  {
    Quantity = new Integer(Quantity.intValue() + nQuantity);
    m_Basket.put( strProductID, new Integer( nQuantity ));
  }
  else if (m_Catalog.isValidProduct(strProductID))
    m_Basket.put( strProductID, new Integer(nQuantity) );
  else
    throw new InvalidProductException( strProductID );
}
```

The code to implement the `addProduct` functionality is shown in Example 5.38. First, we check to see if the product is already in the basket by passing the Product ID to the `get` method of the hashtable. If we receive a valid reference to an integer, we know that the product is in the basket so we simply create a new integer of the sum of the existing quantity in the basket with the newly added quantity. When the new quantity has been determined, we store the new integer in the `m_Basket Hashtable` by calling the `put` method with the same product ID key.

If the Product is not currently in the shopping basket, the call to `m_Basket.get` will return `null`. In this case, we must first check to see if the product is valid by calling the `isValidProduct` method of the `Catalog` object. If the product is valid, we do the same as when we found a product, however, instead of adding the quantity to what exists, we merely allocate a new `Integer` object containing the quantity to add. Finally, if the Catalog does not contain the product we throw an `InvalidProductException` we just built.

5.6.4.3 Changing quantity in the Basket

Changing the quantity of an existing product in the basket is easy now that we have created the `addProduct` method. As with most web applications, this usually encompasses removing products from the basket by setting the quantity to zero. In this context, instead of adding the quantity to what already exists, we simply need to override it with a new value. Furthermore, if the product is not in the basket, it does not make sense to search the catalog—at least in the context of changing quantity. If the product is not in the basket, we simply throw another `InvalidProductException`. The changeQuantity method is shown in Example 5.39.

Example 5.39 changeQuantity method

```
public void changeQuantity( String strProductID, int nQuantity )
  throws InvalidProductException
{
  Integer Quantity = (Integer) m_Basket.get(strProductID);

  if (Quantity != null)
  {
    if (nQuantity == 0)
      m_Basket.remove(strProductID);
    else
      m_Basket.put(strProductID, new Integer(nQuantity));
  }
  else throw new InvalidProductException( strProductID );
}
```

The first task we need to perform when changing the quantity is to look up the product in our `m_Basket` `Hashtable`. As long as a valid reference to the product ID's associated value is returned we can update the quantity. If the product is in the basket, we can update either the quantity or remove the product from the `Hashtable`, altogether. We update the quantity just the same as when we added it to the `Hashtable`. Furthermore, we use the `remove` method to remove an object (and its key) from the `Hashtable`.

Between the `addProduct` and `changeQuantity` methods, we can now support adding products, removing products (passing a zero quantity to `changeQuantity`), and explicitly changing a product's quantity. The last thing we need to implement is a mechanism for generating the XML formatted output that describes the products in the basket. Staying consistent with the previous classes we have implemented, we will provide another `appendTo` method.

Example 5.40 ShoppingBasket.appendTo method

```
public void appendTo(Element parent )
{
  Document doc = DOMManager.getOwner(parent);
  Element basket = doc.createElement( BASKET_TYPE );

  for(Enumeration e = m_Basket.keys(); e.hasMoreElements();)
  {
    String strProductID = (String) e.nextElement();
    int nQuantity = ((Integer)m_Basket.get(strProductID)).intValue();

    Element product = doc.createElement( PRODUCT_REF );
    product.setAttribute( PRODUCT_ID, strProductID );
    product.setAttribute( QUANTITY, Integer.toString(nQuantity) );

    basket.appendChild( product );
  }
  parent.appendChild(basket);
}
```

This implementation is similar to a combination of the `Catalog` and `Product appendTo` methods. In this case, we will be iterating through all of the items in the basket and creating the necessary DOM objects to represent the products in the basket.

The first few lines are the same as all of the other `appendTo` methods. We retrieve the owning document and create our container element; in this case, the type is "basket" as identified by the `BASKET_TYPE` final declaration. Next, we enumerate the list of objects in the `m_Basket Hashtable` by calling the `keys` method of the `Hashtable` object. This is different from the Catalog's implementation—where we called the `Elements` method. As the basket is using the key and its associated value, we need to create our `Enumeration` over the keys so that we can get its value as well. Once we have the key, or the product ID, we can use this to retrieve its associated quantity by calling the `Hashtable.get`.

Once we have extracted the Product ID and Quantity from the `m_Basket` object, we simply create a new DOM Element of type `PRODUCT_REF` and assign the `PRODUCT_ID` and `QUANTITY` attributes using the `setAttribute` method. Remember that the DOM considers all data as being of type String, so we need to convert the Quantity `Integer` to a `String` before assigning it as an attribute value.

This is all there is to the `ShoppingBasket` class. If you have typed in all the examples make sure they compile then give them a test spin by creating a sample testing class.

5.7 Conclusion

Although it may not seem like it, we have accomplished a great deal in this chapter. As one might say, you have to learn how to write Java code before you can read it—we have done just that, in the case for XML.

We have utilized the DOM in a way that is easy to integrate with existing java classes. You should now feel very comfortable creating and manipulating the various elements within the DOM tree.

We have created a framework that we can reuse for other XML-based applications in the future. We took precautions to reduce the impact of switching DOM implementations on application code while still being able to utilize some of the cool features of proprietary APIs. In doing so, we applied the principles of the Factory design pattern and defined a common interface (`DOMFactory`) we can implement to provide a document factory for any DOM implementation. Finally, we created a manager class (`DOMManager`) that could dynamically load these factories, simplify things by providing a few convenience methods, and reduce the amount of code required to manipulate the DOM tree.

Still not satisfied, we put our framework to the test and started implementing the business objects we plan to use for our XML-based website. We have created an `Account` class that will be used to authenticate and register new customers, a `Catalog` class that manages a list of products, and a `ShoppingBasket` class to manage the products a customer wishes to purchase. In doing so, we have gained practical experience working with the different DOM interfaces and covered topics that included multithreading and JDBC.

CHAPTER 6

Building An XML Website

Not surprisingly, the Internet has had a huge impact on many lifestyles throughout the world. Day in and day out, one thing is for sure, no spider could have ever spun a web as large as the World Wide Web (www)! And because of its tremendous size almost everyone in the world has been affected by it in some way. Moreover, success is due to its wide use and reliability and the fact that it is built on technologies that are stable yet easy to learn and use.

Hypertext Markup Language (HTML) provided an easy-to-learn markup that could create relatively interesting web pages in nearly no time at all. Of course, this would not have been possible if the Web was not running on a protocol as reliable as Hypertext Transfer Protocol (HTTP). Although very simple, HTTP provided the mechanism to request web pages from any web server on the planet (We will have to wait for a breakthrough from NASA before we jump this hurdle)! Can you imagine a day when the domain suffix would end with the planet name or a galaxy (*http://yahoo.com.earth.milkyway)*? This would give new meaning to Microsoft's slogan "Where do you want to go today?" slogan.

Move over HTML, there is a new kid in town, and her name is XML. Although HTML and HTTP have made the Web what it is today, we are going to introduce some new technologies into our website. Of course we will still support HTML, but it is merely for backwards compatibility. Using XML technologies, we can use an XSL processor to generate many different formats, such as a modified XML document, HTML, etc. Although our examples will be using an XSL processor to generate HTML, we will provide the necessary abstractions so we can send the XML directly to the browser. In this chapter we will discuss the following topics:

- Java Servlet API;
- Creating an XML-based Java Servlet Framework;
- Creating the Servlet for the website;
- XSL Transformations;
- Parsing XML Documents;
- Processing XML Documents; and
- XSL Stylesheets.

Before we begin this chapter you need to make sure that you have the following tools installed and configured correctly on your workstation.

Because we will be developing a servlet in this chapter, we first need to install the Java servlet development kit (JSDK) version 2.0. This can be downloaded from the Sun Microsystems website at http://java.sun.com. In addition, install the LotusXSL in order to install the XSL processor we will be using for the examples. You can get this at http://www.ibm.com/XML.

Next, you will need to install the Apache web server. The examples in this book have been written and tested using version 1.3 of the WIN32 (Windows NT) binaries. You can get web server at http://www.apache.org. However, make sure you follow all the instructions on how to install and configure the web server. In particular, make sure you have configured it to run as an NT Service. The installation has an icon in the start menu to do this automatically. Furthermore, make sure the web server has been configured to handle requests. You can test this by attempting to bring up the web server's default page. Assuming that you have installed Apache on your local development computer (and it is listening on port 80), open up your favorite browser and navigate to http:/ /localhost. You should see a page that indicates the web server has been installed correctly. Once you are confident the web server is configured correctly, copy the web server image files from the companion CD-ROM to the web server's document root. The root directory is typically the htdocs directory beneath the directory where you installed the Apache web server. When copying the files, make sure that the files remain in their subdirectories as they are stored on the CD-ROM.

Next, you will need to install Apache Jserv version 1.0. This is Apache Group's implementation of the servlet engine. You can get the installation for this at http://java.apache.org. After the installation has been completed and you have restarted the web server, you can test the servlet engine by navigating a browser to *http://YourServerName/jserv/* directory. This should return a page showing all of the servlet engines that are configured, and provide preferences to drill into the servlet zones.

Once the tools are installed correctly, you can continue by configuring the Java Servlet engine (Jserv) by performing the actions as described in the readme file.

6.1 *Java Servlet Specification*

The Java Servlet specification defines a platform-independent API for extending server functionality. Although servlets are similar to applets in their respective environments, they are not the same. Applets are java classes that run inside a web browser. They are subject to the rules of the "sandbox" that include strict security restrictions of the client machine. In contrast, servlets are never downloaded to the client computer. Instead, they run on the web server (although it does not have to be a web server) to perform their functionality. Often, the clients will not even know that a servlet was used to provide the web page they are viewing.

Although commonly thought of as a web server extension, Java Servlets are not limited to web servers. The Java Servlet Development Kit (JSDK) provides the `javax.servlet` package that contains two different layers to begin implementing a servlet. The most generic base layer is called a GenericServlet. This is a very generic layer (thus the name) that cannot provide much functionality because certain key technologies have not been defined. It is primarily useful for creating servlets that are based on uncommon technologies.

Servlets are more commonly implemented by extending the HttpServlet class. Extending this class assumes that the protocol between the client and the server will be HTTP. Knowing the protocol can provide a great deal of functionality. For example, the servlet provides specialized HttpRequest and HttpResponse objects that handle the parsing of the various HTTP method parameters, such as GET and POST. Because HTTP is a connectionless protocol, the HTTP layer of the Servlet API also provides session management, through the HttpSession, using cookies or URL manipulation (depending on the configuration and implementation of the servlet engine) to associate the disconnected clients with a unique session instance. Because we are building a web application we will focus on the HttpServlet.

The first form of "Intelligent" web-based applications on the Internet was known as Common Gateway Interface (CGI) programs or scripts. CGI defined a standard way a web server could communicate with an external program. This allowed logic to be performed at the web server that ultimately modified the contents of the resulting web page in the browser. Written predominately in Perl or C, these programs (in general) had performance implications because each HTTP request would initiate a new process for each request. In contrast, Java Servlets operate in the context of a Servlet Engine. Instead of creating a new process for each request, the servlet engine operates as a daemon process. Although this does add increased complexities over CGI, this enables the servlet engine to remain memory-resident waiting for a request. Although the servlet engine can unload or destroy a servlet to conserve memory, most servlet implementations attempt to keep the servlets in memory to boost performance.

Depending on the web server configuration, a servlet can be invoked by many different mechanisms by a web server. Some web servers can be configured to map file extensions (URL) to a specific servlet. In addition, directories can be mapped to invoke a servlet as well. Some web servers will also make available a mechanism to provide an alias for the servlet. Although typically not used, servlets can also be invoked by their fully qualified class name.

When a web server receives an HTTP request that is mapped to a Java servlet, it forwards the request to the servlet engine. The servlet engine is responsible for loading and creating an instance of the servlet class (if not already loaded), initializing the class (the `init` method), and invoking a method (`service`) to inform the servlet of the request. Typically, the `service` method is not overridden. Instead, the `HttpServlet` base class (which all HTTP servlets extend) provides a default implementation of the service method that will dispatch the request to one of the following methods depending on the HTTP method: `doGet`, `doPost`, `doPut`, `doDelete`.

Typically, servlets are implemented by extending one or more of the aforementioned methods, which is the basis for how servlets interact with clients. Similarly to the applet, a servlet must abide by the rules of the servlet engine. In particular, the servlet specification recommends that instance variables should not be used to store state information. This is because the servlet engine can unload the servlet class (when it is not busy processing a request) to conserve memory resources, etc. Likewise, servlets should be implemented in a thread-safe manner. Although the servlet API does offer an interface (`SingleThreadModel`) that a servlet can implement to declare itself as single-threaded, this can drastically impact the memory consumption in high-traffic websites. This is because the servlet engine must create a new instance of the class for each concurrent request being processed.

Servlets are based on a request/response paradigm. Basically, this paradigm makes provisions for passing parameters to the servlets and providing the ability to return a response. In doing so, this process is always initiated by the client program. Unlike the typical strongly typed methods of Java classes, the servlet framework is more generic to support a wide variety of situations. Instead of explicit parameters, single objects are used to contain the request and response parameters used by the servlets.

Although this allows for any number of parameters, this also means that the servlet implementation must explicitly extract the data from the request object to understand what the client wants it to perform.

When the servlet receives a request, it is free to perform almost anything. Although Java 2 does provide a policy file for custom security settings, security permissions are typically less of an issue because the servlet is running in a server-based environment that is similar to a Java Application environment. Reading files, accessing a database using JDBC, etc., are all achievable because the environment is controllable. Once the servlet has finished processing the request, it must then provide a response of the action to the client. This is traditionally accomplished by streaming back HTML, however, when the support increases this will most likely shift to XML being sent to the browser.

6.2 *XML Servlet Considerations*

The Java Servlet API is well suited for the XML and XSL paradigm. One of the most annoying things about the servlet code at present is that the HTML code is intermingled throughout the servlet. Not only is this annoying, it requires the class to be modified when the site needs a facelift because the data, presentation, and business logic are all compiled together. XSL changes this because now the servlet will only need to focus on generating the XML and the XSL processor, whether it is the server side or the browser that takes care of generating the HTML! Before we start coding, we explore some of the potential issues that can appear with XML centric web applications. In particular, we will be discussing how the client interacts with the servlet and how the servlet responds.

6.2.1 Client-to-server communications

The majority of java servlets being developed are for web-based applications. Hence, most of these servlets extend the `HttpServlet` class to harness additional capabilities for communicating with the client. We will cover the basics of HTTP briefly and look at some of the possibilities that could arise as XML becomes a mainstream language.

HTTP is the protocol that transports the HTML documents across the World Wide Web (WWW). HTTP is a small, lightweight protocol, which runs over TCP/IP used to request documents. It initially started as a stateless protocol that indicated that the connection between the client and the server was terminated after each request. As the popularity of the Internet grew, the recommendation was later revised (HTTP/1.1) to provide better performance using persistent connections and pipelining to improve the efficiency of the network utilization. Typically, HTML pages include many different links to images to enhance the viewing experience. This means the browser made multiple connections to the web server to retrieve each separate image for the web page. As a result, HTTP/1.0 was forced to initiate a separate connection to the server for each different object requested. In HTTP/1.1, persistent connections allow multiple requests from the same server. Moreover, pipelining extended this functionality by allowing web servers to stream multiple packets to the browser without waiting for an acknowledgment.

Most often, browsers request HTML documents using a Universal Resource Locator (URL) and a predefined method such as GET, POST, etc. In addition, parameters can be passed to the server. Depending on the method used to request the document, parameters can be passed to the web server with the request or separately. In either case, the parameters passed to the web server over HTTP can be thought of as name/value pairs. This means that each parameter has a name and an associated value. For example:

```
http://MyServer.com/book/Chapter6.html?Param1=one&Param2=two
```

This is a typical URL that a browser can use to retrieve a document from a web server. It requests the `Chapter6.html` file in the `/book/` directory from the `MyServer.com` server. In addition, the request also passes two name/value pair parameters. The first parameters name is `Param1` with a value of "one" where as the second parameter is `Param2` with a value of "two." Name/value pair parameters work fine for HTML pages, however, XML as well as many other technologies have more complex data structures.

Obviously, XML documents are not constrained to merely name/value pairs. The data structure of an XML document is extremely flexible because it is based on a tree or node data structure. XML documents have the flexibility to be just about anything that is conceivable as long as it is well formed. This creates a dilemma because the way the HTTP protocol passes parameters is not the ideal mechanism to pass XML documents to the server. For example, consider the following family tree data structure:

```
<family>
  <child name="Mr. Bill">
    <child name="Billyboy"/>
  </child>
</family>
```

Although name/value pairs could be used to describe these data in the example, it really is not appropriate as the data structure grows in depth. This is unfortunate because this can impact the capabilities of the XML servlet we are building. The initial URL example utilizes the HTTP GET method. The GET method states that the parameters are passed with the directory and file requested. There are other mechanisms that can be used to pass parameter data differently to web servers. The POST method actually passes data to the web server completely separate from the URL.

A good example of this is submitting an HTML form and the parameters did not show up on the address line of the browser. These types of HTTP requests are known as POST methods. Posting requests to web servers simply means that the parameters will be transferred after the request directory and file from the web server. As the address line is limited in size (varies across the different browsers) this method is typically used to pass large amounts or sensitive data (such as passwords) to the web server. As a result, the HTTP specification allows the client or requester to specify the content type of the data being POSTED.

For the most part, the content type of the posted data is the default text/plain content type that browsers send. In contrast, many proprietary technologies have utilized the content type and POST method to "tunnel" a different protocol through HTTP. The advantage to this is that existing security mechanisms (firewalls) already implemented at websites can still be utilized. Hence, all traffic on a website can be contained within HTTP requests thus firewall security is not compromised.

> **NOTE:** Another W3C working group (HTTP-NG) is currently looking at redefining the HTTP protocol. Although the scope of this effort is very broad, in particular, the group is looking at the message transport mechanism and making it more modular, some day, this could provide a better mechanism to transfer XML documents over the HTTP protocol.

Although this may not be optimal, it is an acceptable solution for transferring XML documents to a web server as well. There are websites on the Internet that are using HTTP to communicate between websites. Moreover, they are utilizing XML because of its inherent benefits to define vocabularies that enable these businesses to communicate.

Although we will only be implementing a website that predominantly communicates with web browsers, it is important to know this before developing an XML-based Java Servlet so that we can design accordingly. These are the types of things that increase the cost of ownership of applications because of extensive modifications to support additional functionality.

6.2.2 Server-to-Client Communications

Next, when designing an XML-centric servlet we must consider how the servlet responds to the client. This is important because we must respond to the client in a language that the client can understand. As we are primarily focused on implementing a website, we can further narrow the scope of client application to the few (most-used) browsers that are used to surf the Web today. In particular, this is Microsoft Internet Explorer and Netscape Navigator.

Web browsers, in general, have primarily been focused on rendering HTML markup. Hence, it seems each browser has a slightly different way of displaying the same markup. In addition, this was amplified with client-side scripting languages. Netscape released JavaScript and Microsoft countered with VBScript and their own (slightly deviated) version of JavaScript,

JScript. The result of these "browser wars" has caused a great deal of work for web developers. At a minimum, this has caused HTML designers to extensively test websites thoroughly with all browsers. In some extreme cases, this has resulted in multiple versions of HTML source specifically written for certain browsers.

XML and XSL are definitely the next evolution beyond HTML. Microsoft Internet Explorer 5 (IE5) has also included the ability to display an XML document using the XSL working draft specifications, and Netscape has similar plans; this offers new possibilities to web developers.

Currently, many dynamic websites are built on proprietary technologies that enable dynamic construction of a web page "on the fly" when the web server receives a request. Technologies such as Active Server Pages (Microsoft), Java Server Pages, and Cold Fusion offer a great deal of flexibility for relatively easy scripting languages to query databases or call into distributed systems. While all of the technologies are great, they do have their downsides because they are based on a proprietary foundation. XSL, based on much broader open standards, will offer much of the same functionality for dynamically generating web pages.

The process of running the aforementioned scripting languages on the server consumes a great deal of computing resources. As a result, scalability is affected because there are a limited number of server resources to accomplish the formatting tasks on the server. Having a standard formatting language offers the possibility that browsers will implement the XSL processing. This means the process of formatting the user interface can be moved to the browser running on the client computer thereby distributing the workload of dynamic websites. By standardizing the data format (XML) and the presentation language (XSL), this process could be accomplished by the browser (on the client computer) creating a more efficient distributed application.

Before we get too excited, we should take a page out of the history book. Just as we have seen with HTML, DHTML, and JavaScript, each browser seems to implement this functionality in a slightly different way. In learning from this experience, we want to avoid the same pitfalls that have occurred before HTML. Although client-side parsing would be great, we should not assume that all browsers will support XSL processing or that the browsers would implement this functionality in a consistent manner. Exactly as in the early stages of XML, it is easy to get excited about XSL, but do not forget that XSL is not a standard yet!

We do not have the luxury of specifying which browsers we are going to support in many cases. E-commerce has revolutionized the way businesses think about selling products because they can reduce overall operating costs while broadening their customer base. Instead of driving your car to the local store, you now can navigate a web browser to a website. The last thing a business can afford is to mandate the type of browser you can use. That would be like saying only people who drive Corvettes are allowed to shop at our store!

6.2.2.1 Summary

We have spent a good amount of time discussing the major technologies we will have to consider for implementing the website. How the client requests data from our servlet and how the servlet responds are very important topics when developing a web-based XML application/site. In particular, the standard name/value pair mechanism we are used to on the web is not well suited for the possible data structures of XML. To overcome this, some companies have already taken the "tunneling" approach by passing XML content though as an HTTP requests Post data.

On the other hand, XSL offers new possibilities on how the servlet communicates with the client. Based on a open standard, the process of formatting and presenting a user interface could potentially be moved to the browser to increase scalability of high-traffic websites. Assuming when (and if) XSL is a published standard, this is also contingent on the browsers implementing the formatting in a consistent manner. If not, we will be left with many of the same problems that we are currently facing with HTML, DHTML, and JavaScript.

As we have seen in the Servlet overview, the API has an object-orientated design that provides additional functionality as the type of servlet becomes more specific. The `GenericServlet` provides rudimentary functionality primarily because it is intended to be abstract based to implement more specific types of servlets. In doing so, the `HttpServlet` extends the `GenericServlet` to provide additional functionality based on the HTTP protocol. In consideration for XML, we will follow suit by extending the `HttpServlet` again to provide XML specific capabilities. In doing so, we will take special considerations for the issues that we have just covered.

6.2.3 XMLHttpServlet

As XSL is still an evolving technology, this class will provide an important layer that can be used to ease the transition when XSL becomes a standard. For now, we will use this layer to transform the XML document and XSL stylesheet into an HTML document before it is sent to the browser. In doing so, we will be able to support all browsers immediately.

Even when XSL is an official recommendation, we can not be certain that each browser will implement XSL consistently. Moreover, there will be a period of transition where browsers start to implement the standard. The HTTP headers passed by the browser can be used to determine if we should process the stylesheet on the server or pass the document back to the browser for stylesheet processing. Essentially, this will make *where* the XSL processing occurs transparent to the application code. When XSL becomes a recommendation and browsers support it, the XSL processing can be transparently offloaded to the browser thus improving web server scalability and maintainability of the servlet.

If nothing else, we will be able to clean up all of the ugliness (embedded HTML) that is embedded in many Java Servlets today. Although this class will not actually implement any application functionality, it will limit the response to a creating an XML document that will influence usage of the DOM API. In doing so, the application servlet will only be concerned with producing the data requirements (XML document) for the request and providing a stylesheet that can be used to format and present the data in HTML format. As a result, we will have provided a strong mechanism for separating the presentation requirements from the business logic of the system.

We will start by creating a new class that extends the `javax.servlet .http.HttpServlet` class, as shown in Example 6.1. From the example, you can see that we have extended the `HttpServlet` class and created a function that overrides the `service` method. Furthermore, we have also created a doXML method. In contrast from using the doGet, doPost, etc., methods that are typically used when writing servlets, we have created a new type because the processing will be slightly different. Although this method still receives an HttpServletRequest object, we have defined a new XMLHttpServletResponse object for the response (we will cover this in more detail after this class). We have changed the response mechanism to conform to the DOM recommendation. As a result, we will utilize the DOM API to dynamically generate the response as an XML document.

Example 6.1 XMLHttpServlet class

```
public abstract class XMLHttpServlet extends HttpServlet
{
  public void service( HttpServletRequest req, HttpServletResponse res)
    throws ServletException, IOException
  {
    ...
  }
  public abstract void doXML( HttpServletRequest req,
                              XMLHttpServletResponse res);

  protected boolean transformAtServer( HttpServletRequest req )
  {
    return true;
  }
}
```

Notice that this class is defined as abstract. An abstract class is somewhere in between an interface and a class at the same time. Where Interfaces only define the methods but does not provide an implementation, an abstract class only provides part of the implementation and requires the descendant class to implement the rest. We will implement the service method, however, we are leaving the implementation of doXML for the descendant class. This is a subtle way of saying, "Your class will not work unless you override the doXML method!"

There will be more to our class but for now we begin implementing the service method. This is a very crucial method to the server. If you can imagine, every thread of execution (client request) will pass through this function. In doing so, this method simply needs to create an XMLHttpServletResponse object, and call the doXML method so the descendant class can process

> **NOTE:** This is slightly different from the `HttpServlet` class in that it is not defined as abstract. This is primarily because the `HttpServlet` class offers many different methods to override to implement a servlet but it is only required to override one of them. Uncertain of which method will be overridden, the `HttpServlet` class provides a default implementation for each of the methods. Although this is not as explicit as using abstract methods, it is better than requiring each `HttpServlet` descendant to implement all of the `doXXX` methods.

the request. Once the `doXML` method returns, the remainder of the method can focus on streaming the response back to the client.

When the `doXML` method is completed, the `service` method can then transform the XML document from the `XMLHttpServletResponse` into HTML using the XSL stylesheet processing instruction from the document.

The first part of the service method is relatively simple. First, we create a new instance of the `XMLHttpServletResponse` object by passing the `HttpServletResponse` object as a parameter to its constructor. If the class name has not already given it away, the `XMLHttpServletResponse` will extend the functionality of the `HttpServletResponse` interface. Do not worry about this object too much right now because we will cover it in detail later. The important thing to note is that the object will be providing additional XML-specific functionality above and beyond the HTTP functionality normally found in the `HttpServletResponse` interface. In particular, a `getDocument` method will return a reference to an XML Document interface. The following code snippet illustrates the first part of the `service` method logic:

```
public static final String DEFAULT_CONTENT_TYPE = "text/html";

...

try
{
  XMLHttpServletResponse xres = new XMLHttpServletResponse(res);
  res.setContentType( DEFAULT_CONTENT_TYPE );
  doXML( req, xres );

  ... // Generate HTML from the XML Document
```

```
}
catch(Exception e)
{
  log( e.getMessage() );
  throw new ServletException( e.getMessage() );
}
```

After the `XMLHttpServletResponse` object has been created, we will assign a default content type for the response. In this case, we have assigned `DEFAULT_CONTENT_TYPE`, which evaluates to "text/html." As we will predominantly be streaming HTML markup to the browser, this helps the browser determine what it is receiving.

Next, we call the `doXML` method to invoke the logic in the application layer (descendant class) of the servlet. In doing so, we will use exception handling just in case the servlet is misbehaving. This will allow us to log the error in the servlet engines log file. Finally, we also added a default content type for the response because this is a commonly forgotten task during servlet development.

The remaining aspects of the service method deal with streaming the results back to the client. As we have discussed previously, depending on the client, we want the ability to stream HTML or the XML document back to the browser. We have already written a rather extravagant solution for stream `Document` objects; however, the HTML part is not quite as clear. Generating HTML from an XML document is done using an XSL processor. In general, an XSL processor needs two XML documents to operate. The first document is an XSL stylesheet that specifies the presentation and the second document specifies the data. Through a rather intensive process, the XSL processor walks the DOM tree of the presentation (XSL) document performing queries on the DOM tree of the data document. During this process, the processor fires events in a formatter object that presents the elements in a specific format. We will use the XSL processor as a stopgap solution until the XSL working drafts become official and there is mainstream support for this technology across multiple browsers.

If this is not complicated enough, there is no standard way of interacting with the XSL processors either. Although we will not go into as much detail as we did for the DOM factory objects, we will also need to consider abstracting how the XSL transformations (XSLT) are performed, otherwise we will be tied to a particular implementation. Not doing so would make all the work we have done so far with the DOM factory and writers less useful.

In order to abstract the transformation process we first need to understand how the two documents (presentation and data) are related. In Chapter 3 we saw that the presentation (XSL) document was related to a data document with the following processing instruction:

```
<?xml-stylesheet href="[URI to stylesheet]"?>
```

This processing instruction, which is part of the data document, signifies a separate XML document that can be used to present the XML data. The `href` attribute of the processing instruction indicates the URI, relative to the data document, to retrieve the stylesheet. Easy right? At first glance, yes, but what is it relative to when dynamically generating XML documents? This is a little trickier when it comes to basing a relative path on something that physically does not exist, but it is really important because the browsers will be expecting to process a relative URI. We will need to add some specialized processing so the server-side XSL processor can function in the same way as a browser.

Having said this, we will design a new interface that provides XSL processing that is independent of the implementation. As we have done for the `factory` and `writer` interfaces, we will create an interface as shown in Example 6.2. Since we are not really sure how the different implementations of XSL processing will function, we have designed the interface for the least common denominator. Instead of getting fancy, we have provided a single method to transform the document.

Example 6.2 XSLTransformer.java

```
package com.ctp.dom;
import org.w3c.dom.Document;
import java.io.Writer;
import java.net.URL;

public interface XSLTransformer
{
  public static final int FORMAT_HTML = 1;
  public static final int FORMAT_XML  = 2;
```

```
  public static final int FORMAT_TEXT = 3;

  public boolean transformDocument(Document doc, URL urlBase, Writer
writer, int nFormatType, String strDocType)
    throws TransformerException;
}
```

The `transformDocument` method takes five parameters: a reference to a Document-base URL; a `java.io.writer`; an integer indicating the output type; and finally a String which indicates to append to the beginning of the document.

The `Document` reference should be the source or data document. We will extract the stylesheet URI from the document, in the same way that a client-side browser do. Because the document was dynamically generated it does not have a URI. We will use the `urlBase` parameter so we can process stylesheets that are associated with relative URLs.

The last three parameters will provide the necessary information for the output after the transformations occur. First, the `writer` interface will be used to output the resulting tree. The `nFormatType` parameter will be used to determine how the result tree will be formatted. We have provided three common formats: FORMAT_HTML, FORMAT_XML, and FORMAT_TEXT. Finally, the last parameter strDocType will be used to prepend a string of text to the document. XSLT provides a mechanism to generating the DOM tree; however, sometimes we will need to add additional information to the beginning of the document, such as an XML Prolog or a DTD.

Now that we know what the parameters will be used for, we will look at the different actions we need to accomplish:

1. Query the document for the stylesheet processing instruction;
2. Apply a context to the relative stylesheet URI;
3. Load and parse the stylesheet into an XML document;
4. Select the appropriate Formatter based on the option selected; and
5. Use an XSL processor to process the two documents sending the formatted output to the `Writer` interface.

Although it may seem as if we are offloading considerable work on the transformer, this leaves the question of how the XSL processing occurs very open. This is good because some XSL processors actually provide processors that encapsulate all of the aforementioned steps within a single method. Furthermore, it is very important that we keep the server-side XSL processing similar to the recommendation because we want to make where the processing occurs (client or server) transparent to the application servlet. In doing so, we should begin to "turn off" server-side XSL processing and offload this to the client (browser).

> **TIP:** Keeping the XSL processing location transparent will also take some discipline within the application servlet. Because the XSL stylesheet processing instruction specifies where to find the stylesheet, it will be important to use a URI that both the client and the server can process. In other words, make sure we always use URLs to specify the stylesheet instead of file system paths because they will refer to different locations on the client and the server.

If you have not already noticed, this looks a lot like the `DOMWriter` interface we created in Chapter 5. In fact, we could have simply created a different implementation of the `DOMWriter` that would include an XSL processor to process the document prior to streaming through the writer object. Although this would work, it will become difficult to control when to transform the document and when to simply stream the document data. Instead, we have created a new interface that will provide a more self-documenting method of transforming the document that will not be confused with simply writing the XML data document. It does make sense to include this functionality in the `DOMManger` class, though. Because XSL transformations are not merely limited to servlets, it makes more sense to include this in the generic DOM package we have already created.

This is relatively straightforward to do, especially as we have done this a few times already. Because the interface has already been defined, we simply need to extend the `DOMManger` class in the `com.ctp.dom` package to include a couple of different variations to set the `Transformer` class, one an instance of the class and the other by class name. Finally, we simply provide a method to retrieve a reference the `XSLTransformer` instance, as shown in Example 6.3.

Example 6.3 XSLTransformer methods in DOMManager

```
public static synchronized void setTransformer( XSLTransformer trans)
  throws TransformerException
{
  m_transformer = trans;
}

public static synchronized void setTransformer( String strClassName )
  throws TransformerException
{
  try
  { Class impl = Class.forName( strClassName );
    setTransformer( (XSLTransformer) impl.newInstance() );
  }
  catch( ClassCastException cast )
  { throw new TransformerException(
            TransformerException.INVALID_FACTORY_IMPL,
                                    strClassName+" is not an XSLTrans-
former.");
  }
  catch( ClassNotFoundException cnf )
  { throw new TransformerException(
            TransformerException.IMPLEMENTATION_NOT_FOUND,
                                    "The class (" + strClassName + ") could
not be found." );
  }
  catch( InstantiationException CantInstantiate )
  { throw new TransformerException(
            TransformerException.CANT_LOAD_IMPLEMENTATION,
                                    CantInstantiate.getMessage() );
  }
  catch( IllegalAccessException Access )
  { throw new TransformerException(TransformerException.ILLEGAL_ACCESS,
                                                Access.getMessage());
  }
}

public static synchronized XSLTransformer getTransformer()
  throws TransformerException
{ if (m_transformer != null)
    return m_transformer;
  else
```

```
    throw new TransformerException(
          TransformerException.NO_IMPLEMENTATION, ERR_IMPL_NOT_SET);
}
```

Because we have covered this several times in the previous chapter, we will not go into too much detail here. The two different `setTransformer` methods work together to assign a static member variable of the `DOMManager` that holds a reference (`m_transformer`) to an instance of an `XSLTransformer` object. The `getTransformer` method simply returns the reference so we can utilize the transformation functionality. Finally, by providing the capability to dynamically set the transformer, it will be very easy to use different implementations in the future.

> **NOTE:** This approach is very useful when we are not really sure if a given XSL processor is thread-safe or can remain persistent. We will be using the Lotus XSL processor to perform the server-side transformations. Currently, the Lotus `XSLProcessor` requires a new instance for every document that it processes. Because we are containing the entire XSL processing in a separate class, we will have the ability to optimize the code when it is appropriate. Ultimately, when the processor no longer requires this special attention, we can simply use member variables in the class to improve the efficiency and optimize the performance of this functionality.

Implementing the `TransformerException` is no different from what we have done for the `DOMFactory` and `DOMWriter` Exception classes. Just like the `DOMFactoryException` and `DOMWriterException` classes, this class will provide a simple generic way of encapsulating any errors that may occur within any given implementation. In doing so, we will store the type of exception and the exception message. This is shown, along with a few additional types, in Example 6.4.

Example 6.4 TransformerException.java

```
package com.ctp.dom;

public class TransformerException extends Exception
{
```

```
  public static final int FILE_NOT_FOUND
= 1;
  public static final int INVALID_DOCUMENT                    = 2;
  public static final int SAX                                 = 3;
  public static final int FILE_IO                             = 4;
  public static final int XSLPROCESSOR                        = 5;
  public static final int MALFORMED_URL
= 6;
  public static final int NO_STYLESHEET
= 7;
  public static final int NO_IMPLEMENTATION                   = 11;
  public static final int IMPLEMENTATION_NOT_FOUND = 12;
  public static final int CANT_LOAD_IMPLEMENTATION = 13;
  public static final int ILLEGAL_ACCESS
= 14;
  public static final int INVALID_FACTORY_IMPL
= 15;

  private int m_nType = 0;
  private String m_strMsg = null;

  public TransformerException( int type, String msg)
  { m_nType = type;
    m_strMsg = msg;
  }

  public String getMessage()
  { return m_strMsg; }
}
```

Now that we have created the infrastructure for how we perform the transformations, the last method we will create will provide a mechanism to determine if we need to transform the document at the server or the client. Because this will be based largely on the client application, we will pass the `HttpServletRequest` object to this method. In doing so, the descendant class can implement specific rules that determine where to process the XSL translations depending on the client application (using the HTTP headers). Instead of defining this method as abstract, we provided a default implementation that forces server-side transformations. This is shown in Example 6.5.

Example 6.5 XMLHttpServlet.transformAtServer method

```
protected boolean transformAtServer( HttpServletRequest req )
{
```

```
  return true;
}
```

Now we can finish the remaining aspects of the service method. After the doXML method returns from the descendant class, we will simply call the transformAtServer method to determine the location of transformation. When this method returns true, we need to get the transformer and call the transformDocument method. Otherwise, when the method returns false, we will use the DOMWriter interface that created in Chapter 5 to stream the (data) XML document back to the client as shown in Example 6.6.

Example 6.6 XMLHttpServlet.service method

```
public void service( HttpServletRequest req, HttpServletResponse res)
  throws ServletException, IOException
{
  try
  {
    XMLHttpServletResponse xres = new XMLHttpServletResponse(res);
    res.setContentType( DEFAULT_CONTENT_TYPE );

    doXML( req, xres );

    Writer writer = res.getWriter();
    Document doc = xres.getDocument();
    if (doc == null)
      throw new ServletException("Document not specified.");

    // Attempt to apply XSL Transformation (server-side)
    if(transformAtServer(req))
    {
      XSLTransformer trans = DOMManager.getTransformer();
      if (trans != null)
      {
        URL urlBase = new URL(HttpUtils.getRequestURL(req).toString());
        trans.transformDocument(doc, urlBase, writer, XSLTrans-
former.FORMAT_HTML, null);
      }
      else throw new ServletException("XSLTransformer not specified.");
    }
    else
    {
      DOMWriter domwriter = DOMManager.getWriter();
```

```
      if (domwriter != null)
        domwriter.writeDocument(doc,res.getWriter());
      else
        throw new ServletException("DOMWriter not specified.");
    }
  }
  catch(Exception e)
  {
    log( e.toString() );
    throw new ServletException( e.getMessage() );
  }
}
```

After the call to doXML returns, we get references to the writer and the document so we know what or where to write our output. If the Document was never set in the XMLHttpServletResponse object, we will throw a ServletException to indicate this.

Next, we call the transformAtServer passing it the HttpServletRequest object. This allows the application servlet (decendant class) to examine the client browser to determine if we should return XML or HTML. If the method returns true, we need to transform the XML at the server probably because the browser does not support XML.

Transforming the XML document is a matter of getting a reference to the XSLTransformer and calling the transformDocument method. Before we can do that, however, we need to set the context of the source XML document so the XSLTransformer can process relative stylesheet URIs. To do this, we call the getRequestURL method of the handy HttpUtils class from the servlet API. By passing it the HttpServletRequest object, this allows it to reconstitute the request URL. Finally, instruct the XSLTransformer to format the resulting DOM tree as HTML.

On the other hand, if the transformAtServer method returns false, we simply get a reference to the DOMWriter and stream back the XML document to the browser. As long as the browser can interpret the XML, it can extract the stylesheet processing instruction and transform the document at the client browser.

6.2.4 Implementing the XSLTransformer class

Now that the `XSLTransformer` interface has been defined, it is time to provide an implementation so that we can begin using it. As we discussed earlier, XSL transformations require two XML documents as input and ultimately produce a single document or result tree. For the most part, XSL processors will usually abstract how the output is written to separate how the output is written from the transformation logic. This is typically accomplished using the Simple API for XML (SAX) events. In doing so, classes can be created that implement the `org.xml.sax.DocumentHandler` interface to provide a specific format of the document. Although this could be another XML document, it could also be an HTML file.

We will use the LotusXSL API to transform the XML documents that we dynamically create into HTML documents. To further narrow the scope, we will primarily be focusing on stylesheet transformations (XSLT) instead of the entire XSL working draft because it is currently stable and working (remember, at the time of this writing XSL is still a working draft). Before we begin working with the XSL processor, make sure that it is installed and the Lotus packages have been added to your CLASSPATH as described in the technical requirements section of this chapter. After the XSL processor has been installed, we can begin by creating a new class, called `IBMTXDOMTransformer.java`. Next, we will want to import the `com.lotus.xsl` package.

With LotusXSL, transformations are accomplished using the `XSLProcessor` class. In order to create a new instance of the `com.lotus.xsl.XSLProcessor`, we must first provide the class with a reference to an object that implements the `com.lotus.xsl.XMLParserLiaison` interface. As the name implies, this class is used as a liaison between the XSL processor and XML parser implementation. It is needed for the same reasons we created the `DOMManger`, `DOMFactory` and `DOMWriter` classes. Because the `XSLProcessor` may have to load and parse XML files, either through `xsl:include` or `xsl:import` tags or having to process XML documents by their URL, the liaison class is needed in order to parse and create `Document` objects for a given implementation. Essentially, this class resolves the deficiencies in the DOM level 1 recommendation, particularly document creation, by providing a bridge between the DOM implementation of the source XML documents and the `XSLProcessor`.

In doing so, each different XML implementation will most likely require a specific `XMLParserLiaison` implementation.

Because we are working solely with the TX classes from IBM, we will also need to import the `XML4Jliaison` class in the `com.lotus.xsl.xml4j2tx` package to provide this functionality. For extensibility, the formatting logic is also separated from the class. Instead of including the formatting logic in the liaison class, Lotus provided a separate interface (`FormatterListener`) for providing the formatting logic. This interface is an extension (inherits) of the SAX `DocumentHandler` interface. Although this is all good to know, we need not be too concerned about this because Lotus has provided three different classes that implement this interface that can be used to format the results in HTML, XML, or plainText.

We can start by creating a class that implements our `XSLTransformer` interface. Implementing the `transformDocument` method is really easy thanks to all of the functionality that LotusXSL provides. For the most part, this method is largely a matter of plugging in the pieces to get the desired output. This is shown in Example 6.7.

Example 6.7 IBMTXDOMTransformer.java

```
public class IBMTXDOMTransformer implements XSLTransformer
{
  protected FormatterListener createFormatterListener( int nFormatType,
String strDocType, PrintWriter pw )
  {
    switch( nFormatType)
    {
    case FORMAT_HTML: return new FormatterToHTML(pw,"UTF-8",strDoc-
Type,true,2);
    case FORMAT_XML:  return new FormatterToXML(pw,"UTF-8",strDoc-
Type,true,2);
    case FORMAT_TEXT: return new FormatterToText(pw);
    };
    return null;
  }
  public boolean transformDocument(Document docXML, URL urlBase, Writer
writer, int nFormatType, String strDocType)
    throws TransformerException
  {
    try
```

```
    {
      // Set up the formatter based on the output type
      PrintWriter pw = new PrintWriter(writer);
      FormatterListener formatter = createFormatterListener(nFormat-
Type,strDocType,pw);

      // Set up the Liasion/Bridge so the processor can communication with
the DOM
      XML4JLiaison liaison = new XML4JLiaison();
      liaison.setFormatterListener( formatter );
      XSLProcessor processor = new XSLProcessor( liaison );

      // get the stylesheet URI and document
      URL url = new URL(urlBase, processor.getStyleSheetURIfrom-
Doc(docXML));
     Document docXSL = processor.parseXML(url.toString(), new String[1] );

      processor.process( docXML, docXSL, url.toString(), pw );
    }
    catch( SAXException saxe )
    { throw new TransformerException(TransformerException.SAX,
                                     saxe.toString());
    }
    catch( MalformedURLException url)
    { throw new TransformerException(TransformerException.MALFORMED_URL,
                                     url.toString());
    }
    catch( FileNotFoundException fnf)
    { throw new TransformerException(TransformerException.FILE_NOT_FOUND,
                                     fnf.toString());
    }
    catch( IOException ioe)
    { throw new TransformerException(TransformerException.FILE_IO,
                                     ioe.toString());
    }
    catch(XSLProcessorException xsle)
    { throw new TransformerException(TransformerException.XSLPROCESSOR,
                                     xsle.toString());
    }
    return true;
  }
}
```

First, the Lotus XSLProcessor requires more than simply a `Writer` to output the resulting tree. As there is special formatting, such as indenting, we will create a new `PrintWriter` that encapsulates the `Writer` object we originally passed to the method.

Next, we need to create the appropriate formatter that will be used to output the resulting tree. Because there are multiple supported formats that could be generated, we have created a separate method, `createFormatterListener`, to allocate the appropriate formatter for the request.

Once the formatter has been created, we can create a liaison class that acts as the glue between the `XSLProcessor` and the particular DOM implementation we are using. By using the `nFormatType` parameter, we select the appropriate formatter. As you can see from the example, we have to pass a few parameters to instantiate the various formatters. For example, the signature of the `FormatterToHTML` constructor is:

```
FormatterToHTML(java.io.Writer writer, java.lang.String encoding,
java.lang.String doctype, boolean doIndent, int indent)
```

The `writer` parameter specifies the output stream to use when writing the document. The `encoding` specifies the encoding that the writer will use. The `doctype` provides the ability to write a custom DTD prior to the result tree, and the last two parameters indicate if the result tree should be indented and, if so, by how many spaces.

Next, we will create a new instance of the `XML4JLiaison` class to provide the bridge between the `XSLProcessor` and the XML parser. Once these objects have been instantiated we can create the `XSLProcessor` object by passing the `XML4JLiaison` class to the constructor.

In order to transform a document, we must call the process method of the `XSLProcessor` (shown just prior to the exception handling). The `process` method is overloaded in a number of ways. Of particular interest is a version that only requires the XML `Document` object to be passed. For this method, the XML Document is queried to determine the stylesheet URL, and loads and parses the stylesheet before ever getting to the transformation. Ultimately, when finished with the transformations, another DOM `Document` object is returned containing the result tree for the HTML document. At first glance, this would seem like the appropriate method to use considering the objects that are passed to this method because we could simply print the document returned from the method using our `DOMWriter` implementation.

Actually, in our situation, this is the least efficient method. Instead of creating a `Document` object for the result tree, a better method would be to stream the results back to client while the transformations are occurring. This is commonly referred to as event-based parsing or processing. Unfortunately, the `XSLProcessor` does not provide a method that only requires the XML `Document` object and a `Writer` object. Instead, we will have to call the process method that requires the `Document` reference for the XML data document and one for the stylesheet. In doing so, we will have to manually retrieve the stylesheet URL and parse it to create the stylesheet document.

The `XSLProcessor` does provide some convenience methods to assist us in this process.

To retrieve the associated stylesheet, we simply call the `getStyleSheetURIfromDoc` method. Once we have retrieved the stylesheet URI, we use the `java.net.URL` class to merge the base url with the URI from the stylesheet processing instruction. Therefore, this essentially allows us to dynamically assign the context to the source Document so relative stylesheet URIs have meaning. Now (finally), we call the `toString` method of the URL to pass the stylesheet URI to the `parseXML` method to create the `Document` object for the stylesheet. Whew!

We can now call the `process` method, passing both documents, the base URI of the stylesheet and the `PrintWriter` object we instantiated at the beginning of the method.

Considering how much is going on inside the `XSLProcessor` can only mean one thing—anything that performs that much work has to throw their share of exceptions! Any number of problems could occur in this process from an invalid URL, not finding the stylesheet or it not being well formed. To handle these situations, we catch the particular errors, and throw our more generic `TransformerException`. In doing so, we simply set the type of exception and duplicate the local exception's message exactly as we have done previously in Example 6.4.

6.2.5 Implementing the XMLHttpServletResponse object

The last thing we must do before the XML servlet infrastructure is complete is to implement the `XMLHttpServletResponse` object. Instead of simply using the existing `HttpServletResponse` object that is provided with the Servlet API we decided to extend it to lock down exactly how the servlet will response to a given client request. In doing so, embedded HTML or now XML will no longer be available because we will limit the response to an XML document, using the DOM recommendation. Although this limits the response generation mechanism, it is still a useful tradeoff because it will enforce good programming practices based on standards.

Therefore, we do not want to have to implement all of the `HttpServletResponse` functionality all over again. The simplest way to do this is to use containment. Containment is very similar to encapsulation because an outer object contains an inner object. This is much different from inheritance. Inheritance describes ancestor classes, whereas containment is merely a fancy term for an instance variable. Thus, the outer object still has complete access to all of the functionality of the inner object, however, it is not directly exposed to the external object. Simply storing the inner object as a private instance variable does this. In order to expose the functionality of the inner object, new methods must be exposed on the outer object. This allows the outer object to limit the methods that are exposed.

In our case, we want to limit how the response is sent to the client to an XML document. In order to do this, we will need to hide the `getWriter` and `getOutputStream` methods. For the most part, the rest of the functionality should be exposed so our descendant class will still be able to perform things such as setting the HTTP result value, creating cookies, and adding HTTP header values. To accomplish this, we will pass a reference to the `HttpServletResponse` object to our `XMLHttpServletResponse` object during construction and simply provide a wrapper method for each of the methods we wish to expose as methods of the `XMLHttpServletResponse` class. This is shown in Example 6.8.

Example 6.8 XMLHttpServletResponse containment of HttpServletResponse class

```
public class XMLHttpServletResponse
{
  private HttpServletResponse m_HttpServletResponse = null;

  public XMLHttpServletResponse( HttpServletResponse res )
  { m_HttpServletResponse = res;  }

  public void addCookie( Cookie cookie )
  { m_HttpServletResponse.addCookie( cookie );    }

  public boolean containsHeader( String name )
  { return m_HttpServletResponse.containsHeader(name);    }

  public void setStatus( int sc, String message )
  { m_HttpServletResponse.setStatus( sc, message);    }

  public void setStatus( int code )
  { m_HttpServletResponse.setStatus( code );    }

  public void setHeader( String name, String value)
  { m_HttpServletResponse.setHeader( name, value );  }

  public void setContentType(String type)
  { m_HttpServletResponse.setContentType( type );  }

  public String encodeUrl(String url)
  { return m_HttpServletResponse.encodeUrl(url);    }

  public String encodeRedirectUrl(String url)
  { return m_HttpServletResponse.encodeRedirectUrl(url);    }

  public void sendError( int code, String msg )
    throws java.io.IOException
  { m_HttpServletResponse.sendError( code, msg );  }

  ... // The rest of the code
}
```

As you can see from the example, the `HttpServletResponse` object is passed as a parameter during construction and stored in the `m_HttpServletResponse` instance variable. Once the instance variable has been set, the methods that we have exposed simply pass the same parameters to the inner objects methods.

Although this is slightly tedious, it is much better than the alternative of having to reimplement all of the methods of the `HttpServletResponse` object!

As we have purposefully excluded the `getWriter` and `getOutputStream` methods from the `HttpServletResponse` (and ancestor classes), it is time to provide similar functionality for the XML servlets. Instead of using streams of text, however, we will expose methods for retrieving and setting an `org.w3c.dom.Document` object, essentially making `XMLHttpServletResponse` a placeholder. As you can see from the following code, this is accomplished by simply adding a couple more set/get methods and a new instance variable to hold a reference to the document:

```
private Document m_doc = null;

public void setDocument(Document doc)
{ m_doc = doc;                          }

public Document getDocument()
{ return m_doc;    }
```

Finally, the last thing we will add to the class is a convenience method for setting the stylesheet processing instruction. Having worked with the DOM recommendation for a while, notice that creating processing instructions is not as straightforward as one might think. The DOM API does provide a `createProcessingInstruction` method on the `Document` interface, however, it still requires some string manipulation. This is because the contents of a Processing Instruction are intended to be passed as is. In many cases, the contents will appear to resemble attributes such as those we find for element nodes, for example, the `href` attribute. Because the processing instructions were not intended to include attributes, the API only provides a `setData` method that sets the entire contents of the node after the name until the closing tag. To overcome this, we create a convenience method that will encapsulate the string manipulation required.

Example 6.9 setStyleSheet convenience method

```
private static final String STYLESHEET_TYPE = "xml-stylesheet";

public void setStyleSheet( String strURI )
{
  String data = "href='" + strURI + "'";
```

```
  ProcessingInstruction pi = m_doc.createProcessingInstruc-
tion(STYLESHEET_TYPE,data);
  Element e = m_doc.getDocumentElement();
  m_doc.insertBefore(pi,e);
}
```

Example 6.9 shows the code to assist the constructions of the stylesheet-processing instruction. As you can see, we have parameterized the URI that will ultimately be the `href` attribute value. Instead of having special APIs for assigning this, however, we have to manually concantenate the attribute name (`href`) with the attribute value. After this, the DOM API can be applied to create the processing instruction. Once the processing instruction has been successfully created, we add it to the document. In doing so, we first call the `getDocumentElement` to retrieve the root element of the document. Whether or not the root element has been set does not really matter in this case. We simply call the `insertBefore` method to insert the processing instruction (pi) before the root element (e). If the root element does not exist, the `insertBefore` simply inserts the node at the beginning of the document.

> **NOTE:** The call to `insertBefore(pi,null)` will not fail. It is actually equivalent to a call to `appendChild(pi)`.

This completes the `XMLHttpServletResponse` class. Although the code was more tedious than thought-provoking, we added some valuable aspects to our XML servlet framework. Through containment we harnessed and exposed the necessary functionality from the `HttpServletResponse` object while restricting access to the `getWriter` and `getOutputStream` methods. Instead we added `setDocument` and `getDocument` methods to manage the response data from the servlet to the client. Last, we created a convenience method for assigning the stylesheet-processing instruction to make the descendant class (application code) more intuitive.

Because the descendant class ultimately decides where the XSL transformations will occur, we can hold off on implementing the transformation functionality until the descendant class has been built. This will allow us to test the code we have written so far, but without a pretty interface to go with it!

6.2.6 Implementing the Servlet Application

Now that we have taken the necessary precautions for issues that may arise when building XML-based servlets, it is time to put what we have built to the test. In Chapter 5 we created the business objects that will be required to implement the website. Furthermore, we just completed extending the Java servlet API to provide specific functionality for XML-centric applications. The remaining piece is the glue that binds these functional components together to make something useful!

As such, the intersection where our technology framework (XML servlet extensions) meets the business objects is the application. Although we have been rather abstract with the code we developed, we will add a context to that code. This class will ultimately be the glue that holds our website together. Because we have approached the design in an object-oriented fashion, this class is really only responsible for handling HTTP requests and calling the various methods of the business objects we created in Chapter 5.

There are many different technologies in the industry at present that are used to dynamically generate web pages on the file. Now, using XSL, we will provide a custom-built infrastructure that is totally abstract from the presentation of the site. If you have not already noticed, after this you will truly understand some of the extraordinary powers of XML and the languages that have already spun from it's web (no pun intended)!

We will now walk through the implementation of the servlet class that will provide the functionality of the website. In doing so, we will follow the lifecycle of the class. In other words, we will start with initialization of the servlet and proceed to implementing the request-handling facilities. Before starting the lifecycle, however, we need to review some of the things the business objects will be expecting from the application in which they will live. If you recall when we were implementing the business objects that we designed these objects to be reusable in many different environments. In doing so, we chose to leave the database connectivity and resource management to the application layer.

Generally, providing database connectivity is straightforward, but although it is slightly more complex because of the threading issues we must consider when designing a servlet, it is still relatively simple. As we will need to provide connection objects throughout the class, we will want to create a separate method that we can call wherever we are in the class.

First, we need to create a new class named `XMLBookServlet` that extends the `XMLHttpServlet` class that we have just implemented. Once this is done, we can create our first method, `getConnection` that will return `java.sql.Connection` instances. Connection to a database using JDBC is really easy, that is, we simply call the `getConnection` method of the `DriverManager` class! In calling this method, we pass a database URL that contains enough information to connect to a specific database. However, there is a catch! Part of the information in the Database URL specifies the JDBC driver that understands how to talk to the database. Thus, it is that simple so long as the `DriverManager` "knows" about a driver that can talk to the database. This is very important because it is the driver's responsibility to inform or register itself with the `DriverManager`. Moreover, this occurs when the JDBC driver is loaded into memory. With that being said, Example 6.10 shows the start of the `XMLBookServlet` class with the `getConnection` method implementation.

Example 6.10 GetConnection method of the XMLBookServlet

```
public class XMLBookServlet extends XMLHttpServlet
{
  private String m_strJDBCDriver                          = null;
  private String m_strDatabaseURL                         = null;

  protected Connection getConnection() throws UnavailableException
  { try
    { Class.forName( m_strJDBCDriver );
      return DriverManager.getConnection( m_strDatabaseURL );
    }
    catch (Exception e)
    { log( e.toString() );
      throw new UnavailableException(this,e.toString());
    }
  }
  ...
}
```

As you can see from the example, we first load the JDBC driver by calling `Class.forName`. Once the driver is loaded, we simply ask the `DriverManager` for a new connection to the database. Between these two lines of code, there are about five different exceptions that can be thrown! As seen in the `DOMManger` class, the `forName` method can throw `ClassNotFoundException`, `LinkageError`, `ExceptionInInitializerError`. Furthermore, the `DriverManager` can throw an `SQLException` if it has any problems connecting to the database or locating the appropriate driver. Although there are all of these different exceptions, they all mean pretty much the same thing to us, that is the site just is not going to work until somebody examines the system configuration! Because of this, we take the simple approach of catching the generic `Exception`, logging the error, and throwing the `UnavailableException` to signify to the servlet engine that our servlet has big problems!

> **NOTE:** This function works well for multi-threaded environments such as servlets. Because each call to `getConnection` returns a new instance of a connection we no longer need to worry about synchronization techniques. However, this can potentially create a different problem of exhausting the limited number database connections. As we are using the JDBC to ODBC Bridge, we also benefit from the capabilities of the ODBC driver, such as connection pooling.

One final note is that we used instance variables to indicate the JDBC driver class name (`m_strJDBCDriver`) and the Database URL (`m_strDatabaseURL`) for connecting with our database. Since this information in more related to system configuration, it is highly likely that it may change while our servlet is still running in a production environment. Whether we outgrow Microsoft Access (most probable!) or simply change where the database is stored (in our case the Data Source Name), we will have to change these values. For data values such as these that can potentially change, the common approach is to load this information from a property file when the class is initialized. We will cover this next.

6.2.6.1 Initialization

In order for our site to function correctly, our servlet class must set up the environment for the business objects and the `XMLHttpServlet` base class to operate correctly. We have already seen that we need to assign values to the two variables required to establish a database connection. We also need to retrieve the class names for the `DOMFactory` and `DOMWriter` (and ultimately the `XSLTransformer`) implementations. Once this is done, we can start to initialize the business objects by creating the shared `Catalog` object.

In order for servlets to initialize themselves, the Servlet API has provided an `init` method that is called prior to any requests, such as `doGet`, `doPost`, or our new `doXML` method for that matter. By overriding this method, we get access to the `ServletConfig` object that can be used to retrieve initialization parameters from the servlet property file. Ultimately, this depends on the servlet engine implementation. Because we are implementing the servlet using Apache group's Jserv implementation, the servlet initialization parameters are stored with the zone properties in the `conf` subdirectory below the Jserv installation directory. The following code shows a portion of the zone's properties file related to our servlet:

```
servlet.startup=Book
servlet.Book.code=XMLBookServlet
servlet.Book.initArgs=Driver=sun.jdbc.odbc.JdbcOdbcDriver,
                      DatabaseURL=jdbc:odbc:XMLBook,
                      DOMFactory=IBMDOMFactory,
                      DOMWriter=IBMDOMWriter
```

> **NOTE:** The `initArgs` parameter is a comma-delimited list of name/value pairs. These are the parameters that will be contained in the `ServletConfig` object when the init method is invoked. Each name/value parameter has been shown on a separate line; however, in the properties file they should be concatenated together on one line.

By default, Jserv will load and initialize a servlet when it receives a request for the servlet. In contrast, the first parameter (`servlet.startup`) instructs the servlet engine to load and initialize the servlet named "`Book`" when the engine initializes. The second parameter simply provides an alias that can be used to refer to our servlet. As shown in the foregoing, a `Book` alias is created to refer to the Java class `XMLBookServlet`. Although the first two initialization parameters are really only utilized by the servlet engine, the third setting will actually provide dynamic configuration information to our servlet.

The first two parameters listed in the initArgs, Driver and DatabaseURL, provide the class name of the JDBC driver and the database URL, respectively. The getConnection method will utilize these to load and connect to our database. The last two parameters, DOMFactory and DOMWriter, specify the implementation class name of the DOMFactory and DOMWriter interfaces, respectively.

Extracting the parameters from the initArgs line is really simple. We simply call the getInitParameter method of the ServletConfig object to retrieve a parameter by its name. For example, to retrieve the value of the DatabaseURL parameter we would simply call ServletConfig.getInitParameter ("DatabaseURL"). In doing so, the value of the parameter would be returned as a String. If the parameter does not exist, null is returned.

Once all of the parameters have been extracted from the ServletConfig object, we assign the implementations of the DOMFactory and DOMWriter using the values we have just extracted from the initialization parameters. Finally, we can create the Catalog object. The entire code for the init method is shown in Example 6.11.

Example 6.11 XMLBookServlet init method

```
public class XMLBookServlet extends XMLHttpServlet
{
  private String m_strJDBCDriver                      = null;
  private String m_strDatabaseURL                     = null;
  private Catalog m_Catalog          = null;

  public void init( ServletConfig config )
    throws ServletException, UnavailableException
  {
    super.init(config);

    m_strJDBCDriver   = config.getInitParameter("Driver");
    m_strDatabaseURL  = config.getInitParameter("DatabaseURL");
    String strFactory = config.getInitParameter("DOMFactory");
    String strWriter  = config.getInitParameter("DOMWriter");
    String strTrans   = config.getInitParameter("XSLTransformer");

    try
    {                         DOMManager.setFactory(strFactory);
                    DOMManager.setWriter(strWriter);
```

```
      DOMManager.setTransformer(strTrans);

                        m_Catalog = new Catalog( getConnection() );
    }
    catch( Exception e )
    {
      log( e.toString() );
      throw new UnavailableException(this, e.toString() );
    }
  }
}
```

The first thing that should always be done when implementing the `init` method of a servlet is to call `super.init`. This allows the ancestors to initialize themselves. Next, we need to retrieve the initialization parameters so we know how to configure the servlet. This is accomplished by calling the `getInitParameter` method of the `ServletConfig` object. In doing so, we pass the parameter name to retrieve its associated value. As long as the parameter exists in the property file, its associated value is returned. Otherwise, the return value is `null`.

Once all of the initialization parameters are read from the `ServletConfig` object, we assign the appropriate adapters for the `DOMManager` using the `setFactory`, `setWriter`, and `setTransformer` methods. Finally, we create a new instance of the catalog object. In order to create the `Catalog` object we have to provide a Connection as a parameter. Thus we simply pass the returned `Connection` object from our `getConnection` method.

A try/catch block to catch any exceptions in unforeseen situations wraps all of the configuration code. Exactly like the `getConnection` method, we would be wasting our time attempting to catch each separate exception because in our case they all mean that the servlet is not going to function. Thus we simply catch the base `Exception` class. In doing so, we use the log method from the `GenericServlet` to write information to the servlet log file and throw an `UnavailableException` to inform the servlet engine that we are unavailable!

6.2.6.2 Implementing the doXML method

Now that we have implemented the initialization code for the servlet, we can move on to the interesting aspects of the application. In order to process requests from clients and make the compiler happy, we need to implement the doXML method. Hence, we will have a common function that every request will enter and can be processed. Because this method will be called by each request, we only want to contain logic that is common to all activities of the site. This is because changes to this method can potentially affect other functional components. Instead, we perform a few common tasks that will need to occur for each request and call separate methods for specific functionality.

For each client request, we have to perform the following. First, the resulting Document object will need to be instantiated. Then, we need to create the root element so that the business object elements can be appended. Because each of the business objects was created independently of the application, the root element will provide the element that can contain each of the business object elements. Furthermore, the real purpose of this data document is to provide information to the XSL stylesheets. As this element is really a representation of the website, we will name it book-session.

Once the document is created, we need to determine what the client is requesting. To standardize on a simple mechanism, we use an HTTP parameter named "Action" to signify what the servlet should do, and using the value of this parameter, we will determine what the servlet should do before sending the response to the client. As previously stated, instead of actually performing the different actions, we will call separate methods specifically designed to accommodate the different types of requests.

After the action has been processed, we need to append the different business object elements to the root element of the response document. This is accomplished by calling the cloneAccount, cloneBasket, and cloneCatalog methods of the business objects and appending them to the root element of the response document.

Breaking down the requirements of the method makes it easier to understand. Creating the response document will be simple because we can use the DOMManager and DOMFactory to create the document. Once the document has been created, we can use it to create the root element book-session and stick it into the response object so the remaining code has a common place to access it.

We can use the HttpServletRequest object to determine the value of the "Action" HTTP parameter, if any. In doing so, we can simply test this variable with specific action codes to determine what we are actually suppose to perform. For now, Table 6.1 identifies the actions codes that we accept and the function we call when we receive the action.

Table 6.1 Method Mapping Based on Action Code

Value	Method invoked
Register	DoRegisterAction
Login	DoLoginAction
AddItem	DoBasketAction
ChangeItem	
Goto	None

With the exception of the basket actions, the rest of the action values will simply invoke their associated method. For the basket actions, AddItem and ChangeItem, either of these values will invoke the DoBasketMethod, because without getting into too much detail here, both of these will require almost identical code. It is not necessary to be concerned with these methods for now, we will cover them shortly.

Finally, we need to append each of the business object's XML representations to the book-session root element. In doing so, we create a separate method to perform this task to make it easier to modify if we add additional business objects to the servlet in the future. The entire doXML method is shown in Example 6.12.

Example 6.12 XMLBookServlet doXML method

```
public static final String BOOK_SESSION                          = "book-
session";

public void doXML(HttpServletRequest request,XMLHttpServletResponse
response)
  throws ServletException, IOException
{
```

```
  Document doc = DOMManager.getFactory().createDocument("1.0");
  doc.appendChild(doc.createElement(BOOK_SESSION));
  response.setDocument(doc);

  String strAction = request.getParameter( "Action" );
  if (strAction != null)
  { if (strAction.equalsIgnoreCase( "Register" ))
      doRegisterAction( request, response);

    else if (strAction.equalsIgnoreCase( "Login" ))
      doLoginAction( request, response);

    else if (strAction.equalsIgnoreCase("AddItem") ||
             strAction.equalsIgnoreCase("ChangeItem"))
      doBasketAction( strAction, request, response);

    else if (strAction.equalsIgnoreCase("PlaceOrder"))
      doOrderAction( request, response );

    else if (strAction.equalsIgnoreCase("Goto"))
      response.setStyleSheet(request.getParameter("ss"));

    else
      log("!! Received invalid Action parameter -[" + strAction + "]");
  }
  else response.setStyleSheet( DEFAULT_STYLESHEET );

  appendElements( request, doc );
}
```

The first few lines should seem pretty straightforward because they do not contain anything that we have not covered previously. Once the `Document` has been created and stored in the `XMLHttpServletResponse` object, we can check to see if the Action parameter was passed by the client browser. To do so, we pass the name of the parameter were are seeking (in our case, "Action") to the `getParameter` method of the `HttpSerlvetRequest` object. This will either return the value associated with the named parameter or `null`.

If the Action parameter was not `null`, we use a series of if tests to determine the appropriate action. For example, if the value of the Action parameter was "Register," we call the `doRegisterAction`, and so forth. Of interest in the `Goto` value, which basically does nothing except assign a dynamic stylesheet based on the "ss" HTTP parameter. We use this to string a series of dynamic pages together without having to call a specific business function.

If the Action parameter was not passed to the servlet we assign a default stylesheet, which happens to evaluate to "/book/catalog.xsl" to the response. Essentially, this will be used to bring up the home page of the site.

Finally, we call the appendElements method. This method must insert the various business object's XML output to the book-session Element. For the most part, this is simply a matter of calling the appendTo methods of our three business objects, as shown in Example 6.13.

Example 6.13 XMLBookServlet appendElements method

```
protected void appendElements(HttpServletRequest request, Document doc)
{
  Element root = doc.getDocumentElement();
  m_Catalog.appendTo(root);

  HttpSession session = request.getSession(false);
  if (session != null)
  {
    Object obj = session.getValue(ShoppingBasket.BASKET_TYPE);
    ((ShoppingBasket)obj).appendTo(root);

    obj = session.getValue(Account.ACCOUNT_TYPE);
    ((Account)obj).appendTo(root);
  }
}
```

Upon entering the appendElement method, we grab a reference to the root element, and immediately call the Catalog.appendTo method to append the catalog and its products to the XML document. Next, we attempt to retrieve the HttpSession that is associated with the user. Passing a false to this method indicates that we do not want to create the session if it does not exist already.

Depending on whether the session exists determines if we append the Account and ShoppingBasket objects. The question you might have been considering is where (and when) the Account and ShoppingBasket classes are stored. Because these classes are really only specific to a single user, we take advantage of the HttpSession object to store these instances. One of the major advantages of extending the HttpServlet class is session management. The HttpServletRequest object provides a getSession method that can be used to retrieve the associated session for the client. In doing so, we must pass the method a `boolean` parameter indicating whether we would like to create the session if it does not already exist. In our case, we passed `false` because we are only concerned with including the business object elements when they exist.

The `HttpSession` object is similar to a hashtable that provides additional methods specific to servlets. Although how this is implemented is up to the servlet implementation, the interface provides methods to set and retrieve objects by name (String). Of course the interface is designed to accept `Object` classes, so all classes can be stored in the `HttpSession` object. The downside is that we have to cast the object back to the appropriate type when we retrieve them, so do not forget what type they are!

Because we have implemented a method that extracts objects from the `HttpSession` we have yet to write any code that places the object into it, it is only prudent to do so now. We have not seen the need for inserting objects into the session yet because we have not started integrating the business objects into the servlet. To do so, we provide a generic implementation that will create the session if it does not exist, and insert new instances of the `Account` and `ShoppingBasket` classes. Although this is relatively straightforward, the key is to know when to create the objects. Using a parameter to signify when to create a session makes many coding tasks very easy. However, this hides knowing explicitly when the `HttpSession` object is created. To the rescue is the `HttpSession` object, which provides an `isNew` method. This method returns `true` when the session has been created but the client application does not quite know it yet! This will provide us enough information to insert our two business objects into the session. To further simplify this process, we create both of the objects whenever the `HttpSession` is "new," as shown in Example 6.14.

Example 6.14 XMLBookServlet.getSession method

```
protected HttpSession getSession( HttpServletRequest request )
{
  HttpSession session = request.getSession(true);
  if (session.isNew())
  {
    session.putValue(Account.ACCOUNT_TYPE, new Account());
```

```
    session.putValue(ShoppingBasket.BASKET_TYPE, new ShoppingBas-
ket(m_Catalog));
  }
  return session;
}
```

As you can see from the example, we have created our own version of `getSession` that is very similar to how the `HttpServletRequest` object operates. The difference is that this method will always attempt to create a new session when it does not exist. Furthermore, we will also always create the two business objects. This will ensure that the objects are readily available for the methods we need to implement for the HTTP Action parameter processing.

6.2.6.3 *doRegisterAction*

Now we can implement the three different methods that will perform the different actions listed in Table 6.1. In doing so, we will finally get the chance to tie in the business objects that we created in the previous chapter. We will start by implementing the `doRegisterAction` method. This method will be responsible for extracting all of the information required (and optional) to create a new customer account, and invoke the create method of the `Account` object. If all goes well, the method will simply set a Successful attribute on the root (`book-session`) element to indicate the action was successful.

During this process, the `Account.create` method can throw either a `SQLException` or a `AccountException`. We can handle both of these exceptions by catching the base `Exception` object. The `doRegisterAction` method is shown in Example 6.15.

Example 6.15 XMLBookServlet.doRegisterAction method

```
public static final String TRUE                    = "true";
public static final String FALSE                   = "false";
public static final String SUCCESSFUL = "Successful";

private static final
String[] keys = { Account.FIRST_NAME,
Account.MIDDLE_INITIAL,
                                          Account.LAST_NAME,
Account.ADDRESS_LINE1,
                                          Account.ADDRESS_LINE2,
```

```
Account.ADDRESS_CITY,
                                        Account.ADDRESS_STATE,
Account.ADDRESS_ZIP,
                                        Account.PHONE_NUMBER,
Account.FAX_NUMBER,
                                        Account.USER_NAME,         Account.PASS-
WORD,
                                        Account.CHALLENGE,
Account.CONFIRM_PASSWORD};

protected boolean doRegisterAction(HttpServletRequest req, XMLHttpServlet-
Response res)
  throws UnavailableException
{
  HttpSession session = getSession( req );  // create it if neccessary
  Object objAccount   = session.getValue(Account.ACCOUNT_TYPE);
  Account acct        = (Account) objAccount;
  Document doc        = res.getDocument();
  Element trans       = doc.getDocumentElement();

  Hashtable hash      = new Hashtable();
  try
  {
    for( int i =0; i < keys.length; i++)
    { String strValue = req.getParameter( keys[i] );
      if (strValue != null && strValue.length() > 0 )
        hash.put( keys[i], strValue );
    }
    Connection conn = getConnection();
    acct.create( conn, hash );
    res.setStyleSheet( "/book/catalog.xsl" );
  }
  catch( Exception e )
  {
    trans.appendChild( DOMManager.createElement( doc, ERROR_ELEMENT,
e.getMessage()));
    res.setStyleSheet( "/book/registration.xsl" );
    return true;
  }
  return true;
}
```

As you can see from the code, extracting the account object is very easy now that we have created the `getSession` method. Because the `getSession` method automatically created the `Account` object we do not need to worry about creating a new one. Instead, we simply extract it out of the `HttpSession` object by passing the key to the `getValue` method. In our case, we used the `Account.ACCOUNT_TYPE` as the key for the `Account` object.

We have to do some work before we can call the `create` method of the `Account` object. Because the account object takes a `Hashtable` of string parameters, we need to create a `Hashtable` and add the HTTP parameters for creating the account. In the process it will be important that we do not reimplement the validation that occurs in the `Account` object. In particular, we do not want any part of knowing whether or not a parameter was required. We simply want to give all the HTTP parameters to the `Account` object and let the business object determine if all the needed information was passed.

To implement this, we used an array of strings, defined in the keys variable, that will be used to identify all the HTTP parameter names we need to insert in the Hashtable. To insert the relevant parameters, we simply iterate through the array, checking to see if the `HttpServletRequest` has the parameter we are seeking. If so, we simply insert it by the appropriate key name into the Hashtable.

Once we have copied all of the parameters from the `HttpServletRequest` to our `Hashtable` object, we get a new database connection by calling `getConnection` and invoking the `create` method of the `Account` object.

Ultimately, the `Account` object will determine whether or not this action was successful. Fortunately, if the action was not successful, we can once again simply catch the generic `Exception` class. In these cases we add a new element of type error to the root of the response document.

Finally, the last task we must accomplish is to assign the stylesheet for viewing the XML document. If the request was successful, we assign the "/book/catalog.xsl" stylesheet so the user will immediately be able to continue shopping. If the method was not successful, we assign the "/book/registration.xsl" stylesheet.

6.2.6.4 doLoginAction

Much like the `doRegisterAction` method, the `doLoginAction` must also retrieve the `Account` object from the `HttpSession` object. This time, however, we check the status of the account before blindly attempting to authenticate the user. Although we are trying to keep all of the business rules in the business objects, we are actually creating an application rule. Recall in Chapter 5 that we did not add any validation to limit when authentication can occur. In doing so, we ensured at the business object level that we could perform "impersonations" whereby a user can reauthenticate as a different user, similar to the su command in UNIX systems. Because this type of functionality is more geared for administrative functions (by contrast, our website is geared towards commerce), we will add business rules in the doLoginAction to ensure that this does not happen. The code for the doLoginAction method is shown in Example 6.16.

Example 6.16 XMLBookServlet.doLoginAction method

```
protected boolean doLoginAction(HttpServletRequest req,
XMLHttpServletResponse res)
                        throws UnavailableException
{
  HttpSession session = getSession( req );
  Object objAccount   = session.getValue(Account.ACCOUNT_TYPE);
  Account acct        = (Account) objAccount;
  Document doc        = res.getDocument();
  Element trans       = doc.getDocumentElement();

  try
  {
    String status = acct.getStatus();
    if (!status.equals(Account.AUTHENTICATED))
    {
      Connection conn = getConnection();
      String strUser = req.getParameter(Account.USER_NAME);
      String strPassword = req.getParameter(Account.PASSWORD);
      String result = acct.authenticate( conn, strUser, strPassword);
    }
  }
  catch(Exception e)
  {
    trans.appendChild( DOMManager.createElement( doc, ERROR_ELEMENT,
e.toString()));
  }
  res.setStyleSheet( "/book/catalog.xsl" );
  return true;
}
```

As you can see from the code in the example, we call the getStatus method of the Account object and compare it to the AUTHENTICATED member of the Account object. As long as the account is not currently authenticated, we extract the relevant parameters (USER_NAME and PASSWORD) from the HttpServletRequest object, grab a database connection by calling the getConnection method, and invoke the authenticate method.

Exactly as in the doRegisterAction method, we only catch a generic Exception object because any exception pretty much means the same thing in this context. When this occurs we simply append an error element to the root element of the response document. Finally, we assign the "/book/catalog.xsl" stylesheet to present the resulting XML document to the user.

6.2.6.5 *doBasketAction*

The last method we need to implement is the doBasketAction method. It will handle both the AddItem and ChangeItem action codes. In doing so, we add the strAction variable to the signature so we do not need to extract the value from the HttpServletRequest object again. The rest of the login pretty much performs the same basic tasks that we have implemented for the last two methods. First, we will extract the ShoppingBasket from the session, extract the parameters from the HttpServletRequest object, and invoke either the AddProduct or ChangeProduct method of the ShoppingBasket object.

Example 6.17 XMLBookServlet.doBasketAction method

```
protected boolean doBasketAction( String strAction, HttpServletRequest
req, XMLHttpServletResponse res)
{
  HttpSession session    = getSession( req );
  Document doc           = res.getDocument();
  Element trans          = doc.getDocumentElement();
  Object objBasket       = session.getValue(ShoppingBasket.BASKET_TYPE);
  ShoppingBasket basket = (ShoppingBasket) objBasket;

  try
  {
    String strProductID = req.getParameter( Product.PRODUCT_ID );
    String strQuantity  = req.getParameter( Product.QUANTITY );

    int nQty = Integer.parseInt(strQuantity);
```

```
    if (strAction.equalsIgnoreCase("ChangeItem") )
      basket.changeQuantity(strProductID, nQty);

    else if (strAction.equalsIgnoreCase("AddItem") )
      basket.addProduct(strProductID, nQty);
  }
  catch( Exception e )
  {
    Element err = DOMManager.createElement( doc,ERROR_ELEMENT,
e.toString());
    trans.appendChild( err);
  }
  res.setStyleSheet( "/book/basket.xsl" );
  return true;
}
```

If this code looks very similar to the other two action-processing methods it is by design. Although a cookie-cutter approach generally gets boring after a few interactions, it is the sign of a good design and consistency. Remember that the `XMLBookServlet` class is really the glue of the application, and the business objects provide the business rules and functionality.

As with the other `doXXXAction` methods, we start by extracting the relevant objects into local method references. Instead of extracting the `Account` object, however, this time we passed the `ShoppingBasket.BASKET_TYPE` to the `getValue` method of the `HttpSession` to retrieve the `ShoppingBasket` object for this user.

Next, we retrieve the product id and quantity attributes from the HTTP request parameters. Because HTTP parameters are all Strings, we must first convert the Quantity parameter to an integer before calling the appropriate method of the `ShoppingBasket` object.

Finally, we test the `strAction` variable that contains the value of the HTTP Action parameter originally extracted in the `doXML` method. Depending on its value we either call the `changeQuantity` or `addProduct` method of the ShoppingBasket class.

Finally, we assign the "/book/basket.xsl" stylesheet to the response object.

Hopefully, implementing the `XMLBookServlet` was easier than first thought. Although working with the DOM repetitively, it is also very quickly learned because the API is so small. As we previously indicated, the `XMLBookServlet` class was simply the glue that will hold the website together. This is the class that ties the technology (XML) with the business objects to provide a solution. Along the way, we covered many aspects of servlet development and used the `ServletConfig` object to dynamically load information from the servlets property file. Once the servlet was initialized, we identified an HTTP parameter "Action" that could be used to invoke specific functionality. With this parameter we began tying together all of the business objects we wrote in Chapter 5. Moreover, the Action HTTP parameter allowed us to decouple the business logic from the presentation tier. This means we will be able to give the site a facelift fairly easily.

6.3 *Implementing the User Interface with XSL Stylesheets*

So far, we have built an infrastructure that provides a great deal of flexibility for creating any user interface. The servlet we just created merely includes the three different business object elements (`Account`, `Catalog`, and `ShoppingBasket`) within a larger `book-session` element that acts as a container. This approach works well for the environment we are creating because it allows access to all the data elements from the stylesheets.

For starters, we create three different stylesheets for the website. The primary stylesheet will present the catalog and allow customers to purchase or place products into their `ShoppingBasket`. The second stylesheet will allow new users to create new accounts. Finally, we need to create a third stylesheet for allowing the users to view the contents of their shopping basket. Of course, these stylesheets will all be based on the `book-session` element that is produced as the response of each request from the servlet we have just created. The elements that are contained within the `book-session` element depend on the action and state of the session at the time the response is created. For example, the following document will be produced when the customer initially hits the website:

```
<book-session>
  <catalog>
```

```
    ... <!-- ellipse for brevity -->
  </catalog>
</book-session>
```

As you can see, the basket and Account elements will not always be included in the book-session element. Looking back at the servlet code, we only created the ShoppingBasket and Account business objects when they are needed. Because the user has not had time to perform any actions related to these objects, neither of them are included in the XML document. The Account object is created when an HTTP "Action" parameter is passed with a value of either "Register" or "Login." Whenever one of these two actions is received, the Account object is created and additional child elements may be included depending on the function performed. If a Login action was received with a valid UserName and Password, the account element might be populated as follows:

```
<book-session>
  <catalog>
    ... <!-- ellipse for brevity -->
  </catalog>
  <basket/>
  <Account Status="Authenticated" CustomerID="01">
    <Address1>123 Main Street</Address1>
    <Address2/>
    <FirstName>Bruce</FirstName>
    <MiddleInitial/>
    <LastName>Weber</LastName>
    <City>Phoenix</City>
    <State>AZ</State>
    <Zip>80025</Zip>
    <PhoneNumber>732-2537</PhoneNumber>
    <FaxNumber/>
  </Account>
</book-session>
```

The important thing to notice here is that the basket element was included. However, the user has yet to add any products to the basket so it is displayed as an empty element. Similarly, the Account element now contains the child elements (FirstName, LastName, etc.) that describe the account and the Status property indicates that the user has been Authenticated. It is very important to understand what data the book-session element will contain when the request is sent to the client in order to know how to process the document.

Typically, the first task that is performed when implementing the HTML for a website is to identify a common look and feel for the entire site. In doing so, many sites modularize specific areas of their website and simply include the boilerplate code in each HTML page. This approach reduces the amount of code written and ultimately reduces the amount of work that is required when changing the look and feel for subsequent modifications. We will also apply this technique by utilizing the `<xsl:include>` element to employ a common code that will provide the shell of the site.

6.3.1 Creating the Shell of the Site

We start creating the shell of the website by creating a new XSL document. This is shown in Example 6.18. This includes creating the XML prolog processing Instruction, and the `<xsl:stylesheet>` root element. Although the XML prolog is not required, it is always a good idea to include this so that the version of the syntax is explicitly declared.

Example 6.18 New XSL stylesheet

```
<?xml version="1.0"?>
<xsl:stylesheet xmlns:xsl="http://www.w3.org/XSL/Transform/1.0"
                  xmlns="http://www.w3.org/TR/REC-html40"
                                  result-ns=""
>
  ...
</xsl:stylesheet>
```

From the example you will notice three attributes that describe the `<xsl:stylesheet>` root element. As we covered in Chapter 3, the `xmlns` identifies the global namespace for the elements in the stylesheet. Similarly, the `xmlns:xsl` attribute identifies the namespace for all the elements within the xsl namespace (elements that start with `xsl:`). Because we will be outputting HTML, the `xmlns` attribute is assigned the HTML 4.0 Namespace URL while the stylesheet namespace (`xmlns:xsl`) is assigned to the version 1.0 transformation URL. Finally, the `result-ns` attribute is used to provide a hint to the XSL processor on how the result tree should be formatted. Although the processor is not required to do anything special with this attribute, assigning an empty string value indicates that the default namespace should be used.

After the XSL processor loads and parses a stylesheet, it then begins to process it. To do so, the XSL processor must match the appropriate template, based on the matching and conflict resolution rules covered in Chapter 3. Typically, stylesheets have a root template that matches all nodes in the data document. In our case, this is the perfect opportunity to apply a standard shell for the website so that all the pages have the same look and feel. As shown in Example 6.19, we match on the root node to begin processing the stylesheet.

Example 6.19 XSL template matching the root node.

```
<?xml version="1.0"?>
<xsl:stylesheet xmlns:xsl="http://www.w3.org/XSL/Transform/1.0"
                    xmlns="http://www.w3.org/TR/REC-html40"
                                    result-ns=""

>
  <xsl:template match="/">
    ...
  </xsl:template>
</xsl:stylesheet>
```

Once the XSL processor matches, the appropriate template execution of the stylesheet begins with the first child element within the template. Furthermore, the current or context node in the data document is set based on the pattern used to match the template. In our case, the root element, `book-session`, is the context node within the template that matches root ("/") document node. The `xsl:template` can include literal elements, such as `<HTML>`, that are simply written to the result tree as they are encountered. Furthermore, the `xsl:template` can also include additional elements from the XSL namespace that can be used to provide minor programmatic capabilities, such as traversing nodes one by one, sorting, simple arithmetic, etc. We will not pay much attention to the literal HTML elements that we encounter throughout these templates. Instead, we will focus on the elements from the XSL namespace.

Most large-scale websites use some form of technology to assist the management of the HTML content. Independent of the technologies, these sites usually have some mechanism that can provide modularity to HTML files, such as including additional files, that can be used to reduce the amount of code. As we covered in Chapter 3, XSL offers similar mechanisms, such as the `xsl:include` and `xsl:import` tags. The tags can be used to make the elements of the external stylesheet part of the current stylesheet. Using these mechanisms, the cost of ownership related to maintenance can be reduced because the common code can be contained in a single stylesheet that effects all stylesheets.

Instead of invoking an `xsl:template` by matching a pattern, we can also invoke a template simply by calling it by name. As seen in Chapter 3, templates can also have a name attribute that can be used with the `xsl:call-template` element. In doing so, the context node of the template does not change as it does when the template is invoked by matching a pattern. This is similar to calling a function in Java. However, the templates will not have a return value. We use the `xsl:include` and the `xsl:call-template` elements to provide a common shell for our website that all of the templates can reuse.

We create a standard header and footer for our website. In doing so, we place the templates for creating the header and footer in a common stylesheet that can be included in different stylesheets designed to present specific information, such as the contents of the `ShoppingBasket`, the `Catalog`, or the user's Account.

6.3.2 Common.xsl

We start by creating a new stylesheet named `common.xsl` and providing the `xsl:stylesheet` element. Next, we create the default `xsl:template` element that matches the root node in the XML document. Inside the template, we start by placing the literal HTML tags necessary to create an HTML table. Inside the HTML table, we add two `xsl:call-template` elements that will be used to generate the top and bottom rows of the table. Finally, we place the remaining HTML elements following the stylesheet elements to close the HTML table and HTML page. This is shown in Example 6.20.

Example 6.20 Default root template

```
<xsl:template match="/" >
  <HTML><HEAD><TITLE>XMLBook Ecomm website!</TITLE></HEAD>
```

```
  <BODY BGCOLOR="#FFFFFF"><CENTER><TABLE BORDER="1" WIDTH="600">

    <!-- Header Area -->
    <xsl:call-template name="ShellTop"/>

    ... <!-- Reserved for content -->

    <!-- Footer Area -->
    <xsl:call-template name="ShellBottom"/>

  </TABLE></CENTER></BODY></HTML>
</xsl:template>
```

As you can see from the example, this template does not do much more than call the `ShellTop` and `ShellBottom` templates to write the literal HTML tags to the result tree. The area between the Top and Bottom templates is reserved for content. As you will see shortly, this template will never actually be used to display a page to a user. Instead, each particular page will provide its own implementation of this template. In doing so, this template can act as a boilerplate layout that required the specific templates to implement the area noted as "Reserved for content."

> **NOTE:** It is unfortunate that each template specific to a section of the site will require its own implementation of a root-matching template. This is primarily because the `ShellTop`, `ShellBottom` and the content areas are contained within the HTML elements. XSL stylesheets must still abide by the well-formedness constraints of XML documents. Thus these HTML documents could not simply be included in the `ShellTop` and `ShellBottom` templates. In order to meet the well-formedness constraints of XML, all of these elements must be contained within another element.

6.3.2.1 ShellTop template

We can continue by implementing the `ShellTop` template. Because this template is being called, the context node will remain the same as the context where it is being called. In this case, it will remain at the root, or `book-session`, element. For now, we simply place our company name and a list of links to other areas of the site at the top of the page, as shown in Example 6.21.

Example 6.21 ShellTop template

```
<xsl:template name="ShellTop">
  <TR><TD COLSPAN="1"><TABLE BORDER="0" WIDTH="100%"><TR>
  <TD WIDTH="*">
    <FONT FACE="Arial" SIZE="4"><I>PDA Plaza</I></FONT></TD>
  <TD><TABLE BORDER="0" WIDTH="100%"><TR>

    <xsl:call-template name="navBar"/>

  </TR></TABLE></TD></TR></TABLE></TD></TR>
</xsl:template>
```

As you can see from the example, this is merely a series of HTML tags. Instead of creating the various links for the site in the `ShellTop`, we actually called yet another template, `NavBar`, to provide the links. As we do not know how much content will be placed in the content area of the page, we take a common approach of many websites by placing the same links at the bottom of the page. In doing so, we only code the links in a single template so we can be assured that the top and bottom links are never out of sync.

6.3.2.2 NavBar template

The `Navbar` template will mostly be a list of links to the other pages of the site. Although we have not implemented these pages yet, they will include the catalog, registration, and basket stylesheets. The registration template will depend on the status of the `Account` object. Users should only be able to register for the site when they are considered anonymous. Instead of blindly including a link to the registration page, we add some intelligence to the `navBar` template to conditionally provide the link to the registration page based on the `Status` attribute of the `Account` element. This is shown in Example 6.22.

Example 6.22 NavBar template

```
<xsl:template name="navBar">
  <TD BGCOLOR="#FFFFFF" ALIGN="RIGHT" WIDTH="100%">
    <NOBR><FONT FACE="Arial" SIZE="1" COLOR="red">
      <A HREF="/XMLBook/Book/">Catalog</A> |
      <xsl:if test="not(//Account/@Status='Authenticated')">
        <A HREF="/XMLBook/Book/?Action=Goto&amp;ss=/book/registration
.xsl">Register</A> |
      </xsl:if>
```

```
      <A HREF="/XMLBook/Book/?Action=Goto&amp;ss=/book/Basket.xsl">Cart</A>
    </FONT></NOBR>
  </TD>
</xsl:template>
```

In order to conditionally display the link to register we use the `xsl:if` element. As seen in Chapter 3, this element will execute its child elements if the expression in its test attribute evaluates to true. In this case, the pattern "`not(//Account/@Status='Authenticated')`" queries the `Status` attribute of any `Account` element within the document. As long as the `Status` element does not equal "`Authenticated`," the condition is true and the child elements are invoked. Furthermore, this test will also return true if the `Account` element *does not* exist in the document.

This template also wrote three links to the different areas of the site. To link to the catalog, we simply used the relative URL "`/XMLBook/Book/`" because the `catalog.xsl` stylesheet is the default stylesheet assigned within the `XMLBook-Servlet` class. For the other two links, the Basket and Registration pages, we passed an Action parameter of "Goto." If you remember back in where we built the `doXML` method, here we can use the `Goto` action to display a different dynamic page without having to call any of the business objects.

> **TIP:** When templates are called the context node does not change; instead, it remains the same as it was when the template was called. When designed templates are called from other templates, it is important to not assume the context of the node. For this reason, we prefixed the Account element with the "//" to avoid knowing the context node. This works well in our situation because we know that the Account element can, at most, only appear once in the document. Furthermore, this pattern does not constrain the parent of the account element. Thus if the root element was changed to a different name in the future this pattern would still function.

6.3.2.3 ShellBottom template

Implementing the `ShellBottom` template will be very similar to the `ShellTop` template. Instead of providing the company name again, we replace this with a status line that can be used to display any errors that occurred while processing a given request. This is shown in Example 6.23.

Example 6.23 ShellBottom template

```
<xsl:template name="ShellBottom">
  <TR><TD>
  <TABLE><TR>
    <TD><FONT FACE="Arial" SIZE="2" COLOR="red">
      <xsl:for-each select="//error">
        <xsl:value-of select="."/><BR/>
      </xsl:for-each>
    <BR/></FONT></TD>
    <xsl:call-template name="navBar"/>
  </TR></TABLE></TD></TR>
  <TR><TD ALIGN="CENTER"><IMG SRC="/book/apache_pb.gif"/></TD></TR>
</xsl:template>
```

As you can see from the example, we used an xsl:for-each element to loop through any error elements throughout the document (signified by the // error pattern). For each error element encountered, we use the `xsl:value-of` element to display its text value. Again, we prefixed the pattern with the "//" locator because we cannot be certain of the context when this template was invoked. Once all of the errors (if any) are displayed, we use the `xsl:call-template` element to invoke the `navBar` template as we did in Example 6.21.

6.3.3 Implementing the catalog stylesheet

To implement the `catalog.xsl` stylesheet, we can create a new file called catalog.xsl and provide the `xsl:stylesheet` element with the same properties previously seen in Example 6.18. In order to use the templates we created in the `common.xsl` stylesheet, we have to use the `xsl:include` element. In doing so, we simply assign the `href` attribute with a value of `common.xsl` to specify the stylesheet we want to include, as follows:

```
<xsl:include href="common.xsl"/>
```

Remember from Chapter 3 that the `href` attribute specifies a relative URL from the current stylesheet. Because we store all of our stylesheets in the same directory, we can simply use `common.xsl`. Once the XSL processor encounters this element, it must locate, load, and parse the `common.xsl` stylesheet and include it as part of the current stylesheet. In doing so, the XSL Processor parses the included files and extracts all of the children below the `xsl:stylesheet` element. This is because the `xsl:stylesheet` cannot contain `xsl:stylesheet` child elements, and because the XSL DTD states `xsl:stylesheet` elements cannot contain other `xsl:stylesheet` elements.

Because we need to provide specific content for the catalog, we cannot use the default template that matches the root node from the include stylesheet. Instead, we have to create our own template that matches the root element. To do this, we can simply copy the same code we used in common.xsl and implement the content by applying a template based on the structure of the XML document.

> **NOTE:** You might be wondering what will happen because this stylesheet will have two different templates that match the root element—the one we will implement in the catalog.xsl stylesheet and a second because we included the common.xsl template. The XSLT working draft identifies this in rather deep detail. The appropriate template is chosen based on importance, priority, and finally as a tiebreaker; the draft specifies that the last occurrence of the template will be used. In other words, when the importance and priorities are equal, the processor will invoke the template that is positioned after the others within the DOM tree. Because the `xsl:include` element precedes all other templates in the stylesheet, this means that the root-matching template in common.xsl will only be used if the outer stylesheet does not specifically implement the template. Refer to Chapter 3 for more information.

Instead of providing the content of the catalog directly inside our root-matching template, we provide a separate template that matches the catalog element. This will allow us to keep the root-matching template very small because it is simply calling different templates. The root-matching template for the catalog stylesheet is shown in Example 6.24.

Example 6.24 Catalog.xsl Template matching the root node

```
<xsl:template match="/" >
  <HTML><HEAD><TITLE>XMLBook Ecomm website!</TITLE></HEAD>
```

```
    <BODY BGCOLOR="#FFFFFF"><CENTER><TABLE BORDER="1" WIDTH="600">

      <!-- Header Area -->
      <xsl:call-template name="ShellTop"/>
      <TR><TD WIDTH="600">
        <xsl:apply-templates select="//catalog"/>
      </TD></TR>
      <!-- Footer Area -->
      <xsl:call-template name="ShellBottom"/>

    </TABLE></CENTER></BODY></HTML>
</xsl:template>
```

As you can see, this is almost identical to the previous template we wrote in the common stylesheet. The only difference is that we are calling the apply-templates element. In doing so, we set the `select` attribute to the pattern for all the catalog elements anywhere in the document (which in our case there will only be one catalog element). Thus, the context node of the template being called will be set to the catalog element when the template is invoked.

Next, we implement the template that will be invoked when execution reaches this element. To do so, all we have to do is create a new `xsl:template` element with a match attribute with an equivalent pattern as the one in the select attribute of the `xsl:apply-template` element, as shown in the following:

```
<xsl:template match="catalog">
  ...
</xsl:template>
```

In this case, we provided the `match` attribute instead of the `name` attribute we provided in the templates created previously. Although we could have provided both, only the `match` attribute matters in this case because the template is being applied based on the result tree from the select attribute of the `xsl:apply-template` element.

As with most e-commerce websites, it is very important that we have a pretty elaborate presentation of the products otherwise the users may go to a different site for their purchases. To accomplish this, we put some of the finer details of the XSL transformations to the test to provide some really interesting features. First, the catalog template will merely traverse through each product in the catalog. In doing so, we order the products by their category and create sections of products based on their category. Finally, will call a separate template to implement the specifics for each product. In this process we alternate the background color of each row.

We use the `xsl:for-each` element to iterate through each of the products in the catalog. As a result, we will add two `xsl:sort` elements immediately following the `xsl:for-each` element to sort the products by their `CategoryName` and `ProductName` child elements. This is accomplished with the following code:

```
<xsl:for-each select="Product">
  <xsl:sort select="CategoryName"/>
  <xsl:sort select="Name"/>
  ...
</xsl:for-each>
```

Because the context node is the `Catalog` element, we are selecting each of the `Product` element children. In the process, we asked the XSL Processor to order these nodes, first by their `CategoryName` child element, and second by their `Name` child element. Inside the for-each element, we style them appropriately.

While we are iterating through each `Product` element, we will provide Row separators within the HTML table that will serve as Category headings. Because the products are ordered appropriately, the rest of the functionality is theoretically simple to implement. By abstract from the technology, we simply want to write the `CategoryName` whenever the `CategoryName` of the current product is different from the previous product and, of course, before the first product is written.

To implement this functionality, we will use the `xsl:choose` element. As seen in Chapter 3, the `xsl:choose` element is similar to a `switch` keyword in Java. The difference between these from conditional statements is that the `switch` statement provides a single expression and multiple result cases,; whereas the `xsl:choose` simply provides multiple tests that may be true, as shown in Example 6.25.

Example 6.25 Providing CategoryName Headings

```
<xsl:choose>
  <xsl:when test="position()=1">
    <TR><TD COLSPAN="3" BGCOLOR="Black">
    <FONT SIZE="+1" COLOR="yellow">
      <xsl:value-of select="CategoryName"/>
    </FONT></TD></TR>
  </xsl:when>
  <xsl:when test="not($prevCat=CategoryName)">
    <TR><TD COLSPAN="3" BGCOLOR="Black">
    <FONT SIZE="+1" COLOR="yellow">
      <xsl:value-of select="CategoryName"/>
    </FONT></TD></TR>
  </xsl:when>
</xsl:choose>
...
<xsl:variable name="prevCat" expr="CategoryName"/>
```

The first `xsl:when` element tests to see if the product is the first element in the list. If this is not the first iteration through the set of nodes, the second `xsl:when` element works in conjunction with the `prevCat` variable assigned on the last line of the example. In this case, the `prevCat` holds the value of the `CategoryName` from the previous context node. In doing so, if the current `CategoryName` is different from the previous one the test is true. In either case, we simply write the value of the `CategoryName` to the result tree. Just prior to completing an iteration, the `prevCat` is reassigned to the value of the `CategoryName` of the current context node. This essentially allows the variable to always hold the previous `CategoryName` value.

The last thing the catalog template needs to do is write the details of each product to the result tree. In doing so, we alternate the background colors to give a striped look to the catalog. In order to accomplish this, we use the modulus operator to determine whether the current product is odd or even within the Node set. The first logical choice would be to implement this using a another `xsl:if` element. Unfortunately, the `xsl:if` element does not provide an else clause as with most programming languages. This is probably because it would be very difficult to implement while adhering to the well-formness constraints of XML specification. Instead, XSL offers an `xsl:choose` element. As you can see from Example 6.26, we use the `xsl:choose` element to provide any alternate to the background colors.

Example 6.26 Alternating background colors

```
<xsl:choose>
  <xsl:when test="position() mod 2=0">
    <xsl:apply-templates select=".">
      <xsl:param name="bgColor">#99CC99</xsl:param>
    </xsl:apply-templates>
  </xsl:when>
  <xsl:otherwise>
    <xsl:apply-templates select=".">
      <xsl:param name="bgColor">#FFCC66</xsl:param>
    </xsl:apply-templates>
  </xsl:otherwise>
</xsl:choose>
```

As you can see from the example, we use the `xsl:choose` element to test to determine if the current node position (in relation to the node set of the for-each element) is an even number. If so, the `xsl:when` element evaluates to true and its children nodes are invoked. However, if the position is an odd number, the children elements of the `xsl:otherwise` element are triggered. In either case, we apply a template that supports the current context node (signified by the dot). The difference between the two cases is how the templates are applied. In order to keep the code base under control we are simply calling a template that is designed to write a single product node to the result tree. In doing so, we are also taking advantage of the variable passing mechanism we saw in Chapter 3. This allows us to utilize the same code base for writing the product row. Depending on the outcome of the modulus test, we either pass a `bgColor` parameter of `#99CC99` or `#FFCC66` to the associated template. Ultimately, this parameter will be used to set the background color of the cells that make up the product row.

Because the context node was a Product when the `apply-template` element was applied, we need to create a template that matches the attribute with a pattern of Product. There is considerable work to be performed for each `Product` element. First, because people are visual, we want to include the `ImageURL` of the product so the user can view the image of the product. Of course, broken links would look unprofessional in a professional website, so we make sure that we filter these out using XSL conditional processing elements. In addition, we display the product name and its description. We finish off the row with the price and quantity available and provide a mechanism to purchase the product. This is shown in Example 6.27.

Example 6.27 Product template

```
<xsl:template match="Product">
  <TR>
    <!-- Start of Product or Mfg Image -->
    <TD ALIGN="CENTER" WIDTH="25" CELLPADDING="0">

      <xsl:if test="not(ImageURL='')">
        <IMG HEIGHT="90" WIDTH="90">
          <xsl:attribute name="SRC">
            <xsl:value-of select="ImageURL"/>
          </xsl:attribute>
          <xsl:attribute name="ALT">
            <xsl:value-of select="Name"/>
          </xsl:attribute>
        </IMG>
      </xsl:if>
      </TD>
    <!-- End of Product or Mfg Image -->

    <TD VALIGN="TOP" BGCOLOR="{$bgColor}">
      <FONT FACE="ARIAL, HELVETTICA" COLOR="blue" SIZE="2">
        <U><xsl:value-of select="Name"/></U><BR/>
      </FONT>
      <I><FONT FACE="ARIAL, HELVETICA" SIZE="1">
        <xsl:value-of select="Description"/>
      </FONT></I>
    </TD>

    <!-- Start of Price, Availability, Buy option -->
    <TD BGCOLOR="{$bgColor}"><TABLE BORDER="0"><TR>
      <TD ALIGN="LEFT" VALIGN="TOP" BGCOLOR="{$bgColor}">
        <!-- Price, buy button -->
        <FONT FACE="Arial, HELVETTICA" COLOR="blue" SIZE="1">
          <xsl:value-of select="format-number(ListPrice,'$0.00')"/>
        </FONT>
      </TD>
      <TD ALIGN="RIGHT" VALIGN="TOP" BGCOLOR="{$bgColor}">
        <!-- Start Buy button/form -->
        <xsl:call-template name="BuyProduct">
          <xsl:param name="ProductID" expr="@ProductID"/>
        </xsl:call-template>
```

```
        <!-- End Buy button/form -->
      </TD></TR><TR>
      <TD ALIGN="CENTER" VALIGN="BOTTOM" COLSPAN="2" BGCOLOR="{$bgColor}">
        <FONT FACE="Arial, HELVETTICA" SIZE="1">
          <!-- quantity availabile -->
          <xsl:choose>
            <xsl:when test="number(Quantity)=0">
              <i>On back order!</i>
            </xsl:when>
            <xsl:otherwise>
              <xsl:value-of select="Quantity"/> in stock.
            </xsl:otherwise>
          </xsl:choose>
        </FONT>
      </TD></TR>
    </TABLE></TD>
    <!-- End of Price, Availability, Buy option -->

  </TR>
</xsl:template>
```

First, to avoid broken links we use the `xsl:if` element to check to see if the `ImageURL` element is not an empty string. If the element contains a value we begin to construct an HTML `IMG` element. In the process, we dynamically assign the `SRC` attribute of the element to the value of the `ImageURL` element. For people with low-speed connections, we assign the Name of the product to the `ALT` tag of the `IMG` element.

For the remaining cells in the row, we assign the `BGCOLOR` attribute of the `TD` element to the `bgColor` parameter that was passed to the template. Inside the second cell, we use the `xsl:value-of` element to write the `Name` and `Description` of the product to the result tree. After the product name and description have been written to the result tree, we write the price of the item. In doing so, we use the `format-number` method to add the currency and decimal places to the price.

Before we get to the implementation of the `BuyProduct` template, the last thing we need to do is display the `Quantity` attribute. As you can see from the example, we display a "On Back Order!" message when the `Quantity` is zero, otherwise we write the value of the `Quantity` element to the result tree.

> **NOTE:** You might have noticed that the <BR/> element following the Name does not look like the typical line-break element in HTML. Remember that the stylesheets must be well formed. Although they are a special type, stylesheets are still XML documents by nature. Because of this, some of the HTML tags, such as `BR`, `HR`, `INPUT`, etc., will require the empty element notation in order for the stylesheet to be considered well formed. Do not worry though, remember this merely writes a result tree; it is the job of the formatter to make the output appear in HTML syntax that all the browsers will understand.

We choose to make a separate template that would write the necessary elements required to add the product to the shopping basket. For reusability, we add this template to the common.xsl stylesheet we previously created. In doing so, we can isolate the `AddItem` action to a single template that can be included wherever a product is displayed. If you can remember implementing the `AddProduct` method of the `ShoppingBasket`, two parameters were required. First, the `ProductID` was required to uniquely identify the `Product` to be added. The second parameter, the number of products to purchase, was also required. In most cases, customers will only want to purchase a single product. In this case, passing only the `ProductID` will suffice. When designing for reusability, however, we do not want to limit the usefulness of the `BuyProduct` template to a single product. Instead, we can use a default parameter in the template to default the `Quantity` to 1 when it is not explicitly passed in the stylesheet. This is shown in Example 6.28.

Example 6.28 BuyProduct template

```
<xsl:template name="BuyProduct">
  <xsl:param-variable name="Qty">1</xsl:param-variable>
  <FORM METHOD="POST" ACTION="/XMLBook/Book/">
    <INPUT TYPE="HIDDEN" NAME="Action"    VALUE="AddItem"/>
    <INPUT TYPE="HIDDEN" NAME="ProductID" VALUE="{$ProductID}"/>
    <INPUT TYPE="HIDDEN" NAME="Quantity"  VALUE="{$Qty}"/>
    <INPUT TYPE="IMAGE"  SRC="/graphics/buy_hand.gif"/>
  </FORM>
</xsl:template>
```

As you can see, we used the `xsl:param-variable` element to provide a default value to the `Qty` variable if it was not explicitly passed when this template was called. The rest of the template is simply writing the HTML elements required to the result tree while binding in the `ProductID` and `Qty` variables.

There is a lot more to the catalog stylesheet than meets the eye. The good news is that we have seen most of the XSL elements hence the remaining two stylesheets will be fairly easy to implement. Also, we have seen a few different ways to invoke a stylesheet, such as by calling a template by name and by applying a template based on a resulting Node Set from a select attribute. We also passed variables or arguments to these templates to make some of the templates more usable in the future. We used the `for-each` element to iterate through a list of Nodes, and the `position` function to provide a stripping effect for the catalog. Finally, we have seen both forms of the conditional elements: `xsl:if` and `xsl:choose`. If you have been following along, give your new website a test spin so you can see what we have developed!

6.3.4 Implementing the basket stylesheet

We will continue by implementing the basket stylesheet that will be used to display the contents of the basket to the user. For starters, we need to create a new file, named basket.xsl, with the XML declaration (processing instruction) and the root `xsl:stylesheet` element that was presented seen in Example 6.18. Furthermore, we also need to include the common.xsl stylesheet to provide the generic templates we will need to use and create a new template that matches the root element (i.e., "/") to provide the entry point for the stylesheet transformations.

Once this is finished, we can begin implementing the basket-specific templates by applying a template that selects the basket element from the document, as shown in Example 6.29.

Example 6.29 Basket root template

```
<xsl:template match="/">
  <HTML><HEAD><TITLE>PDA Plaza -- Your basket</TITLE></HEAD>
```

```
  <BODY BGCOLOR="#FFFFFF"><CENTER><TABLE BORDER="1" WIDTH="600">
    <xsl:call-template name="ShellTop"/>
    <TR><TD><xsl:apply-templates select="//basket"/></TD></TR>
    <xsl:call-template name="ShellBottom"/>
  </TABLE></CENTER></BODY></HTML>
</xsl:template>
```

As noted previously, the "//basket" pattern matches all of the basket elements throughout the XML document. Because we know we will at most only have one basket element, this pattern is acceptable. However, if other elements in the XML document had a basket element, this pattern would select it as well, hence a different pattern may be more appropriate in those situations.

Because the shell (top and bottom) of the page has already been implemented, we need only provide a template that matches the basket. To implement a template to transform the basket element, we simply need to create a new template that matches a pattern of "`basket`." In doing so, the template will be invoked for each basket, which may be present in the document depending on the state of the `HttpSession` object. This template will be required to generate a new table and associated heading rows and to provide totals of all the products in the basket at the bottom of the table. This is shown in Example 6.30.

Example 6.30 Basket template

```
<xsl:key name="ProdKey" match="//catalog/Product" use="@ProductID"/>

<xsl:template match="basket">
  <TABLE BORDER="1" WIDTH="100%"><TR><TH>Qty</TH>
  <TH>Product</TH><TH>Price</TH><TH>Total</TH></TR>

    <xsl:apply-templates select="Product-ref">
      <xsl:sort select="keyref('ProdKey',@ProductID)/ListPrice*@Quantity"
data-type="number" order="descending"/>
    </xsl:apply-templates>
  </TABLE>
</xsl:template>
```

After writing the necessary HTML elements to the result tree, we use an `xsl:apply-templates` element that selects all of the `Product-ref` elements that are children of the Basket element (current context node). In doing so, we also used the xsl:sort element to provide a sort order for how the products are listed. The tricky part is that we are actually sorting the products in the basket by their ListPrice that is a child element of the products in the catalog element.

To accomplish this, we must first set up a key using the xsl:key element. This element is added to a stylesheet as a child to the xsl:stylesheet element. It requires three parameters—name, match, and use. The name is used to identify the key when referenced by the keyref function within a pattern. The match identifies the pattern to indicate the nodes to which the key will apply. Finally, the use indicates the node (element or attribute) that will be used to associate with the context node value. This is the second parameter to the keyref function. This is similar to an equality join in SQL. Because the data we are sorting on are numeric, we need to specify this to the XSL Processor by setting the data-type attribute to "numeric". This lets the XSL processor know that it must convert the LinePrice attribute to a number prior to sorting each element. Furthermore, we also set the order attribute to "descending" so the higher priced lines appear at the beginning of the list.

To implement the Product-ref template we first need to create a new xsl:template that matches a Product-ref element. Then we will be able to apply a new form that will allow the users to change the quantity of the products in their basket, along with seeing the product name ListPrice and the total LinePrice based on the Quantity. This is shown in Example 6.31.

Example 6.31 Product template in basket.xsl

```
<xsl:template match="Product-ref">
  <TR>
    <FORM METHOD="POST" ACTION="/XMLBook/Book/">
      <TD ALIGN="LEFT">
        <INPUT TYPE="HIDDEN" NAME="Action" VALUE="ChangeItem"/>
        <INPUT TYPE="HIDDEN" NAME="ProductID">
          <xsl:attribute name="VALUE"><xsl:value-of select="@ProductID"/></
xsl:attribute>
        </INPUT>
        <INPUT TYPE="TEXT" NAME="Quantity" MAXLENGTH="3" SIZE="3">
```

```
          <xsl:attribute name="VALUE"><xsl:value-of select="@Quantity"/></
xsl:attribute>
        </INPUT>
        <INPUT TYPE="SUBMIT" VALUE="Change"/>
      </TD>
    </FORM>
    <TD><xsl:value-of select="keyref('ProdKey',@ProductID)/Name"/></TD>
    <TD ALIGN="RIGHT">
      <xsl:value-of select="format-number(keyref('ProdKey',@ProductID)/
ListPrice,'$0.00')"/>
    </TD>
    <TD ALIGN="RIGHT">
      <xsl:value-of select="format-number((keyref('ProdKey',@ProductID)/
ListPrice)*@Quantity,'$0.00')"/>
    </TD>
  </TR>
</xsl:template>
```

As you can see from the example there is not a great deal that is new here. To implement the form that will be used to change the quantity of the product in the basket, we dynamically create a value attribute of the `INPUT` element with the `ProductID` attribute. We do the same for the Quantity `INPUT` element by assigning its `VALUE` attribute with the current `Quantity` for the given product. After that, it is simply a matter of using the `xsl:value-of` element to generate the necessary text nodes to display: the `Name` of the product, its `ListPrice`, and the `LinePrice` attribute of the `Product`. Of course, because these values are part of the Product element and not the `Product-ref` element, we need to access these data using the `keyref` function to "join" the different elements together.

That is all that is required to implement the basket stylesheet, and as you will certainly agree, it was much simpler than the catalog stylesheet. You can now test the stylesheet by simply selecting the "Buy" image from the catalog stylesheet. Then you should see a page listing the product you just selected in your shopping basket. Try changing the quantity and watching the totals increase and decrease.

6.3.4.1 Implementing the Registration stylesheet

The last stylesheet we will implement will be the registration stylesheet. For our initial implementation of the registration stylesheet we simply provide literal HTML elements so that the user can enter the customer information necessary to create a new customer account. Although this could be enhanced quite a bit, we will save that as a challenge towards the end of the chapter.

We start the registration template in the same way we started all the other templates. First, we will create a new file named `registration.xsl` and add the `xsl:stylesheet` and `xsl:include` elements. Furthermore, we copy the default implementation of the root node template. Once this is completed, we implement the content for registration by adding a `xsl:call-template` element, as shown in Example 6.32.

Example 6.32 registration.xsl root template

```
<xsl:stylesheet xmlns:xsl="http://www.w3.org/XSL/Transform/1.0"
                                           xmlns="http://www.w3.org/TR/
REC-html40"
                                     result-ns=""
>
  <xsl:include href="common.xsl"/>

  <xsl:template match="/" >
    <HTML><HEAD><TITLE>Xml eCommerce Registration page</TITLE></HEAD>
    <BODY BGCOLOR="#FFFFFF"><CENTER><TABLE BORDER="1" WIDTH="600">
    <xsl:call-template name="ShellTop"/>
    <TR><TD COLSPAN="2"><CENTER>

    <xsl:call-template name="RegistrationForm"/>

    </CENTER></TD></TR>
    <xsl:call-template name="ShellBottom"/>
    </TABLE></CENTER></BODY></HTML>
  </xsl:template>

</xsl:stylesheet>
```

From the root template, we perform the same basic functions, `xsl:call-template` elements triggering the `ShellTop` and `ShellBottom` templates. In the middle; however, we use an `xsl:call-template` element to invoke the `RegistrationForm` template. The `RegistrationForm` template is shown in Example 6.33.

Example 6.33 RegistrationForm template

```
<xsl:template name="RegistrationForm">
  <FORM METHOD="POST" ACTION="/XMLBook/Book/">
    <INPUT TYPE="HIDDEN" NAME="Action" VALUE="Register"/>
    <TABLE BORDER="0"><TR><TD COLSPAN="2">
       <I>Please fill in the form and click <STRONG>Register</STRONG> when
finished.</I>
    </TD></TR>
    <TR><TD COLSPAN="2"><HR/></TD></TR>
    <TR><TD COLSPAN="2" BGCOLOR="#000000" VALIGN="CENTER">
      <CENTER><FONT SIZE="3" COLOR="#FFFF00">Billing Information</FONT></
CENTER>
    </TD></TR>

    <TR> <TD ALIGN="RIGHT"><STRONG>First name:</STRONG></TD>
    <TD><INPUT TYPE="TEXT" NAME="FirstName" VALUE="" MAXLENGTH="50"
SIZE="40"/></TD></TR>
    <TR> <TD ALIGN="RIGHT">Middle Initial:</TD>
    <TD><INPUT TYPE="TEXT" NAME="MiddleInitial" VALUE="" MAXLENGTH="1"
SIZE="1"/></TD></TR>
    <TR> <TD ALIGN="RIGHT"><STRONG>Last name:</STRONG></TD>
    <TD><INPUT TYPE="TEXT" NAME="LastName" VALUE="" MAXLENGTH="50"
SIZE="40"/></TD></TR>
    <!-- Address -->
    <TR><TD VALIGN="TOP" ALIGN="RIGHT"><STRONG>Address:</STRONG></TD><TD>
      <INPUT TYPE="TEXT" NAME="Address1"  VALUE="" MAXLENGTH="50"
SIZE="40"/><BR>
      <INPUT TYPE="TEXT" NAME="Address2"  VALUE="" MAXLENGTH="50"
SIZE="40"/><BR>
      <INPUT TYPE="TEXT" NAME="City"      VALUE="" MAXLENGTH="30"
SIZE="24"/>
      <INPUT TYPE="TEXT" NAME="State"     VALUE="" MAXLENGTH="2" SIZE="2"/>
      <INPUT TYPE="TEXT" NAME="Zip"       VALUE="" MAXLENGTH="9" SIZE="5"/>
    </TD></TR>
    <!-- Phone/Contact information -->
    <TR> <TD ALIGN="RIGHT"><STRONG>Phone Number:</STRONG></TD>
    <TD><INPUT TYPE="TEXT" NAME="PhoneNumber" VALUE=""/></TD> </TR>
    <TR> <TD ALIGN="RIGHT">Fax:</TD>
    <TD><INPUT TYPE="TEXT" NAME="FaxNumber" VALUE=""/></TD> </TR>
    <!-- Account Identity Information -->
    <TR> <TD COLSPAN="2" BGCOLOR="#000000" VALIGN="CENTER">
      <CENTER><FONT SIZE="4" COLOR="#FFFF00">Account Identification Infor-
mation</FONT></CENTER></TD>
    </TR>
    <TR> <TD ALIGN="RIGHT"><STRONG>Login name:</STRONG></TD>
```

```
    <TD><INPUT TYPE="TEXT" NAME="UserName" VALUE=""/></TD> </TR>
    <TR> <TD ALIGN="RIGHT"><STRONG>Password:</STRONG></TD>
    <TD><INPUT TYPE="PASSWORD" NAME="Password" VALUE=""/></TD> </TR>
    <TR> <TD ALIGN="RIGHT"><STRONG>Confirm:</STRONG></TD>
    <TD><INPUT TYPE="PASSWORD" NAME="ConfirmPassword" VALUE=""/><I>(Retype
password)</I></TD></TR>
    <TR> <TD ALIGN="RIGHT"><STRONG>Hint</STRONG></TD>
    <TD><INPUT TYPE="TEXT" NAME="Challenge" VALUE="" MAXLENGTH="50"
SIZE="40"/></TD> </TR>
    <TR><TD COLSPAN="2"><HR/></TD></TR>

    <TR><TD COLSPAN="2"><TABLE WIDTH="100%"><TR><TD>
      <STRONG><I>Note:  Bold fields are required.</I></STRONG></TD>
    <TD ALIGN="RIGHT"><INPUT TYPE="SUBMIT" VALUE="Register"/><INPUT
TYPE="RESET" VALUE="Reset"/>
    </TD></TR></TABLE></TR>
    <!-- End Error row -->
    <TR><TD COLSPAN="2"><HR/></TD></TR>
    </TABLE>
  </FORM>
</xsl:template>
```

As can be seen from the example, the `RegistrationForm` template hardly quantifies for a stylesheet. It is implemented as a stylesheet primarily because we want to harness the `ShellTop` and `ShellBottom` templates to provide the common look and feel across the website. As is clear, this template merely includes the HTML elements necessary to provide a data entry form to create a new customer account. Although there is a great deal we could do with this stylesheet, we will postpone this off until the conclusion of the chapter.

6.3.4.2 Providing the login Interface

There are a few more things we need to accomplish before completing the presentation of the site. First, we need to provide the ability for a customer to log into the website. Then we can provide some rudimentary personalization by displaying the user's name when the user has been authenticated.

Instead of creating an entirely new stylesheet to allow a user to login, we simply implement a tiny form that can be included in the header of each stylesheet that calls the `ShellTop` template. Of course, it would be ridiculous to display a login form when the user has already logged in, so we will make the display conditional based on the Status attribute of the Account element. To implement this functionality, open up the common.xsl stylesheet we have already created and add the template shown in Example 6.34.

Example 6.34 AccountHeader template (common.xsl)

```
<xsl:template name="AccountHeader">
  <TR><TD ALIGN="RIGHT"><FONT FACE="Arial" SIZE="1">
    <xsl:choose>
      <xsl:when test="//Account/@Status='Authenticated'">
        <I>designed for </I>
        <xsl:value-of
       select="concat(//Account/FirstName,' ',//Account/MiddleInitial,' '
,//Account/LastName)"/>
      </xsl:when>
      <xsl:otherwise>
        <FORM METHOD="POST" ACTION="/XMLBook/Book/">
          <INPUT TYPE="HIDDEN" NAME="Action" VALUE="Login"/>
          Login:
          <INPUT TYPE="TEXT" NAME="UserName" MAXLENGTH="10" SIZE="10">
            <xsl:attribute name="VALUE">
              <xsl:value-of select="//Account/UserName"/>
            </xsl:attribute>
          </INPUT><BR/>Password:
          <INPUT TYPE="PASSWORD" NAME="Password" MAXLENGTH="10"
                                                        SIZE="10"/>
          <BR/>
          <xsl:if test="//Account/@Status='Hint'">Here's a hint:
            <xsl:value-of select="//Account/Challenge"/>
          </xsl:if>
          <INPUT TYPE="SUBMIT" VALUE="login"/>
        </FORM>
      </xsl:otherwise>
    </xsl:choose>
  </FONT></TD></TR>
</xsl:template>
```

Earlier when we implemented the Account object, we defined three distinct status values. These were Anonymous, Hint, and Authenticated. Because the Account object is only recreated when needed, another scenario could be presented where the Status of the Account is nothing because the account does not exist yet. Although there are four different situations we have to handle, these can be lumped into two different scenarios for authentication purposes.

To differentiate between an Account that is "Authenticated" and one that is not, we use the xsl:choose element. The first condition, which tests for "//Account/@Status='Authenticated'", will evaluate to true if the Status attribute of the Account object is such. In this case, we provide some personalization by displaying the user's full name. This is very easy using the concat function. As the name implies, the concat function concatenates a series of strings together to form one large string. Thus, we use the concat operator to merge the user's `FirstName`, `MiddleInitial`, and `LastName` elements.

When the `Status` attribute of the Account does not contain the value of "Authenticated," the `xsl:when` element evaluates to false and not all of its child elements are processed. Processing jumps to either the next `xsl:when` element or (if no more exists) to the `xsl:otherwise` element. To handle this situation we display a form to allow the user to self-authenticate. Instead of simply displaying an empty input field, we dynamically set the `VALUE` attribute to the `UserName` child of the `Account` element. Although this element may not exist, the `xsl:value-of` element will not fail but instead resolve to an empty string just as if we had hard-coded the value as an empty string.

When the Account `Status` attribute is Hint, however, we know the user has typed in a valid username but an incorrect password. In this case, the `xsl:value-of` will resolve to the `UserName` previously passed, eliminating the need to retype it. Furthermore, we use the `xsl:if` to test if the `Status` is "Hint" and, if so, we display the `Challenge` element to provide the user with a hint for remembering the password.

The last thing we need to do is modify the `ShellTop` template to call the `AccountHeader` template. We place the form just below the Navigation bar, so we need to call it after the `NavBar` template is completed, as shown in Example 6.35.

Example 6.35 Complete ShellTop template

```
<xsl:template name="ShellTop">
  <TR><TD COLSPAN="1"><TABLE BORDER="0" WIDTH="100%"><TR>
    <TD WIDTH="*"><FONT FACE="Arial" SIZE="4"><I>PDA Plaza</I></FONT></TD>
    <TD><TABLE BORDER="0" WIDTH="100%">
```

```
      <TR><xsl:call-template name="navBar"/></TR>

      <xsl:call-template name="AccountHeader"/>

    </TABLE></TD>
  </TR></TABLE></TD></TR>
</xsl:template>
```

6.4 Challenge

Now that you have seen all of the different technologies, it is time to try some additional work on your own. To put your knowledge to the test, we need to improve the registration stylesheet so that the INPUT fields contain the data typed into the boxes. This will make the registration page much more user friendly should a user fail one of the validation checks within the Account object. At this time, the error message is displayed to the user. However, all of the `INPUT` fields are blank. This will be a good challenge because it will require modifications to the Servlet to include the data in the XML document, and, of course, modifying the stylesheet to retrieve these elements and generate the `VALUE` attributes in the resulting tree during transformations.

6.5 Conclusion

We have covered a great deal in this chapter. For starters, we recapped some of the key points on the Java Servlet Framework and its surrounding technologies. We covered how requests enter the servlet, and how the two objects (`HttpServletRequest` and `HttpServletResponse`) are used to provide the servlet with the necessary information for reading input and writing output. Armed with this information, we extended the framework by creating our XML-centric `XMLHttpServlet` class.

Because XSL is still a working draft, we provided a mechanism to allow the servlet to transform XML documents as the server. Thus the browser will never need to know that the servlet really wanted to send an XML document to the browser. Although the goal is to send the XML document to the browser, we needed this stopgap solution to support the browsers that are currently being used today.

Once all of the business logic was completed, we explored many of the exciting features of the transformation section of the XSL working draft. Although XSL is still a working draft, the XSLT portion of the draft is relatively stable and already has a few working implementations. We covered many different aspects of the XSL transformation, such as including external stylesheets, conditional processing, flow-control, dynamically created attribute nodes for parent elements, and invoking templates either by name or by selecting a node set using a pattern to search the document tree.

CHAPTER 7 *Integrating with the Distributor*

7.1 *Introduction*

Snnnn.... Snnneee....(snoring), "Wake Up!" Oops, you must have fallen asleep in another team meeting. Who can blame you though? You have successfully built the XML website and thrown in the XSL processor on the server to support the Boss's favorite browser! Realizing that the company has not put a down payment on your Ferrari yet, you should open your eyes and see what the boss wants!

"Nice of you to decide to join us," the boss exclaims. He continues with, "Before you get too complacent with the website you've built, maybe you should provide us with some of your wisdom to help us solve our current problem. We just received a letter from our primary distributor of Personal Data assistants indicating that they will be eliminating some of their existing ordering mechanisms to reduce costs. In particular, they will no longer support the EDI channel we use to place orders. Without EDI communication, we need to increase staff to manually fax the orders to the distributor."

As silence fills the room, you begin to wonder if any of the other team members will suggest potential solutions. Overcome with the frustration of waiting, you decide to slowly raise your hand to indicate that you have an idea. "Sleepy has a comment?" your boss questions as the rest of your colleagues chuckle. Clearing your throat, "Well, many companies have been replacing EDI systems will XML-based systems." Before we could continue the boss interrupted, "They mentioned something about XML in the letter; however, they provided some DTD files that I didn't understand and It certainly didn't look like anything you were doing." As the room filled with silence again, you could sense the boss's frustration as he continued, "Since nobody else on this team ever suggests anything, I'll continue this discussion with XML-boy. Meeting adjourned!"

7.1.1 The Scenario

The distributor has a business to business (B to B) Electronic Commerce website that our company, along with other channel partners, uses to obtain product information. In an effort to reduce operational costs, they have decided to migrate to XML for electronic communication between its channel partners. Order processing is their highest priority right now because of the costs associated with their current EDI systems. The alternative is to transmit orders over the Internet to their website.

In doing so, the distributor has extended their website to accept electronic orders that are formatted as XML documents. Of course, the distributor needs to understand the orders. In addition to the documents being well formed, the distributor has also provided Document Type Definitions (DTDs) that describe the content that must be included in the documents to place orders. Although the validation capabilities built into DTDs are limited, it does provide the initial requirements of the content of an order document. In order to maintain their existing security infrastructure, all transmissions must be performed using the HyperText Transfer Protocol (HTTP).

We need to extend our website to transmit orders to the distributor's site. To leave the impression that the customer is purchasing the products from our company, we encapsulate our communication with the distributors web server instead of redirecting the client browser to the distributor's site—where they may find something better to buy! Thus, we will perform the communication from server to server, so the client talks only to our website.

7.1.2 Context

We can do quite a lot in the computer industry with only a desktop computer. As all the programming we do involves entering a different, or abstract world, it is easy to exclude the physical barriers from our mix. Obviously, we do not have a distributor website to accept our order transmissions. Instead, we will create the distributor code while we finish our website. This is what we would do in an actual setting because we would want to test the code to sending it out into production. From a high level, the overall system will look like that of Figure 7.1.

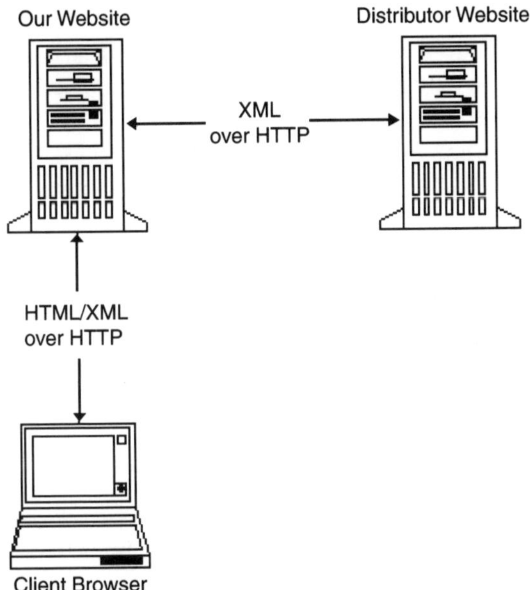

Figure 7.1 External Interactions.

For the most part, adding the order processing capability will simply be a matter of extending the currently implemented functionality. In doing so, we need to extend the user interface by adding another stylesheet. More importantly, we need to extend our servlet quite a bit. Transmitting an order to another website will not be a trivial matter, and when you are done you can boast about your accomplishments with your friends.

We have not really touched on Document Type Definitions (DTD), from a programmatic standpoint yet. Typically, whenever you see XML applied across an industry, DTDs will be the foundation that describes the vocabulary and structure for the transactions between businesses. Thus, we look at the vocabulary the distributor has defined for us so we can better design our portion of the website.

7.1.3 The Distributor's Specifications

Before we dive into coding aspects, it would be prudent to review what the distributor expects from our company. Although DTDs are somewhat limited in their capabilities, these files will at least describe the logical structure of the XML documents we have to send to the distributor. In the process, these documents will also describe some rudimentary validation criteria. Keep in mind that in the real world the Distributor will implement more sophisticated validation above and beyond the capabilities of DTDs.

7.1.3.1 Placing an order

In order for our company to submit an order to the distributor, we must provide a properly formatted XML document. It must also contain the necessary information for the distributor to fulfill the order. An example of an XML document used to place an order is shown in Example 7.1.

Example 7.1 Document used to place order

```
<?xml version="1.0"?>
<!DOCTYPE book-order
          SYSTEM "http://myDistributor/distributor/dtd/book-order.dtd">
<book-order>
  <bill-address>...</bill-address>
  <ship-address>...</ship-address>
  <ship/>
  <payment/>
  <sku/>
  <sku/>
  ...
</book-order>
```

Other than the ellipses that were used to abbreviate the example, the example should resemble the XML documents we have been dynamically generating in the website. The initial processing instruction, or XML prolog, describes that the document will comply with version 1.0 of the XML recommendation. Furthermore, the document is well formed because it has a single (root) element, called `book-order`. Without getting into too much detail about the `book-order` element, we will take a closer look at the mark-up between the prolog and the `book-order` element.

If you have never seen one before, the `!DOCTYPE` is declaring that this document is not simply an XML document, more specifically it is a "`book-order`" type document. If you remember back to Chapter 2, this is how XML documents identify the DTD of the document, which is used to further constrain document structure and the values of its elements and attributes. The `book-order` immediately following the `!DOCTYPE` identifies the root element name or type. If this does not match the root element for the document, the XML recommendation indicates the parser should signal an error.

If this DTD looks too simple compared to others you have seen it is probably because you have been looking at internally defined documents. Internal DTDs include all of the element definitions within the document. Most documents described in books and articles show internal DTDs because they are easier to relate the vocabularies (element declarations) with the actual elements in the document. In our case, we are using an external DTD as indicated by the SYSTEM following the root element name. Finally, the URI to the external DTD follows in quotation marks. This allows a validating XML parser to retrieve the DTD so it knows how to validate the document. Although the example shows an absolute URI, this can also be a relative URI.

> **NOTE:** In the example, the URI to find the book-order DTD indicates that it resides in the myDistributor domain. You will need to modify this to indicate the domain (or IP and port) where you will be storing the distributor DTDs.

7.1.3.2 Book-order vocabulary

As stated previously, the document vocabulary or element definitions are included with the document for internal DTDs. We need to look at the external file to discover the vocabulary of an externally defined document type. The book-order.dtd file describes the logical structure of the document. Just as the DOCTYPE defined the root element type, this file must identify what elements and attributes the root element, in our case book-order, can contain. We will be required to dynamically create this document from the information we currently have about a given customer, and the information we gather while the customer is shopping our website. It is shown in Example 7.2.

Example 7.2 Book-order.dtd

```
<!ENTITY % address SYSTEM "address.dtd"> %address;
<!ENTITY % payment SYSTEM "payment.dtd"> %payment;

<!ELEMENT sku EMPTY >
<!ATTLIST sku ID          ID              #REQUIRED
                          quantity        NMTOKEN         "1"
>
<!ELEMENT bill-address %address-entity; >
<!ELEMENT ship-address %address-entity; >

<!ELEMENT ship EMPTY>
<!ATTLIST ship carrier (Fed-Ex|UPS) 'UPS' >

<!ELEMENT book-order (bill-address,ship-address,ship,payment,sku+)>
```

The first thing to notice is that there is not a DOCTYPE declaration in the file. This should make sense because we declared this in the document from the previous example that pointed to this file for its vocabulary.

The first two lines in the example identify two parameter entities, address and payment, respectively. If you remember from Chapter 2, parameter entities (identified by the %) are slightly different that general entities (identified simply by the !ENTITY). Although both of these types of entities are used to insert replacement text, the different types can only replace text in certain areas of the document. General entities can only replace text within the document content, which would be inside the **book-order** element in our example. Parameter entities are not allowed to replace text in the document content; instead they replace text within the DTD.

As indicated by the SYSTEM and URI indicators, the replacement text for these two parameter entities is defined in external files, address.dtd and payment.dtd, respectively. Again, these URIs are relative; however, the catch is relative to what? As with all URIs in XML, they are relative to the file that references them. In this case, the URI is relative to the book-order.dtd file, not the document. Finally, both of the entities are referenced immediately after they are defined so that they are included in the DTD. For lack of a better term, this is similar to "including" the vocabularies defined in address.dtd and payment.dtd in the book-order.dtd vocabulary. This is how DTDs can be assembled from multiple files.

The next line defines an element of type sku: This is a common acronym that stands for Stocking Control Unit. Furthermore, the `EMPTY` tag contained in the `!ELEMENT` declaration indicates that the element is not allowed to contain any additional child nodes, whether it be text data, other elements, etc. Generally, this means that the sku elements in the document content should be contained in empty-element tags.

Immediately following the sku declaration is an `!ATTLIST` declaration. As the name implies, this is identifying the possible attributes for its associated element, which is the sku element in this case. After the element name, two attributes, ID and quantity, are defined. The first attribute is of type ID (which is also its name). As covered in Chapter 2, attributes of type ID are unique identifiers. In this case, the distributor needs to uniquely identify the product. For the purposes of this book, we assume that the `ProductID` we store with each product in the catalog is the appropriate identifier for the distributor. We will not be able to simply map the ProductID to the sku's ID attribute because the ID attribute must match the Name production in the XML specification. As the Name production cannot begin with a digit, we have to prefix the value. The second parameter, quantity, is slightly less restrictive. As indicated, the quantity attribute must conform to the NMTOKEN production from the XML specification. Although the intent of this attribute is to identify a numeric value of the quantity, the NMTOKEN will actually allow more that simply numeric values but it is the best we can do using a vocabulary. Although we must specify the ID of each sku element, the quantity attribute is not required and will default to 1 when not specified.

The next two element declarations are for the bill-address and ship-address. Different from typical element declarations, these include a reference to the address-entity parameter entity to define the content rules of these elements. At first glance, you would think this DTD is in error because entities must be defined prior to being referenced. Actually, this parameter entity is defined in the address.dtd file, which was previously referenced by the %address; on the first line of the example. We will review both the address.dtd and payment.dtd files once we have finished reviewing this file. These elements will contain the necessary billing and shipping address information that show the distributor the order can be processed.

> **TIP:** Parameter entities provide a powerful mechanism for defining different elements of the same type. Using parameter entities isolates the code to a single place, which will reduce the amount of effort required if the logical structure of the type of element changes.

Next, a ship element is declared an EMPTY element, just as with the sku element. Following the element is its associated ATTLIST declarations that include a single attribute named carrier. Different from the attributes seen for the sku element, the carrier attribute is an enumerated type. As shown in the example, only "Fed-Ex" and "UPS" are valid values for this attribute. Furthermore, if the attribute is not specified for the ship element, "UPS" will be used as the default value. The distributor will use this information to determine how to ship the order to its destination. It would appear that the distributor would only ship orders using either Federal Express (Fed-Ex) or United Parcel Service (UPS). Furthermore, UPS is most likely their preferred carrier.

Finally, the book-order element is defined. Although element declarations can refer to elements that will be defined after the book-order element, we choose to list it after the book-order element to provide a more intuitive flow. If you remember from Example 7.1, this root element will ultimately contain all of the information that describes any given order. As declared, a book-order element must contain a single bill-address, ship-address, ship, and payment elements. Much like the bill-address and ship-address, the payment element was not defined in the book-order DTD. Instead, the payment element is defined in the payment.dtd file to be covered shortly.

Furthermore, at least one sku element is required. However, the plus sign indicates that more than one sku element can be included in the book-order element. Less obvious from the declaration is that the internal elements must be included in the book-order element in the same order as defined in the element declaration.

If you are not in an "information-overload" state yet, congratulations. Many newcomers to XML seem to jump right into coding well-formed documents without paying much attention to the DTDs. In doing so, it seems that once they need to describe a vocabulary they typically end up struggling through the markup and never really take the time to understand capabilities and limitations. To finish the vocabulary defined in the book-order.dtd file we must first look at the two external files that are included. Do not worry, these will not take as long!

7.1.3.3 *Address vocabulary*

Referring back to the book-order.dtd file, the bill-address and ship-address elements referred to the address-entity parameter entity. As such, the purpose of the address.dtd file is to declare the address-entity parameter entity. In doing so, the address vocabulary is used to define types of address elements. The address.dtd file is shown in Example 7.3.

Example 7.3 Address.dtd

```
<!ELEMENT line                          (#PCDATA)>
<!ELEMENT attn                          (#PCDATA)>
<!ELEMENT city                          (#PCDATA)>
<!ELEMENT postal-code                   (#PCDATA)>
<!ELEMENT state EMPTY>
<!ATTLIST state abbrev (AZ|CA|UT|NY) #REQUIRED >

<!ENTITY % address-entity "(line,line?,attn?,city,state,postal-code)">
```

The first four lines should seem familiar. These lines are declaring line, attn, city and postal-code elements, respectively. What may appear new is their content type. The `(#PCDATA)` indicates that these elements can contain parsed character data. If you remember in Chapter 2, this means the contents cannot contain the characters that describe markup, such as the less than (<) and greater than (>) symbols unless they are enclosed in a CDATA section.

If these symbols are needed and a CDATA section is not used, we must use the predefined entities references, such as "`<`" and "`>`", to represent the less than and greater than symbols, respectively.

Reading along, the state element is declared as an EMPTY element. Furthermore, it has one REQUIRED attribute, named abbrev, which is limited to one of the following values: "AZ," "CA," "UT," or "NY." Oddly enough, these are the state abbreviations for 4 states, which appears to indicate that the distributor will (or can) do business in these states, for whatever reason.

Finally, the address-entity parameter entity declares the replacement text that will serve as an element's content restrictions. As the replacement text shows, the first child node must be a line element, optionally followed by another line element. The question mark (?) denotes optional. Likewise, an attn element can optionally be inserted, followed by a city, state, and postal-code elements. The last three are not optional. As we have already seen, the address-entity is referenced as the content types of both the bill-address and ship-address entities in the book-order.dtd file. When the parameter entity is replaced, the content of the bill-address and the ship-address elements will be defined as we just reviewed.

7.1.3.4 Payment vocabulary

The payment vocabulary contains the information necessary for the distributor to charge the customer for the order. In contrast to the address vocabulary, which essentially defined a type of element (by defining the address-entity parameter entity), the payment vocabulary actually defines the payment element that is part of the book-order element content. This is shown in Example 7.4.

Example 7.4 Payment.dtd

```
<!ELEMENT payment EMPTY>
<!ATTLIST payment
          type (Visa|MasterCard|American-Express|Discover)  #REQUIRED>
<!ATTLIST payment     expire-month NMTOKEN                  #REQUIRED>
<!ATTLIST payment expire-year  NMTOKEN                      #REQUIRED>
<!ATTLIST payment card-number  NMTOKEN                      #REQUIRED>
```

As you can see from the example, there is nothing the payment entity or its attributes declare that we have not yet covered. The EMPTY content type specified that the element could not contain any children. Furthermore, the payment method has four parameters that must be included with every instance of the element: type, expire-month, expire-year, and card-number. The type attribute is limited to the following values: "Visa," "MasterCard," "American-Express," or "Discover." The remaining attributes are limited to the NMTOKEN production defined in the XML recommendation.

> **TIP:** What may seem strange is that each parameter is defined in a separate ATTLIST tag. The ATTLIST tag is very flexible. Multiple attributes can be defined per tag; in addition, multiple ATTLIST tags can be used to associate attributes with elements.

There is a lot more detail that one would expect from the DOCTYPE tag in Example 7.1. Order fulfillment is not a trivial task in any organization. Although there was a great deal of detail buried in the multiple layers of the book-order.dtd it should appear relatively straightforward. If you have ever purchased something over the Internet, typically once you place an order you receive another page containing a confirmation number. Customers can use this to track their number. Because the distributor is filling the order, this information must be created in the distributor's systems. Now we will look at the XML document the distributor will send back to us.

7.1.3.5 Order confirmation

When we transmit an order to the distributor, it is either valid or invalid. If it is valid, the order should be placed and we should receive an order confirmation. If the XML document was invalid, either from a logical structure (DTD) standpoint or the contents failed the distributor's additional validation routines, we will receive a declined order confirmation with a listing of errors. In either case, the distributor will send us an XML document in response to the book-order document we transmitted. Example 7.5 shows the vocabulary the distributor will use in response to a book-order document.

Example 7.5 Book-order-confirm.dtd

```
<!ELEMENT order-error (#PCDATA)>
<!ATTLIST order-error
    severity      (error|fatal|warning) "fatal"
    line-number   NMTOKEN               #REQUIRED
    column-number NMTOKEN               #REQUIRED
>

<!ELEMENT order-status (confirmation|order-error+)>
<!ATTLIST order-status status (success|declined) #REQUIRED>

<!ELEMENT confirmation EMPTY>
<!ATTLIST confirmation
          order-num       ID    #REQUIRED
          order-date      CDATA #REQUIRED
>
```

The first line of the book-order-confirm.dtd file declares that a new `order-error` element is defined to contain parsed character data. Furthermore, the `order-error` element will also contain three attributes: `severity`, `line-number`, and `column-number`. The `severity` attribute will have a value of "error," "fatal," or "warning." If the attribute is not explicitly assigned to an element, it defaults to a value of "fatal." The `line-number` and `column-number` attributes will always be present, and their associated values will conform to the `NMTOKEN` production.

The distributor will use the `order-error` element to describe a single error. The contents of the element itself will contain a description of the error. This description will probably be generated from the distributor's validating XML parser, however, the distributor could also provide additional validation. The severity attribute will indicate the significance of the error, with fatal being the worst. Finally, the `line-number` and the `column-number` will indicate the location of the document where the error occurred. These attributes can be useful for debugging purposes.

The next line declares an `order-status` element with a slightly more complicated content type definition. The content type definition declares the `order-status` element that can contain one of two different contents. The pipe (|) symbol is used to signify that the `order-status` element can contain either a single `confirmation` child element *or* one or more `order-error` elements.

The distributor will include a `confirmation` element in the `order-status` element to signify the order was placed successfully. If there were problems during the order processing, the distributor will include one or more `order-error` elements to describe why the order was declined. Although not explicitly shown in the vocabulary, the distributor will use the `status` attribute (defined in the ATTLIST tag on the next line) to signify if the order was successful or not. We can use this to determine which group of elements will be contained in the `order-status` element. As indicated in the DTD, the status element will contain either a value of "success" or "decline."

The final `!ELEMENT` and `!ATTLIST` tags describe the confirmation element that will be included in the `order-status` element. As the `EMPTY` content type defines, this element will not contain any content. It will, however, contain two attributes. The first attribute, `order-num`, can be used to uniquely identify the order within the distributor's system(s). Finally, the `order-date` parameter will signify the date (and time) the order was placed.

If there is still some confusion, this is good. Now that we know the vocabulary of the XML document the distributor will reply with, which is the root element? If you remember the DOCTYPE tag we used to transmit the order, the external file defines only the vocabulary of the document. The root element is not defined in the external file, in this case book-order-confirm.dtd. Instead, the root element is defined in the DOCTYPE tag itself. To complete this triangle, each document the distributor replies with will be formatted as follows:

Example 7.6 Book-order reply document

```
<?xml version="1.0"?>
<!DOCTYPE order-status
  SYSTEM 'http://myDistributor/distributor/dtd/book-order-confirm.dtd'>
<order-status status="...">
  ...
</order-status>
```

That pretty much covers the vocabulary the distributor has provided to us to submit orders and receive confirmations. Before we can implement this functionality in our own site, we need to create a testing stub that will resemble the distributor's order processing system.

7.1.4 Distributor Servlet

As we do not have access to the distributor's system, we will need to create a testing stub before we start implementing our system. Generally, testing stubs are implemented to resemble the external system, however, the internal workings are usually not implemented. Instead, the intricate details are usually handled during integration testing. This means we need to build a system that looks and feels like the distributor's order processing system.

By reviewing the DTDs from the previous section, we have learned how to communicate with the distributor. To transmit and order, we must pass an XML document using the `book-order` vocabulary and structure. Although we are unsure what happens internally in the system when it receives this document, this is not important yet. What is important is how the system responds to the request. We know that the distributor's system will respond with a different XML document with the `book-order-confirm` vocabulary and structure. Of course, these are not simply function calls, this will all transpire over the HTTP protocol.

> **NOTE:** Transmitting sensitive documents such as these across the Internet can raise potential security risks. In most cases, this type of communication is typically encrypted using SSL or some other form of encryption, which is beyond the scope of this book.

After absorbing all of this, you will probably agree that this is essentially what our `XMLHttpServlet` class was designed to accomplish. The Java Servlet API will handle the HTTP aspects of the coding, and the code we implemented will standardize how the XML aspects are accomplished. For starters, we need to create a new Distributor.java file that will contain the initial shell of the Distributor servlet. This is shown in Example 7.7.

Example 7.7 Distributor.java

```
import javax.servlet.*;
import javax.servlet.http.*;
import org.w3c.dom.*;
import com.ctp.xml.servlet.*;
```

```
import com.ctp.dom.DOMManager;

import java.io.*;
import java.util.Date;

public class Distributor extends XMLHttpServlet
{
  public void init( ServletConfig config )
    throws ServletException, UnavailableException
  {
    ...
  }

  public void doXML(HttpServletRequest req, XMLHttpServletResponse res)
    throws ServletException, java.io.IOException
  {
    ...
  }

  protected boolean transformAtServer( HttpServletRequest req )
  { return false; }
}
```

Before we get into what the `Distributor` servlet needs to do, we will review the general implementation of the class. First, the `Distributor` class extends the `XMLHttpServlet`. This allows the class to harness the XML code we created in Chapter 6 while under the covers; all of the HTTP servlet code is still available.

Make sure that the Distributor.java file also contains the function signatures for the `init`, `doXML`, and `transformAtServer` methods. Since the `Distributor` servlet does not need to provide a user interface, XSL transformations will not be necessary. Thus, we need to override to `transformAtServer` method to return `false`. Essentially, this disables the `XSLTransformer`. In doing so, the `Distributor` servlet (server) can return the `book-order-confirm` XML document to the `XMLBookServlet` (client) to complete the transaction.

7.1.4.1 Init method

As we are only implementing a testing stub, we will not need to do much in the initialization routine for the servlet. For the most part, we need to make sure the `DOMManager` class is configured correctly so that we can manipulate documents when requests are received. The complete implementation of the `init` method is shown in Example 7.8.

Example 7.8 Distributor.init method

```
import org.xml.sax.*;
import com.ibm.xml.parsers.TXDOMParser;
...
private Document m_docIncompleteConfirm = null;
private static final String CONFIRM_DTD = "C:\\apps\\apache\\
               websvr\\htdocs\\distributor\\book-order-confirm.xml";
...
public void init( ServletConfig config )
  throws ServletException, UnavailableException
{
  super.init(config);
  try
  {
    DOMManager.setFactory("IBMDOMFactory");
    DOMManager.setWriter("IBMDOMWriter");
  }
  catch( Exception e )
  {
    log( e.toString() );
    throw new UnavailableException(this, e.toString() );
  }
}
```

The first few lines in the example should resemble the `init` method for the `XMLBookServlet` we created in the previous chapter. As always, the first thing we do during initialization is to give the ancestor classes a chance to initialize themselves by calling the `super.init(config)`. Once the ancestors have been initialized, we can assign the factory and writer classes to the `DOMManager` by passing the names of the classes we implemented previously for document creation and writing to the `setFactory` and `setWriter` methods. As this class will never really see production stress, we opted to skip loading dynamic initialization parameters and simply instead will hard code them.

7.1.4.2 Distributor.doXML method

Now that the initialization code is complete we can implement the `doXML` method to handle the `book-order` requests we send to the servlet. As this servlet will be serving HTTP requests that contain XML documents, this will be slightly different from how we implemented the doXML method in the XMLBookServlet class.

In order to resemble the distributor's system, this method needs to accept an XML document from the HTTP POST data. In doing so, we need to parse the post data into a DOM document so that we can manipulate it. Furthermore, we will use a validating parser so that the logical structure of the document can be checked to ensure that it conforms to the book-order DTD. The doXML method is shown in Example 7.9.

Example 7.9 Distributor.doXML method

```
public void doXML(HttpServletRequest req, XMLHttpServletResponse res)
  throws ServletException, java.io.IOException
{
  try
  { // Parse the Document into a DOM doc.
    TXDOMParser parser = new TXDOMParser();
    OrderValidator validator = new OrderValidator();
    parser.setErrorHandler(validator);
    parser.parse( new InputSource( req.getReader()) );
    Document doc = parser.getDocument();

    Document docResponse = handleOrder(doc,validator);
    res.setDocument( docResponse );
  }
  catch(SAXException sax)
  { throw new ServletException( sax.toString() ); }
}
```

Throughout the code we have written so far, we have yet to actually load and parse an XML Document from a file. To accomplish this, an XML parser is used. In this case, we will use IBM's TXDOMParser, which is part of the com.ibm.xml.parsers package. Although IBM provides a few different parsers in this package, the TXDOMParser is compatible with the code we have already written to implement the DOMFactory and DOMWriter interfaces. Essentially, if we choose to use a different parser, this would be like choosing a different XML implementation that would require us to create new DOMFactory and DOMWriter class implementations in order to utilize our DOMManager. Furthermore, as the class name implies, this parser will produce DOM documents. The first line in the try block instantiates the parser and stores a reference to it in the local variable parser.

> **TIP:** It is important to make sure that the parser you use when developing XML applications will produce the output you expect. In this case, we expect a DOM document; however, many parsers do not actually produce a DOM document. Instead, these parsers only produce "events" that can be programmatically implemented to respond to the document structure while it is being parsed. Typically, these parsers are called SAX parsers, the acronym for Simple API for XML. Of course, merely being event-driven does not make a parser as SAX compliant. The parser must adhere to the SAX specification. Although SAX parsers are less intuitive than DOM parsers, they are optimized for speed and resource utilization. Typically, you will see event-driven parsers used when large XML documents need to be parsed. The `TXDOMParser` actually implements the SAX specification as well as produces DOM documents!

To capture the validity constraint errors that a validating XML parser will produce, we provide a mechanism to capture these errors. In order to receive the error messages, we rely on the `TXDOMParser`'s support of the SAX interfaces to notify our code when it encounters an error in the document. To receive these messages, we have to create a class that implements the `org.xml.sax.ErrorHandler` interface. We will create the `OrderValidator` class to accomplish this.

We can receive the error messages once we provide the `TXDOMParser` with a reference to our `ErrorHandler` implementation. This is accomplished by passing a reference of our `OrderValidator` class to the `setErrorHandler` method of the parser.

> **NOTE:** Keep in mind, we are not being as cautious as we were in the previous chapters when considering portability. This is because we are concerned primarily with creating a servlet we can use to test our `XMLBookServlet`. We have relied heavily on the functionality of the XML4J parser and we did so without encapsulating the logic. Other XML parsers may require a different solution.

From the Distributor's specifications (DTDs), we learned how the distributor's system will respond to a `book-order` request. Especially as concerns errors, we need to pass back any errors as `order-error` elements. Furthermore, all of the errors that occurred during the parsing as well as any additional errors the distributor's system might produce will be contained in the `order-status` element. As these events will occur while the document is being parsed, we need to store them so that we can add them to the `book-order-confirm` response document. As you can see, the example uses an `OrderValidator` class to handle the error messages. Using a separate class avoids threading issues because a new instance can be utilized for each request. We will cover the `OrderValidator` class when we have finished reviewing the Distributor class.

Once the `ErrorHandler` has been assigned, we can begin using the parser by calling one of its two parse methods. The easiest way to parse a document is simply to pass a `String` containing the location of the file to parse. This will not work for our situation because we do not necessarily have a `String` containing the location of the file. Instead, we have access to the stream of characters that represents the HTTP POST data. In this situation, we need to use the alternate parse method that takes an `InputSource` as a parameter.

The `InputSource` class is part of the SAX specification and can be found in the `org.xml.sax` package. The purpose of this class it to abstract the different forms of input sources so the parsers are more versatile. In doing so, the `InputSource` provides the capability to parse documents from a system/public identifier (URIs), a `java.io.InputStream`, or a `java.io.Reader` stream. In our case, the Java Servlet API provides access to the POST data stream by calling the `getReader` method of the `HttpServletRequest` object. In doing so, this will return a reference to a `Reader` object that can be passed to the constructor of the `InputSource` class as shown in the example.

The parser will throw exceptions if it encounters problems internally in the `parse` method. First, if the parser has difficulties reading the document from its source it will throw a `java.io.IOException`. Furthermore, an `org.xml.sax.SAXException` will be thrown if problems are encountered related to the document structure. The `doXML` method is already expecting the `IOException` so we do not really need to worry about it. To handle the `SAXException`, however, we will need to catch it and throw a new `ServletException`. On a more opportunistic note, when the parse method completes normally we can retrieve the DOM document by calling the `getDocument` method. In our case, we store the reference to the DOM document in the local variable `doc`.

> **NOTE:** Having a separate method to retrieve the DOM document after it has been parsed by a different method has some significant design considerations in regards to servlets. This was most likely done to conform to the SAX specification, which does not have provisions for the DOM API. In doing so, the parser must internally maintain an instance variable of the DOM document. Although this may appear to be normal, it can present problems in multithreaded environments such as servlets. To avoid threading issues, we simple instantiate a new instance of the parser each time we attempt to parse a document.

Once the `Document` instance has been retrieved from the parser, the `doXML` method is almost finished. The next logical action would be to handle the application specific logic for the document, in this case processing the order. Instead of simply including this logic in the `doXML` method, however, we will create a new method to handle order-processing logic. This method will be called `handleOrder`. This means that the remainder of code in the `doXML` simply needs to dispatch the document to the `handleOrder` method.

Although we have yet not seen the `handleOrder` method, as you can see from the preceding text here it will return a `Document`. The returning document, `docResponse`, will be used as the response document to complete the transaction. Now all we have to do is assign the document to the `XMLHttpServletResponse` object by calling the `setDocument` method. Once the `doXML` method in the `Distributor` class completes, the `XMLHttpServlet` class will stream the document back to the client, which will be our `XMLBookServlet` class.

7.1.4.3 *Distributor.handleOrder method*

The `handleOrder` method will be used to perform the same business functions that the distributor's order processing system would provide. Of course, for our testing stub we will not implement any custom validation. Instead we will use the errors that were generated during the XML parsing in the `doXML` method to determine if the order is valid or not. If you remember back to Example 7.5 on page 326, the distributor's system will return a `book-order-confirm` document as its response to a `book-order` document request. Inside the book-order-confirm.dtd, the root element (`order-status`) can either be a single confirmation element (when there are no errors) or one or more `order-error` elements. In either case we pass both the `book-order` document and the `OrderValidator` class so we can determine which set of elements should be included in the response document. This means the `handleOrder` method needs both the document and the `OrderValidator` object as parameters.

We can start the `handleOrder` method by creating a document. We can do this by using the `DOMFactory` class from the `DOMManager` to create the document. Once the document is created we have a small dilemma. We have yet to create a document with a Document Type Definition. To complicate matters, the DOM API does provide any functionality for creating or manipulating a DTD within the DOM object model. Although the DOM API does not provide for this, IBM's API does.

The XML4J toolkit provides a DTD class (part of the `com.ibm.xml.parser` package) that can be instantiated to create a new DTD Node. Once created, the object itself can be inserted into the DOM tree because it implements the `DocumentType` interface (which extends the `Node` interface). Although we have to deviate from the DOM recommendation, this is the only acceptable solution using the DOM Level 1 recommendation.

> **NOTE:** Just prior to printing, the DOM Level 2 working drafts were released; they contain an open standard for mechanism for creating Document Type Definition Nodes.

To create a new instance of the DTD object we simply call its default constructor as shown in Example 7.10. If you remember Example 7.6, the `book-order` reply document only actually contains an external `DOCTYPE` reference. Furthermore, this external resource is a private or `SYSTEM` resource.

To generate an external `DOCTYPE` reference with the XML4J toolkit we have another IBM-specific class called an `ExternalID`. The purpose of the `ExternalID` class is to provide support for external entities. In doing so, it provides a common object that supports both SYSTEM and PUBLIC resources. The type of `ExternalID` is determined by how the object was constructed. To create a `PUBLIC ExternalID`, we must pass a PUBLIC ID (well-known name of the document) and a SYSTEM ID (`URI`) to the constructor. To create a SYSTEM `ExternalID` we simply pass the SYSTEM ID or `URI` to the constructor. As we need to create a SYSTEM resource, we used the latter constructor and simply passed the URI to the vocabulary of the document (shown in Example 7.10):

Example 7.10 Creating and initializing the DOM DTD object

```
private static final String ORDER_CONFIRM_DTD =
   "http://YourServerAndPort/distributor/dtd/book-order-confirm.dtd";

Document docConfirm = DOMManager.getFactory().createDocument("1.0");

com.ibm.xml.parser.DTD dtd = new com.ibm.xml.parser.DTD();
com.ibm.xml.parser.ExternalID uri =
    new com.ibm.xml.parser.ExternalID( ORDER_CONFIRM_DTD );
dtd.setName("order-status");
dtd.setExternalID( uri );
docConfirm.appendChild( dtd );
```

Once the `ExternalID` object has been created, we simply need to assign the root element name and the `ExternalID` to the DTD object. As was shown in Example 7.10, this is accomplished by calling the `setName` and `setExternalID` methods, respectively. For the name of the document, we used "order-status" because this will be the root element from the distributor's system. Finally, we simply call the `appendChild` method of the document object to insert the DTD in the document structure.

> **TIP:** Notice that we actually declared these objects using their full package syntax. As the `DTD` and `ExternalID` objects are not part of the DOM API, we wanted to make these objects "stand out" from the rest of the code. Instead of simply adding an import at the beginning of the file, we choose to define them fully to make it more difficult to use in other areas of the file.

After the DTD is inserted into the DOM Tree, we can create the root element. To do so, we simply call the `createElement` method of the document passing "order-status" as the name of the element. Once the root element is created, we can append it to the response document we just created by calling the `appendChild` method. This is shown in Example 7.11 to follow. The order of these calls is very important. If you remember Chapter 2, the XML specification indicates (defined in the prolog production) that the DTD must appear before the root element of the tree. Simply calling the `appendChild` method will add the node to the end of the `NodeList`. In doing so, this would invalidate the document if the root element had previously been inserted into the document tree.

Example 7.11 Distributor.HandleOrder method

```
protected Document handleOrder( Document docOrder, OrderValidator valida-
tor )
  throws UnavailableException
{
  try
  {
    Document docConfirm = DOMManager.getFactory().createDocument("1.0");

    // IBM specific functionality
    com.ibm.xml.parser.DTD dtd = new com.ibm.xml.parser.DTD();
    com.ibm.xml.parser.ExternalID uri =
      new com.ibm.xml.parser.ExternalID( ORDER_CONFIRM_DTD );
    dtd.setName("order-status");
    dtd.setExternalID( uri );
    docConfirm.appendChild( dtd );

    Element eRoot = docConfirm.createElement("order-status");

    if ( validator.getErrorCount() == 0 )
    {
      eRoot.setAttribute("status", "success");
      // Save the Document to disk
      File file = File.createTempFile( "Order", ".xml", new
File("C:\\temp") );
      FileWriter fileWriter = new FileWriter( file );
      DOMManager.getWriter().writeDocument( docOrder, fileWriter );
      fileWriter.close();

      //
      // create the confirmation element
      //
      Element eConfirm = docConfirm.createElement("confirmation");
      String strOrderNum = file.getName();
```

```
      strOrderNum = strOrderNum.substring(0,strOrderNum.length() - 4);
      eConfirm.setAttribute("order-num", strOrderNum );
      eConfirm.setAttribute("order-date", (new Date()).toString() );

      eRoot.appendChild( eConfirm );
    }
    else
    {
      eRoot.setAttribute("status", "declined");
      validator.appendTo(eRoot);
    }

    docConfirm.appendChild(eRoot);

    return docConfirm;
  }
  catch( IOException ioe )
  { throw new UnavailableException(this, ioe.toString() ); }
}
```

The remaining portions of the `handleOrder` method are relatively straightforward. After the `order-status` element is created, we also need to check if there were any parsing errors reported to the `OrderValidator` object. To check, we simply call the `getErrorCount` method of the `OrderValidator` object. If there were no errors reported we assume the order is valid and proceed by setting the status of the order to "success."

When the status is "successful," we simply write the file to disk so that we can review it later. In the process, we will let the operating system and/or Java generate a unique file name that we can use as the `order-num` attribute in the confirmation element. To do this, we use the static `createTempFile` method of the `java.io.File` class. Although there are a few different overridden versions of this method, we will use the one that takes three parameters. The first parameter instructs Java as to how the prefix portion of the filename should be generated. Likewise the second parameter instructs the system of the extension of the file to create. Finally, the third parameter is a reference to another file object that represents which directory to use to create the file. As the example shows, we request a new temp file to be created, prefixed with the string "Order," suffixed with the ".xml" extension, in the c:\temp directory. Remember that the backslash character (\) is an escape character in literal java strings, so we used two backslashes to create a single one ("C:\\temp"). Java will use these settings to generate a unique file by inserting a unique character sequence (usually a number) between the prefix and suffix.

Once the file has been created, we simply need to create a `FileWriter` object that can be used to write data to the file. With the `FileWriter`, we can save the XML document to disk using our `DOMWriter` class. Finally, the last thing we need to do is close the `FileWriter`. If we forget to do so, the file will be held open until the `FileWriter` object is destroyed.

After the XML document has been saved to disk, we can resume by populating the order-status element with the confirmation element. In Example 7.5, we saw that the confirmation element contains two attributes, order-num and order-date. As we discussed, we will use the name of the file we just created as the order number. In doing so, we strip off the extension of the file so it does not look like a file name. To accomplish this, we first extract the filename from the file object by calling the `getName` method. Because extension is part of the name, the next like extracts the extension from the filename by using the `substring` method of the String class. The substring method takes two parameters. The first parameter indicates the start position and the second parameter indicates the number of characters to copy into the new string. In our case, as we simply want to strip off the last four characters, we pass a zero to indicate the beginning of the string. We dynamically subtract four from the length of the entire string to determine how many characters to copy. Assigning the order-date attribute is equally simple. We simply create a new Date object and extract its value as a String. To complete the processing for documents without errors, we need to append the confirmation element (`eConfirm`) to the `order-status` root element (`eRoot`).

When the book-order document contains errors, we need to set the order-status's status attribute to "declined." Moreover, when the status is declined, we need to append all of the errors that were collected by the `OrderValidator` class. We use the `setAttribute` method of the `Element` interface to assign "`declined`" to the status attribute. Furthermore, we call an `OrderValidator.appendTo` to append the order-errors elements. In doing so, we pass the `eRoot` Element as the node where the order-error elements will be appended. We will look at this in more detail when we review the `OrderValidator` class.

In either situation, whether the document contains errors or not, we simply return the response document, `docConfirm`, to the calling method, `doXML`. That is all we need to do for the `Distributor` class. Now we need to review the `OrderValidator` class to see how the errors are collected when the document is being parsed, and ultimately how order-error elements are actually inserted into the order-status element of the response document.

7.1.5 OrderValidator class

As already mentioned, the `TXDOMParser` uses the SAX specification to report parsing and validation errors to the application. In doing so, this requires the application to implement the `ErrorHandler` interface, which is part of the `org.xml.sax` package. The `ErrorHandler` interface has three methods: `error`, `fatalError`, and `warning`. The parser will call these methods when it encounters an error. All three of these methods are passed a `SAXParseException`. Furthermore, they do not return any information to the parser. Essentially, these methods provide a way that applications can provide custom error reporting above and beyond the default implementation that disregards warnings and recoverable errors while throwing exceptions when a fatal error is encountered.

For our purpose, we simply want to record each of these messages. Ultimately, these errors need to be included in the response document; however, just like the business objects we have created, we do not have access to the document when the errors are generated. Since we do not have access to the owning document, we will store the errors in `LinkedList` objects until we need to append them to the document.

We can start by creating a new `OrderValidator` class that implements the `ErrorHandler` interface. There is no need to make this class public because the only class that will need access to it is the `Distributor` class. As such, we can simply add it below the `Distributor` class in the Distributor.java file.

We create three separate instance variables for tracking the different types of exceptions that can be raised. We will define final variables to indicate the element type name and attribute names that we will use to output the errors as XML elements. In this case, we need to make sure these names are the same as the book-order-confirm Document Type Definition of Example 7.5. Finally, we will also create another instance variable to track the number of errors generated while the XML document was being parsed. This is shown in Example 7.12:

Example 7.12 OrderValidator Class

```
class OrderValidator implements ErrorHandler
{
  private static final String ERROR_TYPE    = "order-error";
  private static final String ATT_SEVERITY  = "severity";
  private static final String ATT_LINE      = "line";
  private static final String ATT_COLUMN    = "column";

  private LinkedList m_FatalErrors  = new LinkedList();
  private LinkedList m_Warnings     = new LinkedList();
  private LinkedList m_NormalErrors = new LinkedList();
  private int        m_nErrorCount  = 0;
}
```

As you can see from the example, it is declared that our class will implement the `ErrorHandler` interface. This allows the class to participate in the XML Parsing activities because the `TXDOMParser` knows how to communicate with the `ErrorHandler` interface. Next, we defined the `ERROR_TYPE`, `ATT_SEVERITY`, `ATT_LINE`, and `ATT_COLUMN` finals that we will use for the element and attribute names. Finally, we declared three new instances of `LinkedList` objects: `m_FatalErrors`, `m_Warnings`, and `m_NormalErrors` for tracking their perspective types of exceptions. We choose to use a `LinkedList` because we are not interested is searching for a particular error within the list. We are simply going to use the object to store the `SAXParse-Exceptions` until we need to generate the DOM Nodes. Thus, a `LinkedList` is more efficient because the implementations are optimized for inserting elements and iterating through the list from top to bottom.

Because we have instantiated our instance variables where they are declared, we do not need to perform any initializations during the constructor. We can move directly to implementing the methods of the `ErrorHandler` interface.

7.1.5.1 Handling the parser's error events

In order to say that our class implements the `ErrorHandler` interface, we need to implement the `error`, `fatalError`, and `warning` methods. Each of these methods is passed a reference to a `SAXParseException`. This object describes the particular error that the XML Parser encountered. When the XML Parser calls one of the three methods, we will simply store a reference to the `SAXParseException` in the appropriate `LinkedList` so that we can extract the error description and other attributes (line, column, severity) when the class is asked to do so. Last, we will increment the `m_nErrorsCount` instance variable to maintain an accurate account for the total number of errors that we encountered while the document was being parsed. This is shown in Example 7.13:

Example 7.13 ErrorHandler Interface methods

```
public void error( SAXParseException e )
{
  m_NormalErrors.add(e);
  m_nErrorCount++;
}
public void fatalError( SAXParseException e )
{
  m_FatalErrors.add(e);
  m_nErrorCount++;
}
public void warning( SAXParseException e )
{
  m_Warnings.add(e);
  m_nErrorCount++;
}
```

7.1.5.2 Providing the accessor methods

Now that we have added to the code to store the `SAXParseExceptions`, we need to provide a mechanism for retrieving these errors. As we have seen from the `handleOrder` method, the `Distributor` class needs a mechanism to determine if any errors occurred while the document was being parsed. In particular, we have already shown that the `Distributor` class will call the `OrderValidator.getErrorCount` method to accomplish this task. Because we have provided the `m_nErrorCount` instance variable, implementing this method is a matter of returning the value of the instance variable, as shown in Example 7.14.

Example 7.14 OrderValidator.getErrorCount method

```
public int getErrorCount()
{
  return m_nErrorCount;
}
```

Looking back at Example 7.11, if the `getErrorCount` method returns anything other than zero, the Distributor logic will pass an `Element` to the `OrderValidator.appendTo` method. In doing so, it expects us to append the order-error children to the element.

To accomplish populating the necessary order-error elements, we will need to extract the `SAXParseExceptions` from each of the three `LinkedList` instance variables. Although the severity is not actually stored with the `SAXParseException`, we have implicitly stored it because we have used separate instance variables to indicate the `severity` of the exception. Moreover, because we have used the same type of objects to store the exceptions, we can create a `createErrorElements` helper method to reduce the amount of code needed to actually populate the DOM Nodes. This is shown in Example 7.15:

Example 7.15 OrderValdiator.createErrorElement method

```
private static void createErrorElements( Element parent, LinkedList list,
String strSeverity )
{
  Document doc = DOMManager.getOwner( parent );
  Iterator it = list.iterator();

  while ( it.hasNext() )
  {
    SAXParseException err = (SAXParseException) it.next();
   Element e = DOMManager.createElement( doc, ERROR_TYPE, err.getMessage()
);
    e.setAttribute(ATT_SEVERITY, strSeverity );
    e.setAttribute(ATT_LINE, String.valueOf(err.getLineNumber()));
    e.setAttribute(ATT_COLUMN, String.valueOf(err.getColumnNumber()));
    parent.appendChild( e );
  }
}
```

The purpose of the `createErrorElement` method is simple—to avoid having to write three sets of code that perform the same operations, but only on different `LinkedList` objects. The simplest way to accomplish this is to parameterize the `LinkedList` variables. In doing so, each specific instance of the linked list also implies the severity of the exception. Thus, we also need to pass a `String` object indicating the appropriate severity of the `LinkedList` object.

To start off, the method retrieves the owning document based on the parent element that is passed to the method. Furthermore, we create an `Iterator` object by calling the `LinkedList.iterator()` method. An iterator is just what the name implies. It is an object that allows you to iterate through a sequence of other objects. In this case, it allows us to iterate through the objects stored in the `LinkedList`. Thus, we can use it to process each `SAXParseException`, one at a time.

We process each of the exceptions using a while loop. First, we call the `it.hasNext` method to determine if there are any objects remaining in the iteration. On the next line, we extract the next available object by calling the next method, similar to how we fetched rows from the `ResultSet` object of JDBC.

Once we have grabbed a reference to the `SAXParseException`, the rest of the coding is very similar to how we implemented the business object's `appendTo` methods. First, we use the `DOMManager.createElement` convenience method to create type ERROR_TYPE element. Instead of using our document reference directly, we used the convenience method so we could also insert the description of the `SAXParseException` by calling `getMessage`.

Finally, we assign the ATT_SEVERITY, ATT_LINE, and ATT_COLUMN attributes with the relevant information. To extract the line and column numbers from the `SAXParseException`, we call the `getLineNumber` and `getColumnNumber` methods. These methods return an int datatype, thus we use the static `String.valueOf` method to convert the value to a `String` before assigning it as an attribute value.

Whew! That was a lot of work. Because the `createErrorElements` method actually appended the various `order-error` elements, all we have to do from the `appendTo` method is to invoke the `createErrorElements` for each of the three `LinkedList` instance variables, as shown in Example 7.16:

Example 7.16 OrderValidator.appendTo method

```
public void appendTo(Element parent)
{
  createErrorElements( parent, m_FatalErrors, "fatal" );
  createErrorElements( parent, m_NormalErrors, "error" );
  createErrorElements( parent, m_Warnings, "warning" );
}
```

That is it! We are finished with the distributor's system. Make sure the Distributor class compiles and is saved in the XMLBook zone directory. This is the same directory wherein the `XMLBookServlet` class is stored. As this is merely a testing stub, we will not go through the hassle of setting up special configuration parameters. As long as the servlet is in the Jserv Zone that is mounted to the XMLBook directory, we can simply refer to the servlet by class name.

Furthermore, before we continue we need to make sure the DTD files are in the appropriate place. First, we need to create two new subdirectories of the Apache web root directory, typically named `htdocs` below the Apache web server's installation directory. First we need to create a distributor directory and a dtd directory below it (i.e., `<APACHE>/htdocs/distributor/dtd`). Once these directories are created, copy the DTDs from the companion CD to the newly created dtd directory.

7.2 Extending the Website

7.2.1 Introduction

Now that we have the Distributor servlet ready to receive order requests, we need to add this functionality to the website. For the most part, this will require some additional code to all aspects of the system. First, if you remember from our coverage at the distributor's DTD files, we need to collect a little more information for the customer before we can place the order.

The `Account` object we created will suffice for supplying the billing-address element of the book-order document, however, we do not actually capture the customer's shipping address. Because this could potentially change from order to order, it makes sense to capture this information when the customer chooses to place an order. Furthermore, when we are collecting the shipping information, we also need to allow the user to select his/her Shipping carrier and enter their payment information.

Once this information has been captured, we need to extend the servlet to handle this new function. In doing so, we create a new action, "Place-Order," much like the actions we have already created for adding items to the shopping basket, registering, and logging into the site. In the Servlet, the `PlaceOrder` action needs to generate the book-order document dynamically, as defined in the book-order.dtd vocabulary. After the document has been assembled, we will stream the XML document to the distributor's servlet using the HTTP protocol.

7.2.1.1 Linking into the Order Processing

The first place we need to start is by creating a link to start the order processing logic. In order to place an order, we will require that the user is both logged into the site and has at least one product in his/her shopping basket. To implement this, we will modify the template matching "basket" elements in the basket.xsl stylesheet. This is shown in Example 7.17.

Example 7.17 Basket template in basket.xsl

```
<xsl:template match="basket">
 <TABLE BORDER="1" WIDTH="100%"><TR><TH>Qty</TH>
 <TH>Product</TH><TH>Price</TH><TH>Total</TH></TR>
 <xsl:apply-templates select="Product">
  <xsl:sort select="@LinePrice" data-type="number" order="descending"/>
 </xsl:apply-templates>
 <TR><TD COLSPAN="2" ALIGN="RIGHT"><I>Total: </I></TD>
 <TD ALIGN="RIGHT">
  <xsl:value-of
       select="format-number(sum(Product/ListPrice),'$0.00')"/>
 </TD><TD ALIGN="RIGHT">
  <xsl:value-of select="format-number(@TotalPrice,'$0.00')"/>
 </TD></TR>

 <!-- Start Check out link -->
 <TR><TD COLSPAN="4" ALIGN="right">
  <xsl:if
       test="(//Account/@Status='Authenticated' and count(Product)>0)">
   <A HREF="checkout.xsl">Check Out</A>
```

```
  </xsl:if>
 </TD></TR>
 <!-- End Check out link -->

</TABLE>
</xsl:template>
```

As you can see from the example, we added the link just below the total row in the table. Furthermore, we used an `xsl:if` tag to conditionally include the link only if the user is logged in and there is at least one product in the shopping basket. In doing so, the test attribute of the `xsl:if` element first tests the status attribute of the account object in the document. To ensure that the basket contained a product we used the `count` function. As the context node in this template is the `basket` element, we did not need to adjust the context of the pattern. Finally, we used the "`and`" expression to indicate that both of these conditions must be true for the entire expression to be true. If the test attribute evaluates to true, the relative link to a "checkout.xsl" stylesheet is included in the HTML. On the other hand, if the test attribute evaluates to false, the child elements of the `xsl:if` element are not included in the HTML document.

The remainder of the user interface modifications can be contained in the new checkout.xsl file. We will use this stylesheet to handle a few different screens. First, the checkout.xsl needs to present a form to the customer so they can enter the relevant shipping and payment information. In doing so, we need to consider that this form could be presented in two different scenarios. In the first scenario, the form will be displayed when the checkout link is initially selected from the basket page. The form will also need to be displayed when an attempt to place an order was declined. In both of these cases, we need to present the user with either default information, or the same information they entered when the form was submitted. To handle the declined situations as well as the initial shipping and payment entry, we need to make the shipping entry versatile enough to be populated with the values the user entered from different locations within an XML document. Finally, the checkout.xsl stylesheet will also need to present the order confirmation information when the distributor accepts a submitted order.

7.2.1.2 Checkout stylesheet

We can start by creating a new file, named checkout.xsl, with the standard prolog and root stylesheet element, as shown in Example 7.18. Next, we implement the default template that matches the root element of the `book-session` document. In doing so, we will call the templates for the `ShellTop` and `ShellBottom` that are found in the common.xsl file. This will give the page the same look and feel as the rest of the pages of our site. We can finish the root-matching template by handling the forementioned scenarios.

To handle each of these different situations, we use an `xsl:choose` element. In the first condition (`xsl:when`), we check to see if an `order-status` element is contained within the `book-session` root element. Although we have not covered the servlet yet, we will assume that the servlet will be placing the `order-status` element returned from the distributor after an attempt to place an order. It is important to realize that this line does not differentiate between an accepted (status equals success) or a declined order. It merely is checking to see if an order-status element exists in the document tree and, if so, the next line attempts to apply the template that can present this information. See Example 7.18:

Example 7.18 Root template in checkout.xsl

```
<?xml version="1.0"?>
<xsl:stylesheet xmlns:xsl="http://www.w3.org/XSL/Transform/1.0"
                              xmlns="http://www.w3.org/TR/REC-html40"
                              result-ns=""
>
  <xsl:include href="common.xsl"/>

  <!-- Start Main Shell -->
  <xsl:template match="/">
    <HTML><HEAD><TITLE>PDA Plaza</TITLE></HEAD>
      <BODY BGCOLOR="#FFFFFF"><CENTER><TABLE BORDER="1" WIDTH="600">
      <xsl:call-template name="ShellTop"/>

      <TR><TD>
        <xsl:choose>
            <xsl:when test="not(/book-session/order-status='')">
               <xsl:apply-templates select="/book-session/order-status"/>
            </xsl:when>
            <xsl:otherwise>
```

```
            <xsl:apply-templates select="//Account"/>
          </xsl:otherwise>
        </xsl:choose>
      </TD></TR>

      <xsl:call-template name="ShellBottom"/>
    </TABLE></CENTER></BODY></HTML>
  </xsl:template>
  <!-- End Main Shell -->
  ...
</xsl:stylesheet>
```

If the test attribute evaluates to false, the `xsl:otherwise` element is invoked because there are no other `xsl:when` elements to evaluate. At this point we simply apply the template that matches an `Account` element anywhere within our `book-session` document. Immediately after the check-out link is selected from the basket page, the order-status element will not exist. The `order-status` element only exists if the distributor sent an `order-status` document back from a request to place an order. Because we have not made it this far yet, we start by implementing the Account template.

As previously discussed already, the checkout template is responsible for presenting either a shipping entry form or an order confirmation screen. In displaying the shipping entry form, we want to present or default certain INPUT field values. For example, most of the time users will want to ship the products they order to the billing address. As we already have this information in the Account element, we can simply reference the various child elements of the Account object for the VALUE attributes of the HTML INPUT elements.

Before we jump into this, however, the shipping form will also be redisplayed if the information entered by the user fails the validation checks within the distributor servlet. In these cases, we still want to redisplay the shipping entry screen; however, if we always display the values from the Account's children elements the customer will have to retype all of their fields of information. Planning for this ahead of time will drastically reduce the amount of coding involved.

Although we could simply create two different templates to contain all of the shipping entry fields but reference different values from the book-session document, a better way would be to abstract the Shipping entry form and use parameters for these values. Essentially, this is the same as applying good modular techniques to programming in Java. With that said, we can implement the Account template by simply calling a different template, as shown in Example 7.19. In the process, we will pass parameters that the called template can use to display the appropriate information.

Example 7.19 Account template in checkout.xsl

```
<xsl:template match="Account">
  <xsl:call-template name="ShipEntryForm">
    <xsl:param name="ShipLine1" expr="Address1"/>
    <xsl:param name="ShipLine2" expr="Address2"/>
    <xsl:param name="ShipCity" expr="City"/>
    <xsl:param name="ShipState" expr="State"/>
    <xsl:param name="ShipZip" expr="Zip"/>
  </xsl:call-template>
</xsl:template>
```

As you can see from the example, we use the `xsl:call-template` element to invoke the template named "`ShipEntryForm`." Just as we did in Chapter 6, we can pass parameters using the `xsl:param` element. The name attribute indicates the name of the parameter. Furthermore, the `expr` attribute is used to dynamically resolve the pattern to provide the value for the parameter. As always, the `expr` parameter is resolved based on the node context, which is the `Account` element in this template. In layman's terms, the Account template is invoking the `ShipEntryForm` template while passing the following parameters: `ShipLine1`, `ShipLine2`, `ShipCity`, `ShipState`, and `ShipZip`. Furthermore, the values of these parameters are the contents of the `Address1`, `Address2`, `City`, `State`, and `Zip` elements.

Now the `ShipEntryForm` template can be implemented without having knowledge of how the parameters were populated. Instead, the `ShipEntryForm` template is really only concerned with the values of the parameters. The primary purpose of the `ShipEntryForm` template is to insert numerous HTML elements that will present a pretty user interface for entering the shipping and payment information. In doing so, it now has parameters that it can access to assign the values to the different HTML INPUT elements.

Before we subject ourselves to the massive amount of HTML that is required to display the shipping entry form, we need to introduce another interesting stylesheet element that will be used in the `ShippingEntryForm` template.

7.2.1.3 xsl:attribute-set

XML stylesheets offers a mechanism, very similar to Cascading Stylesheets (CSS), which can essentially be used as a mechanism for elements to inherit a set of attributes. To do this, XSL provides the `xsl:attribute-set` element to define a set of attributes. We add this element as a child to the `xsl:stylesheet` element (root element). Furthermore, the `xsl:attribute-set` element requires a name attribute that will be used to refer to the set of attributes by name. Finally, the `xsl:attribute-set` can contain a series of `xsl:attribute` elements that identify the attributes within the set.

For the checkout.xsl stylesheet, we will use the `xsl:attribute-set` to define a default set of attributes for our INPUT elements in the `ShipEntryForm`. For example, most of the INPUT elements that we will be coding will have the following attributes:

Name	Value
TYPE	TEXT
SIZE	40
MAXLENGTH	50

To provide an attribute-set with these attributes, we add code as shown in Example 7.20 as a child to the `xsl:stylesheet` element. Notice that all of the `xsl:attribute` elements are contained within the `xsl:attribute-set` element. Furthermore, the `xsl:attribute-set` element contains a name attribute with a value of "`INPUT-DEFAUTS`." By providing a name, the entire set of attributes can be inherited. Finally, the three attributes (`MAXLENGTH`, `SIZE`, `TYPE`) are defined using the `xsl:attribute` elements from Chapter 6.

Example 7.20 INPUT-DEFAULTS attribute-set

```
<xsl:attribute-set name="INPUT-DEFAULTS">
  <xsl:attribute name="MAXLENGTH">50</xsl:attribute>
  <xsl:attribute name="SIZE">40</xsl:attribute>
  <xsl:attribute name="TYPE">TEXT</xsl:attribute>
</xsl:attribute-set>
```

What makes attribute-sets very useful is how the attributes are applied. To inherit the attribute, we simply need to add an xsl:use element. For example,

```
<INPUT NAME="foo">
  <xsl:use attribute-set="INPUT-DEFAULTS"/>
</INPUT>
```

would produce an HTML element as follows:

```
<INPUT NAME="foo" TYPE="TEXT" MAXLENGTH="50" SIZE="40">
```

Notice that the `xsl:use` element is used to inherit all the `xsl:attributes` from a named set of attributes. Better yet, if the element already contains one of the attributes defined in the set, it will override the attribute from the set. For example, if we wanted the "foo" INPUT element to have a SIZE of "2" we would simple include the SIZE attribute in the element itself. This means the following code:

```
<INPUT NAME="foo" SIZE="2">
  <xsl:use attribute-set="INPUT-DEFAULTS"/>
</INPUT>
```

would produce an HTML element as follows:

```
<INPUT NAME="foo" TYPE="TEXT" MAXLENGTH="50" SIZE="2">
```

7.2.1.4 ShipEntryForm template

We shall put aside the stylesheet elements for the time being. It is now time to look at the `ShipEntryForm` template that is used to generate the Shipping entry form. Unfortunately, there is no way around the amount of HTML code required to produce decent-looking web pages. Do not let this discourage you; instead, pay attention to how the stylesheet and attribute parameter templates are used to dynamically insert values into the HTML elements in Example 7.21:

Example 7.21 ShipEntryForm template

```
<xsl:template name="ShipEntryForm">
  <xsl:param-variable name="ShipLine1"/>
  <xsl:param-variable name="ShipLine2"/>
  <xsl:param-variable name="ShipCity"/>
  <xsl:param-variable name="ShipState"/>
  <xsl:param-variable name="ShipZip"/>
```

```
  <xsl:param-variable name="CardNumber"/>
  <xsl:param-variable name="ExpireMonth"/>
  <xsl:param-variable name="ExpireYear"/>

  <CENTER><TABLE BORDER="0" BGCOLOR="#FFF000">
    <FORM ACTION="/XMLBook/Book/" METHOD="POST">

    <TR><TD BGCOLOR="black" ALIGN="CENTER" COLSPAN="2">
      <FONT COLOR="yellow" FACE="Arial" SIZE="3">Shipping Information</
FONT>
    </TD></TR>

    <TR><TD ALIGN="RIGHT">Attention:</TD><TD><INPUT NAME="ShipAttn"
VALUE="{$ShipAttn}">
      <xsl:use attribute-set="INPUT-DEFAULTS"/>
    </INPUT></TD></TR>
    <TR><TD ALIGN="RIGHT"><B>Line 1:</B></TD><TD><INPUT NAME="ShipLine1"
VALUE="{$ShipLine1}">
      <xsl:use attribute-set="INPUT-DEFAULTS"/>
    </INPUT></TD></TR>
    <TR><TD ALIGN="RIGHT">.</TD><TD><INPUT NAME="ShipLine1"
VALUE="{$ShipLine2}">
      <xsl:use attribute-set="INPUT-DEFAULTS"/>
    </INPUT></TD></TR>

    <!-- City, State, Zip code -->
    <TR><TD ALIGN="RIGHT"><B>City,State,zip</B></TD><TD>
      <INPUT NAME="ShipCity" SIZE="20" VALUE="{$ShipCity}">
        <xsl:use attribute-set="INPUT-DEFAULTS"/>
      </INPUT>
      <INPUT NAME="ShipState" MAXLENGTH="2" SIZE="2" VALUE="{$ShipState}">
        <xsl:use attribute-set="INPUT-DEFAULTS"/>
      </INPUT>
      <INPUT NAME="ShipZip" MAXLENGTH="9" SIZE="9" VALUE="{$ShipZip}">
        <xsl:use attribute-set="INPUT-DEFAULTS"/>
      </INPUT>
    </TD></TR>

    <!-- Carrier (shipping) -->
    <TR><TD ALIGN="RIGHT"><B>Shipping Method:</B></TD><TD>
      <SELECT NAME="ShipMethod">
        <OPTION VALUE="">Not Selected</OPTION>
        <OPTION VALUE="UPS">UPS</OPTION>
        <OPTION VALUE="Fed-Ex">Federal Express</OPTION>
      </SELECT>
    </TD></TR>
```

```
    <TR><TD BGCOLOR="black" ALIGN="CENTER" COLSPAN="2">
     <FONT COLOR="yellow" FACE="Arial" SIZE="3">Payment Information</FONT>
    </TD></TR>

    <TR><TD ALIGN="RIGHT"><STRONG>Credit card:</STRONG></TD><TD>
      <SELECT NAME="PayMethod">
        <OPTION VALUE="">Not Selected</OPTION>
        <OPTION VALUE="Visa">Visa</OPTION>
        <OPTION VALUE="American-Express">American Express</OPTION>
        <OPTION VALUE="MasterCard">MasterCard</OPTION>
        <OPTION VALUE="Discover">Discover</OPTION>
      </SELECT>
    </TD></TR>

    <TR><TD ALIGN="RIGHT"><STRONG>Card Number:</STRONG></TD><TD>
      <INPUT NAME="CardNumber" MAXLENGTH="16" SIZE="16"
VALUE="{$CardNumber}">
        <xsl:use attribute-set="INPUT-DEFAULTS"/>
      </INPUT>
    </TD></TR>

    <TR><TD ALIGN="RIGHT"><STRONG>Expiration:</STRONG></TD><TD>
      <INPUT NAME="ExpireMonth" MAXLENGTH="2" SIZE="2"
VALUE="{$ExpireMonth}">
        <xsl:use attribute-set="INPUT-DEFAULTS"/>
      </INPUT> /
      <INPUT NAME="ExpireYear" MAXLENGTH="2" SIZE="2"
VALUE="{$ExpireYear}">
        <xsl:use attribute-set="INPUT-DEFAULTS"/>
      </INPUT>
    </TD></TR>

    <TR><TD COLSPAN="2" ALIGN="RIGHT">
      <INPUT TYPE="SUBMIT" VALUE="Submit Order"/>
      <INPUT TYPE="HIDDEN" NAME="Action" VALUE="PlaceOrder"/>

    </TD></TR>
  </FORM></TABLE></CENTER>
</xsl:template>
```

Because most of the code in Example 7.21 is HTML-related, we will not cover each single element. First, it is important to understand how the form fits into the overall system. Notice the ACTION attribute of the FORM element (near the beginning of the template). In addition, notice the hidden Action INPUT element immediately following the submit button (near the bottom of the template). These two HTML elements drive how the servlet will treat the request. In this cast, the Action variable has a value of "PlaceOrder." Thus, the servlet will need to process an order request. Furthermore, this action also indicates what stylesheet to use when presenting the results.

The last thing to notice in the ShipEntryForm template before we jump into the java code is how the attribute-sets are utilized. Without getting into specifics, notice that most of the INPUT fields inherit the attributes from the INPUT-DEFAULTS attribute-set. For the INPUT fields that need to deviate from the base set of attributes, such as ShipState, we simply include the actual values with the element to override the attributes in the set. Since we have already added the link to the basket, we can give the template a try once we have completed typing in the template.

7.2.1.5 Implementing the PlaceOrder action

Although we are not finished with the checkout stylesheet, we are at a point where we need to interact with the servlet before we can finish up the checkout.xsl stylesheet. Thus, we will jump into the servlet code and implement the PlaceOrder action.

The first modification is to add some code to the doXML method so we can determine that a PlaceOrder action was requested and route it to a new custom method to support the requirements. To do this we simply need to add another if statement to the group of if statements currently implemented. This is shown in Example 7.22:

Example 7.22 Modifications to DoXML

```
String strAction = request.getParameter( "Action" );
if (strAction != null)
{ if (strAction.equalsIgnoreCase( "Register" ))
    doRegisterAction( request, response);

  else if (strAction.equalsIgnoreCase( "Login" ))
    doLoginAction( request, response);

  else if (strAction.equalsIgnoreCase("AddItem") ||
           strAction.equalsIgnoreCase("ChangeItem"))
    doBasketAction( strAction, request, response);
```

```
    else if (strAction.equalsIgnoreCase("PlaceOrder"))
      doOrderAction( request, response );

    else if (strAction.equalsIgnoreCase("Goto"))
      response.setStyleSheet(request.getParameter("ss"));

    else
      log("!! Received invalid Action parameter -[" + strAction + "]");
}
else response.setStyleSheet( DEFAULT_STYLESHEET );
```

To determine if a `PlaceOrder` action was requested, we simply use the `equalsIgnoreCase` method of the `String` object. In doing so, when the value of the Action parameter is "`PlaceOrder`" we call into a new `doOrderAction` method.

7.2.1.6 Processing the Order

The `doOrderAction` method will encapsulate all of the order processing code for the servlet. In doing so, it must create the `book-order` document, stream the document over HTTP to the distributor's servlet, and finally process the `order-status` document returned by the distributor's servlet.

Although we could use the DOM API to create the `book-order` document, we will use a different technique. Instead, the `XSLTransformer` is used to transform our `book-session` document into a `book-order` document. This may seem strange at first, however, this moves the transformation logic into a markup file instead of compiled code.

Before we can perform this transformation, however, we will need a document to transform! For the purposes of order processing, we need to create a slightly extended version of our typical book-session document. Although we will still include the `Account`, `ShoppingBasket`, and `Catalog` elements, we will add additional ones to represent the `ship-address` and `payment` elements that we saw in the distributor specifications. We need these additional elements so that we have enough information to successfully create the book-order document according to the Distributor's DTD.

7.2.1.7 Creating the book-session document

To encapsulate the logic required to populate our temporary `book-session` document, we create a new method, called `createBookSessionDoc`, to accomplish this task. For the most part, this method will use the existing code already written to create the book-session document in the servlet. Once the book-session object has been populated with the business object elements, we add the HTTP parameters for the shipping and payment information so that they can be included in the book-order document during the transformation process. Example 7.23 shows the createBook-SessionDoc method:

Example 7.23 CreateBookSessionDoc method

```
private String m_strOrderStylesheetPI = null;
private static final String[] ShipKeys = { "ShipAttn", "ShipLine1",
"ShipLine2", "ShipCity", "ShipState", "ShipZip", "ShipMethod"};
private static final String[] BillKeys = { "PayMethod", "CardNumber",
"ExpireMonth", "ExpireYear" };

protected Document createBookSessionDoc( HttpServletRequest req )
{
  Document doc = DOMManager.getFactory().createDocument("1.0");
  ProcessingInstruction pi = doc.createProcessingInstruction(
STYLESHEET_PI, m_strOrderStylesheetPI);
  doc.appendChild(pi);

  Element eBookSession = doc.createElement(BOOK_SESSION);
  doc.appendChild(eBookSession);
  appendElements( req, doc );

  Element eShipping = doc.createElement("shipping");
  for(int i=0; i< ShipKeys.length; i++)
  {
    String strValue = req.getParameter( ShipKeys[i] );
    if (strValue != null && strValue.length() != 0)
      eShipping.appendChild( DOMManager.createElement( doc, ShipKeys[i],
strValue));
  }

  Element eBilling = doc.createElement("billing");
  for(int i=0; i< BillKeys.length; i++)
  {
    String strValue = req.getParameter( BillKeys[i] );
    if (strValue != null && strValue.length() != 0)
      eBilling.appendChild( DOMManager.createElement( doc, BillKeys[i],
strValue));
  }
```

```
    eBookSession.appendChild( eShipping );
    eBookSession.appendChild( eBilling );

    return doc;
}
```

Before we look at the method, notice that we added a few new instance variables to our class. First the m_strOrderStylesheetPI variable was added. This variable will be used to signify the stylesheet processing instruction that will be contained in the document. As this could potentially change, we will load the value for this variable dynamically in the init method and store the value in the properties file.

The other two instance variables are String Arrays indicating the HTTP parameters we need to extract from the HTTP request when we insert them into the book-session document.

The createBookSessionDoc method starts off by creating a new document instance. Next, we use the createProcessingInstruction method of the document instance to create a new ProcessingInstruction containing the information necessary for the XSL Processor to locate the stylesheet.

Next, we perform the usual activities of creating the root BOOK_SESSION element and appending it to the document. Once the root element is in the document, we can pass the document to the appendElements method we created in the last chapter to insert the Account, Catalog, and Shopping-Basket elements into the DOM tree. If you remember from Chapter 6, this is the same method that calls for each request (inside the doXML method) to append the Account, Catalog, and basket elements in the book-session element of the document, just as if we were getting ready to send a response to the client browser.

The last thing to accomplish is to create elements for each of the HTTP parameters that we passed up during the request and that represent the shipping address and payment information.

To simplify this task, we created two constant arrays of Strings (ShipKeys and BillKeys) that hold the parameter names for both the shipping and billing (payment) parameters. The ShipKeys array represents the parameter names for the ship-address elements and the BillKeys array represents the parameter names for the payment attribute values. Essentially, we apply the same concepts we used to implement the `doRegisterAction` in Chapter 6. Instead of searching for each explicit value, we simply search for each value in the array. As you can see from the example, this saves a good amount of code because we can loop through the array. In addition, this makes it very easy to add or remove parameters because we can simply add or remove them from the array.

As each of the two arrays is traversed, we call the `getParameter` method of the `HttpServletRequest` object to retrieve the HTTP parameter's value. So long as the value is valid (not null) and it is not an empty string (zero length), we simply create a new element with the same name and value as the HTTP parameter. Once the element has been created, we append it to either the shipping or billing element depending on the array we are traversing. When we are finished, we append the shipping (`eShipping`) and billing (`eBilling`) elements to our root book-session element (`eBookSession`) and return a reference to our freshly populated document.

Now that we have constructed the `book-session` document, we can transform the document into a `book-order` document. To do so, we will use the `XSLTransformer` we created previously and are currently using to dynamically generate the HTML pages for the client browsers. Remembering back to the `XSLTransformer` interface, the output tree is not returned as a DOM document. Instead it is written to a `java.io.Writer` interface. This means that before we can transform the document we need to set up a `Writer` object to store the resulting document from the transformer. We will use a `java.io.StringWriter` to store the output XML document because this will make it easier to stream the document over the network to the Distributor's servlet. The code required to transform the document is shown in Example 7.24:

Example 7.24 Transforming the book-session into a book-order stream

```
private String m_strOrderProlog = null;
private String m_strDistributorURL = null;

protected boolean doOrderAction(HttpServletRequest req, XMLHttpServletRe-
sponse res)
  throws UnavailableException
```

```
{
  try
  {
    HttpSession session    = req.getSession(false);
    XSLTransformer trans   = DOMManager.getTransformer();
    Document docSession    = res.getDocument();
    Element eSession       = docSession.getDocumentElement();
    StringWriter writer    = new StringWriter();
    URL url     = new URL(m_strDistributorURL);
    URL urlbase = new URL( HttpUtils.getRequestURL(req).toString() );


    // Populate the document
    Document doc = createBookSessionDoc(req);
    // Transform to book-order
    trans.transformDocument(doc, urlbase, writer,XSLTrans-
former.FORMAT_XML,m_strOrderProlog);
    // send to distributor's website
    Document docConfirm = postDocument(url, writer.toString());
    ...
  }
  catch( TransformerException te )
  { throw new UnavailableException( this, te.toString() );
  }
  catch( Exception e )
  { throw new UnavailableException( this, e.toString() );
  }
  res.setStyleSheet( "/book/checkout.xsl" );
  return true;
}
```

Before we delve into this method, notice that we have also defined two more instance variables. They have not been seen yet because they will be initialized in the `init` method, which will be covered shortly. The first variable, `m_strOrderProlog`, will represent the XML declaration processing instruction and the external DTD reference to the book-order DTD. The last variable, `m_strDistributorURL`, will indicate the URL we will use to connect the Distributors website. For testing purposes, we have this pointing to the same website as our servlet, however, it should be easily configurable so the code does not have to be recompiled prior to production release. Ultimately, both of these variables will be loaded dynamically from the servlet's initialization parameters, just like the database information was.

Before you get too concerned about the amount of code that is required here, note that the first seven lines in the try block are merely to set up variables we will be using in the method. We get references to the `HttpSession`, `XSLTransformer`, and the `Document` we be sending back to the client browser. Furthermore, we create a new instance of a `StringWriter` that we will be using to store the resulting tree after the transformation. We create two new URL objects that represent where to send the order after it is transformed and finally, the context of the source document for the transformations.

After we have created the `book-session` object with the call to `createBookSessionDoc`, we are ready to transform the document into a `book-order` document. Thus far we have used the `XSLTransformer` primarily to output HTML; however, this time we want the output tree to be formatted as XML. To do so, we simply instruct the `XSLTransformer` by passing the `FORMAT_XML` flag to the transformer instead of passing the `FORMAT_HTML` flag we used in the `XMLHttpServlet`. This will allow the `XSLTransformer` to choose the appropriate `FormatterListener` (based on its internal implementation) to write the output tree as an XML document.

The other difference is that we must include the DTD in the document. Unlike the HTML documents we have been transforming, this time we need to include a heading to the output stream. Instead of passing a `null` value, as we did for the HTML output in the `XMLHttpServlet` class, we will pass the `m_strOrderProlog` instance variable. This is another instance variable that is assigned when the servlet initializes itself.

Once the transformation is completed, the `StringWriter` will now contain a stream of characters that represents the `book-order` document. Although it would not make a great deal of sense to do, we could essentially reconstitute the document by passing the stream of characters to an XML parser, similar to how the Distributor class parses the HTTP request.

Next, we need to transmit the document data that is inside the `StringWriter` class to the `Distributor` servlet. To do this, we will call a new `postDocument` method, passing the document (as a `String`) and a `URL` we created at the beginning of the method.

7.2.1.8 postDocument method

The task for the `postDocument` method is relatively straightforward. It needs to connect to the Distributor servlet, send the document, and receive a response. As we will be using sockets (TCP/IP) to communicate with the Distributor servlet, we will need to break the URL parameter into smaller pieces so that we can extract the host and port. Furthermore, because we are going to be using the HTTP protocol, we also will need to extract the path or resource on the destination web server we are trying to access. Typically this is a file, however, in our case this will be the path that will invoke the Distributor's servlet.

First, we need to connect to the web server. Because a web server listens on a port, we need to extract the host (server) and port to direct the request. To do so, the URL class provides `getHost` and `getPort` methods. For the most part, there should not be a problem extracting the host from a URL as long as it is an absolute URL. Extracting the port, however, may be more difficult. Most URLs do not explicitly assign the port. Instead, the protocol, such as HTTP, is used to determine the "default" port. The default port for the HTTP protocol is 80. Because we are going to be transmitting over HTTP, if the port is not explicitly assigned in the URL, we will need to use port 80 when we try to connect a socket to the web server. This is important because the `getPort` does not provide the default port of the protocol when it is not specified. Instead, the method will simply return –1 to indicate that it was not specified.

Once we have the host or domain name and port, we can attempt to connect to the web server. In Java this is accomplished using the `java.net.Socket` class. To create a new instance of a socket, we simply pass the host and port to its constructor. As long as a connection to the destination is successful we can continue by hooking into the input and output streams of the socket. Just like all external resources in Java, we use `InputStream`s, `OutputStream`s, `Reader`s, and `Writer`s to read and write data. Essentially, socket programming is no different. Before we can send something to the server, we will need to get a reference to the `OutputStream` of the socket. Moreover, before we can receive data from the Distributor servlet, we need to get a reference to the socket's `InputStream`. To make writing data to the Distributor server easier, we create an instance of a `DataOutputStream` that will write to the socket's `OutputStream`. Furthermore, we will create a `BufferedReader` to read the data from the socket's `InputStream`, as shown in Example 7.25:

Example 7.25 PostDocument method

```
protected Document postDocument(URL url, String strDoc)
  throws Exception
{
  String strHost = url.getHost();
  int nPort = url.getPort();
  if (nPort == -1)
    nPort = 80;

  // Connect to the Web server, setup the streams for input and output

  Socket socket = new Socket( strHost, nPort );
  DataOutputStream out =new DataOutputStream(socket.getOutputStream());
  InputStreamReader temp = new InputStreamReader(socket.getInputStream());
  BufferedReader reader = new BufferedReader(temp);

  // Format the request HTTP/1.0 spec.
  out.writeBytes("POST " + url.getFile() + " HTTP/1.0\n");
  out.writeBytes("Content-type: text/xml\n");
  out.writeBytes("Content-length: "+strDoc.length()+"\n\n");
  out.writeBytes( strDoc );

  // Parse the request into a DOM doc.
  //  HTTP headers will need with a blank line (length zero)

  StringWriter writer = new StringWriter();
  String strLine = null;
  while ((strLine=reader.readLine()) != null && strLine.length()!= 0)
    writer.write(strLine + "\n");

  TXDOMParser parser = new TXDOMParser();
    parser.parse( new InputSource(reader) );

  Document doc = parser.getDocument();
  DOMManager.getWriter().writeDocument(doc, writer );
  log( writer.toString() );

  return parser.getDocument();
}
```

As you can see from the example, the first few lines of code collect the host and port from the URL. If the port was not specified (returns –1), we assign the port to 80 because this is the default for the HTTP protocol. Next, we create a `Socket` object by passing the host and port to its constructor. Although we do not catch any exceptions in this method, if the socket cannot connect to its destination, an exception will be generated. In these cases, we simply pass the exception on to the `doOrderAction` method. If the connection was successful, we continue by creating a `DataOutputStream`. In doing so, we pass the `OutputStream` of the socket to the class's constructor, which enables it to write to the socket (and ultimately the destination web server). Furthermore, we want to use a `BufferedReader` to read the data sent from the web server; however, the `BufferedReader` class does not provide a mechanism to read from an `InputStream`. Instead, we must first create an `InputStreamReader` that reads from the `InputStream` of the socket.

Now that we have successfully attached a `DataOutputStream` to the `Socket`, we can format an HTTP request. To do so, we begin by writing the HTTP method, followed by the resource we want to access and finally the version of the protocol. Notice that all three pieces of information are separated by spaces, and the entire line is terminated with a new line character. In this case, we are using the POST method, accessing the resource based on the result of the `getFile` method of the URL, and we have specified we want to use version 1.0 of the HTTP protocol.

The next two lines specify the HTTP headers to be passed to the web server. They are in the form of name, colon, space, value, and new line character. This means that we are passing to HTTP headers. First, a Content-type header is passed with a value of `text/xml`. Second, a Content-length header is passed with a value equal to the length of a document's character stream.

Although we did not actually check for a content-type in the Distributor servlet, it is good practice to assign the appropriate content-type based on the data that follows the HTTP headers. In this case, we assign `text/xml` to indicate that it is an XML document. The `Content-length` header is used to inform the server as to how long the data is that follows the headers.

Notice that the line that writes the `Content-length` HTTP header includes two new line characters at the end. The HTTP protocol does not limit the number of HTTP headers. To differentiate the POST data from the headers, a blank line must be inserted between the two entities. After the blank line, we can stream the document to the web server. As it is already in string form, we simply pass it to the `writeBytes` method of the `DataOutputStream` object.

This is all that we need to do to post the XML document to the server. At this point we have communicated with the web server, requested the Distributor servlet, and passed two HTTP headers and our `book-session` document. Now the web server can hand the request to the servlet engine, which in turn passes the request to the `Distributor` servlet. We communicate indirectly, never directly with the `Distributor` servlet.

Now we wait until the web server sends a response. When the response is returned, it will also contain HTTP headers. As we are really only interested in the XML document that will follow the HTTP headers, we simply read each line into a temporary string (`strLine`) until we reach a blank line (zero length string). For debugging purposes we have decided to write each line to a `StringWriter` so that we can see the entire data that is passed back from the web server.

Once the end of the HTTP headers has been reached, we can begin parsing the XML document. This is done just as we performed this in the `Distributor` servlet. After creating a `TXDOMParser`, we create an `InputSource` object passing the reader to its constructor and allow the parser to read the data stream and create a DOM document. The last few lines simply write the document to the same `StringWriter` object that originally captured the HTTP headers and then we log the entire HTTP response to the servlet log file. To complete the method, we simply return the document (`order-status`) that was parsed from the HTTP response.

> **NOTE:** As with just about any type of network programming, it is generally not a trivial task. There are far too many aspects of network programming to include in this book. This book focuses mostly on the XML aspects of applications; you should consult a specialized network-programming book for more detailed information about socket programming and the HTTP protocol.

Now that the `postDocument` method is complete, we can finish off the `doOrderAction` method. Upon returning from the `postDocument` method, we now have the order-status document that was returned from the `Distributor` servlet. How the method proceeds is based on the `status` attribute of the `order-status` element. Thus, the first thing we do is retrieve the `order-status` element by calling the `Document.getDocument-Element` method. Next, we can check the `status` attribute by calling the `Element.getAttribute` method.

Example 7.26 XMLBookServlet.DoOrderAction method

```
protected boolean doOrderAction(HttpServletRequest req, XMLHttpServletRe-
sponse res)
  throws UnavailableException
{
  try
  {
    HttpSession session     = req.getSession(false);
    XSLTransformer trans    = DOMManager.getTransformer();
    Document docSession     = res.getDocument();
    Element eSession        = docSession.getDocumentElement();
    StringWriter writer     = new StringWriter();
    URL url      = new URL(m_strDistributorURL);
    URL urlbase = new URL( HttpUtils.getRequestURL(req).toString() );


    // Populate the document
    Document doc = createBookSessionDoc(req);
    // Transform to book-order
    trans.transformDocument(doc, urlbase, writer,XSLTrans-
former.FORMAT_XML,m_strOrderProlog);
    // send to distributor's website
    Document docConfirm = postDocument(url, writer.toString());

    Element eStatus = docConfirm.getDocumentElement();
    String strStatus = eStatus.getAttribute("status");

    if (strStatus.equals("success") && session != null)
    {
      session.putValue(ShoppingBasket.BASKET_TYPE, new ShoppingBas-
ket(m_Catalog));

      Element eConfirm = (Element) findFirstChildNode( eStatus,
Node.ELEMENT_NODE, "confirmation" );
```

```
      Element e = docSession.createElement("confirmation");
      e.setAttribute("order-num", eConfirm.getAttribute("order-num") );
      e.setAttribute("order-date", eConfirm.getAttribute("order-date") );
      eSession.appendChild(e);
    }
    else
    {
      Element eShipping = docSession.createElement("shipping");
      Element eBilling = docSession.createElement("billing");
      appendHttpParamArray( req, eShipping, ShipKeys );
      appendHttpParamArray( req, eBilling, BillKeys );
      eSession.appendChild(eShipping);
      eSession.appendChild(eBilling);

      copyOrderErrors( eStatus, eSession );
    }
  }
  catch( TransformerException te )
  { throw new UnavailableException( this, te.toString() );
  }
  catch( Exception e )
  { throw new UnavailableException( this, e.toString() );
  }
  res.setStyleSheet( "/book/checkout.xsl" );
  return true;
}
```

If the order was placed successfully (indicated by a status equal to "success"), we need to empty the ShoppingBasket and append the order confirmation information to the book-session document so the user will be able to view it.

We can provide the user with a new ShoppingBasket by replacing the existing one that is already in the HttpSession for the user. Essentially, this allows the Java Garbage collector to clean up the old ShoppingBasket instance. Likewise, this ensures that the products the user selects are removed from the basket. To do this, we create a new instance of the ShoppingBasket and insert it into the HttpSession using the same ShoppingBasket.BASKET_TYPE key. This forces the HttpSession object to release its reference to the old basket so it can store the new one.

Conceptually, you would think that inserting the confirmation information into the book-session document would be easy. We have used the appendChild method so many times that we added a macro to type it! Well, it will not work in this case because the confirmation nodes are owned by the document that was returned by the `postDocument` method. With the DOM Level 1 Recommendation, there is no easy way around this. We have to delve a little deeper into the DOM API to accomplish this feat.

Because the confirmation element is a child to the root element (`eStatus` in Example 7.26), we need to search for the Element. There are a couple of ways we could do this. The simplest way is to use the `getElementsByTagName` method of the Element interface. This is a very powerful method that walks the entire tree of children searching for all the elements of a given name. If you have not guessed yet, this can be resource intensive. For server applications, this can be detrimental.

A more efficient but better way is to programmatically examine the Nodes. Although this requires more coding, we are in full control of which Nodes to check. Thus, we can save some computational time on the server by writing a few more lines of code! We create a new method, `findFirstChildNode`, to accomplish this task.

To search for a Node, we need to pass a parent node to provide its context. Furthermore, we also pass in the type and name of the node we are looking for. The `findFirstChildNode` method is shown in Example 7.27.

Example 7.27 XMLBookServlet.findFirstChildNode method

```
public Node findFirstChildNode( Node parent, short nNodeType, String strN-
odeName )
{
  NodeList list = parent.getChildNodes();
  int nLength = list.getLength();

  for(int i = 0; i < nLength; i++ )
  {
    Node node = list.item(i);
    if (node.getNodeType() == nNodeType )
      if (node.getNodeName().equals(strNodeName))
        return node;
  }
  return null;
}
```

First, the findFirstChildNode method retrieves a list of all the parent Node's children by calling getChildNodes(). This returns a NodeList interface that we can interrogate to determine the number of Nodes, by the getLength method, and extract each Node individually with a call to the item method.

Once we have determined how many Nodes are in the list, we simply iterate the list extracting each Node, one by one. After we extract each Node, we check to see if it is the appropriate type by calling the getNode-Type method and comparing it to the nNodeType parameter we passed to the method. If the types match, we need to check to see if the name of the node is what we are looking for. To do so, we call the getNodeName method. If the names match, we return the reference to the Node, otherwise, we keep looping until we find a match or we run out of Nodes.

Now that we have implemented the findFirstChildNode method, we simply call the method passing the eStatus element as the parent, Node.ELEMENT_NODE as the type, and "confirmation" as the name of the node we are interested in. This will return a Node interface so we need to typecast the reference to an Element.

Once we have retrieved the confirmation element from the confirmation document, the rest of the coding is trivial. We simply create a new confirmation element, owned by our book-session document. Next we set the two attributes, order-num and order-date with the setAttribute method. Because we retrieve the confirmation element, we simply call the getAttribute method to retrieve its String value.

Do not get too excited yet because things become a little more complex. When the order is declined, we need to add the shipping and billing elements to the response document just like we did in the createBookOrderDoc method. Furthermore, we also need to add the order-error elements from the confirmation document again. This time, however, there is a potential for multiple order-error elements to add.

We start by implementing the straightforward logic and delegate the order-error processing to a new method called copyOrderErrors. To append the shipping and billing information, like we did when we placed the order, we simply create two new Elements and call the appendParamArray method we used in the createBookOrderDoc. This will populate the shipping and billing elements so now all we need to do is append them to the root element (eSession) of the book-session document.

To append the order-error elements, we call a new copyOrderErrors method. In doing so, we will be passing a reference to source element where the order-errors are located and the destination element where we want the order-error elements. As you can see from Example 7.28, the code to implement the method is very similar to the findfirstChildNode method.

Example 7.28 XMLBookServlet.copyOrderErrors method

```
protected void copyOrderErrors(Element eSource, Element eTarget)
{
  NodeList list = eSource.getChildNodes();
  Document docFactory = DOMManager.getOwner(eTarget);

  int nLen = list.getLength();
  for( int i = 0; i < nLen; i++)
  {
    Node node = list.item(i);
    if (node.getNodeType() == Node.ELEMENT_NODE && node.getNode-
Name().equals("order-error"))
    {
      Element err = docFactory.createElement("order-error");
      Node text = findFirstChildNode(node, Node.TEXT_NODE, "#text");

      if (text != null)
        err.appendChild( docFactory.createTextNode( text.getNodeValue()));

      Element eNode = (Element) node;
      err.setAttribute( "severity", eNode.getAttribute("severity"));
      err.setAttribute( "line", eNode.getAttribute("line"));
      err.setAttribute( "column", eNode.getAttribute("column"));

      eTarget.appendChild( err );
    }
  }
}
```

The first thing the method does is to get a reference to the owner document. We will be using this document as a factory for creating the necessary nodes. Next, we get a NodeList and begin iterating through the nodes much the same way we did in Example 7.27.

Once we have found a match, we create our version of the element. To extract the Text node, we use the findFirstChildNode method, passing a Node.TEXT_NODE type and (the kicker) "#text" as the name. Text Nodes do not actually have a name property, however, when we call the getNodeName method it will always return "#text." Thus, this is a way we can use the findFirstChildMethod to extract the Text associated with the element. The rest is trivial. We simply create the relevant nodes (with our new owner) using the values from the nodes in the source tree.

Before we can test our code, we need to implement the stylesheet that will transform the temporary book-session document into a book-order document. To accomplish this, we will create a new file named dist-order.xsl. This time, we only need to provide the xmlns:xsl attribute of the root xsl:stylesheet element. The other attributes are not needed in this case because we will be generating an XML document. Furthermore, there is no need to include the common.xsl stylesheet that we have been using for our HTML stylesheets. This is shown along with the root template in Example 7.29:

Example 7.29 Root template of the dist-order.xsl

```
<?xml version="1.0"?>
<xsl:stylesheet xmlns:xsl="http://www.w3.org/XSL/Transform/1.0" >

  <xsl:template match="/">
    <book-order>
      <xsl:apply-templates select="/book-session/Account"/>
      <xsl:apply-templates select="/book-session/shipping"/>
      <xsl:apply-templates select="/book-session/billing"/>
      <xsl:apply-templates select="/book-session/basket/Product"/>
    </book-order>
  </xsl:template>
...
</xsl:stylesheet>
```

Referring back to the book-order.dtd file we reviewed earlier in the chapter, a valid book-order document contains a root element named book-order, with a bill-address, ship-address, ship, payment, and one or more sku elements. In looking at Example 7.29, you can see that the root template creates the book-order element and then calls a series of apply templates. It may appear a little deceiving right now, but each of the apply-templates is applied against the source document, which is actually the book-session document. The book-order elements will be created when these templates are actually invoked or applied.

To start, the first xsl:apply-template selects the Account object. Because the Account object holds the bill-address information, this template will create the bill-address element and insert the required child elements, as shown in Example 7.30. As you can see from the example, the Account template first creates the bill-address element, then conditionally includes the various child elements required in the bill-address element. With the exception of the state element, each of the elements is conditionally included depending on whether a valid value from the Account element exists. In the case of the State element, the abbrev attribute is simply assigned to the value of the State element.

Example 7.30 Account template of dist-order.xsl

```
<xsl:template match="Account">
  <bill-address>
    <xsl:if test="not(Address1 = '')">
      <line><xsl:value-of select="Address1"/></line>
    </xsl:if>
    <xsl:if test="not(Address2 = '')">
      <line><xsl:value-of select="Address2"/></line>
    </xsl:if>
    <!-- There is no attention line in our billing info so we'll leave
                                                      it out (optional) -->
    <xsl:if test="not(City='')">
      <city><xsl:value-of select="City"/></city>
    </xsl:if>
    <state>
      <xsl:attribute name="abbrev">
        <xsl:value-of select="State"/>
      </xsl:attribute>
    </state>
    <xsl:if test="not(Zip='')">
      <postal-code><xsl:value-of select="Zip"/></postal-code>
    </xsl:if>
  </bill-address>
</xsl:template>
```

Moving on to the shipping element we inserted for the purpose of creating the book-order document, you will notice that this template operates much like the Account template. Instead of creating the bill-address element, the shipping template creates the ship-address template. Furthermore, it is merely accessing different elements (the elements from the `ShipKeys` array we covered in the `createBookSessionDoc` method) to populate the child elements of the ship-address element. As the shipping element (from the book-session document) contains the carrier, the ship element is also created in this template. See Example 7.31:

Example 7.31 Shipping template in dist-order.xsl

```
<xsl:template match="shipping">

  <ship-address>
    <xsl:if test="not(ShipLine1='')">
      <line><xsl:value-of select="ShipLine1"/></line>
    </xsl:if>
    <xsl:if test="not(ShipLine2='')">
      <line><xsl:value-of select="ShipLine2"/></line>
    </xsl:if>
    <xsl:if test="not(ShipAttn='')">
      <attn><xsl:value-of select="ShipAttn"/></attn>
    </xsl:if>
    <xsl:if test="not(ShipCity = '')">
      <city><xsl:value-of select="ShipCity"/></city>
    </xsl:if>

    <state><xsl:attribute name="abbrev">
      <xsl:value-of select="ShipState"/>
    </xsl:attribute></state>

    <xsl:if test="not(ShipZip='')">
      <postal-code>
        <xsl:value-of select="ShipZip"/>
      </postal-code>
    </xsl:if>
  </ship-address>

  <!-- Carrier Info -->
  <ship>
    <xsl:attribute name="carrier">
      <xsl:value-of select="ShipMethod"/>
    </xsl:attribute>
```

```
  </ship>
</xsl:template>
```

Next the billing template is invoked. The billing element (from the book-session document) is the other element we created explicitly for placing orders. This element contains the elements from the `BillKeys` array that we covered in the `createBookSessionDoc` method. This information is inserted into the payment element in the book-order document. See Example 7.32:

Example 7.32 Billing template from the dist-order.xsl

```
<xsl:template match="billing">
  <payment>
    <xsl:attribute name="type">
      <xsl:value-of select="PayMethod"/>
    </xsl:attribute>
    <xsl:attribute name="expire-year">
<xsl:value-of select="ExpireYear"/>
    </xsl:attribute>
    <xsl:attribute name="expire-month">
<xsl:value-of select="ExpireMonth"/>
    </xsl:attribute>
    <xsl:attribute name="card-number">
      <xsl:value-of select="CardNumber"/>
    </xsl:attribute>
  </payment>
</xsl:template>
```

The final templates applied produce each of the sku elements in the book-order resulting document. Because we only want to include the products that are currently in the shopping basket, the template is applied using the "/book-session/basket/Product" pattern. In doing so, only the Product elements that are children of the basket element will actually instantiate the associated Product template, shown in Example 7.33:

Example 7.33 Product template of the dist-order.xsl

```
<xsl:template match="Product">
  <sku>
    <xsl:attribute name="ID">
      <xsl:value-of select="concat('sku',@ProductID)"/>
    </xsl:attribute>
```

```
    <xsl:attribute name="quantity">
      <xsl:value-of select="@Quantity"/>
    </xsl:attribute>
  </sku>
</xsl:template>
```

This template is slightly different from the rest. Although this template only inserts a single sku element into the book-session element, it will be called for each Product element where a template is applied. As the root template called the apply-templates with a pattern that only matched the Products in the basket, then this template is applied for each Product element in the basket. Also interesting is how the ID attribute value is created. If you remember for the book-order.dtd file, the ID attribute is defined as an ID type. As such, a numeric value, such as our `ProductID` attribute, will not pass the validity checks because it does not match the Name production. In this case we need to prefix the value with the letters "sku" so that the value conforms to the Name production.

7.2.1.9 Finishing up the Checkout stylesheet

This is all there is to the dist-order.xsl stylesheet. The last thing we need to do is finish off the checkout.xsl stylesheet so that it displays the order confirmation screen and redisplays the shipping entry form when an order attempt is declined. We have already implemented the majority of the stylesheet. In doing so, we have already handled the situations when the order-status element is not present in the document. Now we need to handle the cases when it is present. Referring back to the root template of the checkout stylesheet, if the order-status element is present in the document, we simply select a template matching the order-status element.

Although we are simply matching based on the order-status element, XSL is smart enough to choose the most appropriate template for the given element. For example, to handle the cases when the order was declined, we create the template as shown in Example 7.34:

Example 7.34 Declined Order status template

```
<xsl:template match="order-status[./@status='declined']">
  <xsl:apply-templates select="/book-session/shipping"/>
  <xsl:for-each select="order-error">
```

```
    <TR><TD><xsl:value-of select="."/></TD></TR>
  </xsl:for-each>
</xsl:template>
```

As you can see from the example, this template is designed to match only order-status elements with its status attribute equal to "declined." When the status is declined, we first want to display the `shipEntryForm` again; however, this time we want to pass parameters from the shipping and billing elements instead of the Account element. Finally, when the `ShipEntryForm` template has completed, we traverse the order-error elements and display them to recreate a new table row for each element. As the majority of the parameters are in the shipping element, this template simply applies another template with the pattern to match the shipping element, which is shown in Example 7.35:

Example 7.35 Shipping template in checkout stylesheet

```
<xsl:template match="shipping">
  <xsl:call-template name="ShipEntryForm">
    <xsl:param name="ShipAttn" expr="ShipAttn"/>
    <xsl:param name="ShipLine1" expr="ShipLine1"/>
    <xsl:param name="ShipLine2" expr="ShipLine2"/>
    <xsl:param name="ShipCity" expr="ShipCity"/>
    <xsl:param name="ShipState" expr="ShipState"/>
    <xsl:param name="ShipZip" expr="ShipZip"/>
    <xsl:param name="ExpireMonth" expr="../billing/ExpireMonth"/>
    <xsl:param name="ExpireYear" expr="../billing/ExpireYear"/>
    <xsl:param name="CardNumber" expr="../billing/CardNumber"/>
  </xsl:call-template>
</xsl:template>
```

This template basically does the same thing as the Account template, however, it uses different elements to assign the values of the parameters that will be used to populate the `ShipEntryForm` once it is called. On the other hand, the template shown in Example 7.36 is invoked when the status of the order-status element is "success." As you can see, this template also applies a different template to display the relevant information, which in this case is the order confirmation screen. To do so, the template invokes the matching confirmation template because this is the element that contains the data.

Example 7.36 Success Order-status template

```
<xsl:template match="order-status[./@status='success']">
  <xsl:apply-templates select="confirmation"/>
</xsl:template>

<xsl:template match="confirmation">
  <CENTER><TABLE BORDER="1">
  <TR><TD ALIGN="CENTER" COLSPAN="2">
    <B>Your order was placed successfully!</B></TD></TR>
  <TR><TD>
  Your order number is <B><xsl:value-of select="@order-num"/></B>.
  </TD></TR><TR><TD>
  Placed on <xsl:value-of select="@order-date"/>.
  </TD></TR>
  <TR><TD>Please retain this information for your records</TD></TR>
  <TR><TD ALIGN="CENTER" COLSPAN="2">
  Your <xsl:value-of select="//billing/PayMethod"/> will be billed.
  </TD></TR>
  </TABLE></CENTER>
</xsl:template>
```

7.3 Conclusion

Congratulations! By using the process of creating the order processing functionality for the website we have explored a few more aspects of programming XML applications. For starters, we took a detailed look at DTDs, and in doing so, we saw many different ways elements and attributes could be defined. In addition, we saw how DTDs can enforce the logical structure of a document by requiring one or more elements, or in the case of the order-status element have two different internal structures. Furthermore, we saw how we could use parameter entities to chain multiple DTDs together so that they can inherit definitions from other DTDs.

Once we finished reviewing the distributor's vocabularies, we tackled parsing XML documents the hard way. Most of the time, XML documents are simply parsed from a file. Instead, we implemented a servlet that could receive XML documents, parse them, and manipulate the DOM document afterwards. Of course, we moved back into the XMLBookServlet and implemented the code that would send XML documents over HTTP. In the process, we saw some of the internal workings of HTTP protocol.

Finally, throughout the chapter we saw about as much as one could handle of XSL Transformations (XSLT)! We created a stylesheet that would transform the book-session document to a book-order XML document. Up to that point, we had only transformed XML documents into HTML documents. Furthermore, we saw a few more really interesting aspects of XSLT. Keep in mind that XSL (thus XSLT) is still only a working draft, so it will most likely change somewhat before it becomes a recommendation.

CHAPTER 8

XML Related Technologies

In addition to the XML-related specifications described in the previous chapters, many others are being developed. This chapter will try to summarize and point out some of these new specifications that could be used with XML to develop even richer applications. We will cover the following XML technologies:

- XML Namespaces;
- XML Resource Definition Format (RDF);
- XML Document Content Description (DCD);
- XML Channel Definition Format (CDF); and
- Event-driven XML Processing Using the Simple API for XML (SAX).

8.1 Namespaces in XML

One of the difficulties in working with XML documents retrieved from multiple sources is that the meaning of application-specific tags may sometimes become unclear. For example, if a financial application merged two

XML documents—one from a Canadian bank, the other from an American bank—into a single document, and then came across the tag `<dollars>` while processing it, how does it know whether the contents of that element refer to *Canadian* dollars or *American* dollars? As you will see, in such cases XML namespaces will allow users to eliminate ambiguity in the meaning of XML elements and attributes. namespaces allow users to qualify element and attribute names by associating them with namespaces that are tied to URI references. Namespaces are defined in the W3C recommendation "Namespaces in XML" (REC-xml-names-19990114).

8.1.1 What is a Namespace?

Before examining XML namespaces, we first discuss "namespaces" in a more general sense using some everyday examples. A namespace can be thought of as a context; it is a setting, which gives a specific meaning to what might otherwise be a general term. For example, consider the term "bill." What does "bill" mean? Without further information, you might venture to say that "bill" is a shortened version of the name "William," which is a common first name for males who happen to live in the United States. We then provide some context and see what that does to the meaning of the term "bill."

For starters, say that our context is "the personal computer software industry." Does the term "bill" then take on any new meaning? Well, like many folks who follow the software industry, the use of the term "bill" in this context immediately brings to mind a person, namely, Bill Gates. In a phrase such as "Bill is clever," uttered over coffee at an early morning meeting to discuss desktop software, "Bill" almost certainly refers to Bill Gates. By providing a context, the generic term "Bill" has taken on new meaning; "Bill" is no longer simply a common first name, but rather refers to a specific person. Now notice our interpretation of the term "bill" if we switch contexts.

Here, we switch our context from "the personal computer software industry" to "the legislative branch of the United States government." If you know only a little about the US government, then you will easily recognize "bill" as the term that refers to the elements of work that flow through the US Congress, for example, "The House voted two-to-one to pass the bill." In this new context the term "bill" has a completely different meaning than it did before. If you heard someone say that their congressman had crafted a unique piece of legislation, you might venture to say that the "bill is clever."

The question now arises is this the only interpretation of the term "bill" in this context? We answer this with another question: What interpretation would you give the term "Bill" if our context was made slightly more specific, say. in reference to the US Senate, a part of the legislative branch of government, during the early part of 1999. In this more specific context, the term "Bill" could certainly take on new meaning. Then it could likely refer to the President of the United States, Bill Clinton, who was the subject of impeachment hearings. The phrase "Bill is clever" now has a completely different meaning than in the other two contexts. Following along these lines, if we switched contexts to an accounting department of a corporation, "Bill" would likely take on a new meaning, as it would if the context is birds? Needless to say, the meaning of the term "bill," when standing alone, is quite ambiguous, but it is the context that gives meaning to the term.

The point here is that people quite naturally use contexts to find meaning in terms, and thus we can think of these contexts as being "namespaces." Now we look at a somewhat longer, completely fictitious statement: "I hear Bill is going to lobby hard to get the bill protecting spotted-bill owls through the House."

Here is how you might have interpreted this statement, paying special attention to the meaning of the several "bill" terms. "I hear (U.S. President) Bill is going to lobby hard to get the (U.S. Congress) bill protecting the (birds) spotted-bill owl through the House."

Here we have added "US President," "US Congress" and "Birds" as contexts or namespaces that you may have used to give meaning to each of the "bill" terms in the statement. In fact, you probably also mentally mapped the term "House" to the context "US Congress" as well, for it is clear that the "house" referred to in this case is not a "single-family home" but rather a part of the US government. As humans we do this type of namespace or context mapping quite automatically.

Unfortunately, computers are notoriously bad when it comes to automatically figuring out what the context of an individual element should be based on its relationships with other elements, which may not have their context specified either. In fact, it would probably require a state-of-the-art artificial intelligence program in order to have determined the contexts in the forementioned examples. Thus, in general, determining contexts accurately is extremely difficult. (As a test, see what your wordprocessor suggests as a substitution when it finds the term "de facto" misspelled in a sentence, for example, as "defacto." Maybe wordprocessors have a better sense of humor than we think.)

Because computers are so notoriously bad at performing context inferences, and because the creator of the information knows exactly what context is intended, it is much more sensible to permit the creator of the information to explicitly specify contexts. This is what XML namespaces are intended to do for XML documents as they are designed to make life easier for users of XML, whether these "users" are people or (more likely) programs that must read, interpret and act upon the information in the XML. Namespaces in XML are simply a way of allowing the creator of an XML document to qualify elements and attributes in these documents with a context so that the meaning of the XML elements and attributes is not ambiguous.

8.1.2 Using Namespace in XML

The abstract for the W3C Recommendation on "Namespaces in XML" (REC-xml-names-19990114) gives the following concise description: "XML namespaces provide a simple method for qualifying element and attribute names used in Extensible Markup Language documents by associating them with namespaces identified by URI resources."

Recall that the namespace URI is merely an agreed-upon string and need not point to any "real" resource. In particular, namespaces are not pointers to DTDs that define the elements and attributes for that namespace. With this description in mind, we start with a simple example and observe namespaces in XML. We say that you are writing a personal finance application, and that for part of this application you need to keep a record of the yearly earnings for individuals. In this case, you are tracking individuals by their Social Security Number (SSN). Then you need to keep track of their earnings for different years, and by "earnings" we mean their income, as well as the federal and state taxes they paid that year. An example of XML that captures this information for a fictitious individual named Mick E. Mouse, Social Security Number 123-456-7890, who lives in Southern California just outside of Los Angeles is given as follows.

```
<Earnings>
   <SSN>123-456-7890</SSN>
   <Income>100,000</Income>
   <Year>1998</Year>
   <FederalTax>30,000</FederalTax>
   <StateTax>10,000</StateTax>
</Earnings>
```

Now, because we know the context of this document, namely, personal finance, we can deduce that element <SSN> refers to Social Security Number, rather than being a classification for nuclear-powered fast-attack submarines. (For example, the USS Seahorse, SSN 669, is the US Navy's 47th nuclear-attack submarine.) In order to eliminate any possibility of ambiguity should we ever share data with other applications, for example, with an application that does personal finances for US Navy submariners, we need to specify the context of SSN precisely.

To specify the context of "SSN" precisely in our application, we need a namespace in which SSN is defined to mean "Social Security Number," and we need to associate our `<SSN>` tag with that namespace. The US Government happens to have an agency called the Social Security Administration that oversees social security affairs. Thus what we would like to be able to do is to say that our <SSN> element should be interpreted in the "context" of the "Social Security Administration."

To do this, we need a Universal Resource Indicator (URI) that represents the Social Security Administration. However, for now we will pretend that the URI for the Social Security Administration, in particular, the definition of their technical terms, is "http://www.ssa.gov/Defs." We need to tie this URI to a namespace in XML, and we can do this within XML code with a statement such as the following: xmlns:soc="http://www.ssa.gov/Defs."

This means that there is an XML namespace (the "xmlns" indicates that we are referring to an XML namespace), which we will refer to in our code as "soc" (we could have chosen any legal XML attribute name), and that this namespace corresponds to the URI "http://www.ssa.gov/Defs. " We can now use the namespace "soc" to qualify our <SSN> element tag. The syntax for qualifying the <SSN> element with the "soc" namespace is to simply pre-append the namespace onto the element, separating them with a colon, resulting in the namespace qualified element <soc:SSN>. The XML for this could be coded as follows if the syntax for namespaces is starting to look ugly, do not despair! We will see shortly how the syntax can be simplified, but for now our goal is to be explicit):

```
<Earnings>
   <soc:SSN xmlns:soc="http://www.ssa.gov/Defs">123-456-7890</soc:SSN>
   <Income>100,000</Income>
   <Year>1998</Year>
   <FederalTax>30,000</FederalTax>
   <StateTax>10,000</StateTax>
</Earnings>
```

Now when an application accesses the <SSN> element, for example, through a DOM interface, the application will be able to determine the namespace to which the <SSN> element belongs, namely the namespace that corresponds to the URI "http://www.ssa.gov/Defs."

In order for XML namespaces to be effective, there must be agreement beforehand as to the context or meanings of the particular namespaces. That is, in order for applications to agree on the meaning of elements, the applications must share a common vocabulary. In effect, namespaces provide a means for applications (or perhaps more likely, the writers of the applications) to agree on a common vocabulary. What we have done in the foregoing example above is to state that the element <SSN> should be interpreted in the context (e.g., namespace) of the Social Security Administration.

It is expected in the near future that industry sectors will come to agreements on XML "vocabularies" for their individual business sectors, and that the namespaces for these vocabularies will be given well-known URIs so that applications that operate in these domains can make use of them. For example, personal finance application writers might agree that the URI for all social security related terms are "http://www.ssa.gov/Defs. " If this were the case, when programs that encountered an element such as `<SS-5>`, qualified with a namespace that points to this URI (e.g., `<soc:SS-5>` using the same namespace declaration as in the forementioned example, xmlns:soc="http://www.ssa.gov/Defs"), the application would know that "SS-5" refers to the application form for a Social Security card and not, perhaps, a supersonic jet aircraft.

Because namespaces can act as qualifiers for element names, it is perfectly legal for different namespaces to include the same element name, each giving it a different meaning in its own context. For example, suppose the US Navy decides that Los Angeles class nuclear submarines will be referred to in XML by element name `<SSN>`, and suppose the URI for the US Navy submarines is http://www.navy.gov/SilentService." As we saw in our forementioned code, the Social Security Administration could choose to also use the element name `<SSN>`, but mean for it to refer to Social Security numbers. If our friend Mick E. Mouse decided he wanted to become a submariner, and were stationed aboard the USS Seahorse, which happens to be SSN 669, then the following XML code would capture this information unambiguously:

```
<Submariner>
   <usn:SSN xmlns:usn="http://www.navy.gov/SilentService">669</usn:SSN>
   <soc:SSN xmlns:soc="http://www.ssa.gov/Defs">123-456-7890</soc:SSN>
</Submariner>
```

Now that we have taken our first look at the syntax for XML namespaces, we can examine it further.

8.1.2.1 Qualified Names

We have seen examples of how namespaces in XML allow simple element names to be qualified. For example, in the foregoing, `<SSN>` is a simple element name whose two instances have been qualified with different namespaces, namely, with "soc," which corresponds to the Social Security URI, and with "usn," which corresponds to the US Navy submarine service.

8.1.2.2 Declaring Namespaces

The syntax for the forementioned namespace examples can be cleaned up quite a bit if we understand more about how namespaces are declared, how they can be applied to elements (and attributes) and how namespace defaulting works.

In the foregoing examples, we have always declared the namespace directly within the element tag that is being qualified by the resultant namespace. However, namespaces have scoping properties that are analogous to variable scoping properties in programming languages such as Java, C++, C, etc. If a namespace is declared in a higher-level scope, then that namespace attribute is available for use within elements contained therein. The following example shows how two namespaces can be declared in a parent element and used within the children elements:

```
<Submariner xmlns:usn="http://www.navy.gov/SilentService"
            xmlns:soc="http://www.ssa.gov/Defs">
   <usn:SSN>669</usn:SSN>
   <soc:SSN>123-456-7890</soc:SSN>
</Submariner>
```

As you have seen in these examples, a namespace is declared using a family of reserved attributes. Thus far, the attribute names all have "xmlns:" as a prefix (for example, "xmlns:soc" or "xmlns:usn"). In general, namespace declarations may take two forms. The first form is the type we have seen thus far, where "xmlns:" is a prefix for the namespace attribute. This type of declaration creates a namespace that can be used to qualify both XML elements and attributes. (Thus far we have only used it to qualify elements.)

The second form of namespace declaration is used to provide a default namespace, which can be thought of as automatically "prefixing" any nonprefixed element. (Note: automatic/default prefixing applies only to XML elements not to XML attributes.) As an example, expand the forementioned example somewhat, introducing an additional element that represents the submariner's rank:

```
<Submariner xmlns:usn="http://www.navy.gov/SilentService"
            xmlns:soc="http://www.ssa.gov/Defs">
   <usn:SSN>669</usn:SSN>
   <usn:Rank>Ensign</usn:Rank>
   <soc:SSN>123-456-7890</soc:SSN>
</Submariner>
```

Notice that the "usn" namespace is used by two of the elements, <SSN> and <Rank>. Because this is the case, it might be convenient to have "usn" be the default namespace. A default namespace is declared with an XML namespace attribute statement such as: xmlns="http://www.navy.gov/SilentService."

This default declaration can be used in our examples as follows (cleaning up the syntax somewhat):

```
<Submariner xmlns="http://www.navy.gov/SilentService"
            xmlns:soc="http://www.ssa.gov/Defs">
   <SSN>669<SSN>
   <Rank>Ensign<Rank>
   <soc:SSN>123-456-7890</soc:SSN>
</Submariner>
```

Recall that we noted earlier that default namespaces only apply to XML elements, and not to XML attributes. If we wanted to add an attribute to the submariner's rank that indicated their current status (e.g., active, retired, etc.), our code would appear as follows:

```
<Submariner xmlns="http://www.navy.gov/SilentService"
            xmlns:usn="http://www.navy.gov/SilentService"
            xmlns:soc="http://www.ssa.gov/Defs">
   <SSN>669<SSN>
   <Rank usn:Status="Active">Ensign<Rank>
   <soc:SSN>123-456-7890</soc:SSN>
</Submariner>
```

Note here that the URI representing the US Navy submarine service, "http://www.navy.gov/SilentService," is both the default namespace for nonprefixed elements, and is declared as namespace "usn" so that it can be used to qualify the Status attribute (because defaults do not apply to attributes). Note also that attributes do not have to be given a namespace prefix as we have done with the Status attribute of the Rank element in the foregoing. You would likely want to use a namespace prefix for an attribute if you thought that someone else might define another attribute for that same element, but give it the same name as your element. (For example, if someone else used a Status attribute in the <Rank> element to mean "Present" or "AWOL," etc.)

8.1.3 What Problems Do Namespaces Address?

Now that we understand how namespaces can be declared and applied to XML elements and attributes, we will discuss the types of problems that namespaces were designed to alleviate. In general, these problems relate to ambiguity in the meaning of element and attribute names within XML documents. There are a number of ways that ambiguity can sneak into XML documents, but fortunately XML namespaces can eliminate them.

First, we need to give a little thought to how XML will be used in Web applications. XML can be used simply as a data structure inside an application, but its real strength is as a data-interchange format, that is, as a means of communicating information between applications. Any time that multiple information sources are used, there is the potential for naming collisions. A naming collision occurs when two pieces of information that have different types or different semantic meaning are tagged with identical element or attribute names.

We saw naming collisions occur with Social Security numbers and US Navy submarine classifications, both of which might have been encoded with an element `<SSN>`. Because the meaning of "SSN" is different in these two contexts, if `<SSN>` elements from both contexts are used in the same document and are not qualified with an explicit namespace, we would say that a naming collision has occurred.

Naming collisions can arise for a number of reasons, perhaps the most common one being the case where data from multiple sources are merged into a single document. For example, the Computer Science department of a University may offer a class on Java programming. This class is called "CS250" and is encoded in XML as `<Class>CS250</Class>`. Now, as any Java programmer who is reading this will know, one of the fundamental concepts of Java (and Object Oriented programming in general) is that of the "class." (Classes are used in Java as templates to create Objects.)

Course materials would undoubtedly make references to classes; for example, information on graphical user interface design might be found under `<Class>JScrollPane<Class>`. Clearly, an application that accessed an XML document containing the following Class elements would have difficulty due to the ambiguity, not to mention the difficulty that would arise if someone created a Java class called "CS250" that was to be used as code by the students in the CS250 class:

```
<Syllabus>
   <Class>CS250</Class>
      ...
   <Class>JScrollPane</Class>
      ...
</Syllabus>
```

Clearly, these naming collisions, and the resulting ambiguities, can be eliminated by appropriately qualifying the XML elements, for example, as follows:

```
<Syllabus xmlns:univ="http://www.IvoryTower.edu"
          xmlns="http://www.JavaRocks.org">
   <univ:Class>CS250</univ:Class>
      ...
   <Class>JScrollPane</Class>
      ...
</Syllabus>
```

Perhaps the most important problem that namespaces address is the need for common, agreed-upon definitions for vocabulary terms that can be used by Web applications within industry sectors. The problem is similar to that of naming collisions that result from merging data. For example, consider the questions that a shopping agent must consider when comparing prices of items. First, what exactly does "price" mean when it is encountered in a document? Second, does it mean the amount of money that must be tendered in order to purchase a product, or perhaps something slightly different. (Does "price" include tax? Shipping?) Third, if an application finds a price that is $100, encoded as `<dollars>100</dollars>`, is this price being quoted in US dollars, or perhaps Canadian dollars?

Information sharing and data reuse will become commonplace on the Web of the future, and XML will play a central role in making this happen. In this future world, data producers and application developers must ensure that the meaning of their data (e.g., what the tags represent) is clear at all times, and XML namespaces provide users with exactly this capability. As we noted already, industry sectors will likely standardize XML vocabularies, and such standardized vocabularies will enable business partners to perform precise transactions. For example, using a namespace that references an appropriate URI (such as xmlns:usa=http://AmericaTheBeautiful.org), $100 American dollars could be expressed as <usa:dollars>100</usa:dollars>.

8.1.3.1 Related Technologies

XML namespaces are an integral part of many XML technologies, including the Extensible Style Language (XSL), Resource Description Framework (RDF), and the Document Content Description (DCD) proposals. In general, anywhere XML elements and attributes need to be precisely specified, XML namespaces will be employed for that purpose. It should be cautioned, however, that namespaces are not fully compatible with DTDs. Until XML Schema is released, a document will have to decide between namespaces and validation. More up-to-date information can be found at the W3C's website at http://www.w3.org.

8.2 Resource Description Framework (RDF)

The Web is a fascinating place. It provides users with access to vast quantities of information, information that is continuously changing and being updated. While this abundance of information is welcomed by users, it brings new challenges to both application developers and users of the Web who must be prepared to handle these ever-increasing quantities of data. As will be shown, a powerful means of addressing this type of problem is through the use of meta-information and meta-data. Resource Description Framework (RDF) provides application developers with a solid foundation for the processing of meta-data, which will become a necessity for the next generation of interoperable Web applications. The RDF Model and Syntax Specification (REC-rdf-syntax) is currently a W3C Recommendation, and the RDF Schema Specification (PR-rdf-schema) is a Proposed Recommendation.

8.2.1 What is Meta-Data?

In the years to come, developers will face a number of challenges as they create the next generation of interoperable Web applications, and XML will play a key role in helping to meet many of these challenges. One of the challenges that developers will face is cross-application interoperability. The crux of this problem is reliably exchanging data among disparate, applications that will have been created by different development teams, at different times, using different technologies.

A great deal of interest in using XML on the Web focuses on its role as a means of exchanging data between applications. XML turns data into "smart data" by incorporating semantically meaningful content-oriented tags, and enables application designers to agree upon the meaning of these tags through the use of namespaces. Sharing data among applications is greatly simplified when the applications use a common vocabulary (i.e., qualified XML elements and attributes) to describe and reference data.

Another challenge facing Web application designers is information scalability, which in general, is an important property that application designers must always keep in mind. For example, applications must be designed so that they continue to function smoothly as the number of users increases, as the sizes of files they process increases, and so on. These issues are extremely important, and are well addressed by books on software design and software architectures. However, the scalability problems that we will discuss here are more encompassing than those specific performance-related issues. Specifically, they concern the ability of applications (and indeed users), to cope with the sheer volume of information that is available on the Web and to continue functioning intelligently as the volume of data grows ever larger.

It is well-known that there is a large difference between "random" facts and useful information. Information is valuable when it is organized and, of course, when it is accessible. While these may seem to be trivial observations, they begin to address the root causes of the challenges facing the Web, in particular, the challenges faced by developers who wish to write applications that make use of the vast information resources on the Web.

In order to explore the problems relating to information and information scaling, first consider a pre-Web example of "information technology," and see how challenges of information scalability were handled with that technology. The pre-Web information technology we will consider is books, which are a tremendous source of information even in these days of the high-tech Web. A large part of their usefulness comes from the way they organize and present information.

For the moment we will concentrate on nonfiction books, perhaps a reference book or a book on Web programming such as this book. Books such as these contain a great deal of information, and are typically broken down into chapters and sections, and these sections contain paragraphs and figures, and so on. Now consider the Table of Contents. While it is certainly part of a book, it really talks *about* the book. In this way, we say that the Table of Contents is a source of "meta-information" for the book, that is, information about information contained in the book. In the case of the Table of Contents, the meta-information tells us about the structure of the book's content (namely, the various chapters and sections, etc.), the relationship between chapters and sections, and so forth. The meta-information also tells us where the pieces of content are located; for example, that Chapter 4, Section 8.3 begins on page 135. Many books contain additional meta-information in the form of an Index, or perhaps a List of Figures.

Now, consider this in a more general sense and see if we can come to some conclusions about good ways to organize information. We can all agree that books are a valuable source of information. If we consider technical books as our example for the moment, we see that their value as a source of information is due to several complementary reasons. One way to explore this idea is by starting with the lowest-level information and seeing how value is "added" to the information in the book as we work our way up the information hierarchy.

The first way in which a technical book provides value is as a source of low-level facts. For example, if sentence one, of paragraph two, in section three states that "The device is removed by depressing the latch and turning the device counterclockwise," you will find the book valuable (at some level) if this information turns out to be true.

We all know that a good technical book, however, is more than simply a random collection of true facts. This brings us to our second point: a technical book increases in value if the information contained within it is well organized. This generally means that the individual pieces of information have been successively arranged, perhaps hierarchically, in an order that makes sense to us. For example, a book on automobile repair may have a chapter on the engine, another chapter on the drive system, another on the electrical system, and so forth. Clearly, the value of a book comes not only from the correct low-level information contained within it, but also from the organization it applies to this information. We now ask if there is yet another higher-level way that value can be added to the information in such books?

Our answer to this question is "yes." A third way in which the book can increase its value is by providing meta-information about the content of the book. This meta-information is found in the Table of Contents, List of Figures and the Index; all of which provide information about information in the book. We think you would agree that the "value" of a technical book is greatly increased by such meta-information, and, in fact, in our experience the pages in the Index and Table of Contents are sometimes the most often referenced.

The point we are making is that it is not simply the low-level information plus the organization of that information that constitutes all of the value a book provides to the user. In addition to these very important items, meta-information (information about this information) adds value by making the information easier to use and easier to find. This concept of meta-information increasing the value of the information it describes can be applied at even higher levels. In our book example, consider the information structure used to organize books in a library. Libraries have a catalog that allows users to obtain information about books. The library catalog is clearly meta-information about books, which increases the value of the books in the catalog by making them much more accessible to the end users.

In our discussion we have been referring primarily to "information" and "meta-information" as opposed to "data" and "meta-data." This is really a reflection of who might be the intended user of the information. We tend to think of people as using "information" and computers or programs as using "data." The case we have made for meta-information increasing the value of information can readily be applied to meta-data increasing the value of data.

It should be clear that the distinction between information and meta-information (or data and meta-data) is not necessarily precise (nor need it be). That is, the Table of Contents is meta-information about the contents of a book, but the Table of Contents is also part of the book. However, to a library catalog program, the book is simply data. The fact that the Table of Contents can be considered meta-data in one context and data in another is a reflection of the hierarchies of information organization, and does not detract from the data/meta-data's usefulness (indeed, it makes it much richer). The mutability between data and meta-data should come as no surprise to programmers familiar with modern object-oriented concepts. Simply put, data objects can play different roles depending on their context.

Hopefully, you now understand how meta-data increases the usefulness of data, and thereby increases the data's value to the user. As we will see later, the Resource Description Framework (RDF) is a foundation for processing meta-data.

8.2.2 What Problems Does Meta-Data Address?

RDF is intended to provide an infrastructure that facilitates the automated processing of Web resources by allowing applications not only to find data, but also to obtain pertinent information about that data. RDF will play an important part in many application areas, including the following:

- **Resource Discovery**—RDF will enable search engines to more easily discover resources on the Web.
- **Cataloging**—RDF will enable users to better describe the content and content relationships that are available at their Websites. This includes describing content and content relationships at many ranges of scale, from entire websites to portions of webpages, from entire digital libraries to individual XML elements.
- **Intelligent Software Agents**—RDF will allow software agents to more intelligently find, harvest, filter and merge data.
- **Content Rating**—RDF will allow content to be rated.
- **Intellectual Property Rights**—RDF will allow users to more easily express and enforce intellectual property rights.

- **Privacy Preferences and Privacy Policies**—RDF will allow users and websites to clearly express privacy preferences and sitewide privacy policies that can be interpreted by applications.
- **Digital Signatures**—RDF will play a role in creating digital signatures, allowing users to reliably extend a level of trust to other users and applications.

8.2.3 What Does RDF Look Like?

RDF is a foundation for processing meta-data around for our purposes, it is primarily useful as a means of describing Web resources using an XML-based syntax. It is interesting to note that the creators of RDF, using considerable foresight, have not defined RDF as merely a means to describe Web resources using XML syntax. Naturally, RDF can perform this function, but it is also much more. At its most basic, RDF is simply a foundation to model meta-data; in fact, the data that the meta-data describes need not be Web resources, although they almost certainly will be in our case. And it turns out that XML code is but one of many possible syntaxes that could be used to describe these meta-data models. In a sense, RDF is really an abstract idea, that of modeling data about data, which happens to be implementable using XML syntax.

The RDF syntax that we will discuss is based on XML, as are many of the resources we describe (e.g., websites, XML documents, etc.), but neither of these is required to be the case. For example, it is possible for other (non-XML-based) language syntaxes to be used for modeling meta-data, and for such a purpose languages such as the Universal Modeling Language (UML) immediately come to mind. Fortunately, as long as these various language syntaxes model meta-data in the same way, as delineated by the RDF specification, it should be a simple matter to convert a model created using one syntax into a corresponding model based on another syntax. Such a conversion process should not require human intervention, but rather should be fully automated.

The question may arise concerning what the advantages are of having multiple language syntaxes support the same meta-data modeling foundation as RDF. The answer again is one of context; that is, it may depend on who (or what) is intended to be the user of the meta-data. Computers are ideally suited to crunch even the most arcane syntax, whereas humans are not. The adage about a picture being worth a thousand words works in both directions, depending upon whether it is from the vantage point of a human or from that of the computer. More graphical notations, characterized by "node and arc diagrams," are generally better suited for humans, whereas (seemingly arcane) low-level syntax such as XML's is often better left to computers. Fortunately, the designers of RDF have seen fit to allow for multiple syntactic representations of the meta-data models using current languages, and also leaving room for as-yet-unspecified languages and implementations.

The foundations for RDF come from a long history of data modeling. The basic premise of RDF involves specifying one or more properties of a given resource, and supplying values for these properties. The value of a property can be a literal (such as a string), or another resource, which too may have properties associated with it, and so on. When we say "resource," we mean something that can be described by a Universal Resource Indicator (URI), and for our purposes this will generally be a resource that is available on the Web, such as a website, an XML-based or non-XML-based document, or even a portion of a document.

RDF allows us to specify that a particular resource (say, a document) has a property (e.g., it has a "Creator"), and that this property has a specific value (perhaps a person's name). Because the value of a property can itself be a resource, RDF allows us to create very rich, deeply nested information structures that describe Web resources. When we use RDF, we will be making what are called RDF Statements. An RDF Statement sounds much like a simple English-language statement consisting of three parts, namely (1) a Subject, (2) a Predicate, and (3) an Object.

8.2.3.1 An RDF Example

For our first example we will make a statement about the W3C document that describes the RDF Model and Syntax. Our statement concerns the date on which the document was last revised and could be stated in English as follows: "The RDF Model and Syntax Specification was last revised Feb 22, 1999."

The RDF document about which we are making the statement has URI "http://www.w3.org.TR/REC-rdf-syntax." Using a node and arc diagram, this statement could be depicted as shown in Figure 8.1.

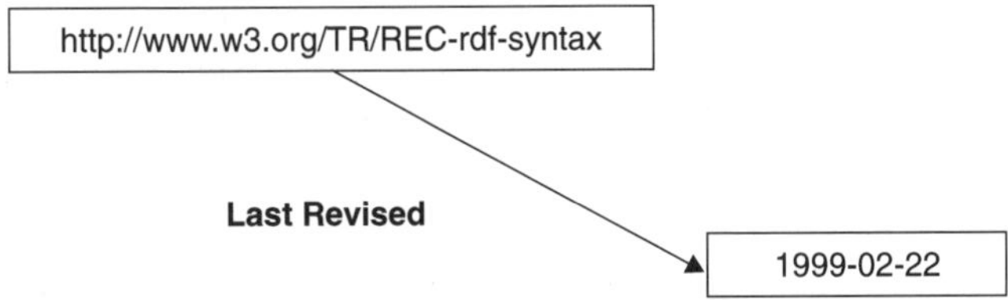

Figure 8.1 RDF statement depicted as node and arc diagram.

We can identify the Subject, Predicate and Object in this RDF statement as follows:

```
Subject   = "http://www.w3.org.TR/REC-rdf-syntax" (Resource)
Predicate = LastRevised    (Property)
Object    = "1999-02-22"   (Literal)
```

Before we show the RDF in XML syntax, we note that RDF requires that Property names be associated with a schema. This can be done by qualifying the element names with a namespace prefix to unambiguously connect the property definition with the corresponding RDF schema, or by declaring a default namespace. RDF schema serve several purposes, including defining what are valid properties, as well as the classes of resources that properties may connect. We will cover these in more detail later, but for now we will assume that an appropriate RDF schema exists at URI "http://description.org/schema/." In our XML code we will refer to the schema at that URI with a namespace that we create and refer to as "s." This allows us to encode our RDF statement in XML as follows:

```
<rdf:RDF xmlns:rdf="http://www.w3.org/1999/02/22-rdf-syntax-ns#"
                xmlns:rdfs="http://www.w3.org/TR/1999/PR-rdf-
schema-19990303#"
                xmlns:s="http://description.org/schema/">
    <rdf:Description about="http://www.w3.org.TR/REC-rdf-syntax">
        <s:LastRevised>1999-02-22<s:LastRevised>
    </rdf:Description>
</rdf:RDF>
```

Although this looks a bit cryptic, it is actually quite straightforward once you become familiar with it. We take a closer look at the required syntax by breaking this example apart line by line. First, the enclosing `<rdf:RDF>` elements act as a wrapper that identifies the enclosed code as XML syntax for RDF. We are declaring an XML namespace called "s" that refers to an

RDF schema via a URI. We next encounter the <Description> element, whose "about" attribute indicates the subject of the RDF statement. The names of the elements enclosed within the <Description> block correspond to the properties we are associating with the subject. Here, the <LastRevised> element, qualified with the namespace "s," corresponds to the predicate of the RDF statement, namely, "LastRevised." Finally, the value of the property element corresponds to the object of the RDF statement. Here the object is a literal date of "1999-02-22." This is the same information represented in the diagram in Figure 8.1.

We noted in the foregoing that RDF requires that all Property names be associated with an RDF schema. In our example we used the namespace "s" to associate a schema at (hypothetical) URI "http://description.org/schema/" with the LastRevised property. RDF schema are being formalized at present by the W3C in the RDF Schema Specification (PR-rdf-schema). The RDF Schema at our hypothetical URI might be the following:

```
<rdf:RDF xmlns:rdf="http://www.w3.org/1999/02/22-rdf-syntax-ns#"
             xmlns:rdfs="http://www.w3.org/TR/1999/PR-rdf-
schema-19990303#">
    <rdf:Description ID="LastRevised">
        <rdf:type rdf:resource="http://www.w3.org.TR/REC-rdf-
syntax#Property"/>
        <rdfs:label>LastRevised</rdfs:label>
        <rdfs:comment>The date of last revision in format YYYY-MM-DD.
        </rdfs:comment>
    </rdf:Description>
</rdf:RDF>
```

As you have no doubt noticed, the syntax for defining an RDF schema bears a striking resemblance to RDF syntax, but includes a number of additional elements. In addition to the "label" and "comment" elements, RDF schema can include elements that constrain the domain and range of Property values. RDF schema definitions are similar to type definitions in object-oriented programming languages, and the RDF Schema Specification has provisions for inheritance and schema subclassing, very similar to what is available for Java classes. The purpose of these inheritance constructs is to allow developers to use (and reuse) common base schemas when deriving new domain or application-specific schemas. This object-oriented approach should significantly reduce the effort required to create new schemas and should promote cross-application interoperability of the resultant data and meta-data.

Continuing with our example, as you might expect, the subject of an RDF statement is permitted to have more than one property associated with it. To illustrate this we will expand upon the previous example. As you may know, technical reports produced by the WC3 fall into categories that indicate the current status of the work being reported on; there are currently four WC3 Technical Report categories: Notes, Working Drafts, Proposed Recommendations and Recommendations. At present, the W3C technical report on the "RDF Model and Syntax" has the status of Recommendation. We can update our English statement to include this information as follows: "The RDF Model and Syntax Specification that was last revised Feb 22, 1999 has the status of Recommendation."

This statement can be represented with a node and arc diagram as shown in Figure 8.2.

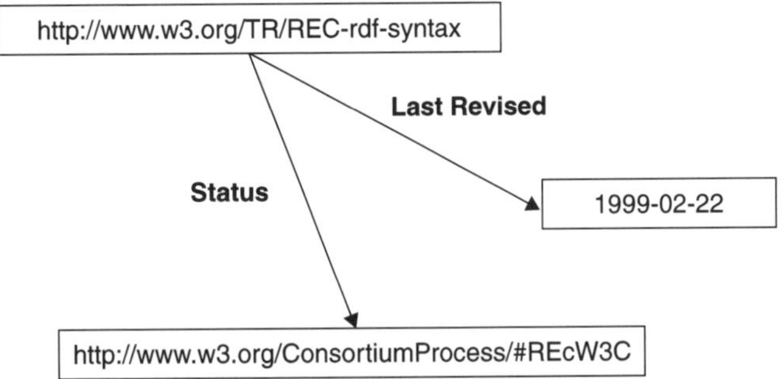

Figure 8.2 Multiple RDF statements depicted as node and arc diagram.

This statement corresponds to two RDF statements; here we can identify the Subject, Predicate and Object terms as follows:

```
Subject   = "http://www.w3.org.TR/REC-rdf-syntax" (Resource)
Predicate = LastRevised   (Property)
Object    = "1999-02-22"  (Literal)

Subject   = "http://www.w3.org.TR/REC-rdf-syntax" (Resource)
Predicate = Status  (Property)
Object    = "http://www.w3.org/ConsortiumProcess/#RecsW3C" (Resource)
```

In order to create XML code for these RDF statements, we need to first update our schema at URI "http://description.org/schema/" by adding a second entry for the Status property:

```
<rdf:RDF xmlns:rdf="http://www.w3.org/1999/02/22-rdf-syntax-ns#"
              xmlns:rdfs="http://www.w3.org/TR/1999/PR-rdf-schema-
19990303#">
    <rdf:Description ID="LastRevised">
        <rdf:type rdf:resource="http://www.w3.org.TR/REC-rdf-syntax#Prop-
erty"/>
        <rdfs:label>LastRevised</rdfs:label>
        <rdfs:comment>The date of last revision in format YYYY-MM-DD.</
rdfs:comment>
    </rdf:Description>
    <rdf:Description ID="Status">
        <rdf:type rdf:resource="http://www.w3.org.TR/REC-rdf-syntax#Prop-
erty"/>
        <rdfs:label>Status</rdfs:label>
        <rdfs:comment>The status of a W3C Technical report, which can be a
                  Note, Working Draft, Proposed Recommendation or
                  Recommendations.
        </rdfs:comment>
    </rdf:Description>
</rdf:RDF>
```

This allows us to encode the updated RDF statement in XML as follows:

```
<rdf:RDF xmlns:rdf="http://www.w3.org/1999/02/22-rdf-syntax-ns#"
              xmlns:rdfs="http://www.w3.org/TR/1999/PR-rdf-schema-
19990303#"
              xmlns:s="http://description.org/schema/">
    <rdf:Description about="http://www.w3.org.TR/REC-rdf-syntax">
        <s:LastRevised>1999-02-22<s:LastRevised>
        <s:Status rdf:resource="http://www.w3.org/ConsortiumProcess/
#RecsW3C">
    </rdf:Description>
</rdf:RDF>
```

Note that as the value of the Status property is a resource (rather than a literal as is the case for the LastRevised property), it is indicated by setting the "resource" attribute of the Status element.

8.2.3.1 Syntactic Variations

The RDF syntax we have been using thus far is known as the Basic Serialization Syntax; which is very explicit and at times can seem verbose. Fortunately, RDF supports a more streamlined syntax (referred to as the Basic Abbreviated Syntax) that can make the RDF code both more readable and shorter in length. The Basic Serialization and Basic Abbreviated syntax differ primarily in their emphasis on XML elements and XML attributes, respectively. Basic Serialization syntax uses XML elements to encode Properties, whereas Basic Abbreviated syntax allows Properties to be encoded as XML attributes. The previous example, which was coded using the Basic Serialization syntax, can be recoded using the abbreviated syntax as follows:

```
<rdf:RDF xmlns:rdf="http://www.w3.org/1999/02/22-rdf-syntax-ns#"
         xmlns:rdfs="http://www.w3.org/TR/1999/PR-rdf-schema-19990303#"
         xmlns:s="http://description.org/schema/">
  <rdf:Description about="http://www.w3.org.TR/REC-rdf-syntax"
    s:LastRevised="1999-02-22">
    <s:Status rdf:resource="http://www.w3.org/ConsortiumProcess/#RecsW3C">
  </rdf:Description>
</rdf:RDF>
```

As can be seen, the LastRevised property has become an XML attribute of the Description element. This is permissible as the value of the property is a literal rather than a resource. Because the value of the Status property is a resource it cannot be made into an attribute and remains an element. Despite these syntactic changes, both this encoding of the RDF statements and the previous one are equivalent for RDF purposes.

We make our example somewhat more complex by adding an additional piece of meta-information. The document that we have been using in our example, the RDF Model and Syntax Recommendation, is part of the W3C website; thus we could say that the W3C website at URI "http://www.w3.org" references this document. We will update our English-language statement to reflect this information. (Note that at present the URI for the RDF document indicates that the RDF document is indeed part of the website; both URIs make reference to "http://www.w3.org." However, at some point the location of the RDF document could change; for example, it could be moved to a website at URI "http://www.rdf.org." In either case the W3C website would still "reference" this document, which is the information that we wish our RDF meta-data to convey.) "The W3C website references the RDF Model and Syntax Specification, which was last revised Feb 22, 1999 and has the status of Recommendation." This statement can be represented as shown in Figure 8.3.

We will not show the updated RDF schema, which would need to be changed to reflect the addition of the References property. Rather an

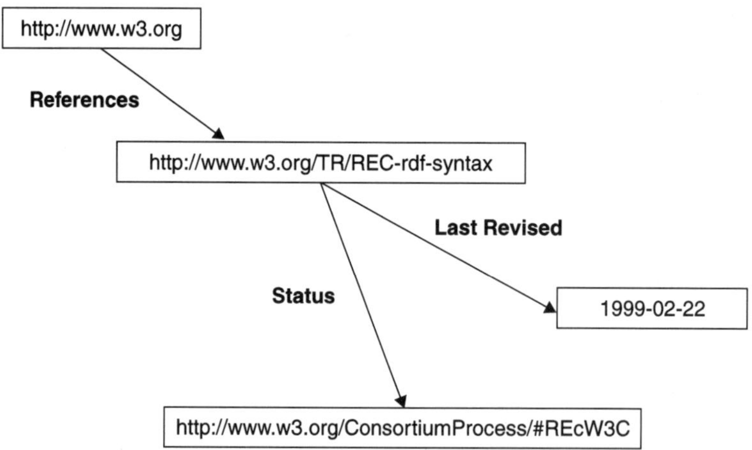

Figure 8.3 Multilevel RDF statements depicted as node and arc diagram.

additional stanza much like the ones for LastRevised and Status would have been added. Assuming this update to be in place, the RDF statements could be encoded using the basic serialization syntax as follows:

```
<rdf:RDF xmlns:rdf="http://www.w3.org/1999/02/22-rdf-syntax-ns#"
         xmlns:rdfs="http://www.w3.org/TR/1999/PR-rdf-schema-19990303#"
         xmlns:s="http://description.org/schema/">
   <rdf:Description about="http://www.w3.org">
      <s:References>http://www.w3.org.TR/REC-rdf-syntax<s:References>
   </rdf:Description>

   <rdf:Description about="http://www.w3.org.TR/REC-rdf-syntax">
      <s:LastRevised>1999-02-22<s:LastRevised>
      <s:Status rdf:resource="http://www.w3.org/ConsortiumProcess/
#RecsW3C">
   </rdf:Description>
</rdf:RDF>
```

This encoding captures the information and makes it clear that two resources are being described as the subjects of RDF statements, namely, the W3C website and the RDF Model and Syntax document. However, to a human reading the RDF code, it is not immediately obvious that a relationship exists between the two resources, namely, that the object of the first RDF statement is in fact the subject of the second. We can employ the abbreviated syntax to remedy this shortcoming, arriving at the following encoding that is semantically equivalent for RDF purposes:

```
<rdf:RDF xmlns:rdf="http://www.w3.org/1999/02/22-rdf-syntax-ns#"
         xmlns:rdfs="http://www.w3.org/TR/1999/PR-rdf-schema-19990303#"
         xmlns:s="http://description.org/schema/">
   <rdf:Description about="http://www.w3.org">
      <s:References>
         <rdf:Description about="http://www.w3.org.TR/REC-rdf-syntax">
            <s:LastRevised>1999-02-22<s:LastRevised>
             <s:Status rdf:resource="http://www.w3.org/ConsortiumPro-
cess/#RecsW3C">
         </rdf:Description>
      <s:References>
   </rdf:Description>
</rdf:RDF>
```

This encoding makes it clearer to the human reader that a relationship exists between the resources for the W3C (URI "http://www.w3.org") and the RDF Model and Syntax Specification (URI "http://www.w3.org.TR/REC-rdf-syntax"), and that this relationship is a property called References.

Due to the sheer volume of information that is available on the Web, application users and developers are being confronted with a new set of challenges. One of these challenges is being able to deal intelligently with these ever-growing information resources. Meta-information makes information more usable by making it more manageable and accessible, thus increasing its value to the end user. RDF provides application developers with a solid foundation for the processing of meta-data, which will become a necessity for the next generation of interoperable Web applications.

8.3 Document Content Description (DCD)

The Document Content Description (DCD) for XML is an RDF vocabulary designed for describing constraints to be applied to the structure and content of XML documents. A DCD is a set of properties used to constrain the type of elements and names of attributes that may appear in an XML document, the contents of the elements, and the values of the attributes. Although "Document Content Description for XML" (NOTE-dcd-19980731) is currently a Note made available by the W3C for discussion purposes only, the ideas expressed within it provide us with insight as to the type of capabilities that are likely to be added to XML in the near future. Work to define XML schemas is also currently underway in the form of W3C Working Drafts on XML Schema Part 1: Structures (http://www.w3.org/1999/05/06-xmlschema-1/) and Part 2: Structures (http://www.w3.org/1999/05/06-xmlschema-2/). The reader is encouraged to seek out these resources at the W3C site for the latest information.

8.3.1 Why Does XML Need DCDs?

In order to understand the importance of Document Content Descriptions (DCDs), it is necessary to understand the changing role that XML is playing on the Web. As XML's role changes over time, it should come as no surprise that users will find areas where XML's current capabilities could stand improvement. For example, at present, XML provides only minimal support for explicit data types (e.g., decimal numbers, double precision values, etc.) and type checking, and therefore significantly lags modern programming languages in these respects.

Fortunately, XML was designed to be flexible and extensible, which enables issues such as these to be addressed without significant language disruptions. In the case of DCDs, XML code is being used to augment XML's current facilities for describing constraints on instances of XML documents. DCDs are an example of how XML is able to bootstrap itself to provide additional capability to users.

We need to gain some perspective on XML's changing role on the Web, which was originally a collection of webpages written in HTML and hyperlinked to one another using the Internet as an underlying transport medium. As the Web grew, so did the difficulty of finding relevant information when it was needed. One of the reasons for this was that the tags used to mark up the information, that is HTML tags, are entirely presentation-oriented and reveal little or nothing about the content stored within a document. This lack of context made searching for information on the Web a trial-and-error activity. To locate information, users would try typing a few keywords into their favorite search engine, and if that did not work they would try different keywords, and so on.

The hit-or-miss nature of information discovery is a major problem inherent in the present HTML-based Web. XML was originally envisioned as a means to improve information discovery by making document content more readily accessible via Web-based tools. XML allows users to apply semantically meaningful content-based tags and structure to information. When the resulting documents are made available on the Web, content-directed searches can more easily locate relevant information.

XML's role in document mark-up has been substantial, which comes as no surprise as its heritage is based on SGML, the veritable king of document mark-up languages. XML has been called "SGML-lite," and for good reason. It provides most of the capability of SGML, but does so with less complexity in terms of syntax and processing overhead. SGML was designed to allow users to proficiently manage document-based content, and not surprisingly, some of its most successful applications have been in managing documentation for very large projects.

Despite the success of the full-featured SGML in areas such as these, the lighter-weight XML technology is already rapidly becoming the de facto standard for representing structured documents. This is evident from the strong support of document companies such as Adobe and Microsoft, which already support XML in their products and that have pledged full support for XML in the future. This is important to end users because the use of XML to structure and manage Web-based documents will make it easier to locate information via the Web, which means documents can be meaningfully cataloged, searched and retrieved. XML is well on its way to solving the problem it set out to address, namely, how to make it easier for users to locate document-type information on the Web.

However, this is not where the story ends, but it is rather where the interesting part begins. The ease with which XML could be used to describe the content of documents was not lost upon the Web application-development community, who foresaw the need to transfer data between applications on the Web. We will now explore XML's role on the Web from an application-centric perspective, rather than from a document-centric perspective as was just done.

We saw that in its first incarnation the Web was mostly a large repository of data whose structure was optimized for presentation. These data took the form of HTML-based webpages that were displayable by Web browsers. CGI programming and servlets took static webpages a step further by creating HTML files dynamically rather than simply returning an existing HTML file. In these scenarios, HTML pages were created on the server, often by querying a database using input parameters gathered from the user. Moving forward a step in time we find that by storing documents in XML format on the back-end tier, server-side applications can more readily query document content to create data that can be shipped to the user for display. XML's ability to meaningfully structure data based on content as opposed to presentation makes it much easier for users to locate information and documents than was possible with HTML-based systems. In addition, XML allows documents to be much more precisely searched and located.

Although our perspective is now application development, notice that up to this point the role that XML has played is still largely one of structuring documents so that their content can be more readily located and retrieved. The true promise of XML, however, is not only in its utility in structuring documents, but will come from its use as a universal data-interchange format that allows applications to share information across the Web. It is one thing to allow users to more precisely locate XML-based documents using improved search capabilities, and entirely another to have XML-based application seamlessly interoperate with one another across the Web and collaborate on behalf of the user. Naturally, cross-application interoperability requires that applications be able to intelligently share data across the Web, and this is the role now being entrusted to XML.

This brings us to a somewhat subtle and not necessarily precise distinction—the difference between "documents" and "data." To a degree, the distinction may simply be one of perspective, however, it goes deeper than this. It seems fair to say that a structured document would always be an example of structured data. Yet, it seems less fair to turn this statement around and say that structured data are always an example of a structured document. In other words, it would seem that the set of structured documents is a subset of the set of structured data rather than vice versa. We raise this point because XML's role as a means of describing data is expanding. It has grown from its original role of describing structured documents to where it now serves as a means of describing richly structured data transferred between Web-based applications.

Thus, XML's role on the Web has grown from merely being a replacement for HTML, and is rapidly becoming the universal data-interchange format. What was originally envisioned as simply a better way to mark-up documents for the Web is being thrust into the role of being a universal data-typing system in the programming-language sense. That is, XML is the data format (e.g., underlying data structure) that Web-based applications will use to exchange data.

As is known, the variety of programming languages in which Web-based applications will be written includes almost anything and everything; for example, Java, C++, Perl, Python, C, and the list goes on and on. In effect, XML is being thrust into a new role as a universal data-typing system that will allow applications written in various different languages to share data with one another. Data in XML format will be the very glue that binds these collaborative applications together, which is a tall order indeed. It is incredible that all of this developed from a mark-up language whose humble beginnings were in document mark-up!

8.3.2 DTDs and DCDs: XML's Present and Future Typing Systems

The mechanism that XML currently provides for defining new document types is the Document Type Definition (DTD). DTDs enable users to specify grammars that define new classes of valid XML documents. They are how users define new elements, define the attributes associated with elements, and define what constitutes a valid combination of these elements.

We start off by first expressing a document type as a DTD, and then show how the corresponding representation would look as a DCD. For our example we will capture information about a book, in particular, the book title, author, ISBN, price, and also the language in which the book is written. A simple Book document type can be defined with the following DTD:

```
<!ELEMENT Book ( Title, Author, ISBN, Price)>
<!ATTLIST Book Language CDATA #REQUIRED>
```

```
<!ELEMENT Title (#PCDATA)>
<!ELEMENT Author ( FirstName, LastName )>
<!ELEMENT FirstName (#PCDATA)>
<!ELEMENT LastName (#PCDATA)>
<!ELEMENT ISBN (#PCDATA)>
<!ELEMENT Price (#PCDATA)>
```

This same information can be represented in the following DCD. We will cover DCD syntax in more detail later, but for now see if you can get a feel as to how DTDs and DCDs go about encoding the same information here. Note how the <Group> element is used to group elements together, serving much the same purpose as the comma-separated parentheses in the DTD in the foregoing.

```
<DCD>
   <ElementDef type="Book" Model="Elements">
      <AttributeDef Name="Language" Occurs="Required"/>
      <Group>
         <ElementDef type="Title" Model="string"/>
         <ElementDef type="Author" Model="Elements">
            <Group>
               <ElementDef type="FirstName" Model="string"/>
               <ElementDef type="LastName" Model="string"/>
            <Group>
         </ElementDef>
         <ElementDef type="ISBN" Model="string"/>
         <ElementDef type="Price" Model="string"/>
      </Group>
   </ElementDef>
</DCD>
```

In DCDs, element definitions (as denoted by ElementDef tags) have scoping properties much like programming-language variable declarations. In this DCD, all elements and attributes are defined locally, with the exception of the outer Book element whose scope is that of the DCD. The scope of each local definition does not extend beyond its enclosing block. An alternate and probably more useful approach is to give the various element and attribute types broader scope, as is done in the following example.

Here, all elements and attributes are defined so that their scope is the entire DCD. This allows them to be used within other element definitions, including within element definitions in separate DCD files as we will see later. Notice how using elementDef statements to define elements is similar in principle to how types (e.g., structures, classes, etc.) are defined in a programming language. This enables complex XML document types to be constructed by combining simpler ones in much the same way, for example, Java classes can aggregate other Java classes.

```
<DCD>
  <ElementDef type="Book" Model="Elements">
    <Attribute>Language</Attribute>
    <Group>
      <Element>Title</Element>
      <Element>Author</Element>
      <Element>ISBN</Element>
      <Element>Price</Element>
    </Group>
  </ElementDef>

  <ElementDef type="Author" Model="Elements">
    <Group>
      <Element>FirstName</Element>
      <Element>LastName</Element>
    <Group>
  </ElementDef>

  <AttributeDef Name="Language" Occurs="Required"/>
  <ElementDef type="Title" Model="string"/>
  <ElementDef type="FirstName" Model="string"/>
  <ElementDef type="LastName" Model="string"/>
  <ElementDef type="ISBN" Model="string"/>
  <ElementDef type="Price" Model="string"/>
</DCD>
```

In this example we see that DCDs perform much of the same function as DTDs. The syntax is perhaps somewhat closer to that of a programming language, where the nesting of types is more explicit, but its functionality in this example remains basically the same. However, DCDs do not merely provide the same functionality as is available with DTD, but they also allow you to do much more. In effect, a long-range goal of DCDs appears to be bringing a full-fledged typing system to XML, much as what is found in programming languages. DCDs provide the following improvements over DTDs:

- **Constraint Checking**
- **Better Provisions for Combining Types**
- **Inheritance**

We shall take a look at each of these in the following.

8.3.2.1 *Constraint Checking*

At present, XML has no means to enforce within the language that the content of elements must conform to specific types, such as integers or floating point numbers. That is, the XML 1.0 specification defines roughly 10 data types that are used to constrain attribute values, but essentially only 1 data type, PCDATA, that is used for element content.

DCDs provide users with a much richer set of basic data types and constraint capabilities that can be applied to both attribute and element content, and which will allow document instances to be validated against these constraints through the XML parser. By adding support for a variety of data types and constraints within the language (via DCDs), XML parsers will be able to verify whether or not a particular document instance indeed conforms to the type definition that now includes such constraints.

For example, if you had an element named Quantity that you wanted to limit to integers in the range of 10 to 100, you might code such a requirement for a Quantity element in a DTD as follows (for simplicity, we have bundled the Quantity elements inside an element called Quantities in these examples):

```
<!ELEMENT Quantities (Quantity+)>
<!ELEMENT Quantity (#PCDATA)>
<!ATTLIST Quantity
         Datatype CDATA #FIXED "int"
         Min  CDATA #FIXED "10"
         Max  CDATA #FIXED "100">
```

Consider the following Quantities instance of XML data, whose first Quantity element value falls within the specified range, the second whose value does not, and the third whose value to begin with is not numeric.

```
<Quantities>
   <Quantity Datatype="int" Min="10" Max="100">55</Quantity>
   <Quantity Datatype="int" Min="10" Max="100">4</Quantity>
   <Quantity Datatype="int" Min="10" Max="100">Hello</Quantity>
</Quantities>
```

Although the values of the second and third instance are not semantically valid (the first is out of range, and the second is of the wrong type), all of these Quantity elements will parse successfully. With the current DTD approach, this type of constraint or data-type mismatch error must be checked for by the application code. To the parser, Quantity values of "4" and "Hello" both meet the DTD requirements, namely, they are acceptable PCDATA. Thus we see that when using DTDs the XML parser provides no real constraint checking, although it would hiccup if we were to leave out the element value itself (e.g., eliminate the "4" or "Hello" altogether).

Now we revisit this example using a DCD instead of a DTD. The Quantities and Quantity document types could be defined with a DCD named, for example, quan.dcd using the following XML syntax:

```
<DCD>
   <ElementDef type="Quantities" Model="Elements">
      <Group>
         <Element>Quantity</Element>
      <Group/>
   </ElementDef>

   <ElementDef type="Quantity" Model="Data" Datatype="int" Min="10"
Max="100"/>
</DCD>
```

Now consider the following Quantities instance that is based on this document content description. Here, we are using a default namespace to identify the Quantities and Quantity elements:

```
<Quantities xmlns="http://YourDCDs.org/quan.dcd">
   <Quantity>55</Quantity>
   <Quantity>4</Quantity>
   <Quantity>Hello</Quantity>
</Quantities>
```

In this case we see that the attributes for Datatype, Min and Max are not included with the Quantity instance, but the DCD that is referenced via the namespace contains this information. Using this information, an XML parser would be able to determine that the Quantity elements with values "4" and "Hello" contain constraint errors. Note that in this case, unlike the previous case, the XML parser as opposed to the application logic can perform constraint checks.

Shifting the responsibility for constraint checking from the application code to the XML parser provides a number of benefits. First, it reduces the total amount of code that application programmers must write, because each application that uses a given document type will no longer need to write a custom constraint-checking code. Instead, this functionality can be performed automatically for each application by a DCD-aware XML parser.

Second, in addition to simply reducing the amount of code that needs to be written, this approach provides for much more consistent checking of constraints across applications. The uniformity of constraint checking essentially having been moved from application-level functionality (performed by code written by many individual application developers) to system-level functionality (performed by an XML parser), which is shared across multiple applications.

8.3.2.2 Better Provision for Combining Types

One of the benefits of DCDs is that they will simplify the sharing of definitions of document types. At present, it is possible to share elements of DTDs across other DTDs; however, the syntax for doing so Quickly becomes cumbersome, involving parameter entities and such. DCDs significantly simplify the sharing of element definitions through the use of namespaces.

For example, we can easily create a new document type that leverages the Quantity type as defined in the previous quan.dcd document content description. Suppose that the new document type must keep track of information for a "part" by storing a PartNumber and a Quantity. Then we can create a document content description named partinfo.dcd for this as follows:

```
<DCD xmlns:q="http://YourDCDs.org/quan.dcd">
   <ElementDef type="PartInfo" Model="Elements">
      <Group>
         <Element>PartNumber</Element>
         <Element>q:Quantity</Element>
      <Group/>
   </ElementDef>

   <ElementDef type="PartNumber" Model="Data" Datatype="number"/>
</DCD>
```

Note how this DCD creates a namespace named "q" that is used to qualify the Quantity element, making it refer to the previous DCD named quan.dcd. Using this new DCD, which we will assign a URI of "http://YourDCDs.org/partinfo.dcd," a PartInfo instance might appear as follows:

```
<PartInfo xmlns="http://YourDCDs.org/partinfo.dcd">
   <PartNumber>9999</Quantity>
   <Quantity>12</Quantity>
</PartInfo>
```

By using XML namespaces in combination with DCDs, sharing document-type definitions across Web applications is greatly simplified.

8.3.2.3 Inheritance

Although the current DCD submission discusses only object-oriented inheritance as a future possibility, there is every reason to believe this is the direction that DCDs will take. It seems clear that the initial DCD submission very wisely wishes to create a solid foundation upon which future DCD capabilities, such as inheritance, can be built. Inheritance in typing systems has proven extremely valuable for object-oriented programming, and will likely have significant impact on XML schemas in the future. Inheritance will enable XML users to more easily leverage commonality in document types they create and to more easily extend the work of others.

8.3.3 From the Ground Up: How DCDs Are Coded

Now that you have been given the overall concepts for DCDs, we will take a closer look at the syntax for defining elements and constraints. As you may have guessed from the examples given, new document types are created in a DCD by assigning properties to objects of type ElementDef. Considering this in terms of programming languages, an ElementEef statement is very similar to a Class statement in Java or a struct statement in C; and an ElementDef statement is how you define a new type.

Suppose you wanted to define a new type that will hold information about a company employee. We will expand upon this example as we go along, but we will start by simply defining a new element type named Employee, which can be accomplished by the following XML code:

```
<DCD>
   <ElementDef Type="Employee">
<DCD>
```

This DCD code is not really of much value because it simply states that a new element type named "Employee" exists. This would allow us to create XML code that uses this definition, such as the following:

```
<Employee>Don L. Duck</Employee>
```

This simple code is using several defaults. In particular, the Model attribute of the ElementDef takes a default value of "Data" if another value is not specified. Thus we can rewrite this definition more explicitly as follows, also adding a Description property to the new type, and a Namespace property to the DCD:

```
<DCD>
   <Namespace>http://URI.ForThisDCD</Namespace>
   <ElementDef Type="Employee" Model="Data">
      <Description>Information about an employee.</Description>
   </ElementDef>
<DCD>
```

We can infer from the Model attribute that Employee elements may only contain data, and may not contain children elements. You will notice that the foregoing example happens to satisfy this constraint because the value of the data is simply the string "Don L. Duck," and contains no elements. The Model attribute plays a key role in specifying constraints for the newly defined type, so we examine it more closely. The Model property indicates which of five broad classes of constraints should be applied to the content of elements. The Model property must be one of the following values:

- **Empty**—Elements of this type must have no content.
- **Any**—Elements of this type may contain text and child elements of any declared type.
- **Data**—Elements of this type may contain only text, but must not contain any child elements. This is the default for the Model property is Data.
- **Elements**—Elements of this type contain only child elements. The types of the child elements that may appear are controlled by the Group and Element properties.
- **Mixed**—Elements of this type may contain text and embedded child elements. The types of the child elements that may appear are controlled by the Element property.

We take a closer look at what happens when the DCD code specifies that Model="Elements." This property states that such elements may only have other elements as children, and cannot contain text. The DCD specification states that child elements must be collected together into Groups, which have Order and Occurs properties. The order of occurrence of the children is declared using the RDF collection-ordering facility. The RDF:Order property can take on a value of either "Seq," in which case children must occur in sequential order as specified, or a value of "Alt," in which case only one of alternative children elements may occur. The Occurs property specifies how many occurrences of an element are required in a Group. Finally, the Group property can take one of the following values:

- **Required**—The element occurs exactly once; this is the default.
- **Optional**—The element occurs zero or one time.
- **OneOrMore**—The element occurs one or more times.
- **ZeroOrMore**—The element occurs zero or more times.

Now we put this all together with an example. The following example creates an Employee document type where the first and last name are required, but the middle initial is optional, and where each employee has either a full-time salary or hourly wage, but not both.

```
<DCD>
   <ElementDef Type="Employee" Model="Elements">
      <Group RDF:Order="Seq">
         <Element>FirstName</Element>
         <Group Occurs="Optional">
            <Element>MI</Element>
         </Group>
         <Element>LastName</Element>
         <Group Occurs="OneOrMore" RDF:Order="Alt">
            <Element>FullTimeSalary</Element>
            <Element>HourlyWage</Element>
         </Group>
      </Group>
   </ElementDef>

   <ElementDef Type="FirstName" Model="Data" Datatype="string">
   <ElementDef Type="MI"        Model="Data" Datatype="string">
   <ElementDef Type="LastName"  Model="Data" Datatype="string">
   <ElementDef Type="FullTimeSalary" Model="Data" Datatype="number">
```

```
    <ElementDef Type="HourlyWage"     Model="Data" Datatype="number">
<DCD>
```

The following are two examples of XML Employee document instances that meet all of the constraints:

```
<Employee>
   <FirstName>Don</FirstName>
   <MI>L</MI>
   <LastName>Duck</LastName>
   <FullTimeSalary>75000</FullTimeSalary>
</Employee>

<Employee>
   <FirstName>Curious</FirstName>
   <LastName>George</LastName>
   <HourlyWage>75000</HourlyWage>
</Employee>
```

We have seen that XML's role on the Web is changing and now includes that of universal data interchange format for Web-based applications. In order to perform this task more effectively, XML needs additional data typing, constraint-specification and constraint-checking capability. Document Constraint Descriptions are an approach being considered for this purpose by the W3C, and provide insight as to the types of capabilities likely to be added to XML in the near future.

8.4 Channel Definition Format (CDF) and Channels

8.4.1 What are CDF Channels?

Channel Definition Format (CDF) is a technology designed to make life simpler for Web users who visit a particular set of sites on a regular basis. Normally, such users would need to visit these sites to determine whether or not the content there has changed. However, with CDF, users can ask to be notified when the content of a website they are interested in changes. They can also have this updated content automatically retrieved on their behalf and stored locally for subsequent browsing.

CDF is an XML-based specification that enables a website to provide meta-information about itself in a standard format so that it can be used by applications such as web browsers and web crawlers. CDF meta-information allows a website to publish, for example, a schedule indicating when its content will be updated, which allows applications to automatically retrieve the updated information on behalf of the user. The CDF technical specification was submitted to the W3C in March of 1997 by the Microsoft Corporation, and is available for downloading at http://www.w3.org/TR/NOTE-CDFsubmit.htm.

8.4.2 How Is Information Organized on the Web?

The Web is a large, loosely structured collection of information that changes constantly and grows larger every day. New pages are added to websites and old ones are deleted, content on pages is updated and additional information is posted, entire new websites come online and new homepages are created all the time. Needless to say, the Web is a dynamic entity, one that brings satisfaction to users when they find what they want, but also brings them frustration when they cannot find what they are seeking.

One of the great challenges to Web developers is determining how to best make information accessible to its intended users. If we look at how this problem has been addressed at individual websites, on a site-by-site basis, we find useful patterns developing that can be applied to the much larger Web as a whole. In the early history of the Web, many sites were simply collections of webpages that had been linked together, sometimes almost seemingly at random.

Finding information on such websites was largely a matter of trial-and-error; for example, clicking on a link and seeing where you landed, back-tracking if you hit a dead-end, continuing this process until you found what you were looking for, or more than likely, found something else more interesting at the moment and followed that train of thought for a while. An hour later, when you realized you still had not found what you had originally set out to find, you may have begun your search anew, or perhaps given up in desperation deciding to try again another day.

At present, the user's experience at a website is generally much more productive than what was depicted in the preceding scenario. This is due in large part to the following three reasons:

- Content Organization
- Site search engines
- Sitemaps

One of the reasons it is easier to find information on websites today is that website designers have learned a great deal about how to organize information on their sites so that its structure facilitates its discovery and actually helps convey the information to the user. Hierarchical organization by topics, such as provided by Yahoo, makes it easier for users to traverse large volumes of information yet maintain the focus of their discovery process.

The organization of the information can be revealed, in varying degrees, either implicitly or explicitly. In different contexts, one approach will be more suitable than another, and indeed implicit and explicit organizations may indeed be combined. An example of implicit presentation of organization would be a hyperlink of a word in a paragraph to its definition in a glossary of terms at the end of the document. That is, the visual presentation of the paragraph, in this case, gives no explicit indication of the relationship between the word and its definition. However, upon clicking the link and being taken to the definition, the user discovers information about the (implicit) organization of the document.

On the other hand, an example of explicit presentation of organization would be a webpage that presents a document in outline format, where the user might see that information on "How to Add a User" can be found under the "System Administration" section of the document.

Good organization certainly makes it easier for a user to locate information by manually traversing individual pages, starting at the top-level homepage. However, websites often provide alternate paths that are much more useful and indeed take advantage of such organization. The first of these is a "site search engine," where you typically type in a word or two and get back a list of pages that contain those words on that site. As you probably know from experience, you never really know what will turn up when you have typed in your words, but often these site searches are quite effective.

A second technique that websites often provide to aid the discovery of information is a "site map," which typically displays the website's organization as a hierarchy. For example, clicking on the Site Map icon might bring you to a page where you will see that information on "Employment Opportunities" is located under the "About Our Company" webpage, which is accessible from the top-level homepage. The site map is intended to give you a high-level view of the organization of the website and is an example of meta-information about the website. We will see that one of the things that CDF does is to permit a website to publish meta-information much like a "site map," in a format that can be used by web browsers and web crawlers to provide more intelligent access to information at the site.

8.4.3 What is a Channel?

Before discussing channels on the Web, we take a moment to consider what a channel means in other contexts. (Actually, it is from these other contexts that the term "channel" has been borrowed for the Web.) When we say "channel" we often use it to mean a "television channel," such as a sports channel, weather channel, or news channel. Even before we turn on our television set, we know what kind of information we expect to find on each of these channels.

For example, if you turn on the weather channel when visiting a new city, you may find that it provides information on local weather, national weather or both, but the information is (not surprisingly) always about weather. The same goes for sports channels, news channels, cooking channels, and so on. Therefore, you always know what kind of information you will be getting, although the specific content (i.e., programming) will vary.

Thus we see that a channel is really just a means of grouping similar information. For example, in television each day many people in network programming decide whether or not particular pieces of information will be seen by you on any given channel. It is certainly possible for the same information to appear on multiple channels (e.g., consider a sports channel and a news channel). Major sporting events are newsworthy, thus even an all-news station often reports scores and shows sports highlights.

It is important to keep in mind that the concept of a channel is merely a tool for organizing information into useful categories whose contents may overlap. If information belongs in both categories put it in both as there is no restriction that information may only be in one category when using channels.

Other analogies for channels include radio stations, some of which broadcast news, others broadcast easy-listening music, classical, rock-and-roll, country, and so forth. With a car stereo, you typically set the radio so that by pressing a button you are automatically switched to one of your favorite stations. Over time, as your tastes change (or perhaps when you lend your car to someone else), the buttons on the radio will be set to other favorites.

The car radio allows you to select a number of stations and to automatically access them by simply pressing a button. This mode of operation provides benefits to users who want to access several radio stations on a regular basis; you do not have to remember the station's broadcast frequency, and you can automatically bypass the stations that you do want. (Of course, these other stations are still available by tuning to them directly, so functionality has not been taken away.)

This brings us to Web channels, which, as we will see in a moment, are defined using CDF. Web channels are intended to provide Web users with the sort of benefits and conveniences that are analogous to those provided by traditional channels such as television and radio. We will see how Web channels allow users to automatically steer their browsers to sites based on content, for example, to find the equivalent of the "sports channel" on the Web, the "news channel," and so forth.

We will also see that Web channels provide Web users with conveniences that have no current counterpart with the previous channel examples, for example, having the channel notify them when new information has arrived. (Can you imagine your radio station calling you to tell you that they just received a new batch of CDs that they are about to start playing on the air?)

8.4.4 Why Does the Web Need Channels?

Channels are a relatively new idea on the Web. They are designed to enhance the user's Web-browsing experience by eliminating a number of difficulties routinely encountered by Web users. The traditional approach to Web browsing results in several recurring problems that detract from the user's experience:

- **Difficulty Finding Information**—It is often very difficult for the user to find information of particular interest. Web search engines are helpful but they are not enough. We saw above that site search engines are well complemented by site maps, which provide meta-information about a website. Channels provide a website with the ability to export meta-information about the contents of the website. This meta-information can be used by both users and Web search programs to more effectively locate information on behalf of the user.
- **Difficulty Tracking Website Changes**—Web browsers should give users access to the most up-to-date information; and by simply visiting a webpage, the browser automatically retrieves the latest information. This is very good in theory, but it also works to the users disadvantage. For example, in order to get the latest information, the user must visit that webpage. That is, if the user visits the webpage, he or she automatically obtain the latest information, but will not know if the information has changed since the webpage was last accessed? That is, there is no way to know whether or not it is necessary revisit the webpage? At present, the user must access the page, retrieve the content, and visually determine if changes have been made. It would be very desirable if webpages could inform users when their content changed. In this way, users would know without having to visit the website whether or not information at the website has been updated.
- **Slowness of Downloading Webpages In General**—The speed with which users access the Web has continually increased, starting for many with a 9600 baud modem, which perhaps now is replaced by a 56.6k modem, or even direct access via a T1 line. Despite all of these improvements, we often find ourselves waiting for a long time for webpages to download. Also, despite continued improvements in Web bandwidth, it will always be faster to access pages locally on your machine than it will be to download them as needed over the network. CDF channels provide a

mechanism whereby web tools can download entire portions of a website to your machine so that they can be accessed locally to give a much higher level of interactivity (e.g., pages load instantaneously). The automatic downloading of these pages can be scheduled to occur when the website changes its content. Also, CDF channels enable such tools to perform the downloads intelligently, only downloading those pages that have changed rather than all pages at the website.

8.4.5 What Do Channels Look Like?

A channel is simply an XML file that provides meta-information about a website using the set of XML tags as defined in the "Channel Definition Format (CDF)" W3C document (http://www.w3.org/TR/NOTE-CDFsubmit.htm). We will start off with a simple example of a channel, adding features as we go along.

Suppose you manage a hypothetical website called "Popcorn-n-Candy.com" that provides users with information about movies that are currently showing in theaters in the New York metropolitan area. The website has information on movie show times, reviews, and previews of upcoming movies. Information on the site is updated on a daily basis late at night. As we will see, our channel asks users to update their local information in the early morning hours between 2:00 am and 6:00 am. A simple channel for describing the website would be the following:

```
<? XML version="1.0"?>
<CHANNEL HREF="http://www.yoursite.com/Channel/homepage.htm"
       LEVEL="4"
        BASE="http://www.yoursite.com/Channel/">
   <TITLE>Popcorn-n-Candy: Your Guide to the Movies</TITLE>
   <ABSTRACT>Popcorn-n-Candy is a hypothetical website devoted to
            movies that are showing in the New York City area.
            Popcorn-n-Candy provides movie showtimes, reviews and
            previews of current and upcoming films.
   <LOGO HREF="logo_wide.gif" STYLE="IMAGE-WIDE"/>
   <LOGO HREF="logo_norm.gif" STYLE="IMAGE"/>

   <SCHEDULE STARTDATE="1999-02-29">
      <INTERVALTIME DAY="1" />
      <EARLIESTTIME HOUR="2" />
      <LATESTTIME   HOUR="6" />
   </SCHEDULE>
```

```
        <ITEM HREF="showtimes.htm">
         <LOGO HREF="showtimes.gif" STYLE="ICON"/>
         <TITLE>Movie Showtimes</TITLE>
         <ABSTRACT>Showtimes for movies appearing at local theaters.</
ABSTRACT>
      </ITEM>

      <ITEM HREF="reviews.htm">
         <LOGO HREF="reviews.gif" STYLE="ICON"/>
         <TITLE>Movie Reviews</TITLE>
         <ABSTRACT>Reviews of movies appearing at local theaters.</
ABSTRACT>
      </ITEM>

      <ITEM HREF="previews.htm">
         <LOGO HREF="previews.gif" STYLE="ICON"/>
         <TITLE>Movie Previews</TITLE>
         <ABSTRACT>Previews of movies to appear at local theaters.</
ABSTRACT>
      </ITEM>

   </CHANNEL>
```

Here we take a minute to go over some of the finer points of this file. First, the CDF file could have been named ourChannel.cdf, and stored in a directory located at http://www.yoursite.com/Channel/; you can see in the <CHANNEL> element that the BASE attribute points to this location. The HREF attribute indicates that the HTML file homepage.htm at our website under the Channel directory should be loaded when the channel is initially accessed.

As we will discuss in more detail later, the LEVEL attribute specifies the depth to which links from the HREF URI should be traversed and their contents cached locally on the client. A LEVEL value of 0 would store only the contents of homepage.htm on the client, while a link value of 1 would also cache all webpages linked to homepage.htm, and so forth. The <LOGO> elements provide the browser with images of varying sizes that will be loaded as the user navigates the channel.

Of more interest is the <SCHEDULE> element, which indicates how often and during which hours the website should be accessed by the web browser in order to retrieve updated information. We discuss briefly how CDF channels operate, and how they address two of the forementioned problems, namely the difficulty in tracking website changes and the slowness encountered by users when downloading webpages. CDF channels use a technique called "smart pull" to address these problems.

8.4.5.1 *Smart-Pull: Combining the Best of Push and Pull*

The Web is primarily a pull-based system, and by this we mean that from the user's perspective, information is accessed by "pulling" it down from a Web server. The Web server's job is to idly wait for requests from Web browsers and then respond to these requests, for example, by returning the requested information to the browser client.

We see that there are two parties involved in this scenario—the client browser and the application server running on the Web server. To be more precise, the "pull" paradigm indicates that the party who initiates the transaction is the client browser, and the party who reacts to the transaction is the application server. In general, the direction of the flow of information for the transaction is toward the initiating party rather than away from the initiating party. In a typical Web scenario, when webpages are accessed the client sends an HTTP GET request to the server to "pull" down a webpage. In this case, the client is initiating the transaction and the information flow (i.e., the webpage data being transferred) moves towards the initiator.

The opposite of pull technology is "push" technology, and as you might have guessed, with push technology the server rather than the client initiate transactions. In this paradigm we consider a server as "pushing" data out to clients, that is, the server is deciding that it has new information that it wishes to distribute to the clients, and in effect simply delivers it to the clients.

An example of push technology is radio. In this case, a radio station is continuously broadcasting updated information (in the form of electronic signals that encode music, news, etc.) that can be received by a radio. In order to deliver a news item, for example, the radio station broadcasts the news item directly. It sends this news item out over the airwaves, and any radio that is tuned to the appropriate frequency may receive it.

In many respects, push and pull are thus quite similar in concept, and only the roles of the parties have been reversed; that is, the server now initiates transactions rather than the client. This reversal of roles, however, causes considerable difficulties for the "client-server" centric Web. With pull technology, the server has to know very little (next to nothing) about clients. It waits for a request message (e.g., HTTP request), which tells the server all it needs to know to complete the transaction. Servers get hits from thousands, even millions, of different clients each day. They can react to each of these requests on a one-by-one basis as each request is self-contained. With push technology, on the other hand, the server must now have explicit prior knowledge of each of the clients with which it must interact. It cannot sit idly by waiting for transaction requests, instead it must initiate the transactions.

Client software in a push paradigm is also more complex than in the pull paradigm. Here, the client software must essentially be able to accept and process update requests that originate from the server; its role also has changed. At this point, push technologies on the Web have been largely proprietary and considerably more complex than the standard, highly successful pull technologies (the basic client browser and Web server combination). Push seems like a promising idea, in that it is able to inform clients when information has been updated, but it seems fraught with difficulties. Is there another way to implement push-like functionality without the difficulties inherent in push?

The answer to this question is yes, and it uses a paradigm that will be familiar to object-oriented programmers, in particular those familiar with the JavaBeans event model. If you are not a Java programmer, there is no need to worry because the concepts are very simple and have everyday analogies. CDF delivers push-like functionality using what is known as "smart pull." Smart pull is similar in concept to the use of "call backs" in object-oriented programming. We first explore this in a more general sense and then see how it applies to CDF.

Suppose that you are an amateur meteorologist who likes to keep a record of the daily high temperature in a notebook. Also, suppose you have a friend who uses a thermometer to monitor the air temperature continuously. Well, one approach would be to ask your friend to call you every day when the temperature reached its peak value. If you were on the go, your friend might have difficulty reaching you, and just to complicate matters, your answering machine is unreliable. After a few weeks of this arrangement, you find you have missed several readings and notice some exasperation on the part of your friend, who is not only calling you daily, but also trying to call other interested parties to deliver the same information to them (also with mixed results).

Your temperature "server" friend has a better idea: because you have his number, why not just call *him* at the end of the day instead? That is, you can think of this as "calling him back," perhaps at a specified time such as 8:00 pm to get your updated information. You agree not to call him at all hours of the day and night in order to get your updated information, but rather you agree to "pull" it from him at an agreed-upon time. Of course, your temperature-server friend agrees to have the information ready by this time, at which time you "pull" it down from him. In effect, what this call back is doing is providing push-like functionality, although somewhat more granular, to those parties who understand how and when to "call back" to the server to get the information.

Smart pull uses cooperation between the client and the server to deliver updated information to the client. Clients request information from servers at specified intervals that could range anywhere from daily to hourly or even more frequently than this. The proper interval to use depends both on how frequently the information changes, as well as how up-to-date you require your client to be. (Is it satisfactory if they pick up updates every hour? Probably "yes" if it's an informational news service, and probably "no" if such news is time-critical to your business.) Figure 8.4 depicts how pull, push and smart-pull technology work.

It was shown that smart pull gives clients a means to regularly access up-to-date information on the server. However, smart pull, as envisioned by CDF provides several additional capabilities that improve upon this. Setting up a schedule to receive updates enables the client to maintain a reasonably up-to-date copy of the information resident on the server. As we noted already, just how "up-to-date" the information needs to be is a matter to be worked out through the update schedule. We can think of the client as maintaining a cached copy of information that would normally have been retrieved from the server. Moreover, keeping a cached copy of this information on the client has a number of benefits for users. We already mentioned that accessing the locally cached copy of this information will likely be much faster than accessing the same information over the network.

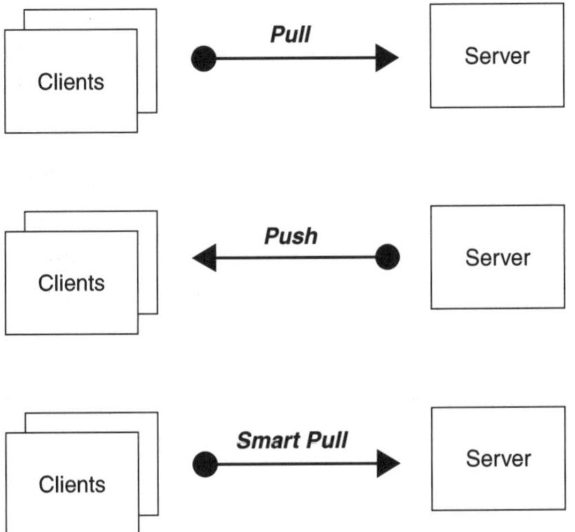

Figure 8.4 Pull, push and smart-pull Web paradigms.

An additional benefit is that keeping a locally cached copy of the information allows the user to disconnect from the Web yet still access the information as if they remain connected. This can be of tremendous value to users of mobile computers who can periodically connect to the Web and "sync up" their locally cached copy with that on the server.

When we say that the client pulls down a copy of the information to be stored locally, keep in mind that most of the time only a few of the files at the website may have changed, and thus only these files need to be downloaded. Intelligent caching of the local data avoids the redundant downloading of unchanged web ages. In addition, channels can specify how "deep" a copy of the data on the server should be maintained as a cached copy using the LEVEL attribute.

8.4.6 How Smart-Pull Is Implemented With Channels

Now that you understand how smart pull works at a high-level, we will revisit the foregoing CDF example and look more closely at the <SCHEDULE> element. The schedule element may contain a STARTDATE attribute, which indicates a time at which the channel service begins, and also a STOPDATE attribute, which indicates a time at which the channel service ends. These attributes let websites inform clients about forthcoming channels, which will be made active at a future date, as well as when the last updates to a particular source of information will be posted. In the <SCHEDULE> element of the forementioned example, we see that this channel became active on a leap year day, February 29th, 1999.

```
<SCHEDULE STARTDATE="1999-02-29">
   <INTERVALTIME DAY="1" />
   <EARLIESTTIME HOUR="2" />
   <LATESTTIME   HOUR="6" />
</SCHEDULE>
```

The three subelements, INTERVALTIME, EARLIESTTIME and LATESTTIME, determine the schedule that channel clients should follow in order to update their local information. This example indicates that the time between updates should be one day; and the website indicates that it updates information on the site on a daily basis. The EARLIESTTIME and LATESTTIME attributes provide the client with a window in which the client should download the updated information from the server. The values in this example indicate that the server should be contacted and the channel data updated between 2:00 am and 6:00 am.

An <ITEM> element defines a webpage as being a subitem under the enclosing element, which in our example makes them sub-items of the <CHANNEL> itself. We see that <ITEMS> have <TITLE> and <ABSTRACT> subelements also, as does the top-level channel. In our example, "Movie Showtimes," which will automatically display the "showtimes.htm" file, is a subchannel of the "Popcorn-n-Candy" channel. It is also permissible to have <ITEMS> contain further <ITEM> elements, and so on, creating even more specific channels.

```
<ITEM HREF="showtimes.htm">
   <LOGO HREF="showtimes.gif" STYLE="ICON"/>
   <TITLE>Movie Showtimes</TITLE>
   <ABSTRACT>Showtimes for movies appearing at local theaters.</
ABSTRACT>
</ITEM>
```

There are a number of additional CDF elements and attributes defined in the CDF specification that we have not covered here. These include elements for <AUTHOR>, <PUBLISHER>, <LASTMOD> date as well as <RATINGS>. You are encouraged to visit the W3C website (http://www.w3.org/TR/NOTE-CDFsubmit.htm) and the Microsoft website (http://www.microsoft.com) to learn more about the world of CDF channels.

8.5 *SAX: The Simple API for XML*

If you plan to develop Web applications that process XML data, it is almost certain that you will be using one of the standard XML application programming interfaces (APIs) to access and manipulate the XML data. The most well-known API for accessing XML data is the Document Object Model (DOM), which we covered in Chapters 2, 4, and 5. It turns out that DOM is not the "only API in town," and indeed there are places where DOM would be the wrong choice of API (the reasons for which we will discuss in detail later).

The Simple API for XML (SAX) is another API for XML. However, SAX is not a "competitor" to DOM, rather it is a complementary API. There are things that DOM does well that SAX does not, and vice versa. The choice of whether to use DOM or SAX will really depend on what it is you are trying to do. DOM implies storage behind its API, permitting random access to the entire document; on the other hand, SAX provides no storage and presents the data as a stream. With SAX, if you want to refer back to anything seen earlier you have to provide those mechanisms yourself. For example, you cannot really edit a SAX document because there is no stored document to edit—you would have to do it by filtering the event streams—whereas DOM provides this capability. Choosing the right one to use in a given situation will make your life as a developer much easier. Toward this end, we will discuss when each API is appropriate and give you guidelines that help you make the right choice.

To get you thinking about this, for now we will say that, in general, DOM is a good choice when you need to build an XML document, or to navigate an XML document repeatedly. For example, if you are capturing input from the user and adding it to an XML document, you would probably manage the XML document through the DOM interface.

SAX, on the other hand, is most useful when all that is required is a fast, single pass through the XML document to "strip off" information that you need. For example, if your application created plaintext summaries of XML documents by extracting their <Title>, <Author> and <Abstract> components, SAX would probably be a good choice for this. On the other hand, SAX's storage advantage may evaporate if you have to reinvent a persistent storage mechanism.

Keep in mind that a single application could use both DOM and SAX to manage its XML documents. For example, if the forementioned example was to create XML summaries from XML documents, SAX could be used to strip the `<Title>`, `<Author>` and `<Abstract>` data from the original documents, which would then be added to a new XML document (the XML summary) via a DOM interface.

The SAX API is the result of an effort by the XML-DEV community, coordinated in large part by David Megginson, who wrote the proposal for the SAX interface as well as its Java implementation. Visit http://www.megginson.com for more information and a complete history of the effort.

8.5.1 Tree-based and Event-Based XML APIs

We have mentioned that DOM is good at some things and SAX is good at others, and you may be wondering if there is an underlying reason for this. Well, the answer is "yes." It turns out that DOM is an example of what is known as a "tree-based API" for manipulating XML. There are actually two major classes of APIs for accessing XML data: tree-based APIs and event-based APIs. While DOM is an example of a tree-based API, SAX is an example of an event-based one.

- **DOM**—Tree-based API
- **SAX**—Event-based API

A tree-based API such as DOM compiles an XML document into an internal tree structure, and then allows an application to navigate and manipulate this tree structure via a number of methods. With a tree-based API, the application "sees" the XML document as a tree made up of nodes that it can traverse, inquire or set element and attribute values on, as well as add-to and delete nodes from. In a tree-based API such as DOM, a parser is used to build the internal tree structure. Only after the parser has finished building the internal tree structure may the application begin its navigation and manipulation of the resulting structure.

An event-based API such as SAX takes an alternate approach. Rather than constructing an internal tree structure, the parser begins reading the XML document from the top and merely reports parsing "events," such as when it encounters the start and end of elements. We will observe what happens when we use an event-based API such as SAX to process the following XML document

```
<?xml version="1.0"?>
<Report>
   <Title>SPECTRE Operations</Title>
   <Author>Dr. No</Author>
   <Abstract>Don't Ask</Abstract>
   <FullText>Since you asked...</FullText>
</Report>
```

An event-based API would report the following events:

```
Start document
Start element: Report
Start element: Title
Characters: SPECTRE Operations
End element: Title
Start element: Author
Characters: Dr. No
End element: Author
Start element: Abstract
Characters: Don't Ask
End element: Abstract
Start element: FullText
Characters: Since you asked...
End element: FullText
End element: Report
End document
```

As you can see, the event-based API has taken the hierarchically structured XML document and converted it into a linear series of events. When an event occurs in this example, we are merely printing out a message to the effect that the event has occurred, along with any relevant information (e.g., the name of the element encountered).

In general, in order to process these events an application must provide event "handler" methods, which are designated application methods that are automatically called (by the parser) when an event occurs. In object-oriented programming terminology, we would say that the event handler gets a message each time an event occurs. We will discuss event handlers for SAX in more detail in the section "SAX Implementation: the DocumentHandler Interface" in the following. For now, though, we will continue with our comparison of tree-based APIs such as DOM and event-based APIs such as SAX.

It is interesting to compare the internal tree structure created and used by the DOM API with the events generated by the SAX API. Figure 8.5 shows how the DOM structure for the forementioned example would look. Notice what happens if you perform what is known as a depth-first traversal of this tree, starting at the uppermost document node. A depth-first traversal of the tree structure is shown in Figure 8.6.

During this traversal, we will perform some processing at each node as follows, in order to produce the event output stream in our forementioned example. The first and last time you encounter the document node, you would print "Start document" and "End document," respectively. Each time you encounter an element node X for the first time, you would print out "Start element: X," and each time you leave an element node X for the last time, you would print out "End element: X." When you encounter an element's value node with value Y, you would simply print out "Characters: Y." You should be able to verify that by applying a simple depth-first traversal with this type of node processing to a DOM tree structure, the result will be the linear sequence of events we saw produced in the foregoing.

You should also be able to verify that the reverse is also true, namely, that it would be possible to create the corresponding tree structure by processing the series of events in strict linear order one at a time. That is, it is possible to create the data structure used internally by a tree-based API from the output of an event-based API, and to create the events generated by an event-based API given a tree-based API. Essentially, this is saying that both APIs convey the same information, namely, the structure of the XML document.

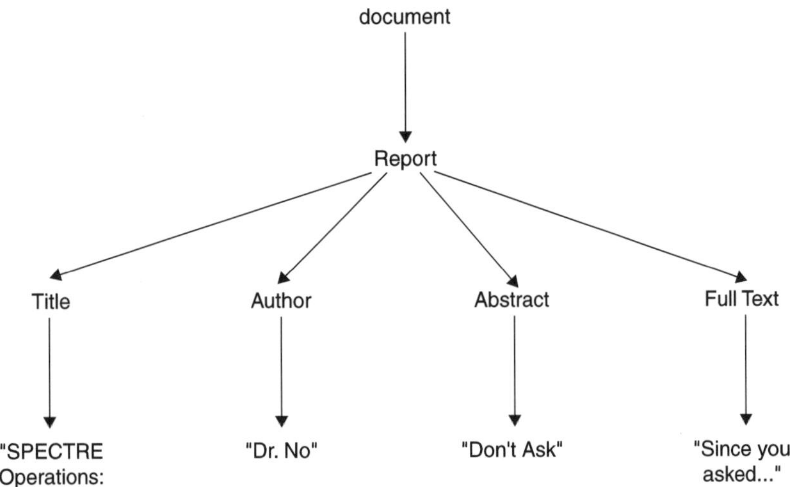

Figure 8.5 *Internal tree structure corresponding to DOM object.*

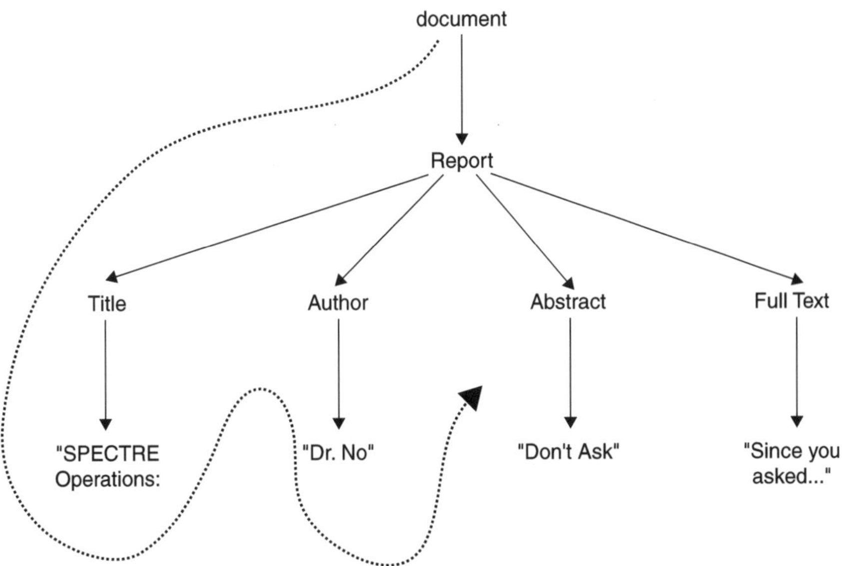

Figure 8.6 *Depth-first traversal of tree structure that generates SAX event stream.*

8.5.2 Choosing a Tree-based or Event-based API

Now that you understand how tree-based APIs such as DOM and event-based APIs such as SAX work, it is time to consider the advantages and disadvantages of using each type. The primary advantages of SAX over DOM are that SAX is faster and requires much less memory space when run. If this is the case, why not always use SAX? Well, it turns out that you cannot always use SAX. For starters, SAX only processes XML documents by reading them and does not have provisions for inserting element nodes, and so forth.

In contrast, tree-based APIs such as DOM are appropriate when you need to create an XML document by building one internally in the application. That is, the SAX API reads XML documents (and reports on parsing events) but does not have provisions for automatically updating them by inserting arbitrary nodes, as does DOM. Thus, if your application will be creating XML documents, you will likely want to use DOM for this purpose.

However, if your application is processing XML documents in order to retrieve information from them, SAX may be a viable alternative, but there are a number of issues to consider. As we saw in the earlier example, an event-based APIs like SAX reports the hierarchical document structure as a linear series of events, which are processed by the application's event handler methods. It is important to realize that it is not possible to "rewind" this sequence of events, as they are not being read from a file (where you could easily back-up one line), but instead are being generated by the parser. Once an event has been handled by your code, unless you have saved it yourself, it is gone.

Event-based APIs such as SAX represent a single, unidirectional (e.g., forward) pass through the XML document. If you encounter an event near the end of the document and wish you had saved some piece of information from an earlier event, it is too late. Your only recourse is to stop the current SAX processing and have the SAX API start again from the top and reprocess the entire document. Note that if your application happened to be reading its XML input from standard input rather than from a traditional file, it might not be possible to reprocess the input because your application may have already consumed it. The one-pass nature of the SAX API needs to be a consideration in the design process.

The SAX API is appropriate for tasks such as filtering XML documents, or for neatly stripping data off of an XML document. UNIX shell programmers who are familiar with utilities such as grep, lex and yacc and are familiar with one-pass filtering in that domain may want to think of SAX processing as providing a (roughly) similar type of functionality.

If you think that either DOM or SAX will work for your application and are not sure which to choose, remember that SAX is typically faster and generally uses much less memory space. How much less memory space, perhaps maybe an order of magnitude, or even several orders of magnitude.

Recall that DOM builds an internal tree structure corresponding to the XML document, but SAX does not. Early APIs for DOM required large amounts of RAM to store the internal tree structure. At present it is not unheard of for a 1 megabyte XML disk file to result in a 10 megabyte DOM object in the program's memory at runtime. At runtime, SAX would use but a tiny fraction of this memory. If the size of the input XML file were increased to 10 megabytes, the DOM object could require upwards of 100 megabytes of RAM; SAX would likely require only the same memory as in the previous case. This happens because the SAX API is processing the XML file linearly, and need not read in or store in memory the entire XML file in order to generate the parsing events. It is worth keeping in mind that the efficiency of DOM implementations has been improving steadily, and although DOM will likely *always* use more memory than SAX at runtime, the actual amount of memory used may be well within the demands of your particular application and platform. Making such determinations keeps software design interesting.

8.5.3 SAX Implementation: the DocumentHandler Interface

In order to create a Java-based SAX application, you will first need to download and install the necessary Java libraries. At the time of this writing, such libraries are available at no charge from a number of software vendors and organizations. The Java libraries you will need are the following:

- **SAX interfaces and classes**—These are currently available for downloading at http://www/megginson.com
- **XML parser that supports SAX**—A number of SAX-compliant XML parsers are available; the one which we use is the "XML for Java" parser (xml4j) from the IBM Corporation. Visit http://www.alphaWorks.ibm.com/tech/xml4j for information about downloading this parser.

After you have downloaded them, do not forget to add them to your CLASSPATH so that the Java compiler and runtime environment can find them. When we run our example in the following, we will need to know the full classname of the SAX driver for the parser; for the ibmxlj parser it is com.ibm.parser.SAXDriver.

In order to process parsing events, you will need to create event handlers that will be informed of events as they occur. In the SAX API, the primary event handler is the DocumentHandler, which receives events for the start and end of elements, as well as events signifying that the parser has encountered character data, processing instructions, and other basic XML structure.

The DocumentHandler interface includes the following public abstract methods, all of whose return types are void, and all of which throw SAXException. (The complete specification, from which the information here is taken, is available at http://www.megginson.com.)

- **startDocument()**—Receive notification of the beginning of a document. The SAX parser will invoke this method only once before any other methods in this interface.
- **endDocument()**—Receive notification of the end of a document. The SAX parser will invoke this method only once, and it will be the last method invoked during the parse.
- **startElement(String name, AttributeList atts)**—Receive notification of the beginning of an element. The Parser will invoke this method at the beginning of every element in the XML document; there will be a corresponding endElement() event for every startElement() event (even when the element is empty). All of the element's content will be reported in order before the corresponding endElement() event. The attribute list provided will contain attributes with explicit values.

- **endElement(String name)**—Receive notification of the end of an element. The SAX parser will invoke this method at the end of every element in the XML document; there will be a corresponding startElement() event for every endElement() event (even when the element is empty).
- **characters(char ch[], int start, int length)**—Receive notification of character data. The SAX parser will call this method to report each chunk of character data. SAX parsers may return all contiguous character data in a single chunk, or they may split it into several chunks.
- **ignorableWhitespace(char ch[], int start, int length)**—Receive notification of ignorable whitespace in element content. Validating parsers must use this method to report each chunk of ignorable whitespace (see the W3C XML 1.0 recommendation, section 2.10).
- **processingInstruction(String target, String data)**—Receive notification of a processing instruction. The SAX parser will invoke this method once for each processing instruction found.

The SAX implementation includes an adapter class, HandlerBase, that provides default implementations of all of the methods of the DocumentHandler interface. This allows you to create a class that extends HandlerBase, and only requires you to implement the particular DocumentHandler methods you need. This is the approach used in the following small application that uses SAX to process XML documents. The application in this case simply prints a message when parsing events are received, for example, when the document begins and ends, each time an element starts or ends, etc.

```
import org.xml.sax.HandlerBase;
import org.xml.sax.AttributeList;
import org.xml.sax.Parser;
import org.xml.sax.SAXException;
import org.xml.sax.helpers.ParserFactory;

public class SAXDemo extends HandlerBase {

   public void startDocument () {
      System.out.println("Start document");
   }

   public void endDocument () {
      System.out.println("End document");
   }
```

```
    public void startElement (String name, AttributeList attributes) {
       System.out.println("Start element: " + name);
       for (int i = 0; i < attributes.getLength(); i++) {
          System.out.println("  Attribute: "+attributes.getName(i)+' '+
          attributes.getType(i) + " \"" + attributes.getValue(i)+'"');
       }
    }

    public void endElement (String name) {
       System.out.println("End element: " + name);
    }

    public void characters (char ch[], int start, int length) {
       System.out.print("Characters: ");
       System.out.println( new String(ch, start, length) );
    }

    public void ignorableWhitespace (char ch[], int start, int length)
    { }

    public void processingInstruction (String target, String data) {
       System.out.println("Processing instruction: " +
                                          target + ' ' + data);
    }

    public static void main (String args[]) throws Exception {
       if (args.length != 1) { System.err.println(
          "Usage: java -Dorg.xml.sax.parser=<classname> " +
                            "SAXDemo <document>");
          System.exit(2);
       }

       Parser parser = ParserFactory.makeParser();
       SAXDemo handler = new SAXDemo();
       parser.setEntityResolver(handler);
       parser.setDTDHandler(handler);
       parser.setDocumentHandler(handler);
       parser.setErrorHandler(handler);

       parser.parse(args[0]);
    }
}
```

This example creates a SAX Parser object by supplying a class name to the ParserFactory, instantiates the SaxDemo class, registers the handler with the parser, then parses all URLs supplied on the command line. The example can be compiled with the following command: the classpath we are using assumes that the sax.jar file is located in the root directory `c:\` and that the Java JDK1.1.7B is being used.

```
javac -classpath "c:\sax.jar;c:\jdk1.1.7b\lib\classes.zip" SAXDemo.java
```

In order to run our application, we will need an XML file and its corresponding schema coded as a Document Type Definition. An example of each of these is presented as follows:

```
report.dtd:

   <?xml encoding="US-ASCII"?>

   <!ELEMENT Report (Title, Author, Abstract, FullText)>
   <!ELEMENT Title (#PCDATA)>
   <!ATTLIST Title PublicationDate CDATA #IMPLIED>
   <!ELEMENT Author (#PCDATA)>
   <!ELEMENT Abstract (#PCDATA)>
   <!ELEMENT FullText (#PCDATA)>


report.xml:

   <?xml version="1.0"?>
   <!DOCTYPE Report SYSTEM "report.dtd">
   <Report>
      <Title PublicationDate="1963-01-23">SPECTRE Operations</Title>
      <Author>Dr. No</Author>
      <Abstract>Don't Ask</Abstract>
      <FullText>Since you asked...</FullText>
   </Report>
```

The application can be run with the following command:

```
   java -classpath ".;c:\xml4j_1_1_4.jar;c:\jdk1.1.7b\lib\classes.zip"
        -Dorg.xml.sax.parser=com.ibm.xml.parser.SAXDriver SAXDemo
report.xml
```

Here we are using the IBM "XML for Java" parser, whose classfiles are located in the c:\xml4j_1_1_4.jar jarfile. Note that we are specifying the SAX driver as a command-line argument; in this case the parser is named com.ibm.xml .parser.SAXDriver. The output from the program is shown below.

```
Start document
Start element: Report
```

```
Start element: Title
   Attribute: PublicationDate CDATA "1963-01-23"
Characters: SPECTRE Operations
End element: Title
Start element: Author
Characters: Dr. No
End element: Author
Start element: Abstract
Characters: Don't Ask
End element: Abstract
Start element: FullText
Characters: Since you asked...
End element: FullText
End element: Report
End document
```

SAX provides a lightweight, event-driven interface for processing XML documents. SAX should not be viewed as a replacement for the Document Object Model (DOM) API. Instead, the SAX and DOM APIs are complementary, and one of your jobs as an XML application developer will be to determine which one is more appropriate for any given situation.

8.6 The Future of XML

If someone had told you ten years ago that the Internet would one day be huge, and that major corporations would vie with one another for consumers on this medium, you probably would have politely excused yourself and gone on about your business. Of course, these predictions have come true, and with the advent of the Web it happened much faster than many thought possible.

It is interesting that even as little as five years ago some of the largest software corporations still "did not get it" about the Internet. The standalone personal computer, where users ran applications that came on CD-ROMs, was one vision of the future that has since been replaced by the globally interconnected model of the Web. Sooner or later, everyone seems to "get it," realizing the importance of being connected in our globally networked world.

So what does this all have to do with the future of XML? Well, partly it is to tell you that predicting the future is a very difficult thing to do. However, predicting the future is something we all like to do, and we are certainly happy when our predictions come true, not that they always do. However, if we base our predictions on solid foundations, and make reasonable assumptions, we may not be that far off when the dust has settled and the future has arrived.

With all of that said, it is time to talk about the future of XML. XML currently seems to be enjoying its time in the spotlight with great popularity. It also seems well on its way to delivering upon many of its promises, namely, a more navigable and interoperable Web. However, no technology can last on hype alone. It must provide value to users, and must be able to solve real-world problems.

As we all know, the Web, and information technology, in general, has its share of challenges ahead. Making applications interoperable not only on the user's desktop but across the Web as well, is certainly an ongoing challenge, and one for which XML is ideally positioned. XML promotes interoperability by being a universal data-interchange format. XML is not just a "future technology," but is available here and now, and it can solve this problem. Information about the ongoing W3C efforts is available at http://www.w3.org, and the many technical reports and publications maintained by the organization are available for downloading at http://www.w3.org/TR/. In order to understand how XML can solve these problems, you need to not only understand the problems, but also the technologies that can solve them. Your experience as a Web application developer will certainly benefit you on the first of these; the W3C website is clearly the place to keep abreast of the latter. In addition, there are a number of standards bodies and groups playing active roles in XML, including XML.ORG (http://www.xml.org) whose purpose is to provide a credible source of accurate, timely information about the application of XML in industrial and commercial settings and to serve as a reference repository for specific XML standards such as vocabularies, DTDs, schemas, and namespaces. OASIS, the Organization for the Advancement of Structured Information Standards (www.oasis-open.org) is a nonprofit, international consortium dedicated solely to product-independent data and content interchange. These are excellent resources to consult for the latest information.

In terms of forthcoming XML technologies, it appears that many of them will be driven by XML's increasing role as a universal data-interchange format. XML technologies are under development that enable richer data structures to be represented, using more robust document linking, for example. Work is also underway to use XML as a means serializing and transporting objects across the Web. New XML technologies that simplify using XML as the medium to disperse meta-data about Web resources will undoubtedly continue to be developed.

Although it is difficult to predict the future of any technology, especially one as new as XML, it seems clear that XML has a very bright future ahead. You are encouraged to follow the progress of XML not merely as a spectator but by actively participating in its development and adoption by building the next generation of interoperable Web applications using XML.

8.7 *Conclusion*

We have explored a number of new and upcoming XML technologies that are designed to help you build even richer Web applications. Some of these technologies are available here and now, and others are perhaps farther down the road. With all of the excitement about XML and with new technologies that support XML being developed almost daily, it is important to keep abreast of the latest developments. We hope that this chapter has helped you in this regard. The future of XML seems very bright, and we suspect that you agree.

Index

C

E

L

M

N

W

X

About the Author

Reaz Hoque is a web technologist who specializes in cutting edge e-business technologies. He has written six other books on technologies such as CORBA, JavaBeans, and Components. All his books demonstrate how technologies can be used to maximize e-business initiatives. As a well-known speaker, Reaz travels all over the globe to deliver speeches on net technologies. In his years of computing, he has had the pleasure of working for companies such as General Electric, Netscape and EC Cubed, Inc. He is the founder of supara.com and varsityfun.com

About the Contributing Authors

Vishal Anand is a software engineer and object-oriented design consultant. He has been consulting on development of large-scale client/server systems for the last four years. Recently he has been devoted his energy to streaming live content over the web. He has worked before with Reaz on two books on CORBA. He would like to express his thanks to his family and friends for support throughout this book.

Mike Alexander has 15 years experience designing large-scale software systems in both scientific research and business settings, including Wall Street. He has a Ph.D. in Computer Science (University of Virginia), was at one time a University professor, and is now President of Metadapt Design Systems, Inc., a company he recently founded. When not tinkering with code, he enjoys traveling abroad with his wife Sally, reading novels, and listening to and playing surf-guitar music.

Bruce Weber started out in the software development industry by developing client/server and intranet solutions for Scottsdale Insurance Company. Moving into e-Commerce, Bruce cocreated a large business-to-business web site for ECAdvantage, a subsidiary of MicroAge. Currently, Bruce is a technical architect with Cambridge Technology Partners specializing in electronic commerce projects. Bruce would like to thank his wife Robin Weber for putting up with all the time he has spent working on the book. He mentions that he loves her dearly!

Related Titles from Morgan Kaufmann

http://www.mkp.com

- **CORBA FOR REAL PROGRAMMERS**
  Reaz Hoque
  1999 ISBN: 0-12-355590-6

- **WEB PUBLISHING WITH XML IN SIX EASY STEPS**
  Bryan Pfaffenberger
  1998 ISBN: 0-12-553166-4

- **ENTERPRISE XML CLEARLY EXPLAINED**
  Robert Standefer
  2000 ISBN: 0-12-663355-0